T0403292

Single-Camera Video

This book contains everything a student needs to know about planning, shooting, and editing a single-camera video project.

Steve Price takes students through the entire single-camera video production process, from pre- to post-, showing students how to expertly plan, light, capture audio, shoot, edit, and color-correct their work successfully and effectively. In addition, he teaches students how to translate their skills to any single-camera genre in the industry through dedicated chapters on fiction and non-fiction projects, such as narrative films and series, commercials, music videos, documentary films, news packages, and corporate and freelance videos. Each of these chapters discusses how preproduction, production, and postproduction differ between the genres, featuring tailored tips and tricks for each individual mode of production, as well as a case study that helps demonstrate the differences and similarities between each one.

This book is a must-have for any filmmaking, media production, and communications students taking a class in single-camera video production.

Stephen Price, Jr. is a professor at the University of Central Missouri and has worked in the media industry for almost 30 years. He started out in sports radio, but has since produced TV news, commercials, music videos, corporate videos, and documentary films. He was the president of the Missouri Broadcast Educators Association for 6 years, and has been the Chair of the Production Aesthetics and Criticism Division of the national BEA organization. He's been teaching for over 20 years across four different universities, with classes that cover every type of video production, including scriptwriting, cinematography, video editing, documentary film production, and corporate and freelance production.

Single-Camera Video
From Pre- to Postproduction

Stephen Price, Jr

Routledge
Taylor & Francis Group

LONDON AND NEW YORK

Designed cover image: Getty Images

First published 2025
by Routledge
4 Park Square, Milton Park, Abingdon, Oxon OX14 4RN

and by Routledge
605 Third Avenue, New York, NY 10158

Routledge is an imprint of the Taylor & Francis Group, an informa business

British Library Cataloguing-in-Publication Data
A catalogue record for this book is available from the British Library

ISBN: 978-0-367-44557-7 (hbk)
ISBN: 978-0-367-44558-4 (pbk)
ISBN: 978-1-003-01035-7 (ebk)

DOI: 10.4324/9781003010357

Typeset in Sabon
by codeMantra

Contents

Part I

Preproduction (Chapters 1–3)

Preproduction is the most important phase of any project. Regardless of the genre, preproduction sets the foundation for everything that comes after it. Beginning with an idea is important, but it's only the first step towards visualizing your project and giving your crew a blueprint so they can help you on your journey towards a polished final cut. It's important for you to be able to convey your idea in a way that allows others to visualize it and put everything together as you focus on the very specific parts that need your attention. Efficiency is the key. I've seen many projects where the student producer or Director knew exactly what they wanted, but they didn't take the time to do proper preproduction, and the crew sat around waiting to be told what to do instead of working independently on their portion of the setup and then tweaking it once everyone came together.

Good preproduction creates a plan for everything. The script gives the actors and Director the dialogue and general context of everything. Storyboards and other previsualization techniques let the entire crew know how each shot should be framed and lit. Lighting plots and location maps let everyone know where to place lights, cameras, props, and actors. And good shooting schedules and shot lists make sure everything runs smoothly and on time. Things come up all the time, and changes have to be made on the fly, but having a good plan in place makes it much easier to adapt. Even though students are often tempted to rush the preproduction, time spent in this phase will always save time later on.

DOI: 10.4324/9781003010357-1

1   Scripts and Storyboards

Most good stories and projects begin with an idea. Sometimes, you'll start with something else (commercials often start with an intended outcome, for example), but most often, you'll have an interesting thought or situation or personality or … well, *story*. However, it's important to take that idea and sculpt it into something more solid before jumping in with a camera and shooting. This chapter will walk you through the basics of getting your idea planned out in a way that others can visualize. This is important for your crew and talent, but also to secure potential funding sources and potential distribution outlets. Specifically, this chapter will cover:

Beginning with an Idea

Over the years, I've had many ideas pop into my head … sometimes in the middle of the night, sometimes as I'm driving down the road, sitting and watching television, or out mowing the lawn. Regardless of when and where they come, these ideas seem to disappear if I don't write them down. Maybe there's a specific project I'm working on and I'm brainstorming solutions to a problem. Or maybe I'm just feeling overly creative and think of a good plot for a short film. Whatever the case may be, I've started keeping a journal at hand (on my phone, actually) where I can get these ideas down in writing the minute they come to me, so I don't forget them. Sometimes when I come back to them later, I realize that they weren't really all that good to begin with. When that happens, I go ahead and delete those ideas from my journal and move on with my life. Other times,

DOI: 10.4324/9781003010357-2

though, I think that I've struck gold. When I have an idea like that, it's time to take the next steps.

One of the first things I do when I realize I've got an idea that can be developed into a short film or storyline for a commercial or promotional video, or if I've discovered an issue I want to explore further in a documentary film, is to run the idea past other professionals I know and see what they think about it. Often, the idea dies right there. I'm fortunate to have colleagues who will be lovingly honest with me and tell me when an idea really isn't as great as I think it is. While this might seem like my dream is being crushed, it's an important step in the creative process. If I can't get others to see the merit of my idea, or convince them that it is, in fact, a good idea, it probably isn't actually a good idea. Or, it's at least not an idea that translates into a media product easily or well. In those instances, I might leave the idea in my journal in case I think of a better way to develop it later. But often, I go ahead and delete those ideas as well.

If my idea relates to a specific project I'm working on, and especially if I'm working with others or for someone else, I'll typically polish the idea a little bit and then run it past my co-workers or my employer. When I freelanced and shot instructional videos, it required constant contact with my employer so that I knew I was on the right track. With other genres like music videos, commercials, and event videography, the process of checking in with your employer is something that needs to be worked out ahead of time. Some are more willing to let you be as creative as you want and just report in during the postproduction phase. Others want to be updated regularly and approve ideas and concepts before you even shoot them. Be sure you understand the expectations your employer or funding partner has for their level of involvement and oversight ahead of time.

If everyone thinks an idea might actually be good, then it's time to get to work. At this point, writing a treatment and outlining your project is a good idea. And then you're off to write scripts, develop your previsualization, and get everything ready to move on to the production phase.

Developing a Treatment

There are many formats for treatments, each depending on the genre. Film treatments are entirely different from treatments for commercials, documentary films, music videos, or other projects. All of them have some things in common, though. Every treatment should be able to simply and effectively convey the concept. This should include any and all details in the plot structure, as well as character arcs and backstories. For a film, it's important to convey the entire plot. For other genres, like commercials and promotional videos, it's also important to provide an account of everything you know about your audience, including any research you can do, and define your desired outcome. Once complete, the treatment becomes your guiding document. It's the thing you'll show a potential backer for funding or what you'll use to pitch your idea to the company that hired you to make their commercial. In corporate video, the treatment is what you'll pitch to your boss to make sure you're heading in the right direction, before you've invested so much time and effort in a project that it becomes unreasonable to stop and change everything. The treatment comes before the script because it helps guide the script as you develop it. In general, treatments should address the desired outcome, the concept (including the message), and the audience.

The Desired Outcome

For many projects, especially in corporate or freelance production, you'll be hired to perform a specific task. For example, commercials are often made to sell a new product. Sometimes, though, commercials are made to enhance the image of a brand. Still other times, commercials are created to raise the visibility of the good work the brand is doing in some area other than the one they are known for, like an advertisement for shoes that starts with shots of plastic and other waste floating in the ocean, then transitions to show and tell the story of how Brand X shoes uses recycled materials in their products and renewable energy to power their manufacturing. In that case, the desired outcome is not to sell shoes (although that is certainly an ancillary outcome). The desired outcome is to convince consumers that Brand X is environmentally responsible, and probably more so than the competition. In many genres of video production, the desired outcome is the most important thing. In commercial production, promo videos, and instructional videos, the desired outcome should be at the heart of every decision. Even in fictional films, there's often a desired outcome, even if it isn't overt.

I remember a Super Bowl commercial a few years ago where the brand was relatively unknown and the desired outcome was obviously to create brand recognition. The commercial was incredibly clever, and almost everyone was talking about it the next day. But even as they discussed it, almost no one remembered what the name of the company was or what the company did. The concept was brilliant, but the desired outcome wasn't achieved. So ultimately, that company paid millions of dollars for a failed result. The converse of that happens when commercials that aren't remarkable still find ways to stick in your head. There are commercials for law firms, products, and restaurants that you can probably think of now where the concept was so bad that you remember it. And you probably even remember the brand name or the product it was selling, even though you thought the concept was terrible. Ideally, the concept will be good AND the desired outcome will be achieved. But given the choice, I'd rather accomplish the goal for my client than have something that the audience finds amusing.

Concept (Message)

The concept in a treatment is what you would traditionally think of as the outline, description, or summary of your project. Sometimes, especially in film, the words "concept" and "treatment" will be used interchangeably. What will the film look like? How will it flow from one section to the next? Who are its characters? How do their story arcs progress? In non-fiction, the treatment should address the topic and what you know about it. A treatment for a documentary film might include the angle you intend to take. For example, many documentary films have been made about climbing Mount Everest. But perhaps you want to make a film specifically about the trash that gets left behind on the mountain. A unique perspective will set your project apart from the others that might have come before it.

It's also important to note that a treatment concept should lay everything out. I've seen many student projects where the treatment only sets up the premise but didn't tell the whole story. If you're going to try to get someone to fund your project, they're going to want to know how the story ends, and that you've thought everything through. Same thing for a TV series. Writers might not know what is in store for individual episodes until the scripts are written, but they have a pretty good idea of the story arcs and how the series will end even before they write the pilot script. In freelance or corporate video, you don't want to say to your client or employer, "You'll have to wait to see the ending until I edit it." You want to give them a clear idea of what you're producing for them so they're on board from the start. The last thing you want as a producer is to finish a project only to have someone you're working for (or receiving funding from) say, "That's not what I wanted. You need to try again."

A feature-length film treatment concept may be 30 pages long or more. In order to give enough detail that a financial backer feels confident you can produce it, you may need to write the story arcs for every single plot line and every single character. In commercials, a page is typically enough. For promo videos, instructional videos, corporate videos, and other genres, you may need a few pages. Sometimes, as is the case with some instructional videos, an outline may suffice; bullet points with a short description of what will be seen are often enough to ensure you cover the main ideas and for your client to get an understanding of what the video will be like. For some genres, like music videos, the concept may be broader and outline the general artistic vision, but not the specifics of how the video will flow. Ultimately, the way you write your concept will vary by genre and perhaps even by client.

The treatment concept should not detail every shot. That's what your script and pre-visualizations are for. Instead, the concept is written in prose (flowing sentences, almost like you're writing a book). It's unhelpful to say, "First, you see this. Then you see this." You'll do that in your script anyway. Instead, your prose should flow as much as possible, as if you're writing a fictional novel: "Jane was born in Missouri in 1993 to parents who loved her incredibly. She went to a small, private school where she excelled at math." This will help your pitch by allowing people to visualize what is happening without them getting hung up on specific details. This is also true for commercials and other fictional genres.

For non-fiction, the concept is a bit different because the story won't really come together until the topic is explored fully in production and put together in post. But treatment concepts should still follow the same basic principles. They should be written in prose, give as much detail as possible, and be written in the best way possible to help potential funding sources and others to visualize the way it will look and feel. For example, when pitching a short documentary about Alcatraz, I wrote about the different angle I planned on taking (Mohawk activist Richard Oakes's occupation of the island in 1969) and how I would mix in poetry from Native Americans to give the documentary a unique personal perspective from indigenous people who are no longer around to give interviews on camera. The specific details of the end result weren't exactly what I anticipated, but the overall look and feel of the piece were. And I don't think my crew or colleagues were surprised in the end when the film had an experimental feel to it because of the mixture of imagery, interviews, and poetry.

Audience

In almost every treatment, it's important to think about who your audience is before you get any further. Even fictional films have a desired audience. That audience determines the rating you want ("R," "PG," etc.), the style of humor you use, and the actors you might cast to play certain characters. For instructional videos, knowing how to connect to your audience is almost as important as the outcome you hope to achieve. For commercials and other projects, you might have a secondary audience, but your primary audience in every media project needs to be narrowly and specifically defined. If you aim for "everyone," you'll miss your target almost every time. Instead, think about who it is you want to reach and what you know about them. Then in your treatment, write about the research you've done on your audience and give examples of media messages that have resonated with those audiences before.

There are two ways to view media artifacts: as art and as communication. Great films, commercials, instructional videos, and other media projects should be seen as both. As an art form, films don't necessarily define their audiences narrowly. Superhero movies, for example, often appeal to children and to adults. But producers and Directors are rarely under the illusion that they're trying to appeal to everyone. Younger children may not be mature enough for the violence they see in a superhero movie. Others may just not like the genre. Instead of trying to appeal to an audience that likes musicals, superhero movies generally ignore some audiences and instead try to really appeal to their niche audience. Doing so has made the genre extremely profitable.

As a communication form, even fictional films have messages they want their audiences to understand. A film about an animal in captivity might actually be targeting audiences to think harder about the nature of amusement parks and zoos. Certainly non-fiction, commercials, instructional videos, and corporate videos have an audience and a message in mind. But you should avoid delivering a message without finesse. If the message is targeted to the right audience, but doesn't appeal to them visually, your message won't be effective. Finding the best way to appeal to that audience is important, and it starts with researching and writing down everything you know about them.

When I'm thinking about my audience, I begin most often by simply writing out the demographic information. Demographics include things like age, ethnicity, gender, occupation, income level, and other information that can be used to segment populations into more easily identified groups. Once I know the demographics, I can do some research about their tastes and what media messages have resonated with those groups before. For example, Nielsen data (ratings) is available for 18–34-year-olds who watch specific television shows. Knowing what shows have done well in that age group can help me target the same age group with my media message. The time of day or desired distribution outlet has an impact on who the audience will be as well. Online viewing data can help determine which distribution platform might be best to reach a specific audience. There are many places to find data about audiences, including the clients who might hire you to produce their message. Perhaps you're producing an online training video for a company who wants to automate their onboarding (employee training) process. They already know the type of people they try to hire, and they might even have data about those people. You can use that data to research the things that resonate with that demographic so you can connect your message with them and achieve your desired outcome more easily.

There are other ways to break down audiences as well. Psychographic information segments populations based on their habits, hobbies, attitudes, political views, etc. Psychographics are often more useful than demographics, but they're much more difficult to collect. It's useful to know that 18–34-year-olds are more likely to spend money on expensive coffee. But it's also useful to know that even within the 18–34-year-old demographic, there are people who prefer to save up and purchase things that are high-quality and expensive, and there are also people who prefer to get "a deal" regardless of the perceived quality. Crafting a message about the low cost of something is only going to appeal to one of those groups. Knowing audience psychographics is important.

In freelance and commercial work, your audience is often prescribed to you. When I produced a commercial for the State of California, I knew exactly who my audience was from the start. I still needed to research that audience and find the best ways to appeal to them to get my message across. As another example, I was on an airplane a couple years ago and the video screens dropped down to play the safety message. Even though everyone on the plane is the target audience for that message, I rarely paid attention to them. They were dry, boring, and contained information I heard every time I boarded a plane. This time, however, the video was humorous. The flight attendant in the video wore a rubber ducky tube around their waist when the voiceover talked about a water landing. When the flight attendant told a person in the video not to smoke on the plane, it was a fire-breathing dragon. You get the point. I paid attention to the entire video. The people who produced that video learned how to reach their audience and they used humor to connect that audience to the desired outcome. Even though their audience was determined by the fact that we were passengers on a plane, and the desired outcome was to convey basic information, the video connected with the audience because the producers knew that humor would reach people who are nervous about taking off, bored at the thought of a long flight ahead of them, or who typically don't pay attention because they've just seen the standard message too many times.

Although this isn't something I've used professionally, the example treatment in Figure 1.1 shows the type of planning that might go into a short commercial project for a client. If this really were for a client, I would probably spend a bit more time developing the concept and do more audience research, but this should give you the general idea behind what to put in a quality treatment. For other genres, there will be differences. I'll give examples of those differences in the later chapters where I break down the production process by genre.

Desired Outcome:

To associate Brand X shoes with environmentalism and concern for the planet.

Concept:

The ocean. Majestic. Beautiful. Deep Blue. A whale slowly surfaces. But wait. What's that white stuff floating over there? It's trash. A lot of it. So much trash that it fills the ocean. Trash is everywhere, infecting our water, preventing us from enjoying the beach, and worst of all, hurting the majestic animals that call the ocean "home." Brand X shoes. Beautiful. Majestic. And made from 50% recycled materials. The shoes are comfortable. They're fashionable. They're great for work, great for play, great for parties, and great for relaxing. The manufacturing plant is solar powered. You can see that the company really cares. The workers smile because they know that they work for someone who cares about the future of their planet. Brand X Shoes. The shoes that care.

Audience:

According to "Identifying the green consumer: A segmentation study", by Arminda M Finisterra do Paco, Mario Lino Barata Raposo, and Walter Leal Filho (Journal of Targeting, Measurement and Analysis for Marketing, March 2009, Volume 17, Issue 1, pp 17-25), this type of commercial appeals to conscientious people that generally care about outdoors space and the environment. These consumers are willing to spend a bit more money on something if they believe in it, knowing that the extra cost will allow the company to maintain expensive, but ethical, business practices. These are typically younger people and people who have disposable income.

Figure 1.1 An example of a commercial treatment.

Scriptwriting

Once you've done the research and developed your idea into something that will resonate with your audience, it's time to work out exactly what will happen in each scene of the project. Writing a script is often the most creative part of the entire process, and a lot of thought and care needs to go into the details in the script. The script is the document that will guide the Director and actors through the production process. There are many books out there that cover scriptwriting in great detail, so my aim here is to briefly discuss the two types of scripts that are commonly used in single-camera production and to give you examples of each. Single-column scripts are typically used in dramatic productions, such as fictional films. Often, commercials will also use single-column scripts, but it depends on whether the production team is coming from the film industry where single-column scripts are common, or the television industry where two-column scripts are the norm.

Single-column Scripts

Single-column scripts are written in prose. Like a novel, the script should flow in a way that is easy for actors and Directors to visualize the action and dialogue, but typically without the camera details that might distract and create a disjointed reading experience. For example, a single-column script might describe the visuals by saying, "The sun rises over the ocean and shows the vast, blue horizon." A single-column script will typically avoid directing camera shots or writing things out in a technical way. Writing with too much technical detail prevents the Director and actors from being able to get into the flow of the action and dialogue. Likewise, dialogue should be written in a way that sets it apart from the shot descriptions so actors can simply read their lines as they rehearse. In Figure 1.2, you can see that the dialogue is inset so that the actors can read through it with ease. Each scene will typically specify whether it is an interior (INT or indoors) or exterior (EXT or outdoors) shot. These scenes and shot directions are in bold and all upper-case. The scene descriptions written below these shot directions are written in flowing prose to describe the action in the scene. Finally, if the writer gives the actor directions on how to deliver their lines, this will be centered and in parentheses underneath the character's name who is speaking. This practice has evolved in film scripts, though, and is becoming less common. Instead, the script is seen more as a guide, and the Directors and actors are allowed more creative latitude to deliver the lines as they want.

The script example below takes the idea from our example treatment and develops it further. In this case, there are no actors, but a voiceover that must be scripted out with the shots. A new scene is typically specified anytime we change location, concept/theme, or time.

Two-column Scripts

Two-column scripts are typical in live multi-camera television production, such as news and talk shows. But because a fair amount of single-camera production is done at television stations, two-column scripts are sometimes used even in single-camera projects. News packages, instructional videos, promotional videos, and even commercials will often use the two-column format. You'll see commercials use two-column scripts when the commercials are locally produced by the creative department of a television station, or by a production house.

In a two-column script, the writing is broken down into shot descriptions (video instructions) in one column and the dialogue (audio instructions) in the other. A variation is often used in live television production that includes a column for timing information. For commercials that are only 30–60 seconds long, the timing column is typically absent, although I encourage students to keep it there to help their pacing and to keep the project under the time limit.

1   **EXT. THE OCEAN WITH THE SUN COMING UP**   1

The sun comes up over the vast, blue ocean. We sweep along the surface. It's a beautiful place,filled with life.

Marine life exists in abundance. Dolphins are playing, whales are swimming. We see some under water life as well. Coral reefs, clown fish, and a fascinating eco system exist.

NARRATOR
(with energy,as if narrating a nature documentary)
The open ocean. A beautiful eco system. Home to some of the world's largest and most majestic creatures. A place to relax and take a vacation.

2   **EXT. THE HARBOR, WHERE TRASH HAS COLLECTED**   2

There is a bit of trash in the open ocean. Mostly plastic (probably). Then more trash. And more trash. Finally, some shots of the harbor, where people are trying to get out on their boats, marine life is all but absent, and the situation seems hopeless.

NARRATOR (CONT'D)
But the oceans have a problem. Trash lines the shores, keeping vacationers away. Marine life is in peril. This beautiful eco system is in danger. Man has created too much waste for the world to handle.

3   **EXT. BRAND X SHOE BEING WORN BY A PERSON**   3

The shoe is beautiful, majestic, and comfortable. The person wearing it walks off down the beach, away from the initial camera shot. They continue to walk in the sand, demonstrating how the shoe is one with nature.

NARRATOR (CONT'D)
Brand X shoes are made for this environment. Made from 50% recycled materials, Brand X shoes were designed to lessen the impact people are having on the planet, so we can enjoy the planet.

Figure 1.2 An example of a single-column script.

4   EXT. THE BRAND X SHOE FACTORY   **4**

The factory has a wind turbine and solar panels. It is a bright sunny
day, and workers can be seen working hard, but enjoying
themselves.

NARRATOR (CONT'D)
And Brand X shoes aren't just using recycled
materials to make the most comfortable walking
shoe on the market. They're also using renewable
resources to power their factory to lessen the impact
on the planet.

5   GRAPHIC BRAND X SHOES AND TAGLINE   **5**

The Brand X Shoe logo appears on the screen, with the tagline, "Brand
X Shoes. Made for this environment."

NARRATOR
Brand X Shoes. Made for this environment.

Figure 1.2 (Continued)

In a two-column script, the shot descriptions are often more technical and specify
exactly what type of shot is to be used, what is seen within the shot, and the action that
occurs. Unlike a single-column script, this is not written in prose. Because live television
production has to stay focused on timing, the shot descriptions are brief and sometimes
they aren't even complete sentences. Dialogue is written in a similar way to single-column
scripts, and anything that is not to be read aloud should be put in parentheses.

Previsualization and Storyboards

Previsualization (previz) used to be the same thing as storyboarding. Basically, it means
to develop visuals that are detailed enough to guide the production phase of the process.
Detailed storyboards were always better than vague ones, and computer-enhanced previsualization (animatics) has taken this step in the process to an entirely new level. But
knowing the basics is still important, and few students have access to the tools that Hollywood has at their disposal. Regardless of how it's done, in order for previsualization
to be helpful, it must have visuals that show the Director and Cinematographer what
each shot should look like. Previsualization should also contain the details about each
shot that will be necessary when setting up and recording the action. For example, will
there be dialogue in the shot? Sound effects? Will the characters move during the scene?
All of these details should be identified at this point to enable efficiency once the cast
and crew are on set and shooting. Students often see this step as a waste of time because
they think they have a clear vision in their head about what will happen in each shot
and each scene. But when they get on set to direct the cast and crew, they realize that no
one else knows what the shot should look like, much less how to set up the lighting and
camera. Good previsualization allows the entire crew to be on the same page. It makes
everything run more smoothly because the Cinematographer can set up the camera and

Time (TRT 30 seconds)	Video	Audio
:30:00	CU of the ocean, zooming out to a LS of the sun rising over the water	(Narrator, as if narrating a nature doc) The open ocean. A beautiful ecosystem. Home to some of the world's largest and most majestic creatures. A place to relax and take a vacation.
	MS of a whale or dolphin playing	
	Underwater LS of a reef thriving with life	
:25:00	CU of trash in the ocean	(Narrator) But the oceans have a problem. Trash lines the shores, keeping vacationers away. Marine life is in peril. This beautiful ecosystem is in danger. Man has created too much waste for the world to handle.
	LS of piles of trash in the open water	
	LS of trash in the harbor and on the beach	
:20:00	CU of a Brand X shoe being worn by someone as they walk along the beach	(Narrator) Brand X shoes are made for this environment. Made from 50% recycled materials, Brand X shoes were designed to lessen the impact people are having on the planet, so we can enjoy the planet.
	LS of that person walking away	
:15:00	LS (drone flyover) of factory with solar panels and wind turbines	(Narrator) And Brand X shoes aren't just using recycled materials to make the most comfortable walking shoe on the market. They're also using renewable resources to power their factory to lessen the impact on the planet.
	CU of solar panels	
	MS of workers and factory	
:05:00	Graphic with logo and tagline	(Narrator) Brand X Shoes. Made for this environment.

Figure 1.3 An example of a two-column script. The shot descriptions are brief, but specific. This is the same commercial as above, but scripted in two-column format.

frame the shot without any input from the Director. The audio crew knows exactly how close they can get to record dialogue, and whether or not there are sound effects they will need to capture while on set. The Lighting Director will know what the lighting should look like based on the visual image and the shot description, and the Grips will know what equipment will be needed and whether they'll need to assist with any camera moves. If previsualization is done well, a Director isn't even needed until they're ready to say, "action," although issues always seem to pop up during setup that require the Director's attention.

Another thing I've learned from my experience across a variety of genres is that you want your previsualization to be planned down to the shot level. Many students stop at the scene level, drawing or shooting one single image to represent an entire scene full of shots, reverse shots, actor movements, camera movements, and so on. Unless a scene is a basic seated dialogue scene between two actors (with a standard 2-shot, shot, reverse shot, setup), you'll want to draw new visuals for every single-camera setup or actor movement. Anytime you move the camera or the actors, your lighting might change, the description might become more intricate, and the expectations for your crew might change.

Previsualization is also the step in the preproduction phase where the visuals help you pitch your project to a client, a potential funding entity, or a distribution outlet. Being detailed with your visuals will help those audiences see what the project will look like when it's completed. Along with the script, this is often where projects are tweaked to make sure that they accomplish their goals and desired outcomes.

Visuals

The visuals in your storyboard should show exactly what the shot will look like through the lens of the camera. This can be done in a variety of ways. I've drawn entire storyboards using nothing but stick figures, because I'm not much of an artist. What is important is that everyone in the crew understands how to frame and light the shot. With affordable access to DSLR and phone cameras now, it's easier sometimes to just snap a shot of what the visuals will look like, although that requires setting up a little bit of lighting and getting someone to stand in for your actors. If you have talent with 3D modeling software, you could even create animatics (animations that show the actors, their movement, the camera movement, and the shading on each object). At some point, though, you have to do a cost-benefit analysis and know that previsualization is best when it is done both quickly and thoroughly enough to ensure the crew can be efficient once they're on set preparing to shoot. Any work beyond that is wasted time, no matter how good it looks.

Detailed Descriptions

When storyboarding or doing any other kind of previsualization, you should include as much detail about each shot as possible. My preference is to have an entire set of information on each frame of my storyboard. Even when using digital images or animatics, it's important to have notes for each shot about the audio requirements, the camera movement, the actors' movements, and anything else necessary to execute the shot efficiently and to get the best results from the shoot. Many of the details will be repeated from one panel to the next, and many of the details will be duplicated elsewhere in your preproduction shooting schedules, crew lists, prop lists, equipment lists, and other places. It is always better to have too many details planned out than too few, but it does require paying delicate attention to those details so they correspond across your planning documents.

The next section on the template is the image box. This is where you would draw your shot as it would look through the camera, or insert a digital image to show how to frame and light the shot. If you're using animatics, the clips should be cut together as

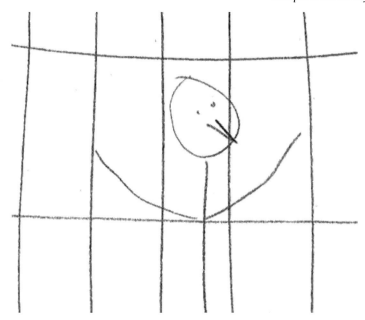

Figure 1.4 A stick figure drawing I used in storyboards to produce a music video. Even though there aren't a lot of visual details, the crew can easily see that it will be a medium shot, with the lighting up front on the bars and on the actor.

Figure 1.5 A much more detailed drawing that a student did for that same music video. In this drawing, the crew can see that it will be a long shot, with a police car in the foreground, a streetlight in the middleground, and the suspect's house in the background. The moon shows that it's night outside, with the streetlight providing a bit of light on the main part of the shot, spilling out onto the house and the police car.

Figures 1.6, 1.7, and 1.8 A series of digital images I used to storyboard a commercial project. The commercial depicted a woman shopping in a grocery store and using her debit card, directly addressing the camera at times to tell the audience about the card's new features. Although this is easily the most detailed way to visualize your shots, it might not be worth the time to get locations, actors, and equipment lined up to shoot these images. Then again, it might be, depending on your production timeline, your budget, and how large your crew is.

you actually plan on editing them, but notes and details for each shot should still be kept on a separate planning document, and the shots in the animatics should be labeled with on-screen graphics so shots can be easily matched to the detailed notes.

The template contains audio information next, including whether there will be dialogue to record on set or if it will be MOS (without sound). I also include whether or not there will be sound effects or music so that my audio crew knows how to treat the audio they're capturing on set. For example, if sound effects are needed, I would expect my audio crew to make sure they get at least one clip of the sound effect as it is produced on set during shooting. Even if they are planning on creating the sound in post by using Foley techniques or canned sound FX, it is still important to capture it on location to make it easier to replicate or sync up to the Foley sound later. Maybe it will sound great and the crew won't end up needing to do Foley. Knowing that there will be music added over the shot in post also allows my sound crew to know that they'll be able to mask certain room tones or small noises that might otherwise ruin a take. The template also includes a section to write out the details about the audio. For example, if the dialogue is a whisper

Figures 1.6, 1.7, and 1.8 (Continued)

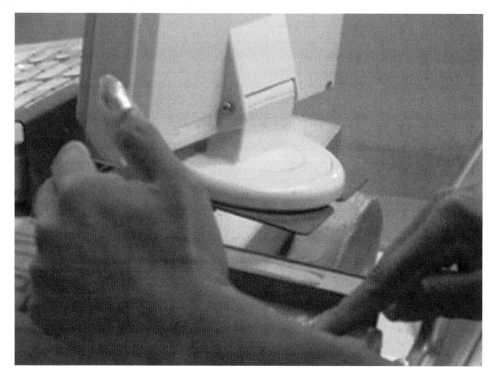

Figures 1.6, 1.7, and 1.8 (Continued)

Title _____   Scene _____   Page ____

Figure 1.9 A fairly traditional storyboard template. I might use this type of template earlier in the planning and visualization of my project, but by the time I'm ready to shoot, I hide these away somewhere. They're great for helping others visualize the action, but don't typically contain enough detail to actually help once I start shooting.

that isn't supposed to be heard clearly, the audio crew will need to account for that during the shot. Actual dialogue to be spoken by the actors does not go here. The entire cast and crew will also have a copy of the script that contains the lines. The description should specify *how* the audio should be recorded, not the lines themselves.

Similarly, the shot details section shouldn't contain the entire scene description or shot description from the script. Instead, it should specify what the shot should look like, and the function of the camera while shooting. For example, you might say, "The shot starts in tight on the water, then zooms out and tilts up to show the vastness of the ocean. Probably shot from a boat or a drone, it will need to be stabilized and on a pan-tilt head." This way, the entire crew knows how to set up and get the shot, with little need for the Director to micro-manage.

Information about location, equipment, and cast/crew needed will most likely be repeated from shot to shot within a scene. But it is important information to have on your storyboard as you plan your shooting schedule. Sometimes, it might make the most sense to organize your days around specific locations so you're not transporting crew and equipment around needlessly. Other times, you have limited days with your actors, so you might need to shoot all the shots they're in within that time frame. In other instances, you might have specialized equipment that you need to rent for a few shots taking place across different scenes, so you might shoot those shots in the same day to minimize your rental costs. Having this information on your storyboards allows you to quickly scan through all your shots and pull the ones out that all need the same location, the same actors, or the same equipment (a process called "pulling shots"), and organize them in

Scene Title_____Scene Number_____ Shot Letter_____

Audio: □ Dialogue   □ Music   □ Sound FX   □ MOS   □ Other

Audio Details:

Shot Details:

Location:

Equipment Needed:

Cast/Crew Needed:

Figure 1.10 The storyboard I typically use for my projects and share with students so they can use it for theirs. It contains substantial space to fill in the details about each shot. Occasionally, I will "brainstorm" my visuals in a storyboard template like the one in Figure 1.9, but most often, I use a storyboard template like the one in Figure 1.10 when I'm planning out my shots. The template starts at the top by naming the scene, for example, the "wide-open ocean" scene from the commercial script examples above. Then it has spaces to write in the scene number (Scene 1 in our example) and the shot letter. It's helpful to storyboard each shot in the scene because there are a number of them. Shots are sometimes numbered, but I prefer to start lettering them at this point, so when I'm slating the takes on set, I can match each shot up to the corresponding storyboard image easier. Continuing from the Brand X shoe commercial example, shot 1-A begins close in on the water and zooms out to show the vast ocean. Shot 1-B shows the marine life. Shot 1-C is an underwater shot of a coral reef.

any way you need to shoot them in any order, like using information tags when sorting through a database.

Planning in a Way that Everyone Can See

Anything worth saying is worth saying again. When planning your project, it is always best to do it in a way so that everyone can see it, visualize it, and work toward making it happen with little input from you, if possible. When I taught a class where students produced a live 30-minute newscast, I felt like I accomplished my job at the point in the semester where I could walk in, sit down, watch everything unfold, and walk back out without hardly saying a word. I knew at that point that I had taught and prepared my crew and enabled them to make the creative choices necessary to go beyond my initial vision for the show. Even though this is an example from live television, the thought applies to any project I've ever worked on and any crew I've ever worked with.

As a producer/Director on a commercial set, I aim for the same empowerment. I plan everything out meticulously so that I don't need to give anyone instructions as they set up for shots. I give them scripts and storyboards ahead of time so they can visualize each shot before even arriving at the location. And I'm more than open to suggestions as the Cinematographer frames the shot, the Lighting Director works on the highlights and shadows, and the audio crew sets up to acquire the best sound. With everyone on the same page, it becomes fun to creatively discuss ways to enhance the shot with your crew instead of focusing on the basics of where to put the camera and how to frame the shot. As I tell students, video production is a team sport. You still have a coach to whom you should ultimately defer, but everyone has to work together toward a common goal to have the best possible outcome. If you're the producer working on the preproduction, your job is to prepare in a way that you or your Director can coach the cast and crew toward that outcome.

How Scripts and Visuals Are Used on Set

Once your cast and crew are on set and shooting, the script and storyboards remain important tools for the process. Obviously, actors will still refer to their scripts at times when they need to refresh their memory on their lines. The Director and crew will refer to the storyboards and scripts as they set up, in order to refresh their memory about what the shot should look like and what needs to happen once they start rolling. The script and storyboards are also important tools to help the clapper/loader fill out the slate for each take, to take notes on about continuity, to indicate whether a take is good or not, and to generally keep a log of what has been shot and what still needs to be shot.

For most productions, a Script Supervisor is a fairly essential position. The Script Supervisor takes notes on a copy of the script (or, as I encourage my students to use, the storyboard template for each shot for their notes) about eyelines, the axis of action, the position of props, wardrobe, and lighting. The Script Supervisor also uses a shot list as a checklist to make sure each shot was actually captured during the day's shoot. It seems a bit silly until you've been on a set for the third 12-hour day in a row, but sometimes a crew simply forgets to capture a certain shot. Often, it's an insert or cutaway, where something a character glances at needs to be shot, or a shot needs to exist in order to smooth a transition in post. But having someone who simply checks off each shot and makes notes about each take is important.

Figures 1.11 and 1.12 On the set of a short film about a poker game, it was essential to have a Script Supervisor (Figure 1.11) to ensure continuity. In this case, stills were taken as we shot so we could reference exactly which cards were on the table in order to maintain continuity from long shots to close ups and from flashbacks to present time.

Chapter 1: Scripts and Storyboards Main Points

- When shooting single-camera videos, regardless of the genre, it is always important to develop an idea beyond a simple tagline and run the idea past potential audiences to ensure its quality.
- Treatments vary by genre, but should always address the concept of the project in a detailed way from start to finish.

- Many single-camera projects require you to think about the audience and the desired outcome of the project before crafting your message or developing your concept.
- There are basically two different kinds of scripts: single-column and multi-column. Each has advantages and disadvantages, and the use of each varies by genre.
- Previsualization should be done in a detailed way so that everyone on crew understands what each shot entails. Good previsualization is all about making sure the time spent on set is as efficient as possible.
- Ultimately, good scripting and previsualization gets you to the starting line for the race. But it is incredibly important to lay the groundwork as well as you possibly can to ensure success and to look back and make notes as you shoot. That way, you can move forward confident that you will have everything you need once you get to postproduction and start putting the project together.

2 Locations

Unless you're shooting entirely in a studio (and even then, at times), securing and scheduling locations will be an essential part of your production process. And although this chapter comes before the one on scheduling, location availability will be one of the things you have to think about when making your schedule. Specifically, this chapter will cover:

Location Scouting

The first thing to think about with locations is whether or not it will even work for your story. This seems obvious, but I've seen lower-budget projects settle for locations that were convenient to access or cheap to rent. A recent student film I watched was shot in a classroom, even though that location made absolutely no sense in connection with the plot of the film. It made it difficult to follow the narrative because the setting didn't give any clues about what was happening in the story. An office setting, although a bit more difficult to secure for these students, would have made a lot more sense.

On the other hand, sometimes specific locations are less important, but the general ambience is essential. Working as crew on a well-known reality show, I helped secure a

DOI: 10.4324/9781003010357-3

secondary location when our first one became too noisy. We started out in a local restaurant, but ended up in a personal residence that worked just as well to convey the "feel" of the interviews we were conducting. Even though the script called for a restaurant, it actually turned out that a house was just as effective as a backdrop for the interviews. It's important to think about the narrative structure, the story being told in the scene, the general ambience, and the specific needs of the project when walking into a location to see if it will work for you.

Ambience

Ambience refers to the look and feel of the location. A smoky nightclub obviously has a very different feel than a bright playground at a park. But even two different playgrounds can tell the audience two very different things. A playground that only has one slide and a few swings, one that has old mulch or weeds growing instead of grass, conveys loneliness and neglect. A playground like that tells the audience that this was once a happy place, but it's outlived those days and is a shell of what it once was. Whether that's the truth about that specific playground is irrelevant. The thing that matters most when considering the ambience of a location is, "what will this communicate to the audience?"

At this point, you should also take some photos of the location. Location stills will help the Director, the writer, and the crew understand the ambience of the location. Stills rarely include details to assist in setup, but if there is an important aspect of the location for setup, it never hurts to have a lot of pictures of a place to help everyone envision the space. Something like a stained-glass window that might cause problems, or a hard-to-find location of a power outlet are examples of pictures or notes you might take to help the crew prepare for the location. The goal as you begin your location scouting is to collect as many details as you can about the space. These details will help the Director understand the shots they need to capture at the location, and they will help the crew understand what needs to happen with equipment to make that vision come to life.

Figure 2.1 This playground is new and modern. The slides are shiny and the plastics have a smooth feel to them. This tells the audience that this playground is a happy place that gets used and is regularly maintained.

Figure 2.2 This is a playground I used for a music video. Even though it has the same color palette as the playground in Figure 2.1, it conveys something completely different. In the video, we wanted to tell the audience that this was a sad and lonely place, where happiness recently existed but doesn't anymore. The chain-link fence set off in the background and the tall grass suggest neglect. The playground in Figure 2.1 would not have worked for this.

I can't stress enough how important the ambience of the location is. If the ambience isn't right for the scene, then it doesn't really matter how convenient it is, how cheap it is, how much natural light it has, or what the sound qualities are like in the space. It just won't work for the story. When scouting a location, this should be the first consideration. And if the ambience isn't right (and you can't really do anything to fix it), you don't even need to go on with the rest of your checklist.

Lighting

The natural lighting in a space can be extremely helpful and save you a lot of time as you set up additional light sources. You can always block out natural light and add your own lights, reflectors, and diffusers to a scene to get the story just right, but that can take a lot of time, equipment, and people to get it done. If a location has good natural light for the story being told, then it can be much easier to just use it. Chapter 5 is all about specific lighting techniques, so the main point here is what to look for when scouting a location.

When you do decide that a location works well for you, it's important to take some notes. What direction(s) is the light coming from? What might cast shadows? If you're shooting indoors, make a note of window locations so you can bring black fabric to block the light if you need to. Pay attention to things that might reflect light or pass light through in specific patterns that might be distracting. Make notes about lamps and other lights in the room and whether they're fixed or moveable. Maybe they'll work as practicals (lights that are part of the scene), or maybe you'll have to find the switch to shut them off completely before adding your own lights.

If you're shooting outdoors, be careful of things that cast unwanted shadows, either on the background or on your subjects. Shadows are something that our brains filter out easily when we're looking at something in person, but they become very distracting on a screen. The same thing goes for reflections. Windows, doors, signs, and even the eyeglasses the subject is wearing can all create distracting reflections and moving "hot spots" that distract your viewers. I see this especially in interview settings for news packages and documentary films. In those shooting situations, it's easy to overlook the surroundings and focus on the subject while shooting. Scouting those issues ahead of time will make it much easier to anticipate and look out for them.

Sound

The sound qualities of the space do matter, and they might even be harder to overcome than lighting if they're not appropriate for your shoot. These might seem as obvious as some of the lighting issues mentioned above, but our brains are remarkable filters with sound issues as well. We rarely pay attention to air conditioning noise, the hum of a refrigerator, the rustle of tree leaves in the wind, the sound of running water, or other ambient sounds that might help tell the story, but are often just distracting to the audience. This is also why room tone is so important: if a sound is constant, audiences actually have an easier time ignoring it. I once shot some b-roll in the largest kitchen in the world. Even though I could understand what the supervisor was saying while we were shooting, none of the audio was usable for the project because of the ambience. I have no idea what the sound was even coming from because it was just everywhere. And the acoustical properties of the room were a nightmare.

When scouting for sound, besides listening for unwanted noises, you also need to pay attention to surfaces. Outdoors, this isn't usually a problem. But indoors, any hard surfaces will bounce soundwaves and create unwanted reverberance (not quite an echo, but the bounce can make dialogue difficult to understand). You should make notes about the surfaces when you scout a location to know what kind of sound equipment you might need, as well as what materials you might bring to knock down or trap the sound waves to "deaden" the reverb. Chapter 6 talks about audio gear in more detail.

Time of Day

When thinking about lighting and sound, it really is essential to scout the location at the same time of day (and time of year, if applicable) that you'll be shooting. Shadows and the direction of the light obviously change throughout the day (and year), so the only way to ensure the light quality is the same when you're shooting is to scout the location at that time. When shooting schedules aren't planned according to the direction of the light, shots are often too bright or too dark, they're backlit, or they have a range of other issues. This matters especially when shooting outdoors, and it's easy to overlook that even 30 minutes can make a huge difference. Directors often try to shoot during the "magic hours" that happen around sunrise and sunset, where the light is diffused evenly across the sky. The actual amount of time varies, but being off by 30 minutes here is not going to be good.

Surprisingly, ambient sounds also change throughout the day (and year). Outdoors, many trees lose their leaves in the fall and sound different in the wind. Insects might be more active during the cooler morning hours than the afternoons. The heater might run more at night than during the day. Once, when shooting a commercial at a grocery store (see Figures 2.3, 2.4, and 2.5), we negotiated after-hours access so we didn't have to worry about people chatting and other distracting noises. But we only scouted the location during the day, so we focused so much on the people that we failed to anticipate just how much noise the freezers made in the store and how much that sound echoed throughout the space. We ended up changing the concept for the commercial and doing a voice-over for the entire thing instead of a direct-address (where the subject talks to the audience on camera) like we had planned. Likewise, the reality show mentioned above, where we had to move locations, was planned for a restaurant in the morning before

Figures 2.3, 2.4, and 2.5 We planned to shoot this with the talent directly addressing the audience, but the acoustic properties of the space made that almost impossible. Luckily, we shot enough b-roll to change up our concept in the editing phase to incorporate a narration instead.

Figures 2.3, 2.4, and 2.5 (Continued)

they opened. Because the location wasn't thoroughly scouted, we failed to realize that the restaurant had a coffee shop above it. During the morning hours, that coffee shop was extremely busy and you could easily hear the footsteps above us, forcing us to waste time moving to a secondary location.

Other Considerations

It seems like a lot to think about already, but there are a few more things you have to make notes about when you scout a location. None of these things will prevent you from using a location like a poor fit, bad lighting, or bad sound qualities will, but they're still things that will waste a lot of time if they're not thought through completely.

Locations of Cameras, People, and Backgrounds

When you do location scouting, it's important to have your storyboards with you. That way, you can start to plan out where cameras might be placed to get the shots planned. When thinking about camera positions and drawing them out on location sketches, pay attention to what objects might be around that will interfere with the shot. Think about what the focal length of the lens might be for that shot, and therefore how far away from the subject the camera will need to be. And especially look for backgrounds that might be distracting. It's easy to accidentally sketch out a map of the location that puts the camera and actors in an ideal spot without realizing that the background will be too busy or too bright. We've all seen interviews on the news where the people walking past in the background are actually more interesting than the person talking. This should never happen when you have time to thoroughly plan your camera locations.

Power Requirements

Power outlets are often crucial to a production. These days, LED lights and cameras are easy enough to power with batteries, but if you're shooting on a location for more than an hour, you'll want to plug everything in so you don't waste valuable time swapping out batteries, or worse, have the batteries die on you in the middle of a shot. If you're not using LED lights, it's essential to scout your power outlets and breakers so you know just how many lights you can plug into each outlet. In a residential setting, an entire floor might be on the same breaker, so you would need to bring stingers (extension cords) to run lights to different floors and split the load between the circuits. With LED lights, it's definitely less of an issue, but you can still overload a circuit if you're not careful. There are websites and formulas online that can tell you exactly what load each circuit can hold, but in general, you don't want to plug in more than two 600-watt lights into the same 15-amp circuit, which means that even for a 3-light setup, you might be running one of them upstairs. You can plug eight to ten equivalent LED lights into one circuit, but you'll still want to make note of where the outlets are, where each light will be placed, and where you will run your power cables. This will speed things up tremendously during setup.

The breaker box in most houses is labeled, and getting access to it is important to see what is on each circuit. It also helps to know the breaker box location while you're shooting in case you do trip one of them. I once set up a 3-light interview in a home that was built in the early 1900s. I was so nervous about plugging in the lights that I ran one stinger all the way to the carriage house just to make sure it was on a different circuit. If LED lights had been an option for me, I wouldn't have had any reservations. When you draw your location sketches (more on this below), you'll want to mark the locations of all of the outlets, the breaker box(es), and which ones are on each circuit.

Director and DIT Stations

Although every Director is different, almost every one will want an external monitor. Sometimes this is a handheld monitor that allows them to be right next to the Cinematographer. But sometimes Directors prefer a large monitor placed on a desk or stand in a location specifically designed for them to see what the camera sees. The handheld monitor allows them to be right next to the action, but the dedicated station allows them to remove themselves a bit and look at things as an audience member would. Neither is necessarily better, but when you scout your location, you'll want to look for a spot to create a dedicated Director's station.

You can easily combine the Director's station with the DIT station if there is enough room. The DIT (Digital Imaging/Intermediate Technician) essentially manages the data on a shoot. Sometimes this means they just have a laptop and they're pulling clips off the SD card or other media that the camera uses, backing up the data, wiping those cards, and getting them back into the camera to help the crew continue shooting efficiently. When shooting 4k or higher, cards often have to be re-used even when shooting just one scene. The DIT manages the hard drives or servers that are being used to store all the data. On a larger set, the DIT will also need monitors to go with their computers and

Figures 2.6, 2.7, and 2.8 The DIT stations for a short film about life, love, and poker. It was essential for the Director, shown working with the DIT in Figure 2.6, to see previous shots so the continuity of the playing cards on the table could be maintained. In one location, the DIT moved from room to room as we shot in multiple rooms so she could have a quiet space to work.

Figures 2.6, 2.7, and 2.8 (Continued)

storage devices. This allows immediate playback so the Director can see a shot and decide whether they want to move on or re-shoot. The DIT station might also be used to screen the dailies (the clips that were shot that day), but often this is done in a dedicated screening room. Regardless, you'll want a space close to where the shooting is happening for the DIT to set up their gear. My preference is to do this in a separated space so the DIT can work and not worry about making noise while the crew is shooting.

Bathrooms, Craft Services, and Other Emergencies

It is so easy to overlook things that become emergencies quickly at a location. I once worked on a TV episode about living a minimalist lifestyle. At one location, the only bathroom was an outhouse and there wasn't any running water. Knowing where the closest bathroom was, how far away it was to drive there, and how to access it became really important really fast. Most locations won't be that challenging, but it's still important to plan and take notes for life's necessities.

In a similar way, Craft Services (setting up food and snacks) is also a really important thing to make the crew happy and efficient. Even on low-budget shoots, it's a bad idea to think a few granola bars will sustain your crew through a long day. And purchasing sandwich fixings and chips is way less expensive than taking everyone out to a restaurant. If you're working on a larger-budget project, hiring a caterer to bring food in and set everything up is a great idea to save time driving to a restaurant. It's a good rule of thumb to have snacks available continuously throughout the day and plan for at least two or three filling meals, depending on how long your shooting schedule has the crew working that day. When producing a TV show called, "Bay Area Views" in San Francisco, we set up a green room (place to relax and eat) in a hallway for the crew and the guests who would come on the show. Even though the show was shot live and was only an hour long, we were often there for about 2 hours setting up before the shoot, so the food helped everyone, especially the guests, relax and settle in for the production. Finding a nice relaxing spot for your cast and crew is an important part of scouting a location.

Finally, I've never been on a set where it was necessary to take someone to the ER, but I still put the address in my location scouting notes just in case. I was a Boy Scout, and I still think being over-prepared is a good thing. As you plan, you might want to put together a simple first-aid kit for your shoot. Know where the nearest access for an ambulance will be, what the address is for the location you're shooting, and have a plan in case something goes terribly wrong. And then hope that you never, ever, have to implement that plan.

Permissions

There are a number of things to remember when securing permissions for your locations. The first thing to check is to see whether the location is a privately owned property or if it is public. If it's privately owned, then you'll need a contract with the property owner. The contract should specify the date(s) and time(s) the property will be used, the fees involved, a description of any changes to be made to the property and how it will be left when shooting is complete, and a list of anything the business is to provide or provide access to (for example, bathrooms).

Permits

If the property is public, then you have to find out if a permit is needed or not. In general, larger cities require permits to shoot and smaller ones often don't. A permit allows the city

Location Scouting Checklist
Comm 3050 Cinematography

1. Camera Locations
   a. Shot List (LS, MS, CU)
   b. Actor Locations
   c. Set/Prop Locations
2. Location of Other items
   a. DIT Station
   b. Cable Runs
   c. Emergency Room and Other Emergency Items
   d. Bathrooms
   e. Craft Services and Green Room
3. Lighting
   a. Location of Existing Natural and Artificial Light Sources
   b. Additional Lighting Needed
   c. Location of Lighting Gear and Cable Runs
4. Power Requirements
   a. Location of Power Sources
   b. Equipment Needs
      i. Number of Power Cables
      ii. Length of Power Cables
   c. Potentially Overloaded Circuits and Location of Circuit Breaker
5. Sound
   a. Acoustic Properties
   b. Cable Runs
   c. Ambient Sounds that Might Cause Problems
6. WiFi Password (if needed)
7. Permissions Needed

Figure 2.9 A location checklist I give students in my Cinematography class to guide their notes as they scout a location. While there might be other things to look for that apply to a specific shoot, this covers the general things.

to control the flow of traffic, if any roads need to be blocked off or police presence needs to be coordinated, and alerts local businesses about possible disruptions. Cities can't legally prevent you from using a location because you're part of the public, but they can control all of the logistics so the city can function properly around the distraction of your project.

A while back, I shot a short documentary film on Alcatraz Island, and I could have approached permissions two different ways. I could have purchased ferry tickets, packed up a light package of gear, and gone out as a tourist would and shoot some footage on the island. I knew that this was legal and probably unobtrusive enough that I wouldn't be hassled. Of course, I didn't use that approach. Instead, I contacted the Park Rangers – Alcatraz is a national park – and talked with them about what I was doing. They actually coordinated with me to send a crew and full set of gear out to the island with the rangers' morning ferry for free. We had to leave at 5am, but once we got to the island, we were allowed to shoot anywhere it was safe, and we had the entire island free from tourists for several hours. We also got to interview the head ranger for the film, and his voicework ended up being essential to the narrative structure.

It's also worth noting that there are some locations that are public that you will not be allowed to shoot without securing permissions first, and those permissions are difficult to come by. I shot part of a promotional video in an active maximum-security prison.

The only reason I had access was because my client was actually the State of Missouri Department of Corrections. The amount of security my crew and I had to go through was unreal, but it was an amazing experience. I also recently completed a documentary film about a mental healthcare institution in Georgia, Central State Hospital. Getting access to a mental institution that still houses patients is exceptionally difficult, and we had to be accompanied the entire time we were shooting. Mentally ill people are a very protected population, and the one day we rolled up and started shooting outside without making arrangements ahead of time, we were met by several police officers within minutes. Even though this is technically public (state-owned) property, there are restrictions.

Colleges and universities have similar restrictions. If you're outside, they won't likely prevent you from shooting, although you should still check ahead of time. But if you try to shoot inside a building or classroom without permission, it would be very disruptive and you would be removed pretty quickly. I've only had one situation on a campus where the police were called on a student, and it was because they were shooting a news package outside of the Student Health Center on STD awareness/testing day. When I discussed the situation later with the university's legal counsel, I was made aware that even though the student was shooting in public at a location where people had no expectation of privacy, the university can control freedom of speech when it might disrupt business operations or have a chilling effect on others' rights. Because things might be different at each school, it's worth exploring what permissions you might need before you go shoot anywhere, even on your school's campus.

Situations Where You Don't Need a Permit or a Contract

If you are shooting in a public space and a permit is not required, then there are still things you'll want to keep in mind and be respectful of. Even though you might be doing things legally, you still need to consider the ethical lines you might draw for yourself and how you might approach those situations. For example, shooting at a public park may be legal, may not require a permit, and you may be within your rights to show people's faces who are playing there, but this might cause a lot of people there to be uncomfortable. It would be wise to do your best to scout a time when the park might not be as crowded, locations within the park to be less obtrusive, and plan a way to inform the public there what your purposes are so they feel more comfortable being there. The First Amendment allows you access to people and locations where people don't have an expectation to privacy, but that doesn't mean you have to be unreasonable about it. As a pool manager for a local parks and recreation growing up, I had to ask people to put away their video cameras, as I received complaints from patrons who were there sunbathing and swimming. Legally, I knew I couldn't make them put away their camcorders. But I also knew that I could call the police and scare them a bit for creating a nuisance at the pool. They almost always complied, and even seemed embarrassed that they hadn't realized the effect the camera was having on the people around them. Of course, that was before every cell phone had a camera built-in, so I'm sure the public's expectations are different now.

It's also worth noting that for some spaces, it will be impossible to figure out if they're public or private; or if they're private, to track down who owns them. County records offices often have the name of the property owner, but that doesn't mean you'll be able to get in touch with them. In these situations, some filmmakers will use the property with confidence, knowing that there won't likely be any repercussions. I draw my ethical line in a different place, though, and I won't use a property unless I'm sure I've exhausted my search for the permission granter *and* I'm sure it's public property. If it's private and I can't

UCM Media Network Location Release Form

Producer Name _____

Project Title _____

I_____(please print full name)

Hereby consent to the photography, recording, filming, and use of my property, located at:

_____

| Street | City | State | Zip |

for the purpose of photographing and recording scenes for the above program produced by the UCM Media Network. These materials will be used only as part of the UCM Media Network's programming and publication that may include DigitalBurg, The Muleskinner, CTV, or UCM Radio-The Beat. The Materials may also be submitted to contests and festivals on behalf of the students and/or faculty in the Department of Communication at UCM.

Permission includes the right to bring personnel and equipment onto the property and to remove them after completion of the work. The permission herein granted shall include the right, but not the obligation, to photograph the actual name connected with the premises and to use such name in the program(s).

The undersigned hereby gives to the UCM Media Network, its assigns, agents, licensees, affiliates, clients, principals, and representatives the absolute right and permission to copyright, use, exhibit, display, print, reproduce, televise, broadcast and distribute, for any lawful purpose, in whole or in part, through any means without limitation, any scenes containing the above described premises, all without inspection or further consent or approval by the undersigned of the finished product or of the use to which it may be applied.

The UCM Media Network hereby agrees to hold the undersigned harmless of and free from any and all liability and loss which the UCM Media Network and/or its agents may suffer for any reason, except that directly caused by the negligent acts or deliberate misconduct of the owner of the premises or its agents.

The undersigned hereby warrants and represents that the undersigned has full right and authority to solely enter into this agreement concerning the above described premises, and that the undersigned hereby indemnifies and holds the UCM Media Network and/or its agents, harmless from and against any and all loss, liability, costs, damages or claims of any nature arising from, growing out of, or concerning the use of the above described premises except those directly caused by the negligent acts or deliberate misconduct of the UCM Media Network or its agents.

Signed: _____ Date: _____
(Signature of Authorized Property Representative)

Figure 2.10 A typical location release form for someplace where a contract or permit isn't needed. This document doesn't have a date or time on it like a contract would, but I've found that having release forms like this on set saved confusion when someone questions whether or not we're allowed to be shooting there, even if we don't legally need permission.

track down the owner, I'll typically move on and look for other spaces that will work for my story. I've also been pretty fortunate that when I do freelance work, my clients mostly provide locations and permissions, so I'm not often securing my own locations.

Location Sketches

When scouting a location, you should also make sketches. You might be able to scout the location multiple times, in which case your sketches might get more detailed each time. But you might only be scouting once, so you need to try to be as thorough as possible.

A location sketch is essentially a map of the area. That map will help guide the crew when they arrive to set up equipment because it will have the locations of the important things on it: camera locations, lighting positions, locations for DIT and Director, actor positions, and the layout of the space. It should have the locations of power outlets, furniture, and props.

Visuals

The visuals are important, but you don't have to be a great artist or use sophisticated CAD (Computer Assisted Design) software to convey your ideas to the crew. A simple, hand-drawn map is sufficient. And if you're using the location for more than one shot, say a Master Shot (a wide establishing shot) and two Singles (a CU of each actor), then you might even want to draw a location sketch for each shot. If the shots at the location are simple enough, then one sketch for the entire scene might be appropriate. Because the positions of the camera(s) and lights might change from shot to shot, things can get messy fast. The most important thing is to convey to the crew setting up the camera and lights where they need to place everything. This will allow the Director to focus on the actors and their lines and movements, instead of taking their time telling every single crew member what to do.

Detailed Descriptions

Either as part of your map, or as notes that accompany the location sketches, you should have descriptions. Sometimes, this means putting a "key" on the map so everyone knows what your symbols mean. Sometimes this means having lines below the location sketch that explain exactly what will happen in the shot. The important thing here is that the ideas are being conveyed to the crew doing the setup. It doesn't have to follow a specific template, and it doesn't require a lot of words, but bullet-points and explanations only enhance the communication about the location.

Planning in a Way that Everyone Can See

I've seen this on many student productions. The preproduction is inadequate, so when everyone arrives on location, the Director spends most of their time guiding the crew. The lighting crew is sitting around while the Director works with the Cinematographer to figure out placement and lens choice, and then the Director moves on to the lighting crew. Meanwhile, the sound crew and the actors are sitting around waiting to get instructions. Eventually, the Director has made the rounds, but too much time has passed and now the shots are rushed to stay on schedule. Or the schedule is just thrown out and everyone feels like they were lied to about how long it would take for the day. More on scheduling later, but the point here is that good location sketches and storyboards will guide everyone during setup. If this preproduction is done well, then copies of the preproduction binder can be handed out to the Cinematographer, Lighting Director, and sound mixer, and the Director can be confident that the basic setup will take place. Tweaks will still be made before the actual takes, but having confident crews who don't need oversight during setup is one of the keys to an efficient shoot.

When it comes to preproduction, and especially storyboards and location sketches, the visuals help everyone stay on the same page. If the vision for the day's shots are only in the Director's head, then it's going to be a long day. If everyone understands and shares the vision and plans for the shots, then the Director can focus on directing the actors and getting a good performance, not micro-managing the crew.

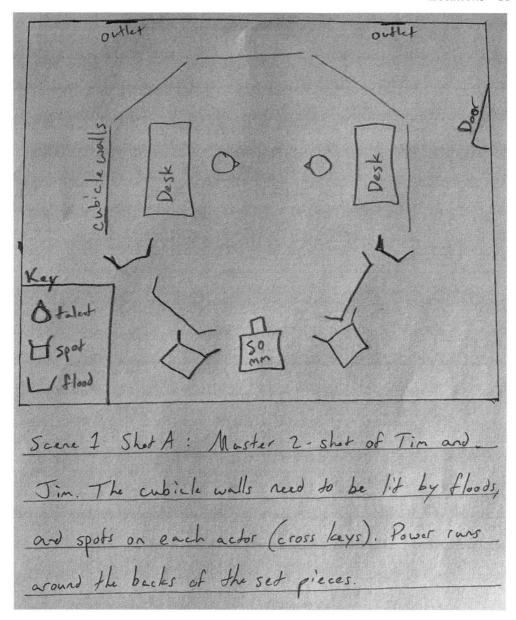

Figure 2.11 A location sketch for the Master Shot of a short film my colleagues and I produced about two temp office workers. This isn't great art, and it didn't require dedicated software, but it's effective in communicating locations to the crew setting everything up.

Shooting in a Studio or Soundstage

Planning to shoot in a studio or on a soundstage is slightly different, but the preparation needs to be approached with the same amount of attention to detail. In a studio or soundstage, you might already have access to a lighting grid. There may be c-stands and backdrops that can be picked up and moved at a moment's notice. Everything is very convenient, which is why many films shoot on a soundstage greenscreen instead of flying to some remote location. You'll be tempted to forego location scouting and making a location sketch because you're already familiar with the layout of the studio and the locations of power outlets and cameras. But I've also seen studio shoots that have become inefficient endeavors because the Director had to spend all their time supervising each part of the setup. And then the acting suffered because the Director was too busy with the crew. And the schedule pushed back late to the point that the crew became frustrated.

With the exception of a news show or other serialized studio shoot, each time you're in the studio you should draw out a location sketch and take notes. When I worked for the local news station, we definitely didn't do any of this. Instead, an outside construction firm was hired once every so many years to come in a re-design the set. At that point, you can imagine that everything was planned out meticulously. There were CAD drawings of set pieces, locations of monitors and chairs, and a detailed map of the new lighting setup. After that, we rolled in each morning and didn't have to think about moving set pieces or camera locations. All of that was planned out thoroughly during the construction phase.

If everyone is familiar with the space and you end up planning more thoroughly than is necessary, you will perhaps waste a few minutes of your time in preproduction. But if you under-plan, you'll waste more than a few minutes of everyone's time.

Chapter 2: Locations Main Points

- Ambience is the first thing to look for when scouting a location. If the ambience is wrong for the scene, then move on.
- Take more notes than you think you'll need when scouting a location. Pay attention to power, lighting, sound, bathrooms, access to emergency services, and a place that's out of the way for the crew and talent to relax.
- You should scout your locations at the same time of day you plan to shoot.
- Figure out who you need to sign off and allow you access to a location. Whether you need to have a contract, a permit, or just a location release form, get it in writing.
- Sketch out a map of the area and include as much detail as possible. This helps others visualize what your notes are already telling them and speeds up setup when you arrive.
- Even if you're shooting in a location that everyone is familiar with, you should be thorough in your location scouting.

3   Scheduling

Scheduling is where all of the details you've collected in your preproduction get together into a plan for production. Specifically, this chapter will cover:

Introduction

When I first began producing videos, I was really bad at scheduling. Like many students, I got the basic pieces together – the script, storyboards, locations, and talent ("talent" is a generic term that refers to the actors or participants who appear in your project) – and tried to schedule as I went. "Hey, I'm free this weekend. What's everyone's schedules look like?" This kind of planning might even work okay for small projects where you're not on a specific timeline. And when you have friends who are working as your crew. But once you take on larger projects with more moving pieces, you need to get pretty good at logistics. You might line up your actors for a weekend when your location isn't available. Or you might have everything in place, but not enough crew to make it happen.

Imagine putting a puzzle together. You wouldn't just pick up one piece and then try every other piece until you find one that connects. You develop a system. Maybe you look for outside pieces first. Or perhaps you group colors together first. Then you look for patterns and try pieces together based on certain characteristics. Putting a shooting schedule together is a lot like that. You might start with your locations if you can only access them at certain times. Or perhaps your outdoor location needs to be shot at a specific time of day or time of year. Either way, that's going to be more important to scheduling than whether or not your crew can work at that time – you can likely find or hire different crew, if needed.

DOI: 10.4324/9781003010357-4

Or perhaps you've contracted specific actors or talent for your project. Their schedule might be tight, or their contract might only allow for a certain number of days. In those cases, their availability might override the scheduling of the location, so you might start with your talent's schedule first. Or there is a possibility, especially if you're doing a class project, that your equipment is only available at a specific time. We often get students who want to shoot their films over break so they have more flexible schedules and they can reserve the equipment for much longer periods of time than during the school year. Regardless, I always begin my schedules with the part that will be the most difficult to nail down. Then I work systematically from there, moving on to the next most difficult thing.

Scheduling Overview

As you start to put the pieces together for your schedule, you'll inevitably start by focusing on an overview schedule that plans in terms of days, weeks, and possibly months. For example, if your actors are only available on the weekends, then you'll start to schedule out crew, equipment, and locations for those weekends. You'll probably get a sense of what shots and what scenes you might shoot on each day. Scheduling out weekly is a great thing, and you need a general idea of your overall timeline for the project. Eventually, you'll need a very detailed daily shooting schedule. More on this below. But you have to put together your overall timeline and an overview of the schedule for the entire project first.

Deadlines

If you have a specific date, like a class due date or a festival entry deadline, then mark that date and work backwards from there as you put your schedule timeline together. Or if that date is further away (or you don't actually have a deadline), give yourself an artificial deadline to work towards. These do actually help. I recently completed a feature-length documentary film I've been working on for over ten years. I did all of the interviews and shot all the b-roll the first year I took on the project. But after that, I just never made it a priority. There wasn't a client or funding source with deadlines to hit, and other things always came up. I only recently finished it because I hired an editor and he and I worked out some deadlines for festivals that we wanted to enter the film into. Having that deadline actually made us push ourselves in a way that I hadn't been able to for almost a decade.

Changes to the Schedule

Changes are bound to happen. Having an overview schedule will allow you to look at everything holistically as you shift things around when an actor gets sick or something else derails your progress. It's just as important that you look at the schedule for other days to see if you can shift gears and shoot something different so you don't get behind. When shooting a music video once, I had an actor get sick for the storyline shots we were planning. About two days out, I got notice that we wouldn't be able to shoot that person for the full Saturday we were planning. It was also too late to coordinate our other actors and locations to shoot different scenes. We were able to salvage some of our shooting schedule, though, by taking a few of the crew who were scheduled for that day, the equipment we already had reserved, and the travel arrangements we already had planned, and shooting some of the b-roll we had planned for a different day. We got some exteriors we needed, as well as some of the filler shots we used later for visual interstitials (clips that can be inserted as transition shots). We didn't make up all the time we missed for that day, but it certainly kept us from getting an entire day behind, and the crew were already scheduled to work, so they appreciated a lighter day than what they expected.

This is probably a good place to mention that this is a textbook covering the basics. There are many more things that you'll have to account for as a producer for a major film or other very large projects. For example, you might have to know union rules for scheduling your Cinematographer, Director, Actors, or others on a film set. Unions might require a specific amount of time for breaks, or that changes to the schedule require a certain amount of notification. Full disclosure: I have never hired or scheduled union workers, but I have worked on a set with them. I've also never had to coordinate flights for cast, crew, and equipment. This can be an enormous headache, but letting everyone schedule their own can be a bad idea as well. I've definitely heard horror stories about unexpected flight cancellations or equipment ending up in a different city when flights aren't centrally coordinated. I am not an expert on these types of scheduling situations, and you'll want to do additional homework before planning a production on that scale.

Re-shoots

For many types of projects, you'll need to set aside some days in your schedule at the end for re-shoots. Even on small projects, it's common to get into the editing phase and find that a shot just won't work the way you imagined it. Maybe you saw some issues in the daily screenings and you need to re-shoot the next day (which will bump another day further down the schedule). Or maybe later, as you edit, you realize there isn't anything wrong with either shot in isolation, but it will be a continuity error if two shots are juxtaposed. Either way, having specific days set aside where there isn't anything else scheduled, but your cast, crew, and equipment are ready to go, is an important part of preproduction. The only thing you can't necessarily line up for your re-shoot days is the location because you may not know which location(s) you'll need. Actors can be a bit tricky as well, because not every actor will be needed for every scene.

The smaller the project, the less time you'll need to set aside at the end for the re-shoots. For a short promo video or commercial, one day might be enough; for a music video, one or two days. For a narrative film, even a short one, you'll probably want at least two days. When I shoot documentary films, there aren't any re-shoots, per se. Instead, I like to set aside a day or two (or a week or two for long-form projects) to get b-roll footage that's missing once I put the rough cut together. In documentaries, the interviews often drive the narrative, and you may not know exactly how the story will fit together visually until you're mostly done editing. Like news packages, though, you can shoot some of the visuals as you conduct interviews and hear the common themes coming through in the words. About the only type of shooting that doesn't require re-shoots is news. A reporter might do their standup more than once, or shoot multiple interviews and questions that don't make it into the final cut. But they rarely have the time to come back a day or two later and re-shoot any of the footage before their package airs.

Shooting Schedule Overview
No More Victims Music Video

Date	Shots	Talent	Locations	Crew	Equipment
05/25/2022	1-A, 1-B, 1-C, 1-D (artist shots)	Johnnie, extras	Prison (indoors)	Dir, Cam, Lights, Grip, Grip	Lights, Cam, Slider, Tripod, Dolly
05/26/2022	2-A, 2-B, 2-C, 2-D, 2-E (artist shots)	Johnnie	Playground (outdoors)	Dir, Cam, Grip, Grip	Reflectors, Cam, Flycam, Tripod
05/27/2022	3-A, 3-B, 3-C, 3-D, 3-E, 3-F, 3-G, 3-H (story shots)	Mada, Policeman	Playground (outdoors) House (indoors)	Dir, Cam, Lights, Grip, Grip	Lights, Reflectors, Cam, Tripod, Slider
05/28/2022	4-A, 4-B, 4-C, (story shots)	Johnnie, Mada, extras	Prison Boardroom (indoors)	Dir, Cam, Lights, Grip, Grip	Lights, Cam, Tripod, Slider
06/13/2022	Re-shoots	Johnnie		Dir, Cam, Lights, Grip, Grip	Lights, Reflectors, Cam, Tripod, Slider
06/14/2022	Re-shoots	Johnnie, Mada		Dir, Cam, Lights, Grip, Grip	Lights, Reflectors, Cam, Tripod, Slider

Figure 3.1 An overview of the schedule for a music video. The "artist shots" are the ones where the artist plays all the way through their song. Each shot would be a different angle or camera move. The "story shots" are ones that give the music video a narrative element to help it flow and to convey the inner emotions of the artist as they play through the song. Notice the two days set aside at the end for re-shoots, and that this overview doesn't have specific times or details about the equipment or the shots.

Daily Schedules

Many of my students do a good job of planning their overall schedules, but very few go beyond that level of planning without being forced. And stopping with an overview is a recipe for disaster once you're actually getting ready for an intense day or week of shooting. Instead, a daily shooting schedule needs to be planned down to the minute for each and every day you're shooting. Otherwise, you won't know if you're running on schedule or not. And when you do take a break for lunch, you won't know how long you can allow your cast and crew to relax. For that matter, you won't even know what time each person needs to be on set in the morning. It's a bad idea to have an actor waiting around for hours until they're finally needed on set. That's either going to cost you a lot of money, or cause ill will if they're doing the shoot for free.

It might seem cliché at this point, but time spent in preproduction saves time spent in production. When I'm producing something, my daily schedules are where everything comes together. There's a reason the storyboards in Chapter 1 (Figure 1.10) are labeled for each scene and each shot. This allows me to schedule each shot for each day and pull the storyboards for those shots easily when it's time to shoot. At the bottom of the storyboard is the planning I already put in for each shot – what equipment I will need, what props I will need, what is happening in that shot, etc. So, as I schedule that shot in my daily shooting schedule, I can cross-reference the storyboards and the script to make sure I'm consistent in my planning. There is computer software out there to help this planning (one such program is called *Movie Magic*), and it is much easier than doing everything with spreadsheets in a "production binder" (literally a three-hole binder with all your planning documents hole-punched or in sleeves where they can be easily removed for the day's shoot). The software keeps details in a database, so when you create your storyboard details, it automatically populates and cross-lists the information into other areas, like your daily shooting schedules. But, as of writing this book, there are no free options out there for any of these software programs, so you'll have to weigh their benefits against their cost.

Your production binder will have your script, storyboards, location sketches, schedule overview, daily schedules, shot lists, and call sheets in it. And if something exists on one sheet in the binder, it should be accurate anywhere else it appears. For example, if the script says Scene 1, Shot A is a close up (CU) of the main character, then the storyboard panel for 1-A needs to be a drawing of the CU shot. The storyboard panel will specify the location for shot 1-A, so your location sketches for 1-A need to be a map of that location with the camera and lights in place for a close up. The storyboard panel for 1-A will also list the crew and equipment needed for that shot, so my daily schedule will list those things as well. When I make my schedule overview, I also know which locations we need for each shot, so I'll make sure we have those secured. And my daily schedules will detail the exact times that I've dedicated to each shot. So, my daily schedules will specify which location is needed at certain times, especially if I'm shooting more than one location in a day. When I crewed for a reality show a few years ago, we actually shot three locations in one day, so it was important to schedule each location ahead of time and to specify in the contracts what time we would be at each and for how long.

Locations

As part of the daily schedule, you need to specify start and end times for your locations. This needs to include setup time and time to strike your equipment at the end. This is one place where it's easy to get overzealous and schedule things too tight. Especially if you're paying for access to a location or you're concerned about overstaying your welcome, it's easy to assume things will go perfectly when putting your schedule together and underestimating the amount of time it takes to set everything up. This is a broad generalization, but I would allow a minimum of 30 minutes for setup time. If your lighting or audio setups are more complicated, then an hour to an hour and a half might even be pushing it. Most scenes I've shot have taken a minimum of 3 hours. And some shoots I've been on spend half a day or more at a single location. The short poker film I was the Cinematographer on was shot in two (very long) days. The entire first day was at one location – the "basement" scene where the poker match was actually taking place. And we were only able to knock out that location in one day because we spent several hours the previous day setting up lights and blocking out camera movements. We still pushed our shooting schedule because of microphone issues and some lights that had to be moved while we shot.

We shot that scene in the back room of a local business. We contracted with the business for the setup day and the day of the shoot. And even though the narrative was told through flashbacks, the poker scene tied everything together. Think, *For Love of the Game*, but with poker as the backdrop. The scene itself was very important to get right. It was worth dedicating the entire day for that one location. And shooting all of the shots and all of the coverage in one day allowed us to transport gear after wrapping for the day, allowing the actors to leave after what wasn't an especially taxing day for them.

They were needed the next day, but only after all the equipment was brought to the next location and set. Because of the set construction, we knew that we wouldn't get a chance for re-shoots at the business, so we made sure that we paid attention to our continuity Director and took stills of every hand. Even though I wouldn't always suggest taking the time, we reviewed footage as we shot to make sure we got everything right. This slowed the day down, but kept us from making mistakes. Sometimes it's better to schedule an important location for longer than you think you'll need. That way, you can be sure to get it right and that you have enough coverage (extra shots that can cover up continuity errors or just fill out a scene to make it less boring) for the edit. It's a beginner's mistake to schedule only enough time for the one or two shots on the storyboard, without allowing time for the Director to find new shots and interesting angles.

And don't forget to bring your contract, permit, or location release form with you in the binder. You don't want to waste any time arguing over whether or not you have the right to be there shooting. Part of your call sheet should include contacting your location owners the day before a shoot, just to verify that everything is ready for you.

Cast and Crew

I often include a call sheet as part of my daily schedule, but if you're using templates or software, you can easily produce a separate call sheet. And if you want to keep things simple for your talent, a separate call sheet is a good idea. A call sheet contains everyone's phone numbers (to, you know, call them), the scenes being shot that day, locations, emergency contact information, break times, and times that everyone is needed on the set. Those call times are different for crew and for talent. The call sheet often includes a weather forecast for the day, but this is just general information for the crew to tell them how to plan and dress for the conditions. If weather can possibly throw off your shooting schedule, you need to be looking several days ahead so you can move things around if necessary. The call sheet also has times for sunrise and sunset, but this info should also be on your location scouting notes and your daily shooting schedule as well.

Whether you only use a daily shooting schedule, or if you also have a separate call sheet, you need to be very clear about what time the crew is to arrive and what time the talent needs to be there. If an actor is only needed later in the day, don't schedule them to come early "just in case" you're ahead of schedule. It's much more likely that they will be sitting around doing nothing and lose their concentration. Same thing goes for specialized crew. If a drone operator is only needed for the afternoon scenes, it will cost money to have them sitting around all morning for the unlikely event that you're running ahead of schedule. Often, the crew will arrive an hour or two before the talent gets there. It's easy enough to have a Grip or production assistant stand in for the talent while lights and cameras are being set.

On a smaller-scale shoot, or something where you're including the client as talent, you might have the cast and crew call all at the same time. In the case of a commercial, for instance, it's not a bad idea for the person paying you to see how much effort you're putting in. Or if you're shooting a music video, the band might even help out with the creative process while you're setting up. More than once, I've seen artists "goofing off" on the set of a music video and gotten inspiration for some coverage shots.

Equipment

I encourage students to put together overall equipment lists. This helps them track down all of the items they'll need for the entire production. If they want to use a flycam rig,

Golden State Advantage Commercial
Call Sheet

Crew Call: 7pm

Date: 03/15/2001
Day: 6

Location: Rainbow Grocery
1745 Folsom, San Francisco

Sunrise: N/A
Sunset: 7:19pm

Weather: 65 degrees, Partly sunny

Times:	Gear Transport	6:00pm (meet at BECA Rental to pick up gear)
	Crew/Setup	7:00pm
	Talent	8:00pm
	Break/Reset	9:30pm
	Talent Wrap	10:30pm
	Crew Wrap	11:00pm
	Gear Transport	03/16/2001 at 7:00am (meet at BECA Rental to unload)

Gear Transport Team

| | Bob Smith | 415-555-5555 |
| | Jane Doe | 415-555-5555 |

Crew

Cam	Bob Smith	415-555-5555
Dir	Steve Price	415-555-5555
Lights	Jane Doe	415-555-5555
Grip	David Jones	415-555-5555
Grip	Harold Johnson	415-555-5555

Talent

| | Sarah Miller | 415-555-5555 |

Hospital: 1001 Potero Ave, San Francisco
415-555-5555

Figure 3.2 An example call sheet. It has phone numbers, but also times for people to be on set, emergency information, and sunrise and sunset times.

for example, they need to know where to rent one. But it's more important to develop a daily equipment list for your shooting schedule. This way, you plan exactly what you need for the day and you're not hauling around (or paying for) extra gear. If you're shooting entirely outside, for example, you probably won't need light kits. But you might need reflectors, diffusers, and flags. And your daily equipment list becomes your checklist as you load in the equipment for transport, both to and from your locations.

It's also tempting to leave small things off your daily list. Batteries are fairly common items, and we tend to overlook them as an essential part of the equipment. Until we don't have one. On one shoot I worked, I spent an entire day driving to the city we shot at the day before, just to pick up the batteries that we accidentally left there. They were expensive rechargeable batteries – worth the trip – that were necessary for the project.

The crew was able to make it work while I was gone with what they had that day, but it was an important lesson for me: always consult your checklist when you load in or load out gear. Taking 2 seconds to consult the list would have told us that the bag of batteries wasn't in the car as we loaded up. But it was a veteran crew and it had been a long drive and a long day of shooting, so we didn't take the time. On a different shoot, it was power cables for my lights. On my checklist, I had, "Light Kit," so when I loaded the kit, I thought everything was good. But I never opened the case to make sure it had everything inside. When I got to my location (after hours, miles away), I found out the rental house hadn't checked the kit and I only had one power cable for six lights. Needless to say, my shots from that night were not great. At first, I was furious at the rental house. But I eventually settled down and realized that I was just as much at fault for not checking over my gear. A daily equipment checklist needs to be detailed enough, and you need to be thorough enough when loading up gear, so that these kinds of mistakes don't happen.

It's also easy to put something like "Camera" on your checklist without writing out all of the other things a camera needs to make it work. If you're using your own gear, or gear from a rental house that you're very familiar with, you can probably get away without having to list each lens, filter, battery, battery charger, tripod, camera plate, or rod. But if you're using rented equipment, or even using your own gear, it really doesn't hurt to take the time to list everything out. When I go up each year to Michigan to shoot the highlight video for the Wakonse Conference on College Teaching, I always create a checklist. Even though I'm using my own camera, lenses, tripod, and camera rig, I'm traveling far enough away that I won't have access to anything I forget to load in. And since I'm also packing a suitcase and camping gear, my car ends up being full of stuff I'm hauling. When I'm packing up to come back home, I rely on my list again to make sure I don't leave anything there. Although I did leave my favorite insulated coffee mug up on Lake Michigan somewhere (before I got so meticulous with my lists), I've never left any camera equipment there. If I did, I'd be making the 14-hour drive back there and my wife wouldn't be too happy that I'd be gone two more days.

Props

Creating a daily schedule for your props is as important as scheduling out your equipment. And for the same reasons. You don't want to have to carry around all of the props for the entire project everywhere you go. And it's too easy to forget one or two things if you don't have an exact list of what you need at the beginning of each day. Like equipment, you'll want to develop a prop list overview early on in the planning phase so you can track everything down. But you'll want your daily shooting schedule to include the specific props you need for each scene you're shooting that day, and you'll want to have a plan for transporting the props in a way that won't damage them.

Case Study: Preproduction on a Promotional Video for Campus Club Milledgeville

When I lived in Milledgeville, Georgia and taught at the university there, I had the opportunity to be the Executive Producer on a promotional video for Campus Club Milledgeville (CCM) (now CREATE, Inc.). Campus Club Milledgeville is a summer program that engages the middle Georgia area with STEAM activities, targeting an underserved population. The project was a great learning opportunity for my students, and it gave me a chance to give back to my community. This case study will take you through all of our preproduction planning, from our initial conversations with our client to our pitch, to our finalizing plans with our shooting schedule.

We spent the first six weeks of the semester in preproduction. We started by assessing the goals of the client. In this case, they had two major aspirations, so we created treatments for two separate videos. The first statement of purpose was, "To promote Campus Club's art enrichment program while showcasing student opportunities, activities, and successes." The second statement of purpose was, "To promote Campus Club's art enrichment program while attracting potential donors, volunteers, and students." We pitched both treatments back to our client, along with storyboards for each. They decided that the concept for the second video was the one they wanted to go with. So, we dove into the preproduction for the video.

Concept 2: Sponsors

Open with a montage of shots and interviews on location of kids saying "because of Campus Club I..." This should show how Campus Club has allowed kids to grow in ways they never thought possible such as: reaching their dreams, and recognizing talents, changing lives, etc. The montage should contain four or five kids with the final montage shot about the Berkeley scholarships awarded. The montage should vary the shots of each person.

All interviews should be shot on location somewhere to differentiate the background and show that the kids are active in the community. The music will begin to build during these shots. Next, have Toyia talking about the goals and dreams of Campus Club and how they've achieved that this year. Then, go to a shot of the teens performing the song they created. Next, have a shot of Greg talking about how they want to provide more for their kids, but have limited resources. Then, have a shot of the kids working together while Greg's V.O continues. Then show one teen talking about what they would have missed out on if it had not been for Campus Club, where they came from, and what Campus Club has given them. These shots should frame a small story of how they have changed because of Campus Club such with stories such as "when I was a kid, the idea of college seemed impossible" or "when I was a kid, I never knew music could change the world'

This should be about 5 interviews with different shots showing different angles the teens while talking. The interviews will take place all in one room to give the viewer the idea that Campus Club is growing and impacting young teens and kids. This should be set up as a montage using different camera angles to give the shots personality, even having teens in the background. At the end of the montage the camera should pull out to a long shot showing all the kids at the end saying "Campus Club gave me a future", or something similar. The montage will be followed by Greg and Toyia walking into the frame to describe what Campus Club gave them, and what it is still giving Milledgeville. These should be short interviews. Finally, go to another shot of the teens performing as the music gets louder. To close, fade in the Campus Club logo with one of the teens saying "Campus Club, Join the movement."

Figure 3.3 On this project, the concept came after the statement of purpose.

<u>Audience Research</u>

In doing the research of our primary target audience (children and their parents), several trends were noticed about children residing in the state of Georgia. First, 45% of the children in Georgia live in families that have low-income - meaning they have an annual income of less than $44,100, according to the National Center for Children in Poverty. Campus Club Milledgeville has an appealing factor for these families because CCM is a nonprofit organization.

For our secondary audience (donators and volunteers) it has been shown that a key motivational factor for people to donate their time and money is when they see an organization that contains a minority. "A 2009 survey by the Center on Philanthropy at Indiana University showed the top three reasons people donate are to help disadvantaged folks meet their basic needs, to make the world a better place and to make their community a better place," (Fundly). All of the partners of Campus Club Milledgeville are also involved with furthering students' education and physical well-being. The organizations involved are dedicated to counseling students, providing them with a healthy diet, and educating them. The appealing factors for these groups would include children who are in need of financial assistance, are being deprived of a decent education, and are not receiving sufficient encouragement to be the best they can be.

The target audiences for this video include low-income families and donors and volunteers who are dedicated to assisting children through their personal growth.

BIBLIOGRAPHY

"Behavior Tips: Attention Span." Early Intervention Support.com. Early Intervention Support, 2010. Web. 29 Jan 2012.
Chttp://www.earlyinterventionsupport.com/parentingtips/behavior/attentionspan.asp&xgt

Boyce, Dave. "What Motivates People to Give to Charity? " Online Fundraising Blog. Fundly, 05/12/2011. Web. 29 Jan 2012. <http://blog.fundly.com/2011/12/05/what-motivates-

Cheng, Benson. "Children's Attention Span By Age." My Blog. N.p., 16/04/2010. Web. 29 Jan 2012. <http://bensoncheng.wordpress.com/2010/04/16/children-attention-span-by-age/>

"Children's Defense Fund." Children in Georgia. Children's Defense Fund, 01/2011. Web. 29 Jan 2012. <www.childrensdefense.org>

"Demographics of Low-Income Children." National Center for Children in Poverty. The Trustees of Columbia University, 19/01/2011. Web. 29 Jan 2012. Chttp://www.nccp.org/profiles/GA profile 6.html>

Dorian, Marc, and Patrick McMenamin. "Do We Really Only Care About Ourselves?." 20/20. ABC News, 23/10/2009. Web. 29 Jan 2012. <www.abcnews.go.com/2020>

Figures 3.4 and 3.5   The audience research (done in 2012). Although the client knew some of these statistics, it helps show them that we've done our homework as well. The graphs help to easily visualize the findings.

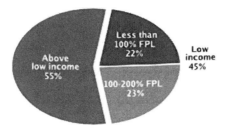

Percentage of Children Living in Low- Income Families

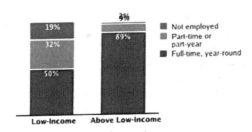

Parental Employment Status in Georgia

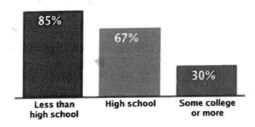

Figures 3.4 and 3.5 (Continued)

CAMPUS CLUB – "SPONSORS"

SHOT OF INTERVIEWEES IN SUCCESSION

We see Campus Club members saying "because of Campus Club I…", with each completing the sentence in a different way. The last one should be of the teenagers who got the music scholarships.

Question: Could you complete this phrase for me: Because of Campus Club I…?

FADE IN MUSIC

CUT TO: TOYIA

Toyia describes the dreams and goals of Campus Club while also telling about everything they have already achieved.

Questions: Could you talk about the goals you have for Campus Club? The ones you have achieved and the ones that you are aiming for in the future?

CUT TO: KIDS PERFORMING SONG

CUT TO: GREG

We see Greg talking about how they want Campus Club to be able to do even more, but they have limited resources.

Questions: Could you talk about what else you want to do through Campus Club, in addition to what you are already doing? Could you briefly talk about what kinds of resources you are going to need to be able to get everything you want to do done compared to what you already have access to?

CUT TO: KIDS WOKING TOGETHER

We see kids working on the song or other projects while Greg continues talking in a voice over.

CUT TO: CAMPUS CLUB MEMBERS

We see kids discussing what they would have missed out on if they had not joined Campus Club one by one.

Questions: What do you feel Campus Club has been able to give you that you couldn't have gotten otherwise? What would you have missed out on if you hadn't joined Campus Club? What differences do you see in yourself that have occurred because of Campus Club?

CUT TO: ALL THE KIDS

Figure 3.6 The script for the project. We used a single-column format because the timing for the video was not all that important, and it allowed us to visualize everything more easily. Also, we couldn't script out the answers to the questions in our interviews. For this type of shooting, scripting the questions is all you can do. But thinking hard about how the answers will cut together is important. Recall that the concept (Figure 3.3) has a montage of the CCM participants saying similar things. This is called a "vox pop" (voice of the people) montage.

Everyone in Campus Club comes together in the shot to say that "Campus Club helped give me a future". Next, Greg and Toyia walk into the shot and speak about what Campus Club has given them and what they believe it is giving to Milledgeville, or could give to Milledgeville.

CUT TO: KIDS PERFORMING

FADE TO CAMPUS CLUB GRAPHIC

We hear a single kid saying "Campus Club, join the movement."

FADE TO BLACK

Figure 3.6 (Continued)

concept 2 : video for sponsors

Teen 1 : " because of campus club, I . . . " (scene 1, shot 1)

Teen 2 : " because of campus club, I . . . " (scene 2, shot 1)

☆ Fade in music throughout these shots

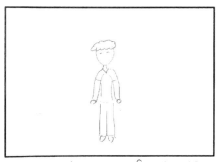

Teen 3 : " because of campus club, I . . . " (scene 3, shot 1)

Teen 4 : " because of campus club, I . . . " (scene 4, shot 1)

Figure 3.7 The storyboard for the project. Although we didn't end up using the storyboard template I suggest (Figure 1.10), these initial storyboards helped the client visualize the concept before we moved ahead with it. You can also see on these storyboards that each panel is a new scene. The first five panels are probably the same scene (Scene 1 with shots A–E). Otherwise, each scene probably is only one shot long. We did not end up taking the time to do the planning on the storyboard templates, but you'll see from the shooting schedule that every detail was meticulously planned out prior to shooting.

Teen 5: " because of campus club, I..." (scene 5, shot 1)

Midshot of Toyia talking (scene 6, shot 1)

Teens performing the song they created (scene 7, shot 1)

Midshot of Greg talking (scene 8, shot 1)

Figure 3.7 (Continued)

kids working together
(scene 9, shot 1)

VO of Greg talking ends here

Teen talking about what
campus club did for him/her
(scene 10, shot 1)

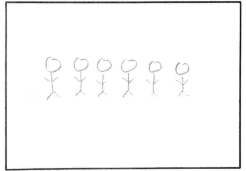

Longshot of teens saying
"campus club gave me a
future!   (scene 11, shot 1)

Greg & Toyia step into frame
with teens and tell everyone
what campus club gave them
(scene 11, shot 2)

Figure 3.7 (Continued)

Teens performing song
(scene 12, shot 1)

cut to black

Fade up campus club logo
(scene 13, shot 1)

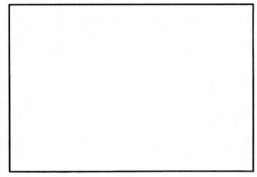

Teen: "Campus club: join
the movement!"
(scene 14, shot 1)

Figure 3.7 (Continued)

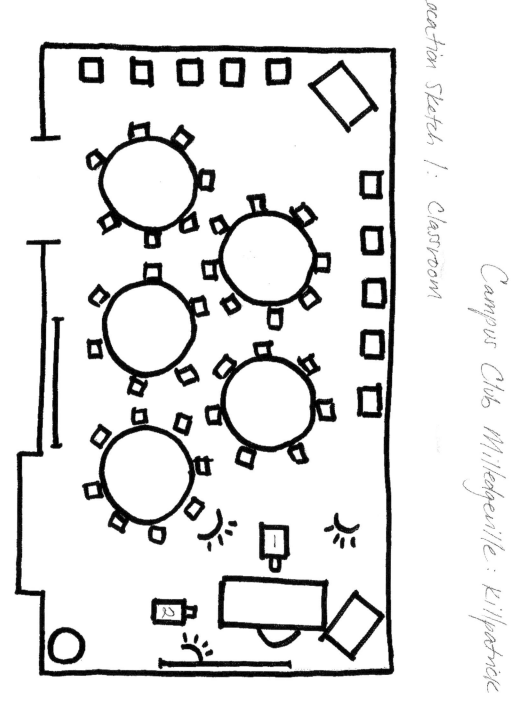

Figure 3.8 The location sketches for the project. If I could go back in time, I'd make sure these had more detailed information in them. They're helpful to set everything up, but they don't differentiate between types of lights, they're missing the location(s) of talent, and there's no text to tell everyone the setup. Still, even this amount of detail can help expedite things once the crew arrives.

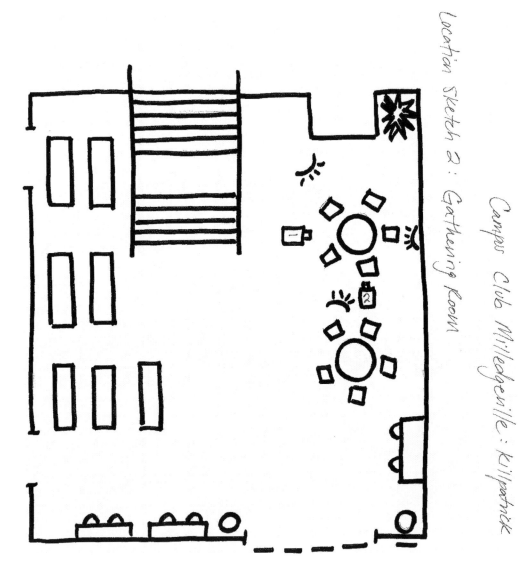

Figure 3.8 (Continued)

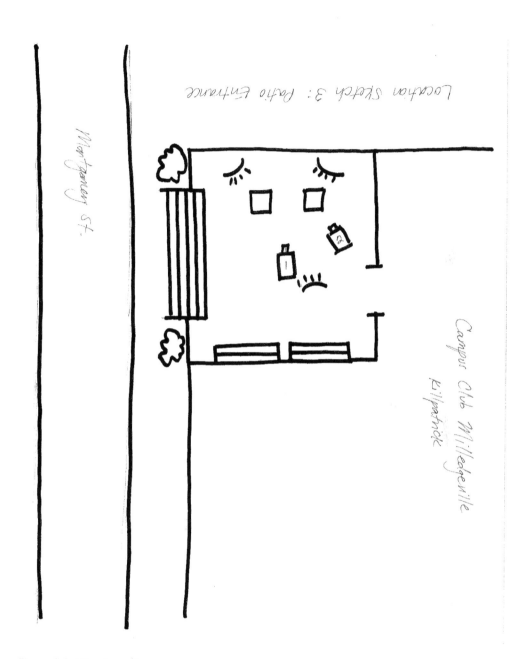

Figure 3.8 (Continued)

Campus Club Milledgeville
Shooting Schedule: Day 1   Thursday, March 1, 2012

8:00-9:00am	Crew Call at 8am/Setup
9:00-9:15am	Talent Call at 9am/Break for Crew
9:15-9:45am	Scene 6 (Toyia Interview)
9:45-10:00am	Break
10:00-10:30am	Scene 8 (Greg Interview)
10:30-11:00pm	Room Tone & Strike

- Location: Kilpatrick Classroom

- Equipment List:
  - Panasonic P2-HD 170 Camera and Bag
  - 2 Panasonic Batteries
  - Manfrotto Tripod
  - Panasonic P2-HD 370 Camera and Bag
  - 2 Anton Bauer Batteries
  - Vinten (Heavy) Tripod
  - Headphones
  - Marshall Monitor
  - 4 L-series batteries for Monitor
  - HDMI Cable for Monitor
  - Lowel Light Kit (3xProLight)
  - Lowel Light Kit (2 Omni/1 Tota)
  - AT 897 Shotgun Microphone and AA Battery
  - Boom pole
  - Elbow XLR cable for boom pole
  - Sony Wireless Lavaliere Mic and Batteries
  - Gaffer's Tape

- Prop List: none
- Crew List:

Director	Brandon	555-555-5555
Camera Operator	Chelsea	555-555-5555
Cam 2 Operator	Chris	555-555-5555
Assistant Director	Kelly	555-555-5555
Audio	Colin	555-555-5555
Lighting Director	Drew	555-555-5555
Grip	Anne	555-555-5555
Producer	Bailey	555-555-5555

- Participants/Talent:

Toyia	555-555-5555
Greg	555-555-5555

Figure 3.9 Day 1 of the shooting schedule for the Campus Club Milledgeville Video. Notice how each scene (each shot, really) is given its own time block. That way, you can know whether you're running ahead of schedule or behind. We were only able to secure a classroom to conduct interviews earlier in the morning, so luckily our talent could get off work then. I like to schedule Room Tone just so everyone on the crew knows we're going to take time to get it before striking and packing up all the equipment. That way, no one gets antsy.

Campus Club Milledgeville
Shooting Schedule: Day 2   Friday, March 2, 2012

3:00-4:00pm	Crew Call at 3pm/Setup
4:00-4:15pm	Talent Call at 4pm/Break for Crew
4:15-5:15pm	Scene 1-5 (student vox pop shots)
5:15-5:45pm	Scene 10 (student vox pop shots)
5:45-6:15pm	Room Tone & Strike

- Location: Kilpatrick Patio

- Equipment List:
  - Panasonic P2-HD 170 Camera and Bag
  - 2 Panasonic Batteries
  - Manfrotto Tripod
  - Panasonic P2-HD 370 Camera and Bag
  - 2 Anton Bauer Batteries
  - Vinten (Heavy) Tripod
  - Headphones
  - Marshall Monitor
  - 4 L-series batteries for Monitor
  - HDMI Cable for Monitor
  - Flexfill Reflectors
  - Diffusion 4x4 Frame & Gel
  - AT 897 Shotgun Microphone and AA Battery
  - Boom pole
  - Elbow XLR cable for boom pole
  - Sony Wireless Lavaliere Mic and Batteries
  - Gaffer's Tape

- Prop List: none
- Crew List: Phone Number
  - Director   Brandon   555-555-5555
  - Camera Operator   Chelsea   555-555-5555
  - Cam 2 Operator   Chris   555-555-5555
  - Assistant Director Kelly   555-555-5555
  - Audio   Colin   555-555-5555
  - Lighting Director   Drew   555-555-5555
  - Grip   Anne   555-555-5555
  - Producer   Bailey   555-555-5555

- Participants/Talent:
  - Patrick   555-555-5555
  - Thomas   555-555-5555
  - Akina   555-555-5555
  - Chassity   555-555-5555
  - Xavier   555-555-5555

Figure 3.10 Day 2 of the shooting schedule for the Campus Club Milledgeville Video. On Day 2, we had to wait for the students to get done with school, so we called the crew at 3pm for setup and then waited until the talent came for interviews. We were also shooting outdoors, so instead of light kits, we had reflectors on the equipment list.

Campus Club Milledgeville
Shooting Schedule: Day 3   Saturday, March 2, 2012

8:00-9:00am   Crew Call at 8am/Setup
9:00-9:15am   Talent Call at 9am/Break for Crew
9:15-9:45am   Scene 7 (Students singing)
9:45-10:15am   Scene 12 (Students singing)
10:15-10:30am   Break
10:00-10:30am   Scene 9 (B-roll of students playing)
10:30-10:45am   Break
10:45-11:30am   Scene 11 (Toyia, Greg, and students' outro)
11:30-12:30pm   Lunch Break (craft services set up at 11am)
12:30-1:30pm   Scene 13 ("Join the Movement" vox pop)
1:30-2:30pm   Pickup shots (re-shoots)
1:30-2:00pm   Room Tone & Strike

- Location: Kilpatrick Patio

- Equipment List:
    o   Panasonic P2-HD 170 Camera and Bag
    o   2 Panasonic Batteries
    o   Manfrotto Tripod
    o   Panasonic P2-HD 370 Camera and Bag
    o   2 Anton Bauer Batteries
    o   Vinten (Heavy) Tripod
    o   Headphones
    o   Marshall Monitor
    o   4 L-series batteries for Monitor
    o   HDMI Cable for Monitor
    o   Flexfill Reflectors
    o   Diffusion 4x4 Frame & Gel
    o   AT 897 Shotgun Microphone and AA Battery
    o   Boom pole
    o   Elbow XLR cable for boom pole
    o   Sony Wireless Lavaliere Mic and Batteries
    o   Gaffer's Tape
- Prop List:
    o   Guitar
    o   Microphone
- Crew List: Phone Number
    o   Director   Brandon   555-555-5555
    o   Camera Operator   Chelsea   555-555-5555
    o   Cam 2 Operator   Chris   555-555-5555
    o   Assistant Director Kelly   555-555-5555
    o   Audio   Colin   555-555-5555
    o   Lighting Director   Drew   555-555-5555
    o   Grip   Anne   555-555-5555
    o   Producer   Bailey   555-555-5555
- Participants/Talent:
    o   Toyia   555-555-5555
    o   Greg   555-555-5555
    o   Students   555-555-5555

Figure 3.11 Day 3 of the shooting schedule for the Campus Club Milledgeville Video. Since it was a Saturday, we had all of the talent there at the same time for the shots that needed everyone. We also took a lunch break and ended the day early enough that we still got good performances. Notice that some "pickup shots" were scheduled as well. Even though these aren't true re-shoots, we knew that if we just couldn't get a shot to work earlier in shooting, we could always come back to it here. Worst case, you either get some candid shots or pack up early. But scheduling this prepares the crew and talent for it. That way, you're not asking them to "stay late" to get these shots.

Chapter 3: Scheduling Main Points

- Scheduling is like putting together a puzzle. Start with the pieces that will be most difficult to schedule (often either the talent or location) and work your way to the easiest piece to schedule (typically the crew or equipment).
- Although you should develop an overview of your schedule for locations, talent, crew, props, and equipment, you should also have a daily shooting schedule that plans every minute of every day you shoot. It's the only way you'll know if you're running ahead or behind.
- Your daily schedule should include equipment, props, talent, and crew. That way, you know exactly what you need for each day and you don't transport a lot of extra stuff or people you don't even need.
- You don't need to schedule everyone to show up at the same time. Often, having your talent call time after setup is almost finished is better than making your talent sit around waiting. However, if your preproduction is thorough enough, your Director can be working with your talent at the tail end of the setup time to make sure they get good rehearsals in and feel good about the shoot.
- Don't be tempted to schedule things too tight. Traveling to a new location and setting up equipment takes time. You don't want your crew or talent to feel pressured to roll with a bad take just to stay on schedule. If you schedule too much time for breaks, no one will be mad. If you don't schedule enough time for breaks, not only will people get grumpy, but their performances will suffer.
- There is software that makes scheduling easier, but you still need to understand the different documents and how each is used. The main advantage of the software is that it puts information into multiple documents all at once and formats everything in fairly standard templates. If you're willing to just double-check all of your paperwork to make sure that everything is cross-listed across documents, then you might find you don't need the software.

Part II
Production (Chapters 4–6)

Good preproduction leads to smoother production. The actual lighting, set design, acting, shooting, and directing is where all the hard work pays off. I enjoy working with cameras and seeing the images come to life. The main goal of this phase, though, isn't to tell the story necessarily. The goal of the production phase is to get enough raw material for the story to be put together in post in a way that flows well and captivates your audience. I've seen students focus on their story too much at this point in the process and end up short when they get to post. For example, a few years ago, I was the advisor for a Master's thesis film. The producer also directed the film. He did an amazing job on the preproduction, but when he was directing, he sped through his shots. He ended up ahead of schedule for many of the shoots, and got some great footage. But when I screened his raw footage with him, we noticed some issues with some of the shots. I asked if he had a different take he could cut in, and he told me that he only had one take of most of his shots. The film came together, and I'm really happy with it, but it could have been even better with more takes and more coverage. The student focused too much on the story, and not enough on shooting coverage (the extra shots to give a scene some depth and to give your editor choices about which shots to use). So, he ended up with too few options in post. When you think of production as the collection of clips, sounds, and performances to be put together in post, you'll get a wider array of options as you tell your story.

DOI: 10.4324/9781003010357-5

4 Shooting

Shooting is where things start to get really fun for me. Knowing how to set the camera up and compose your shots is where the production starts to feel real. It's important to know the best way to set everything up, the different choices you have with equipment, some basic functions of cameras, and how to best compose your shots. This chapter will also teach you how things work on a set and what the protocols and procedures are. You need to learn basic terminology of video shooting so you know what people mean when they say things on set. Specifically, this chapter will cover:

DOI: 10.4324/9781003010357-6

The Tripod and Other Camera Mounts

Never underestimate the value of a good tripod. I still have the first set of "sticks" (film slang for tripod) I ever bought. I've replaced the head on it, but the legs have survived many years of use. There are different kinds of tripod legs and heads, but the main idea is that you need something to mount your camera on. Even light cameras feel heavy after a few minutes of trying to hold them steady.

I prefer tripod legs that have multiple stages, so they collapse smaller and are easier to transport. Some have a spreader that keeps the legs from extending out too far. And most have rubber feet, although some have rubber feet that convert into spikes for use outdoors. Tripod heads also come in a variety of shapes and sizes. You'll want one that is rated for the weight of your camera, and that has a "fluid head," allowing for smoother movements than something slowed by friction. There are other types of mounts for your camera, but all of them are specialty items for specific shots. The tripod is fairly ubiquitous.

Setting Up a Tripod the Easy Way

It may seem trivial, but over the years of shooting, I've even developed a system for setting up my tripod. This is the fastest and easiest way I've found to do it. It seems counterintuitive at first, but if you set up your tripod like this, I think you'll agree with me:

1. If your panning handle is collapsed up against the legs, loosen it and extend it out. You should store your handle like this if your tripod head has a spring-loaded auto-return feature so you don't stretch the springs out. If it doesn't have an auto-return, then you can just tilt the head down to collapse the handle for storage.

Figure 4.1 The panning handle is collapsed for storage. Step 1 should always be to loosen the handle and extend it out. Otherwise, it will prevent the legs from extending outward.

2. Keeping the legs together, extend the top-most section of the leg, making the tripod taller. By keeping the legs together, it should be easier to release and tighten the locks for the section. If your tripod has a spreader in-between the legs, be sure you're extending all three legs at the same time. I usually undo all three locks, extend the legs out, then lock all three in place. Extend all three legs together until the top of the tripod head is about even with your chin. This height will definitely change based on your subject matter and shot composition – for example, a sit-down interview will be

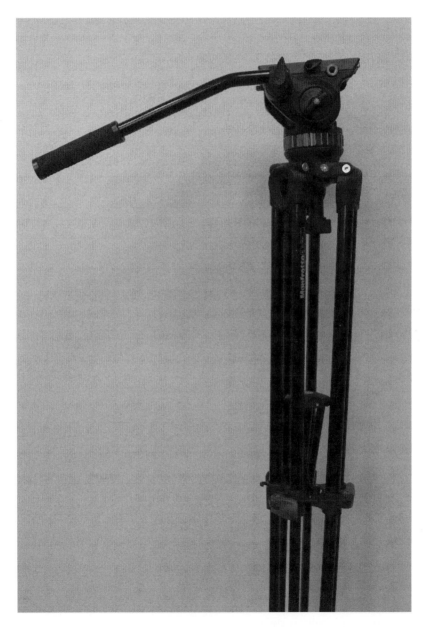

Figure 4.2 It seems counter-intuitive, but I leave the legs together while I extend them. No matter how many sections the tripod has, this speeds up my setup time and keeps the legs the same length, so they're likely close to being level by the time I spread them out.

shot slightly above the subject's eye level, not necessarily at a height that's comfortable for you. But chin-height will put the camera at the most comfortable level for you to shoot from.

3. Spread the legs out. If your surface is level, extending the legs out evenly will keep the legs pretty much level once they're spread out.

4. Most tripods have a ball-head with a level bubble built in. Reach underneath the head, loosen the ball adjuster, and roll the head around until the bubble in the level is inside the circle. Now, your camera will be level once you mount it to the tripod.

5. If your tripod doesn't have a ball head, then your only option is to make small adjustments to the legs to level out the camera. My system for that is to lower one of the legs until the bubble is "pointing" to one of the other two legs. Then, I lower the leg it's pointing to until the bubble is in the middle. If you're adjusting all three legs on a tripod after setting it up, you've done something wrong.

6. Remove the camera plate from the tripod head. There is some variation here, but most camera plates slide on and off from the back (where the panning handle is), and most have a locking mechanism and a release button. Loosen the locking mechanism first, then push the release button as you slide the camera plate off.

7. Mount the camera to the camera plate on the tripod head. You want the camera screw to be fairly tight – I keep a nickel in my pocket to use as a screwdriver – and pay attention to which way the lens of the camera needs to be facing relative to the camera plate. Many plates only slide in from the back (and only slide in facing the front), and you don't want the camera to be on backwards. Camera plates often have a little brass

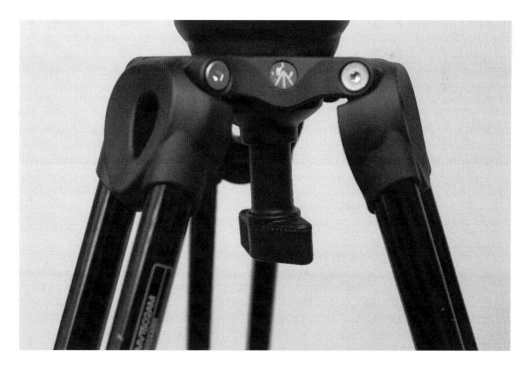

Figure 4.3 The adjustment knob for a ball head. Ball heads certainly make it easier to level the camera. But you have to be careful that your legs are still fairly level so they're stable in their ability to support the camera weight.

Figure 4.4 The bubble level on tripod heads is round. The goal here is to adjust the ball head until the bubble is in the center of the black circle.

knob in front of the screw that helps stabilize the camera on the plate. The last thing you want is for your camera to wobble on your tripod or, worse yet, unscrew and fall off.

8. Slide the camera plate back onto the tripod with the camera attached. You should hear a click as the release button trips. If you don't, you might not have the camera plate completely down into the channel it slides into. Then, tighten the camera plate lock. Don't ever let go of the camera until you've checked to make sure it's secure. I usually lift up a little bit and try to wiggle the camera around before letting go.

Camera Safety

For most professionals, your camera is how you make your living. Even if you own more than one, having a camera break is an expensive and time-consuming event. As a student, the equipment probably doesn't belong to you, so you should be even more careful with it. There are a few things you'll want to look out for as you set up and use your camera.

First off, make sure that when you set up your tripod, the legs are wide and stable. Some spreaders actually extend out, and you'll want to make sure the legs are as wide as you can get them in the space you're shooting. On uneven ground, the legs shouldn't be the same length. Instead, the center of the tripod head should be directly above the center

Figure 4.5 Tripod legs without a ball head attached. In this case, your only option is to make adjustments to the leg lengths to level your tripod head.

of the three legs. And if you're shooting outdoors on an uneven surface like a hillside, there are spikes on your tripod's legs that should be exposed so they stick into the dirt and prevent your tripod from slipping.

You should also make it a rule for everyone on set that the camera gets removed from the tripod and carried separately any time the tripod needs to be picked up and moved. Often times when equipment is being moved to set up a new shot, many people are involved in moving the camera, tripods, lights, and audio gear. It should be clear to everyone that slinging the tripod over your shoulder with the camera attached is not a risk worth taking to save a few seconds.

I also caution against leaving the camera on the tripod during breaks and overnight. This one is easy to forget, and as long as you're keeping an eye on it, it's probably okay to leave the camera on the tripod during a short break. But when everyone breaks for lunch, I would take the time to be safe. When I bought my very first camera as a freelancer, I was shooting a promotional video for a camp. I got done one evening and left the camera set up on the tripod overnight. Sure enough, the next morning some campers were running through the dining hall and knocked over my tripod. Luckily, the camera didn't break. But the weight of it falling snapped the tripod head and broke it. Remember how I told you I've replaced the head, but not the legs? This is why.

Lastly, I try really hard to take care of the lens. Some cameras have lenses that are interchangeable, and some cameras have a built-in lens. Either way, I keep the lens cap on until I'm ready to frame a shot or start shooting. Lenses are made of glass, and they can get scratched. More commonly, though, is that leaving the lens exposed for long periods will allow dust to settle on it. This will cause your shot to be less clear and will take time to clean. Keep a microfiber cloth handy. These are specifically designed to clean your lens without leaving any fibers behind. And be sure to keep the cloth clean as well. If you go to clean your lens and there's dirt on your cloth, you could easily scratch the lens.

Other Camera Mounts

Tripods aren't the only way to mount a camera. For stationary shots, they're the best way. But for shots where the camera needs to move, there are an increasing number of specialty mounts out there. For each type of mount, you should read the manual and watch videos to learn how to use it. There are too many specific types out there, but here are a few and generally how they work:

A three-axis gimbal allows you to hold the camera on a stick (or mount it to a vest of some kind to offload the weight from your hands). The gimbal has motors that constantly adjust as the camera is moved, causing the image to "float" around a little as you move. Gimbals give the viewer a first-person POV (point of view), but aren't nearly as jarring as if you try to hold the camera by hand or rest it on your shoulder as you move.

A jib is an extension of a tripod, but the camera is mounted on the end of a long arm. This allows the camera to go much higher and lower than a tripod, and allows for movements that feel "sweeping." These shots are often used as establishing shots, where you see everything from up high and then sweep down into the action and main characters. Jibs take practice and balance, so the shot can still float a bit if you're trying to use one for a static shot. There are very expensive computerized jibs out there that do a much better job of this.

A slider is a set of rails that a tripod head slides across on ball bearings. These shots are smooth and are best used to create a slow, subtle sense of movement. Good sliders are heavy and need stands at either end to distribute the weight as the camera slides across. There are some lightweight sliders out there that are intended for DSLR cameras and other lightweight cameras. When purchasing a slider, pay attention to the weight limit.

A dolly is a cart that the camera mounts to. Dollies are usually large enough that the cameraperson rides along as the dolly is pushed by a Grip. For even smoother shots, dollies are built on rails, much like a slider. Dollies and rail systems are bulky and expensive, though, so you don't often see them on the set of low-budget projects. There are many DIY hacks out there for creating a similar look, though. I've even used a wheelchair to get a "dolly" shot. And there are "spider dollies" that basically add wheels to your tripod. As long as your floor is pretty smooth, any set of wheels can add movement to your shots.

A steadycam is a shoulder harness with a spring-loaded extension arm to mount the camera to. Much like a gimbal, the spring-loaded arm allows the camera to "float" as you walk around with it. Steadycam rigs have come down in price recently, but they still take a bit of skill to operate. In Hollywood, some people build entire careers as a steadycam operator, and their skill with camera movements is worth the money.

Much like a steadycam, a drone requires a skilled operator. Not just for safety and knowledge of regulations, but flying a drone smoothly enough to get quality shots is a skill that requires practice and coordination. The best drones allow you to mount any camera and control the camera and the aircraft separately so one person can focus on flying while the other one focuses on getting a good shot.

Monopods are not recommended for video work. Still photographers often use them because they are easily transported, but keep the camera steady enough to snap good crisp shots. For videography, a monopod is too difficult to keep still while you're shooting.

There are other mounts out there, but most of them are very specialized and not often seen outside of the film industry. Even some of the ones listed above are often seen on larger-budget shoots, but given how filmmaking techniques are permeating through other areas of video production, it's still good to know what's out there.

The Camera

The camera is the tool you'll use to shoot your video images. Essentially, cameras are a lens that focuses light onto a sensor that records each pixel's color information to the computer inside the camera. The body of the camera houses the sensor and the computer. The size of the sensor matters (more on this later), as does the processing power and computer algorithms the camera uses. The lens might be attached, or it might be interchangeable. There are many different cameras out there, but they fall into three main types: DSLR/mirrorless cameras, camcorders, and cinema cameras.

Types of Cameras

DSLRs began as still photography cameras, but when manufacturers added the ability to record videos, these cameras (along with the newer mirrorless versions) became the main tools of many videographers and Cinematographers. DSLRs have the advantage of good image quality, but often without the expense of a cinema camera. Lenses can become expensive, though, and good quality DSLR lenses can end up costing more than the camera itself. DSLRs also typically have compressed codecs (they don't record all of the image information hitting the sensor), which means the quality of the image is lower than a dedicated cinema camera, even if the lens is high-end "glass" (slang for lens).

Figures 4.6 and 4.7 A DSLR camera being handheld to shoot still photography versus being mounted on a shoulder rig with counterweights to stabilize the shot for video work.

There are an increasing number of books and resources out there for using a DSLR for video production. For the most part, DSLR cameras have the same functions as camcorders and cinema cameras. My main camera these days for smaller video projects is a DSLR, but for many live events, I still use a camcorder because of the ease of transport and use. And of course, when I shoot a film, I'm using a dedicated cinema camera because of the better image quality. I've found that to get the best image from my DSLR often takes more money (for lenses and rigs to mount the camera on) and time (for setting up the rigs) than using a camcorder. Even though the camera itself is typically less expensive and easier to transport, the additional gear needed to make it function like a camcorder often makes it overall more expensive to shoot with a DSLR instead of a camcorder.

Camcorders, sometimes just called, "video cameras," are typically self-contained cameras. Once you have one mounted on a tripod, you're pretty much ready to shoot. Because of the ease of transport – you don't need to carry around a case full of lenses to swap out – and the ease of use, camcorders are the preferred cameras for news and sometimes even documentary films. When I worked for a local TV news station as a production assistant, the reporters were often required to know how to operate the camera. For big stories, a photog (dedicated videographer) would run the camera for them. But for many stories, the reporter needed a camera that was easy enough to set up quickly and use with auto-functions so they didn't have to worry about having to run the camera while also reporting the story.

Camcorders always have a built-in battery plate so you can just slide a battery on and go. Some cinema cameras require a separate battery plate with cables to run to the camera. And camcorders often have a built-in zoom lens. Some have bayonet-mounted lenses, but these are rarely swapped out for other lenses and pretty much feel like they're part of the camera itself. Camcorders usually have XLR audio inputs built into the camera as well. The audio recorders on these cameras are much better than the ones built into DSLRs or cinema cameras because of the need to "run and gun" with camcorders. When shooting with a DSLR or cinema camera, we usually record audio dual-system (record the audio separately and sync it with the video in post), so those cameras don't need higher-end audio inputs or recording hardware.

So why wouldn't you just use a camcorder for everything? They typically have a less "cinematic" look. Even though lenses and camera hardware can be quite good on a camcorder, the sensors are almost always smaller, which leads to deeper depth of field (more on this later). Movies, television shows, and music videos have all shifted toward shallower depth of field for many of the shots, so camcorders look too much like live TV and less like movies. I used a higher-end camcorder for my first feature-length documentary film, and when I watch it now, I have to admit that I'm a little disappointed with the "look" of the images. As I walked the hallways of the mental institution the film is about, I loved the convenience of the camcorder. I could easily zoom using the rocker switch on the handle, I never had to swap lenses, I didn't need special rigs or counterweights to move with the camera as I shot, and the wireless microphones plugged in easily. I finished shooting on the film in 2012, and if I were to shoot the film again, I'm not sure if I would choose the camcorder or a newer cinema camera.

Cinema cameras typically have larger sensors than camcorders, and even lower-cost DSLR cameras. This, along with the availability of very high-quality lenses and high-end computers inside, gives the cinema camera unparalleled image quality. Like a DSLR camera, cinema cameras allow you to change out lenses and require additional gear to make them function like a camcorder. The additional gear typically includes a follow focus

Figure 4.8 The very first video camera I ever owned was this camcorder. It had audio inputs, a zoom lens (the lens could be removed, but the stock lens was really good and I never bought any additional lenses for this camera), a shoulder mount, and recorded to MiniDV tapes. I loved this camera, but now even my cell phone is more convenient and shoots higher-quality video. My current rig is the camera in Figure 4.2. Same conveniences, but the DSLR takes longer to set up.

wheel to allow you to turn the focus ring on the lens without touching the lens (and potentially shaking the shot), a matte box to shade the lens and prevent lens flares, and an external monitor for the Director (and possibly a second monitor for the First AC (Assistant Camera) to adjust focus while the Cinematographer moves the camera. It can make a cinema camera look like a massive machine with cables and things sticking out everywhere.

Types of Lenses

There are really only two types of lenses: those that zoom (change focal length) and those that don't. In a "prime" lens (one with a fixed focal length), you typically get a higher quality lens for less cost. The iris generally opens wider on a prime lens, allowing for a shallower depth of field and better low-light shooting. This is why Cinematographers often shoot their movies using prime lenses. The downside of prime lenses is that you have to physically change lenses if you want a closer shot than the one you have. So prime lenses can be more time-consuming to use. Imagine having to swing away the matte box and slide the follow focus over every time you wanted to zoom in tighter. Good quality cinema zoom lenses cost a lot of money, though. So far, all of my shooting on cinema cameras has been done with prime lenses.

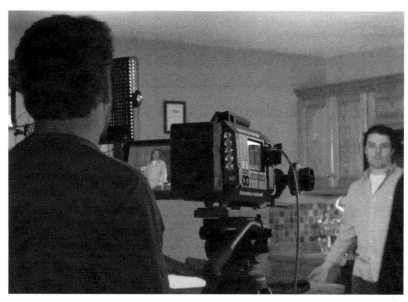

Figure 4.9 A cinema camera with the follow focus wheel sticking out. This camera has several built-in monitors, but there is still a cable running to the Director's monitor. Notice, though, that the camera has extra BNC connectors on the back to connect even more monitors and additional gear.

Figure 4.10 This cinema camera needs a lot more outboard gear – the matte box on the front, the external monitor for the Cinematographer, and the rail system – everything is mounted external to the camera body. Even the battery is attached to an external plate and connected to the camera through an external cable.

Zoom lenses can either be manual, where you turn a zoom ring to shift the lens focal length, or they can have a servo motor built in. The servo motor allows you to zoom automatically using a rocker switch (often labeled "W" for "wide" and "T" for "telephoto"), usually found close to the handle for easy access. Camcorders almost always have a servo zoom, whereas DSLR and cinema camera lenses most often do not. Zoom lenses use a series of internal lenses to alter the focal length of the light entering the lens.

A wide-angle lens will show a wider field of view (the amount of the scene we are able to see in the shot) because of how the lens bends the light inward so rapidly. Wide-angle lenses are lenses with smaller focal length values. For example, a 20mm lens is fairly wide. A 10mm lens would be even wider and show even more of the scene. When someone uses the term "wide shot," what they generally mean is a fairly wide-angle lens shot that includes much of the set surrounding the talent.

A narrow-angle lens will show a smaller field of view. Audiences typically read these shots as being closer in to the talent, but the camera might actually need to be further away to be able to use a narrow angle lens. Narrow angle lenses begin around 50mm and go up from there. The reason there aren't exact values is due to the differences in sensor size. A 50mm lens will look different on a full-frame (typically 35mm) sensor compared to a slightly smaller (cropped) sensor. A 70mm lens will appear slightly closer than what we see with our eyes. A 300mm lens will appear very close, even if the camera is fairly far away.

Focal length values are a continuum, not discrete categories. What this means is that a 600mm lens is very narrow compared to a 300mm lens. And even though a 55mm

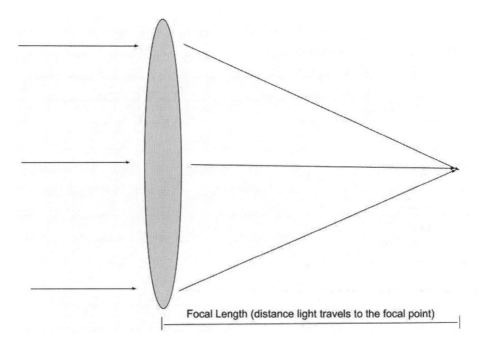

Focal Length (distance light travels to the focal point)

Figure 4.11 The focal length of a lens refers to the distance light travels after the lens "bends" it inward toward the sensor of the camera. It is always measured in millimeters (mm). The longer the focal length, the more "zoomed in" your image appears. An object shot with a focal length of about 35mm (on a full-frame sensor) would appear about the same distance away as our eyes see.

lens might be slightly narrow, it looks very different than a 150mm lens, which is more narrow. And as you get towards the extreme focal length values, your image can become distorted. A lens that is very wide will give you a "fisheye" effect where straight lines appear to bulge outward. A lens that is very narrow will cause objects to appear closer together and will "flatten" the image. When I shoot interviews, I always use a 50mm lens so my subjects appear fairly natural and not distorted. When shooting still photography portraits, however, I will sometimes cheat a bit and use a pretty narrow lens to get a shallow depth of field and flatter my subjects.

Codecs and Shooting Modes

The computers inside any type of camera have to convert light coming in through the lens into binary code (computer language). There are many different codecs (encoding and decoding algorithms) that cameras and computers use to record and reproduce later the color and brightness information. This is an oversimplification of how a sensor actually records the information, but essentially, each pixel (picture element) represents one tiny dot of information. Sensors and screens have millions of pixels and are often referred to by how many dots they have from top to bottom (we call this their "lines of resolution").

Figure 4.12 A fairly extreme wide-angle lens. The focal length is 4.44mm. Since this was shot with a cell phone with a very small sensor, it doesn't look as wide as 4mm would on a DSLR or cinema camera, though. Notice how much of the surrounding scene is in the shot and how the car distorts – the front end looks much wider than the back.

Figure 4.13 A shot of a beach using a 150mm lens. The hills in the background look closer here than they did to my naked eye at the time because this is a narrow-angle lens. Although we see a lot of the background, we don't see a lot of the sides of the scene. We're missing the rest of the beach and the water because the field of view is narrow.

Figure 4.14 A shot of the same beach taken moments later with a 600mm lens. This is an extreme narrow-angle lens that brings everything closer together. The hills are now gone because the shot is so much tighter. And the depth of field (the part of the depth axis that is in focus) is much shallower, meaning that objects that are actually quite close to the subject are out of focus.

HDTV is 1080 pixels tall by 1920 pixels wide. We simplify this to simply say 1080. 4K television is actually 3840 x 2160. 8k is 7680 x 4320.

There are also two different scanning patterns. Scanning pattern refers to the process a television takes to recreate the image, but it also matters in the encoding process as you record the image inside the camera. Interlaced scanning (where the screen reproduces the odd-numbered lines first, then goes back and reproduces the even-numbered lines) is noted by putting an "i" after the lines of resolution. HDTV that is interlaced is shot and reproduced at 1080i. Progressive scanning means that each line is reproduced consecutively. This scanning pattern is noted by putting a "p" after the lines of resolution – 1080p for HDTV. When you shoot video or film, the lines of resolution and scanning pattern is one of the choices you will have to make. I shoot almost everything in 1080p these days because most people are watching content on HD screens and not 4k yet. HD files are also significantly smaller to store and transfer compared to 4k and 8k. All of that image information for each pixel takes up hard drive space on a computer! 4k does have the advantage, though, of being able to crop an image (use only a smaller part of the image itself) without losing resolution. Because of this, I often shoot in 4k with my drone because it has a fixed focal length lens.

Frame rate is another choice that you have to make when shooting. Frame rate refers to how many complete images the camera records and the screen reproduces during each second. For video, common frame rates are 30fps (frames per second) and 60fps. For film, 24fps is the standard. The only reason to use any other frame rate is if you're shooting something you want to put in slow motion in post. By shooting a super-high frame rate, when you put things into slow motion, you can maintain the illusion of movement smoothly. When you add frame rate in, you'll see camera settings like, "1080 60i." This setting would mean you are recording 1080 lines of resolution at 60fps with an interlaced scanning pattern.

Lastly, you'll have to decide the actual codec – the computer language the camera uses to write the information about each pixel – that you want to shoot in. Many cameras can shoot multiple codecs, so you want to be sure you're using the right one. H.264 is a common codec if you're shooting something for the web. QuickTime (.mov files) is another popular one. With many of these codecs, you can specify the video format (1080 60i) and the computer language (Prores) the camera uses separate from one another. It's worth reading a bit more about each one, and your camera manual should be helpful in choosing one. You should also check with your editor or your editing software to see what they prefer. I shot a documentary film once in a codec called, "DVCProHD." At the time, it made sense. Now, it's a dead codec and I had to transcode (change from one codec to another) all 30 hours of footage before editing.

"Shooting modes" refers to the exposure setting you need to have the camera in prior to shooting. On a video or DSLR camera, there is often a wheel you can turn to put the camera into Manual Exposure Mode, Auto Exposure Mode, or some kind of hybrid mode where you can control some settings manually, but the camera will extrapolate the other values to make sure your image is exposed properly. Again, reading this section of the camera manual is worth it so you know what you're getting in each shooting mode. My DSLR camera has a simple wheel that turns and makes it obvious what mode I'm in. The camcorders we use for our live events are totally different. Once you put them in Manual mode, you still have to push buttons to turn off auto control for Gain, Aperture, and Shutter Speed. Otherwise, even in Manual mode, everything will still be set automatically.

I will also say here that I've heard many times that "professionals don't shoot in manual." I completely disagree with this statement, but I understand the sentiment. True professionals use whatever mode will get them the best image consistently, and switch between modes depending on their subject. Sometimes, shooting in auto is a good idea. In a live event where I don't necessarily know what's going to happen next, or where I might need to point my camera, I don't really have the time to make all the manual adjustments needed every time something happens. In those cases, I leave the camera on autofocus and autoexposure. If I'm shooting a fictional scene where I have the time to compose every shot, I definitely don't want to risk the chance of the autofocus jumping to the background or the autoexposure darkening on me. In those cases, I shoot with everything in manual.

Camera Exposure

Exposure is often oversimplified. We tend to think of exposure as overall brightness of the image. But in digital imaging, it's a bit more complicated. With digital technology, we can always change the brightness and contrast values in post. So, when we talk about exposure, what we're really referring to is how much detail is captured in the highlights, the shadows, and the midtones. As long as we allow enough light to come into the lens and get recorded by the sensor, those details can always be adjusted in post. With digital, we only run into real trouble when we overexpose (lose details in the highlights) or underexpose (lose detail in the shadows) and can't recover those parts of the image in post. It's almost impossible to capture the entire range of luminance (brightness) values of a scene, so when we talk about "proper" exposure, we're shooting for a good medium – details throughout many of the highlights and shadows. Even the best cinema cameras can't expose the entire range. The one I use has 16 stops of dynamic range, which is pretty good, but it can't expose the deepest shadows and the brightest highlights at the same time. HDR technology allows cameras to expose a wide dynamic range as well, but it has its limitations too. So, when I shoot a scene, no matter what camera I use, I often have to make choices. Sometimes, those choices are easy. My actors always need to be properly exposed, unless I'm shooting a horror film or something where they need to be in the shadows. If I'm shooting a commercial, the product needs to be exposed well. Of course, we can bring the subject and background into the dynamic range of the camera by adding lights (more on that later), but that isn't always an option. There are really four ways to control the exposure on your camera. The "Exposure Triangle" refers to the settings for your aperture, your shutter speed, and your ISO. The fourth way we can change exposure is to add an ND filter.

Figure 4.15 An underexposed, properly exposed, and overexposed photo of the same subject. In the underexposed photo, details are lost in the shadows, like the lettering on the sign. In the overexposed photo, details are lost in the highlights, like the edges of the sign.

Aperture/Iris

The aperture is the hole through which light enters the lens and is focused onto the sensor. The iris is the blade mechanism that controls how large the aperture is. In reality, we typically use the terms interchangeably. In digital cinema and still photography, we typically use the term "aperture" (no "a" after the "r"). In video, we call it the iris.

As the opening gets larger and lets more light in, your exposure gets brighter, raising the details in the shadows, at the expense of possibly losing details in the highlights. As the aperture gets smaller, less light comes in, and the exposure decreases. In cinema and still photography, we measure the aperture in f-stops. Lenses that open especially wide have a good range of f-stop values. My fixed focal length 50mm lens I use for shooting interviews, for example, goes from f/1.4 (where the aperture is wide open and lets a lot of light in) to f/22 (where the aperture is closed down and lets very little light through). When shooting video, including live TV, we are rarely so precise with our measurements. Instead, the camera person just knows to "iris up" if the image is too dark.

Figure 4.16 The aperture is the hole in the center of the lens. The iris is the blade mechanism that expands and contracts to control how large the aperture is.

The aperture is one of the points on the exposure triangle. The tradeoff when you use the aperture to adjust exposure is that your depth of field changes (DOF refers to the amount of the depth axis that is in focus). When your aperture is wide open (a low f-stop value), the DOF is shallow, meaning that your subject might be in focus while the foreground and background are out of focus. When your aperture is closed down (a high f-stop value), your DOF is deeper, meaning that your foreground, background, and subject might all be in focus.

Shutter Angle/Shutter Speed

In still photography, the shutter speed refers to the mechanism that opens and closes (like window blinds) to allow light into the lens for a certain length of time. Usually this is fractions of a second. In cinema, 1/48th of a second is the most common shutter speed when shooting 24fps. The shutter mechanism on a camcorder operates differently, but the visual effect is the same. For still photography and videography, the goal when selecting a shutter speed is to simply get good exposure without the drawback of getting motion blur. The longer the shutter stays open, the brighter the image. But while the shutter is open, anything that happens in front of the camera will be recorded in the picture or within the video frame. This results in motion blur, and is typically a bad thing when you're shooting. If you're handholding a camera and shooting with a slow shutter speed (typically anything slower than 1/60th of a second), you'll want a tripod to hold the camera steady. Otherwise, you can cause motion blur just from holding the camera – very few people can hold a camera completely still without mounting it on something.

Shutter angle is essentially the same thing, but many cinema cameras use a rotating disc for a shutter instead of the blinds-like mechanism in DSLRs. Because the disc rotates, you control the length of time light enters the lens by how large the angle is in the part of the disc that opens and lets light in. In film, a shutter angle of 180 degrees is common. A larger angle (270 degrees, for example) will potentially create motion blur, but will also brighten up the image. A smaller angle will be darker, but will create a nice, crisp image.

ISO/Gain

In video cameras, the setting is called "gain." In DSLRs and cinema cameras, it is called "ISO." ISO is not an acronym, so it is pronounced, "eye-so," not "I S O." ISO settings are typically exponentials of 200. The lowest ISO on cameras is typically 100 or 200. Then 400, 800, 1600, 3200, and up. ISO (gain) is a measurement of how much signal boost the camera is adding to the sensor, making it more or less sensitive to the light that is hitting it. The higher the ISO, the more the signal is boosted, and the brighter the image is. The lowest ISO value (often 100) means the image will not be boosted, so this setting is typical in well-lit scenes. DSLRs and cinema cameras are constantly coming out with new computers and sensors that can go up to higher and higher ISO values. As I write this, there is a DSLR available with a maximum ISO of 51,200. Cinema cameras are often much lower because we light our scenes well. The cinema camera I used on my latest project had a maximum ISO of 3200. But most cinema cameras also specify a "native ISO" that you should try to shoot at. This is because when you increase ISO too much, it introduces noise into the image. Most often, this noise happens in the shadows, and in the digital world, noise looks like pink and purple pixels in place of what should be the black pixels of the shadows. DSLRs and cinema cameras are also increasingly more capable of

Figure 4.17 A shot with motion blur (the shutter was open for ½ second) and one with a faster shutter to freeze the action (the shutter was open for 1/250th of a second).

cleaner images at higher ISO values, though. My DSLR introduces noise when I shoot around ISO 6400. Newer cameras can go much higher than that before you'll notice.

On a video camera, the gain is measured in decibels (dB). A change of 6dB in gain does the same thing to the image as changing the aperture one full f-stop. As the gain is increased, the image gets brighter. As the gain is decreased, the image gets darker. Like ISO, the tradeoff is digital noise within your image, especially in the shadows. On a camcorder, the gain values are often not specified in the settings, so you're left with "High" (typically adds 18dB of gain), "Medium" (typically 9dB of gain), and "Low" (3dB). Most camcorders also have AGC (Automatic Gain Control), while cinema cameras do not.

Exposure Triangle

We refer to exposure as a triangle because the three settings (aperture, shutter speed, ISO) can all effect the brightness of the image (exposure) independently, but when you adjust one, you can compensate by adjusting another. For example, if I start out with good exposure, but I want my DOF to be shallower, I need to open up the aperture. This will make my image brighter and overexposed. But instead of closing my aperture back down, I can adjust the ISO (make it lower) or my shutter speed (make it faster) to compensate. If I have good exposure but too much noise, I need to lower my ISO. This will make the image darker, but instead of raising the ISO back up, I can open up my aperture (and have shallower DOF) or slow down my shutter (brightening the image, but potentially causing motion blur). Of course, you can make small adjustments in both of the other two values instead of making a larger adjustment in one value. The exposure triangle takes some practice to learn and figure out what compromises you're willing to make in each shooting situation. I highly recommend shooting still photography on a DSLR or mirrorless camera to learn the exposure triangle. Camcorders are too forgiving because of their small sensors, and cinema cameras are often too complex to see immediate changes in the image.

Aperture	Shutter Speed	ISO
(open = brighter)	(slower = brighter)	(higher = brighter)
(open = shallow DOF)	(slower = motion blur)	(higher = noise/grain)
f-stop at 1.4	1/4 of a second	32000
f-stop at 2.8	1/60 of a second	1600
f-stop at 6.2	1/500 of a second	800
f-stop at 11	1/10000 of a second	200
(closed = darker)	(faster = darker)	(lower = darker)
(closed = deep DOF)	(faster = motion stopped)	(lower = crisp/no noise)

Figure 4.18 The exposure triangle. Each of the three settings affects the brightness of the image, but each has a tradeoff.

ND Filters

ND (neutral-density) filters are like sunglasses for the lens. Sometimes, they go into the matte box or screw onto the front of the lens itself. Sometimes, they are built into the camera body. ND filters darken the image without adjusting any values on the exposure triangle. Essentially, ND filters allow you to "cheat" the triangle. In cinema, we use ND filters often, especially when shooting outdoors. This allows us to open the aperture wide and get shallow DOF without overexposing the image. ND filters are measured in optical density, with values that start at.3 (equal to one f-stop of aperture), and going on up to.6 (two f-stops),.9 (three f-stops), 1.2 (four f-stops), etc. On a camcorder, the optical density is rarely specified, but an ND-1 is typically.3, ND-2 is.6, ND-3 is.9, and ND-4 is 1.2. When I shoot with a camcorder, I'm generally not using an ND filter to compensate for changing my aperture because the smaller sensor isn't going to give me shallow DOF anyway. Instead, I use the built-in ND filters on a camcorder to easily darken an overexposed image without having to change all of my exposure triangle settings.

Camera Movement

Moving the camera while shooting can add excitement, interest, and intrigue to a shot. You can use camera movement to keep a shot from getting too boring, or you can move the camera out from behind a foreground to reveal something previously unknown to the audience. I like adding subtle movement to shots when I want the viewer to feel as though they're part of the action. And of course, there are times when the action happening in front of the camera requires movement to follow it. There are several types of camera moves. In live TV, you'll have a Director telling you when and how to move. In scripted single-camera shooting, you'll work out and rehearse any camera moves with the Director before you record the shot. In unscripted projects, you'll often make the moves as you follow the action naturally. In any case, it helps to know what the move is called and what it can convey to the audience.

Pan

A pan is when you move the camera left or right on the tripod head. "Panning left" happens when you direct the camera so the lens points further to the left than when you started (the shot "looks" over to the left). This means when you pan left, you're actually moving the panning handle on the back of the tripod to the right. "Panning right" happens when the camera "looks" to the right. Pans are generally done to follow the action or reveal something to the audience. Occasionally, we incorporate "swish pans" into the scene, where the camera acts like a party to the conversation between two people and rapidly pans back and forth between them, like you would if you were watching two people talk.

Tripods have a pan lock and a pan drag. When you're getting ready to pan the camera, you should always have the lock off. The drag should be tight enough to offer you some resistance, which will make the pan smoother. The drag shouldn't be so tight that the pan will be jerky as you fight against it. When I'm shooting live, unscripted projects, I often keep my pan lock off and my drag a little looser so I can get to the shot I want faster. When I'm shooting scripted projects, I practice the move ahead of time so I know exactly how tight to set my drag.

Tilt

A tilt is when you point the camera lens up or down on the tripod head. "Tilting up" happens when you direct the camera so the lens points further up than when you started (the shot "looks" up). This means you're actually pushing the panning handle on the back of the tripod down. "Tilting down" happens when the camera "looks" down. Tripods also have a tilt lock and a tilt drag. The lock is very helpful when you rest in between shots, but it's easy to forget that you locked the camera down. I make sure I unlock it every time I shoot, and I keep the drag set using the same logic as the pan drag.

This is a good place to give you a piece of advice I've learned over the years: when you know you're going to be doing a pan or tilt where you're going to have to reposition your body as well as the camera, it helps to put yourself into the final position, or as close to it as you can get, before you begin the move. For instance, if I'm going to pan left across an audience, I'll get around the right side of the camera to start the move. Then I lean over so I can track the shot as I make the move. As I begin the pan, I'm slowly moving into a more comfortable position, and I'll end the move in my normal position behind the camera. The alternative is starting the move in a comfortable position, but ending it leaning out and falling over. The shot will be much smoother if you plan from the ending first. This advice goes for any movement where you might have to reposition yourself throughout the move.

Zoom

When you zoom, you're not technically moving the camera. But to the viewer, it still feels like movement. Zooms are often used when shooting on a camcorder, but they're not often used with cinema cameras and DSLRs. Part of this is simple logistics – the lenses for cinema cameras are most often primes (fixed-focal length) that don't zoom. DSLR lenses often zoom, but because the cameras are so light, touching the lens shakes the camera and messes up the shot. There are cinema zoom lenses out there, but they're very expensive. And audiences have grown used to only seeing zooms in live TV and as a special effect. A "push in" means to zoom in slowly while recording. A "pull out" is the opposite.

I also found early on in my career that zooms have to be done very carefully so the viewer doesn't get disoriented. When I shot my very first wedding as a freelancer, I zoomed in quickly when needed, thinking I would just cut the zoom out in post. When I got to the editing bay, though, I realized that I would be cutting out some key moments in the ceremony. I left the zooms in there and sheepishly apologized to my clients, knowing that it looked unprofessional. From then on, I made sure that if my camera was rolling, I did everything slowly and smoothly. Of course, now I shoot weddings with multiple cameras, but I still make sure that all my movements are smooth.

Other Moves

A dolly shot is one where the camera physically moves in closer to your subject. Typically done on a dolly (often on a track), this move requires a Grip to move the platform on which the camera is mounted while the Cinematographer maintains the shot. A third person (the First AC) is typically required to "pull focus" and keep the shot from drifting out of focus. A dolly seems like it would be easily replaced by a zoom, but a dolly shot doesn't change the focal length of the lens like a zoom does. When you dolly, the depth of field and the depth axis remain constant. When you zoom, the depth axis expands or contracts (along with the DOF expanding or contracting) because of the shift in lens focal length.

A "handheld" shot is one where the camera appears to be handheld or floating. This aesthetic makes the viewer feel like a voyeur – a "fly on the wall" – as they watch the scene unfold. It can be effective if that's the message you intend, but it can be distracting and disorienting if not done well. Even in movies where the camera is supposed to put the viewer in the place of a character (a Point of View, or POV shot), these shots are typically done with a gimbal or steadycam to help smooth out the movements. You can adjust the reaction times of a gimbal to make things still seem a bit shaky, but without being completely disorienting. I highly recommend never actually holding the camera in your hand as you shoot. Even a shoulder rig is better and more stable.

There are other "floating" types of shots. Drones, cranes, helicopters, and jibs can all give a floating, sweeping kind of movement to your shot. Unlike a handheld shot, these kinds of mounts offer perspectives that we don't often see through our own eyes. These shots need to be very smooth and typically very slow to be effective. Otherwise, the viewer doesn't have time to take in the surroundings and the reason behind the camera perspective.

Composition

When we say "composition" of the shot, we mean the decisions we make about what to include in the shot, how close to the subject we feel, where we want the audience to look, and how balanced or comfortable we want to make them. An extreme close up (XCU) is typically close enough to the subject that we cut off part of their forehead and chin. A CU probably includes all of the head and a bit of the shoulders. A medium shot (MS) shows some or all of the torso. A long shot (LS) includes some or all of the legs and the environment. An XLS not only shows the feet, but often a good bit of the surrounding scene. Establishing shots show the relationship between the subject and the environment, and establish the time and place of the scene.

Rule of Thirds

The rule of thirds is a composition tool where the screen is divided into thirds from top to bottom and right to left. The idea is that our eyes are drawn to the intersections of those imaginary lines. Using the rule of thirds actually unbalances the shot, but in a way that still feels fairly natural. Instead of simply putting the subject off center, placing them on one of the intersections feels stabile, but with a little bit of intrigue. You're probably already familiar with what this looks like, because many cell phones have the guides built into their camera app. But a word of caution: not everything should be shot using the rule of thirds. When balance and stability is important to the message the shot conveys, the rule of thirds can actually work against you. So, this is a rule you should use sometimes, but not all the time.

Headroom

Headroom is the amount of space above the subject's head in the shot. In general, you want to leave a little space, but the tighter the shot is, the less space you give. In an XLS, for example, we might see quite a bit of the background above the subject. In an XCU, we probably don't leave any headroom. When I first worked in TV news, I thought I understood "proper" headroom meant that you made sure there was a lot of space. Until the Director kept telling me, "Tilt down, tilt down, tilt down, stop" when the news anchor's head was almost touching the top of the frame. I learned that textbooks

Figure 4.19 My eyes are almost on the intersection of the thirds. This shot is not balanced, but it feels more natural than if my eyes were centered or moved even closer to the edge of the frame. My son's head is pretty close to another intersection, and his body follows along the imaginary line, making this shot stabile, but not balanced. This is a fairly close CU shot, but not quite an XCU because of how my shoulders are included.

exaggerate headroom to emphasize the point that you should leave a little space. But I've found that giving headroom is actually something that comes fairly naturally to videographers who grew up watching TV and movies. Do what feels right when composing a shot and don't overthink it.

Noseroom/Leadroom

Noseroom refers to the space you want to leave in front of your subject when they're looking to the side of the frame. Leadroom is a similar concept, but referring to subjects and objects in motion – giving them leadroom means leaving space in front of them. The idea is that when someone is looking in a direction, or when they're moving in a direction, the audience cares much more about where they're going than where they've been. Sometimes this is also called "looking space" or "breathing room." Like headroom, you should try to do what comes naturally. And the further off to the side the eyes are facing, the more space you should give.

Lines

In visual images, lines are an important compositional tool. We see lines that lead our eyes in certain directions (leading lines), like the eyeline in Figure 4.21. Audiences are

Figure 4.20 The headroom in the shot feels natural. There is enough space that the head doesn't feel too close to the frame (making us feel like the ceiling is squeezing down unnaturally), but there isn't so much room that there's a bunch of boring space above my head.

Figure 4.21 I'm positioned off to the side of the shot (noseroom) to allow room for the viewer to follow my eye lines to the drone.

drawn in to the eyes of the actors and talent on the screen, so their gaze is typically the first thing you look at when watching TV or a movie. And wherever the talent is looking is where your eyes are drawn to after that. In Figure 4.21, you probably first noticed my face and my eyes, then you immediately looked down at the drone that I'm looking at in the photo. My eyeline creates a strong directional pull. After figuring out the eyeline, you probably noticed the hard line where the edge of the lake is. This isn't necessarily a leading line, but it does divide up the picture in a way that you can clearly tell a difference between the foreground and the background. Dividing lines are what makes the rule of thirds so effective – we're naturally trying to group things when we look at an image, and lines help us do that.

Depth of Field

I've used the term depth of field a lot in this chapter already because it's one of the things that your aperture and focal length choices affect. To reiterate, DOF (depth of field) refers to the amount of the depth axis (the z-axis in math terms) that is in focus. When most of the depth axis is in focus, we call that "deep" DOF. When the focus doesn't extend very far behind or in front of the subject, we call that "shallow" DOF. Three things determine how deep or shallow the DOF is: the aperture, the focal length of the lens, and the distance between things in the shot. Your sensor size can also affect your DOF. Smaller sensors have inherently deeper DOF. But since you can't change the size or your sensor, you just need to be aware that different cameras will behave differently when it comes to DOF.

Figure 4.22 Shallow DOF. The focal length is 600mm (really narrow) and the f-stop is f/6.3 (fairly open, but not extremely so). The subject is cleanly in focus, but other people who are within 5 feet of them are out of focus, or soft focus. The people two rows in front of the subject are starting to get pretty blurry. The focal plane is clearly set to the text on the graduation cap. The DOF is fairly shallow in front of the focal plane and behind it, so things start to get fuzzy fairly quickly on either side of the focal plane.

Setting Focus Manually

No matter what your aperture or focal length settings are, there is one specific distance away from the camera that is most crisply in focus (this is called the "focal plane"). The depth of field (DOF) is in front of the focal plane and behind the focal plane. Everything inside of the DOF is in "acceptable focus." When you set the distance for the focal plane, you are doing what we call "setting your focus" for the shot. To manually set your focus, you first zoom in as far as you can with the lens (optical zoom). This changes the focal length of your lens to make it more narrow, which compresses the DOF around your focal plane and makes it easier to see where that plane is because your DOF is shallow. Then you adjust the focus ring on the lens until your subject's eyes are in focus (or the most important part of the object you're shooting). Then you can zoom back out and compose your shot, knowing that your subject's eyes are the part of the image that will be most crisply in focus.

Distance

Distance doesn't necessarily change anything about your DOF. Moving your subject further away requires you to re-adjust your focal plane, but it doesn't make your DOF

Figure 4.23 Deep DOF. This picture was shot with the same camera, but with a 24mm focal length (wide angle lens) and an f-stop of f/10 (a bit more closed down than the photo above). The subjects are in focus, but so is the immediate foreground, and so is the arch in the background. Even the clouds are in focus, and they're pretty far away. It's very different from the photo above.

more shallow or deep, like changing the focal length or the aperture does. Distance does, however, make it easier to separate out your foreground from your middleground and background. I've seen many interviews shot where the goal is to focus on the person talking, and the aperture and focal length are setting up a shot with shallow DOF so the background can be de-focused. This is common so the audience pays attention to the person and what they're saying, and not the posters on the wall behind them. But in order for this to be effective, the subject needs to be moved away from the wall and towards the camera. If the wall behind them is close enough to the focal plane and within the DOF, no matter how shallow, it will still be in focus and will be a distraction. Create some room and add distance between your foreground and background and your DOF choices will be much more dramatic.

On-set Procedures

Most single-camera projects will employ the Master Scene Method of shooting. This means that you approach shooting your scene, and the different camera angles within the scene, in a systematic way. The Master Scene Method almost always begins by shooting the Master Shot, or the establishing shot. The entire scene plays out in front of the camera during that shot. For example, a typical conversation scene would begin with the 2-shot (an LS that includes both people). The two actors would have their entire conversation, and the camera wouldn't move. For the next shot, you would shoot one of the singles (an MS or CU that only shows one of the actors) all the way through the entire conversation again. Then, you would shoot the other single. This means you're only moving the camera and lights twice. It also allows the audio crew to get cleaner audio on the single shots because they can get in closer. In post, the editor can choose from any of the three camera angles at any point in time as they put the scene together.

For other types of projects, variations on this might be used. Or for non-fiction, I often try my best to anticipate the action and find it and shoot it, but sometimes I end up "winging it." But when you can plan out and script your scenes, the Master Scene Method is the most efficient. I would also caution you to start out getting really good at shooting scenes with one camera before trying to shoot multiple cameras from different angles at the same time. In the conversation scene example, I could shoot with three cameras and have my actors only say their lines once (assuming a good take). And this seems on the surface like it would save time. But when you factor in the lights and the sound, it actually takes longer. When you light for more than one camera, you spend a lot more time making sure shadows aren't being cast wrong and that highlights are in the right places to maintain consistency between camera angles. For the audio, you can't get in as close because of the 2-shot, so your audio isn't as clean as it could have been on the singles. This means I have to clean it up in post, which takes time. I've found that even when I have access to multiple cameras, it can actually slow things down. The only time I shoot with more than one camera these days is when I shoot a wedding or something else that I can't exactly say, "hold that position while I move the camera."

Crew Positions and Hierarchy

On a typical single-camera shoot, you'll have a Director who runs the operations on the set. The Director focuses on the actors, the shot, and the crew. On set, the Director is in charge. Underneath them, you'll have a camera unit, run by the Cinematographer (sometimes called the DP – Director of Photography). The First AC pulls focus when there's camera movement, and records camera data for each shot – this is extremely helpful if re-shoots are required days or months later. Grips are people on a set who move dollies and other things around.

The Lighting Unit also falls under the Director, although sometimes the DP oversees them immediately. The Lighting Unit is run by the Gaffer, a Gaffer's assistant, called a Best Boy, and on a large film set, there are often electricians under them. Grips also work for the Gaffer on set moving things, but are generally not allowed to do electrical. The Audio Unit falls under the Director as well. The Audio Unit will have a Mixer or Recordist in charge of it, and at least one boom operator who holds the microphone on a long boom arm above the talent.

Of course, on a smaller project, people may have to perform more than one task. Your First AC might also serve as a Grip. Your DP might set up the lights and the camera, and then shoot the shot. A word of caution here, though: the Director should only have one job. If the Director is splitting their attention trying to run the camera or boom the audio, then they're not going to really know if a take was good or not. They need to focus exclusively on the image and sound being recorded. Along those lines, it's also nice to have an Assistant Director on set. The AD's job is to assist the Director, but also to keep time throughout the day and keep the crew on schedule. This allows the Director to focus even more deeply on the shot in front of them. A continuity or Script Supervisor is also handy when scenes become more complex. A Script Supervisor's job is to keep track of positions, props, directions of movement, and other things that might create a continuity error later on. When anything is in question (for example, was that 6 of diamonds on the table when we shot our poker film?), the Script Supervisor should know.

Director's Commands

The Director uses language to tell the crew and actors exactly what to do when. Live television uses similar words, but single-camera shoots can vary slightly. The following lays out the on-set process for the Director and crew on a single-camera shoot:

1. Get the camera and lights set up and ready.
   a. Format the card in the camera.
   b. Check the camera's codec and make sure you're shooting in the correct format.
   c. Check your battery to make sure it has enough juice for the shots/takes you are about to shoot.
   d. Look over the location sketch for camera and light locations.
   e. Set up lights. Use diffusion and other lighting techniques to get the desired effect.
   f. Set up the tripod.
   g. Select the lens that will give you the correct framing and DOF according to the storyboard and script.
   h. Set up a monitor feed for the Director and have them check the shot and lighting.

2. Once everyone is set and you are ready to record:
   a. The Director should check that audio and video are rolling. Director's commands for this are:
      i. Director asks: "Camera Set?" DP answers: "Set."
      ii. Director asks: "Audio Set?" Sound Recordist answers: "Set."
      iii. Director says: "Roll Sound." Sound Recordist answers: "Speed."
      iv. Director says: "Roll Camera." DP answers: "Rolling."

3. The Clapper/Loader (Second AC, First AC, or AD typically) and Sound Recordist make sure to visually and verbally slate each track.
   a. The Visual Slate should include: Name of the Production, Director's Name, Sound Recordist's Name, Date of Shoot, Card/Reel #, Scene #, Shot Letter, Take #.
   b. As the visual slate is held in front of the camera, but before the clapboard is clapped together, the Clapper/Loader should also give the following verbal slate: (Production Title if the unit is working on multiple projects at a time), Scene #, Shot Letter, Take #.

4. Clap after the verbal slate to ensure sync with video. The Clapper/Loader will hold the clapboard for 2 seconds, then remove themself from the shot.

5. The Director yells, "Settle." This tells everyone to get ready and for the camera to shift focus from where the clapboard was to where the talent is, if needed.

6. The Director yells, "Action."

7. During the shot, the Cinematographer will look for any errors and execute any camera movements (along with the Grip if a dolly move is used). The Cinematographer

will pull focus during the shot (unless they are executing a move, in which case the first AC will pull focus).

8. At the end of the track, the Director yells, "Cut."
9. If the mic dipped into the shot or any other visual mistakes happened, the DP/Cinematographer will notify the Director at this point.
10. If there were any audio issues during the take, the Sound Recordist will notify the Director at this point.
11. The Director will either decide to do another take or to move on to the next shot.

Chapter 4: Shooting Main Points

- Camera safety is important. Take the time to set up a tripod or any other kind of mount properly so it's stable and the camera is secure.
- There are different types of cameras and lenses. Take the time to read the manual for your camera and get to know all of the settings and how to change them.
- Make sure you're shooting in the settings that will be best for your project. Sometimes, knowing how the project will be distributed is the best way to choose your codec, frame rate, lines of resolution, and scanning pattern.
- There are several standard camera moves, with terminology and commands you need to be familiar with. When moving the camera during a shot, always rehearse the move ahead of time and plan it out (even where your body will be positioned throughout the move).
- Exposure is determined by the aperture (iris), the ISO (gain), and the shutter angle (shutter speed). Each of these makes up one point of the exposure triangle. You can "cheat" the triangle by using an ND filter, but only to a certain point. Knowing how the points of the exposure triangle inter-relate, and the tradeoffs for adjusting any of the three settings, is extremely important as a video shooter.
- CU, MS, and LS are the three basic fields of view (ways to frame a shot). When composing your shot, there are some helpful tools to keep in mind, like the rule of thirds. You should also pay attention to lines, especially eyelines, and how much room you're leaving between your subject and the edges of the frame (headroom, noseroom, and leadroom).
- DOF is determined by your lens focal length and your aperture. The distance between the focal plane and your camera is determined by your lens's focus ring. A wide-open aperture and/or narrow angle lens will make your DOF shallow. A closed down aperture and/or wide-angle lens will make your DOF deep.
- Knowing how to manually set your focus is vital. You should practice this process so much that it becomes second nature anytime you step up to use a camera.
- The Master Scene Method is the most efficient method of shooting scripted video. Using more than one camera is often less efficient than just shooting with one single camera.
- Knowing the hierarchy of positions, the commands, and the process employed on a film set will help you on any kind of set. Most often, anything scripted will use the same positional chain of command, the same words, and the same protocols as a film set.

5   Lighting

Good lighting is what makes an image look professional. There's not really any other way to say it. If you shoot without putting intentional thought into where your highlights and shadows fall, the quality of the light, and the dynamic range of your shot, your image will look like a home video. When I talk about lighting, these are the things I'm really talking about. Lighting is so much more than just illuminating a subject so you can see them adequately in the shot. Specifically, this chapter will cover:

DOI: 10.4324/9781003010357-7

Lighting Instruments

As I write this book, one of the most exciting areas of advancement in filmmaking is happening in lighting technology. LED lights have opened up an enormous range of ways to light a scene. Instruments have gotten smaller and manufacturers are experimenting with how lights are shaped, how lenses focus the light, and how lights are powered. In this chapter, I won't have the pages to cover all of the emerging technology. But I will try to give an overview of lighting instruments you might have access to. This is obviously changing and requires some generalities to be at all useful.

Types of Instruments

Lighting instruments are most often referred to by how bright they are, how their lens (or lack thereof) focuses the light, and any other features they have built in. As you gain experience working with lighting instruments, you'll understand that naming a light this way actually tells you something about the quality of the light it will cast on your subject or your scene. These days, most lighting instrument manufacturers are producing high-quality LED lights. LED lights are easily my preference. Having worked with older tungsten and PAR (parabolic reflector) lights, there are a few differences. LEDs stay a lot cooler than other bulbs. Tungsten bulbs got so hot that I would have a set of insulated gloves on set just to be able to adjust the barn doors (the flaps that help prevent light from going where I don't want it). They got so hot that if you touch them when they're cool, the oil left by your fingers can heat up and shatter the bulb. Another advantage with LEDs is that you can often control the color temperature (more on this later) and intensity of the light. The only downside I've found with LED lights is that they aren't as bright as the tungsten and PAR lights I used in the past. If I really need to flood a scene with bright light, I'm probably not doing it with LEDs. You can still purchase HMI PAR lights that get up to 18,000 watts, for example. But for pretty much everything else, LED instruments are an easy choice.

A Fresnel light is named that because of the lens the light instrument uses to focus the light. Augustin-Jean Fresnel designed the lens to have ridges that focus the light, allowing the lens itself to be much lighter than a normal convex lens. These days, LED Fresnels might even have a plastic lens inside because the LED bulbs don't get nearly as hot as the Tungsten bulbs in older instruments. Fresnels have a long history in film and television of being portable, efficient, flexible lights. Most often, my key light (the main light on my subject) is a Fresnel. Fresnels can be focused or defocused by moving the lens closer or further away from the bulb. One downside of a Fresnel is that it is typically heavier than an open-faced instrument (a light without a lens). It can also create "hot spots," if not used properly, because of the lens.

Fresnels are so ubiquitous in film and television that names for the different wattage of light bulb have made it into the vernacular: an "inky" is a Fresnel with a 100-watt bulb, a "midget" is 200 watts, a "tweenie" is 650 watts, a "baby" is 1000 watts, a "junior" is 2000 watts, and a "senior" is 5000 watts. Mole Richardson, a popular lighting instrument manufacturer, gave their lights these names and they became shorthand in the film industry. LED Fresnels don't always try to sell people based on the number of watts they use, as it's a fraction of the wattage of tungstens. So, this can make it tricky to figure out exactly how bright an LED instrument is. My old Lowel Omni lights were 600 watts. That was about ten times the energy consumption of an incandescent light bulb in a house was, and it was much brighter (maybe ten times, although watts aren't a measure

Figure 5.1 A Fresnel lens on a 2k (2,000 watt) light. There is a metal grid to protect the lens from being touched or damaged because it gets incredibly hot when the light is on. Notice the metal barn doors (the black flaps sticking out the sides, top, and bottom) that can be used to block the light from shining in certain places.

of a bulb's output, just its energy consumption) than a traditional bulb. The Arri L5-C Fresnel I use often now is 115 watts. It seems about as bright as the 600-watt Omni I used for so long, but I have no idea exactly how it compares in luminance. At first, LED manu-facturers advertised a "watt equivalency" to help people like me make our choices. Some manufacturers still do this. Some don't even list any measure of brightness, or they list the actual wattage of the LED bulb. Some newer instruments are trying to standardize a measurement that will be meaningful, but something like "lumens" doesn't quite give me a good idea of brightness yet. Hopefully the more I work with these instruments, and the closer the industry gets to agreeing upon a measurement, the more my brain will adapt.

Open-faced instruments are making an enormous comeback. An open-faced light doesn't have a lens. Typically, this means a bare light bulb that requires barn doors or other devices to block the light from areas of the scene that you don't want it. The Lowel

Omni light mentioned above was an open-faced instrument that was very difficult to use. Because it got so hot, it was difficult to run the light and shape it at the same time. Now that LEDs are the bulb of choice, light manufacturers are experimenting with different kinds of lenses, reflectors, barn doors, and other accessories to help shape the light and guide it where you want it to go. Many of the new open-faced lights have a unique design, where the bulb is set far up inside a removeable reflector, or the bulb itself is just exposed, allowing a multitude of accessories to be attached. In the past, I've avoided open-faced lights if possible. But now, I think they offer the most flexibility of anything out there. They can be a spotlight on the talent or a light that provides a broad wash across the background. They can be battery powered (more on this below) and are easy to transport. The only downside is that you have to pack around all the accessories that

Figure 5.2 An open-faced light. It doesn't have a lens, just a reflector cone surrounding the LED bulb at the front of the unit. On lights like this one, the reflector cone is removable and can be replaced by other accessories, like a softbox (a silk that surrounds the bulb and diffuses it) or barn doors. These lights are highly versatile and the kits have a lot of tools to help you shape the light. The biggest downsides are that they don't typically get as bright as tungsten Fresnels of the same size, and that they are more complicated to set up and use because of their versatility. Take the time to read the manual and watch instructional videos if you purchase one.

come with it. They can also be more difficult to learn and to set up because of all the additional pieces.

Panel lights are generally flat and wide. The LED bulbs take up most of the broad side of the light instrument, and there is often some frosted diffusion gel covering the individual bulbs (or some LED panels leave all the tiny little LED bulbs exposed). These lights are great for lighting backgrounds and for filling in light everywhere and decreasing the shadows (fill light). If you want an evenly lit scene, these panels work really well. For interviews, for example, panels are perfect. The problem comes if you want to have shadows anywhere. These lights are often so good at filling in shadows that you can't really use them for night scenes or dramatic scenes where shadows help tell the story. For a brief period, panel lights used fluorescent bulbs. You may still see some of these lights out there, but fluorescents were fairly quickly replaced with LEDs. And when we used tungsten and PAR lights, panels weren't usually an option. Instead, we used softboxes around bare light bulbs to create the same effect. LED panels have all of the same advantages that LED Fresnels have, but because they have so many bulbs (diodes, actually) inside, they can get quite bright. So, the main disadvantage here is that panels are almost impossible to shape the light and control spill. Lighting kits often come with a mixture of Fresnels and panels, although increasingly, kits may have only panels or only open-faced instruments.

Figure 5.3 An LED panel. All of those dots are actually tiny LED bulbs. This panel also has barn doors attached, but all those bulbs tend to emit light all over in an unfocused way, so the barn doors do an okay job of blocking spill, but there is still quite a bit.

Setting up Lighting Instruments

When you set up a light, you'll want to set up the stand first. Much like a camera's tripod, the lighting stand should be set up so the legs can be extended out as far as possible, and that it's as stable as possible before you mount the light on it. The light itself will have a sleeve that slides down over the top of the stand (the stud). The light sleeve will have a mounting screw on the side. Be sure that screw is loosened enough that it clears the top of the stud and can tighten onto the stand below the lip. This is very important – if the light becomes loose, it should still remain tight enough that it won't lift up over the stud and fall off completely. Once you've mounted the light, be sure it's secured to the stand before letting go of it. After that, run your power cables to the light and adjust any screws or levers to aim it correctly before raising the stand's sections. Some light stands can extend fairly tall, and it can be a pain (and dangerous) to be reaching way up to make your adjustments. Better to lower the stand to re-aim the light, adjust the brightness, or focus the Fresnel lens. Some of the newer instruments even have remotes or phone apps that allow you to control settings remotely so you don't need to lower the light to make some types of adjustments.

Lighting Safety

You should always tape down your power cables so no one trips over them. Gaff tape (gaffer's tape) is a specialty tape that is as strong as duct tape, but releases from a surface easily when you're done and doesn't leave any residue. It's a bit more expensive than painter's tape (which doesn't leave residue, but isn't as strong) and duct tape (which is strong, but leaves a sticky residue on cables and floors), but it's completely worth the price and it's the only thing that truly works. To tape a cable down, start with a short strip of tape running across the cable perpendicularly at one end of the cable run. Then stretch the cable taught and put another short strip perpendicularly at the other end of the run. If the cable is a tripping hazard and runs longer than about 6 feet, you might need multiple anchor strips like these. After you've anchored the cable, then stick down one end of the roll onto one of the anchor strips and run the tape down on top of the cable for the entire length of it (or at least to the next anchor strip). Tear the tape off the roll and stick it down on top of the cable, trying to center the cable under it as much as possible. If the cable sticks out from under the tape, or if the tape doesn't sufficiently cover the cable, then you'll need to put more tape down lengthwise on top of the cable. You might even need to put additional anchor strips in the middle of your run and then run short parallel pieces of tape between them to cover the part that's sticking out.

You should also use sandbags on light stands and other pieces of equipment that might tip over. This is especially true if you're outdoors where wind might blow a light over, or anywhere the light itself presents a tripping hazard. When using a sandbag, it's best to place it toward the center of the stand, where it straddles one of the braces, and not just on the outside of one of the legs. If the only option is the outside of a leg, you need to sandbag more than one leg so the stand doesn't just slide out from under the sandbag.

I've already mentioned the safety measures for lighting instruments that get hot – use insulated gloves anytime you're handling the light, even if it's turned off. Lights can stay hot for quite a long period of time. I also always assume a light is hot unless I'm 100% sure it has not been turned on yet. I've gotten spoiled with LED instruments, though, and I don't even take gloves with me anymore. The same advice stays true, though: if you're not sure if something is hot, use caution before you touch it.

When working with electricity, you need to be cautious as well. On a union set, only specific people will be allowed to plug something in or unplug it. Regardless of whether you're the one running the power to the lights, though, you should know some safety rules. In Chapter 2 on locations, I mentioned that you want to make sure you don't trip any breakers by plugging too many lights into one circuit. This is worth repeating here. You should also always assume something is "live" unless you can see both ends of the cable and you can verify that it isn't plugged in. Stingers (electric extension cords) are supposedly named that for a reason. Many LED lights can be powered by batteries. This is a good option if you're worried about tripping a breaker or working in a space without access to electricity. Batteries die, though, and often at inopportune times. When I'm given a choice, I'll always plug a light in.

Lastly, lights can be extremely bright. Often when we're working on a darker set, our eyes can be shocked when we turn a light on, as our pupils have to suddenly adjust. For the talent in front of the lights and the crew who might be looking towards the set, we say, "striking" anytime we turn a light on. This is something you'll hear a lot on a film set, but it's good practice no matter what you're shooting. If your talent isn't used to the term, you can warn them some other way before you turn the lights on. I've been known to loan my stand-ins sunglasses while we set up the lights for a scene as well.

Lighting Instrument Terminology

Much like knowing the procedures and terms used on a film set helps regardless of the project you're working on, knowing certain words and concepts about lighting technology is important. These are some of the basic concepts and terms, although there are entire books and courses just on lighting and lighting techniques. This is a very shallow dive into the world of lighting film and video.

Color Temperature

Color temperature is a measurement of how blue-ish or orange-ish the light source is. Our brains do an amazing job of realizing that the sun casts the same light whether it's behind a cloud, setting or rising, or straight up over our heads. Cameras don't have that ability, so we have to tell a camera what color temperature the light actually is. A sunset obviously appears very orange-ish to a camera. The color temperature of the sun at that time is around 3200k (kelvins). At midday, the sun's color temperature is blue-ish and closer to 5600k. Light bulbs for your house actually come in different color temperatures these days ("daylight" bulbs are typically around 5600k, while "soft white" bulbs are around 3200k). Newer LEDs that are "bi-color" lights can typically be adjusted to dial in the color temperature you desire for a scene. But many lights, including some LEDs, are sold as either "daylight" (5600k) or "tungsten" (3200k). Most cinema cameras and DSLRs currently allow you to adjust the color temperature. This should be set to match the color temperature of the light source(s) you're using. For example, if my key light is daylight balanced, I should set my camera to 5600k to match. Typically, we do not adjust either the color temperature of the light or the camera to "color" the image (more on this in the chapter on color grading), although once you become comfortable with color temperature settings, it is a possibility.

Camcorders might have presets, but they rarely have the ability to simply dial in a color temperature. Instead, they may have one preset for 3200k, one for 5600k, and then a manual white-balance (WB) feature. To manually white-balance a camera, you need to zoom in and fill the screen with a white-balance card, then hold the WB button until the camera registers the shot as pure white. There are technical reasons why we use white, and scopes that tell you whether your colors are accurate or not, but basically, white is the reflection from the white card to the camera of all colors at equal intensities. So, when the camera understands the color temperature of light reflecting off the white card, it can accurately record color information of all of the colors hitting the sensor. This means, though, that when you use a white card, it's very important that you use the same card for every shot of the scene. Using a piece of white paper is okay in a pinch, but paper is notoriously flimsy, and using different pieces of paper as you shoot will give you variation in your white balance. Believe it or not, not all paper is the same color white.

Direct Light vs Diffused Light

Direct light travels in rays straight from the light source to the subject or object you're lighting. When you turn on a flashlight, the bulb shines light directly out (although some is reflected within the flashlight itself before shining out) at whatever you're aiming the light at. Direct lights can have a lens or be open-faced, but they don't have any diffusion gel (frosted material) anywhere between the light bulb (or LED) and the subject, and they're not bouncing light off of another surface to light the subject indirectly. Direct light usually creates a fairly harsh look – "deer in the headlights" – and isn't usually desirable. We also call this "hard" light. The only time I use direct light is when I need fairly bright hot spots with fairly fast falloff and deep shadows. This is because direct light doesn't spill out everywhere – it's pretty focused and creates hard lines where the light ends and the shadows begin. This is what fast falloff means: the transition from

Figure 5.4 This shot has very fast falloff. The character is depressed and having dark thoughts, so the lighting reflects that. This is also how you would shoot a night scene – hard, fairly direct light that creates bright highlights immediately next to deep shadows.

highlight to shadow is very abrupt. With fast falloff, you can almost draw a line on the screen where the light ends and the shadow begins.

Direct light and fast falloff are typically found with lighting instruments that focus the light rays as they project out onto the subject. We call these instruments "spot" lights. Although in theater, "spotlights" are typically a specific kind of ellipsoidal focused light that projects at great distance, the generic term "spot" or "spots" for lighting instruments in film and video doesn't necessarily refer to one specific type of instrument. Fresnels, for example, can be spots. Even some LED panel lights claim to be "spots," although I've found that the panels don't typically focus light as well as something with a lens or open face. A specular light source (one bulb instead of many) almost always does a better job of producing direct, hard light with faster falloff, and panels have lots and lots of little bulbs.

Diffused light travels through diffusion material (gels or silks) or bounces off another surface before lighting the subject. Diffused light is softer and produces slow falloff, where the edges of the light aren't hard lines. With diffused light, you can tell where the scene is darker, but you typically can't tell exactly where the light is hitting and

Figure 5.5 This interview uses high-key (flat) lighting to create very slow falloff. Even though there are shadows in places, the subject's face is evenly lit and light fills in nicely. Metaphorically, this shows that you can trust this person and they're not hiding anything because their eyes and face are well lit.

where it isn't. Diffused light is great for filling in shadows because it doesn't create hard shadows like direct light will. We call this kind of light a "flood" or "floods" (versus a "spot").

You can also diffuse light by bouncing it off a surface. A mirrored surface will keep the light rays fairly tight and direct, but a white card, white ceiling, or other bounce material will scatter the rays and cause them to light up your subject in a more diffused manner. On almost all of the sets I light, I use bounce and diffusion as I light my subject. One of my favorite simple techniques is to aim a spotlight up at the ceiling and let it bounce down onto my subject. This turns the hard direct light into a diffused one. And the light comes from a natural direction – humans are used to light coming from above. When you bounce from the side, it can cause shadows in unnatural ways that can disorient viewers (unless there is a lamp or something the viewer sees in the shot that could be the potential light source; this is called a "practical" light).

Spill

I've already used the term "spill" several times in this chapter, so you probably already have an idea of what I mean here. Spill happens when light from an instrument projects out to subjects or parts of the scene where it wasn't intended. Spill is different from fill light (light that fills in shadows) because spill is unwanted, and we use the term to describe a negative effect of the lights we're using. Spill most often happens with floods because the diffused light rays are much more difficult to control. Spots have lenses, and they often have barn doors and other built-in accessories to control spill. We can also use blackwrap (like tin foil, so it can take the heat, but with a matte black panted finish to prevent unwanted reflections) on the light itself to block spill.

Other Instruments that Shape the Light

Like camera mounts, there are too many light-shaping tools out there to make this a comprehensive list. And I've also used household items that aren't on this list when I've needed to get creative. A white bed sheet can make a great diffusion gel, for instance. A piece of cardboard clamped in just the right place can block light from spilling. The list that follows contains some of the most common things out there, but you can imagine that there are a lot more, and many more ways (especially with LED lights that don't get hot) to shape light that I haven't even thought of yet.

C-Stands and Other Mounts

While C-stands don't actually shape the light, they're invaluable tools to have on any shoot. A C-stand is essentially an extra hand – it's a stand that typically has a gobo arm with a knuckle clamp at the top. This clamp can hold a gel frame, a bounce card, a light, a flag, a boom pole for a microphone, and almost anything else you can think of. When using a C-stand, you should always place a sandbag on top of the leg that is closest to the ground for safety. This way, the sandbag straddles the leg, but also rests on the ground so it doesn't slide off. You should also "table" (adjust the clamp so the gel stand, flag, etc. is flat and parallel to the ground) anything attached to the stand during breaks when shooting outdoors. This keeps the wind from turning the item into a sail and blowing it over on top of someone.

Figure 5.6 A C-stand is like having an extra hand on set. You can use the gobo arm and clamp to hold almost anything.

Flags, Scrims, and Barn Doors

Flags are black cloths stretched over a (usually) metal frame. Flags block light completely, and the design makes it so they can be taken down and folded for easy transport. The frame often folds up as well. Flags are important for blocking spill from one part of the set. They can also be used to shade the monitor and Cinematographer (a "courtesy" flag) when shooting outdoors. This way, the Cinematographer can see the shot without the sunlight washing out the monitor. It's the same reason Cinematographers still use eyepieces when shooting – to block out the sunlight.

A scrim is a piece of fabric that stretches over a frame, just like a flag. But a scrim is sheer (sometimes netting), and some light passes through it. This "knocks down" the light spilling out onto the set, but it doesn't prevent it completely. Scrims are great tools when you're trying to use a light for more than one purpose. For example, if I have a conversation scene and I want a light to shine directly onto one talent's face, it will also be hitting the back shoulder of the other talent. Because it will actually be closer to that talent's back, it will be brighter there unless I use a scrim to knock down the light on the shoulder. I can position the scrim so that it doesn't block any light from the other talent's face, though, so I get the effect I want. In a pinch, I can make a scrim out of just about any sheer fabric and some clamps to stretch it tight. Scrims can also be metal (or plastic on an LED light) circular pieces that mount directly onto the light itself. These scrims look like a kitchen strainer, and because they're mounted directly to the light, they pretty much knock down all of the light being projected, not just in certain areas of the scene.

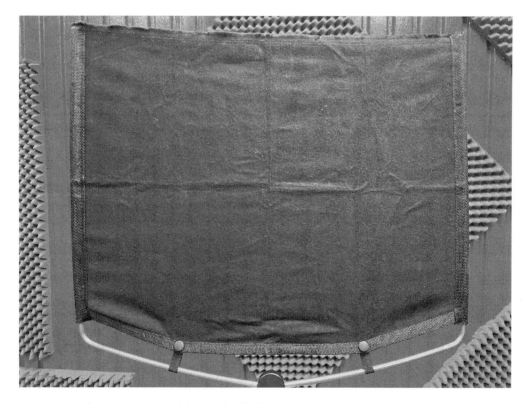

Figure 5.7 A flag is opaque – it blocks all light from passing through.

Figure 5.8 A scrim is sheer – it allows some light to pass through, but knocks down the brightness.

Barn doors are flaps that can be closed in toward the light or opened up wider. You can see the barn doors just on the outside of the lights in Figures 5.1 and 5.3. Barn doors are great at blocking light at the source, and they're much more convenient because they're often part of the lighting instrument itself. But because they're located at the source, they don't necessarily create hard lines when blocking light like a flag will. The light rays travel enough distance after passing through the barn doors that they diffuse slightly. So, in practice, barn doors tend to knock the brightness down a little or prevent light from spilling out completely, but they shouldn't be the only thing you use to shape the light if it's critical to get your shadows and highlights placed accurately.

Diffusion Gels and Silks

A gel is a thin sheet of resin that light shines through. These can be colored (party gels) to project a specific color of light. This is typically done to "wash" the background in a certain color or colors. They can also be colored specifically to match the color temperature of other lights. For instance, CTB gels can turn a tungsten-balanced light into a daylight-balanced light. CTO turns daylight instruments into tungsten-balanced light. To be honest, though, since purchasing bi-color lights that let me dial in the color temperature, I haven't touched my CTO, CTB, or party gels.

Diffusion gels are still incredibly useful, though. Diffusion gels and silks come in a wide range of shapes and materials. Diffusion gel allows light to pass through, but it scatters the light rays as they pass, creating a nice, soft light. Silks do the same thing, but silks are made of fabric and not heat-resistant plastic resin. Even if you have a flood light, you might still want to diffuse it further to soften it even more. Many LED panels even come with specially cut diffusion gels that slide into the light face. Diffusion gel comes in rolls as well, and you can cut a piece and mount it to a gel holder with snot tape (really sticky double-sided tape that stays flexible). You can also find small-sized diffusion gels that you can clip to the barn doors of a light with a C47 (a wooden clothespin that will withstand the heat). Anything you put close to the light needs to be specially designed for heat. I have melted gels before by getting them too close, although with LEDs this is much less of an issue. You can also use a white T-shirt, sheet, or other fabric as diffusion material in a pinch.

Shadows and Highlights

As figures 5.4 and 5.5 show, lighting isn't really about the instruments you use or the tools you have to shape the light. Lighting is about getting the shadows and highlights in

Figure 5.9 A silk is sheer – light passes through it, but it diffuses the light rays. Notice the frame is the same one that the flag and the scrim were mounted on. This is a special kit that contains many different tools you would need on a set and folds up for easy transport. You can also use a silk as a bounce card in a pinch. When you shine light at a silk, the white material also reflects a bit of light that can be used to fill in on the bounce side of the silk.

Figure 5.10 Diffusion gel placed over the same light panel you see in Figure 5.3. This gel is cut exactly to the same width and height of the light itself. It scatters the light rays from the individual LED bulbs and creates a soft look with slower falloff. You can also see the barn doors that are built into the light. With the diffusion gel, the barn doors are mostly unnecessary – the diffuse light will spill out and scatter regardless. But if you need to knock the brightness down on part of the set, they still might serve a purpose.

the right place to tell your story. I was the Cinematographer on a short film a few years ago and we brought in a Lighting Director to set up the lighting schemes for the different locations. The Lighting Director had other obligations during the actual shooting and couldn't be there, so we worked with them to set up lights ahead of time. In one location, this worked fine because we could close the set off in between the light setup and the shoot. In the other location, though, it was a personal residence, and the lights couldn't be kept in place until the shoot. When we went to set things up the way the Lighting Director had laid out, it just wasn't working for our shots. So, I had to devise a new lighting scheme. We ended up bouncing off the ceiling and placing white cards in other locations to get a fairly warm, high-key look. It was the exact same look the Lighting Director had achieved in our run-through, but the tools we had were used in very different ways. This story highlights the fact that, when it comes to lighting a shot or scene, there can be many different approaches that might all get you to the same place. What the shot looks like – the quality of the light (soft/hard) and the locations of the shadows and highlights – is the important thing. Having said that, there are a few lighting schemes that are fairly standard places to start when determining instrument choice and position.

3-point Lighting

3-point lighting is also called "triangle lighting." All other lighting schemes use terms derived from 3-point lighting, so even though I don't always use all three lights, it's probably the most important lighting pattern to learn. In 3-point lighting, you start with your "key" light. This is usually a more direct light, and it's usually brighter than the other two lights that make up the three points of the triangle. The key light is typically aimed at the subject from the camera side, but placed several feet away. If the key light is placed immediately next to the camera, it flattens the subject because the camera doesn't "see" any of the shadows being cast. Think about when you take a picture and the flash is attached to the camera. Not a very flattering shot. Instead, we separate the camera and the key light so the camera can "see" the shadows. It gives your subject shape and texture.

After the key light is placed, we follow up by placing a "fill" light. In 3-point lighting, the fill light is usually a bit softer and dimmer than the key, but it doesn't have to be. The idea is to leave some of the shadows cast by the key light, but to soften them out. This leaves the shape and texture of the subject, but doesn't leave deep, dark shadows. In Figure 5.4, we removed the fill light completely, creating some heavy shadows. In Figure 5.5, the fill is as bright as the key, so the shadows are almost completely removed. As you can see in Figure 5.11, the fill light is placed about the same distance away from the camera as the key, but on the opposite side of the camera from the key. A lot of 3-point lighting kits come with two spots and one flood. With these kits, I generally use a spot as my key and a flood as my fill, which is why Figure 5.11 shows a different kind of light instrument (an LED panel) for the fill.

The third point of the triangle is the back light (or "backlight"). I've often heard it said that using a backlight is what separates the professionals from the amateurs. This is a little bit of an overstatement, but the backlight creates a subtle difference in your subjects by separating them from the background and giving them shape. The backlight in Figure 5.5 is falling on the subject's left shoulder (the right side of the shot). See how the shoulder is black and the chair is black, but yet you can tell where the shoulder ends and the chair begins? It's quite different from the subject's other shoulder where there isn't a backlight (maybe there should have been a second backlight – the way that shoulder blends into the background annoys me to this day). The slow falloff of that backlight as it wraps around the left shoulder also rounds out the subject in a way that gives him depth and shape. The backlight doesn't dramatically change the look the way the key and fill do, but it's still a very important light. It should be placed behind the subject, but off to the side where the camera won't see it. Usually, it will also be higher up than the key and fill (they should be eye level with your subject generally) and shines downward onto your subject.

You can certainly add or subtract lights to 3-point lighting to get your desired effect. For instance, most of the time you'll need to light up your background as well. This may even require more than one background light. Since I often travel with a 3-light kit when shooting interviews, I have to get creative when I'm short on lights. There have been many times when I use a bounce card for the fill light (bouncing the reflected light from the key onto my subject) and then used the flood light from the kit to light up my background instead. This way, there aren't hot spots in the background from using a spot, and my fill is still nice, diffused light that fills in shadows well. You might also add a "kicker" (a backlight coming from below your subject), a "rim" light (a backlight that comes from a bit more of an angle and highlights more of the subject's outline), or an "eye" light (a small, additional key light aimed at the subject's eye to get it to "twinkle").

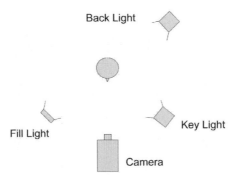

Figure 5.11 A very simple diagram of 3-point lighting. In this case, the key and backlight are spots, but the fill is a flood. This is exactly how I lit the interview in Figure 5.5 to get the high-key lighting and slow falloff I wanted.

High-key Lighting

High-key lighting gets its name from the use of a brighter key light, but when we say, "high key," we are generally referring to a lighting scheme where everything is bright and evenly lit. While there are shadows, they are fairly soft and falloff is slow. High-key lighting is sometimes referred to in television as "flat" lighting (in cinema, we dislike the term "flat," and prefer to say, "high key"). High-key lighting is often seen in documentary and news, because it conveys trust. When there aren't any shadows, metaphorically we're saying that this person has nothing to hide. We also use high-key lighting in narrative TV shows and movies when we want an upbeat mood, or to convey happiness and warmth. When everything is bright, viewers equate that with abundant sunshine.

To set up high-key lighting, I will usually use way more than three lights. I'll start with 3-point lighting, using diffusion and bounce to fill in shadows and spill light out everywhere. In this lighting scheme, floods are better than spots because you want to light everything evenly. High-key lighting is where I'll also bounce lights off the ceiling and walls to spread it around as much as possible. In other lighting schemes, I'll close blinds and turn off the house lights (overheads) so I can control everything. But when I'm wanting high-key lighting, I'll often incorporate natural light into my plans. Let the open window serve as a backlight. Let the overheads light up the background. It just means I have fewer lights to have to set up and place.

Low-key Lighting

Low-key lighting doesn't mean turning down the brightness of the key light. It's a common mistake to think that when you want to shoot a night scene or want things to appear "dark" that you need to lower the overall brightness. Instead, you should dim the fill light or remove it completely. The backlight often needs to be there to outline your subject, and the key light needs to be a hard spot that doesn't spill out into the shadows. But low-key lighting isn't darker; it's just more selective in what is lit and what isn't. With low-key lighting, you want fairly hard lines and fast falloff. You want deeper shadows. You want a background that isn't washed in light but has a few selective patches of it instead. Figure 5.4 is a pretty good example – the actor's shoulder still has light hitting it. This keeps the shape of the shoulder and the depth. The deep shadows right next to the bright highlights on his face give it texture. The face isn't dark; in fact, it's fairly bright. But the half that is shaded is deep in the shadows, and there is a hard line between the lit side of the face and the shadowed side. Usually low-key lighting requires fewer instruments, and it certainly requires you to control any natural light sources. Black out the light coming from windows with flags or blinds. Turn off the overheads. Use barn doors and flags to block light from hitting the background unintentionally. Place lights higher so they spill less onto the set.

Lighting a Night Scene

Some of this was already covered above, but I wanted to give some very specific tips for shooting a night scene, especially outdoors. Night scenes should almost always be low-key lighting. Even indoors, we think of nighttime as being dark. This doesn't mean that there aren't any lights, though. In our houses at night, we still have a lamp or overhead light fixture on. But outside of where that light falls, it's often dark. When I have my family room pot lights on, my kitchen stays in deep shadows. When I'm outside, there are still street lights or moonlight. But outside of that, it is really dark with deep shadows. So, when you shoot a night scene, you're often placing your subject in some fairly bright light – the light that mimics moonlight or a lamp – but the shadows are also very dark and deep. And there has to be fast falloff between the two. This is also called "high-contrast" lighting.

When I shoot a night scene, I really have to think through my lighting on my subject and my background. This is way more difficult than a high-key scene because you have to be so careful that your lights don't spill out anywhere. So, I'm always using a spotlight for a night scene. I'm often closing the barn doors down or using blackwrap on the instrument to block the light even further. And I'm putting distance between my subject and the background so light that's aimed at the subject dissipates before it gets to the background. Better yet, I position the light up high so it aims a bit more at the ground and less at the background (while still being focused primarily on my subject). I also have C-stands equipped with flags to block the spill from the background and from parts of my subject where I don't want light. The same thing goes for the backlight, although I'm tempted to use a kicker from down low, so that if light spills it's doing so outside the frame. Or using a small, very focused light and flags to keep it from hitting my subject too broadly.

The other real trick here is to light the background just as selectively as your subject. With high-key lighting, you can often get away with your background light(s) being broader than you planned. If parts of your background are a bit brighter, it may not matter. But for a night scene, it would be completely disorienting if light appeared to be coming from multiple directions or multiple sources. Your viewers would be confused if the light quality on the background didn't match the light on your subject. If your subject looks like a street light is illuminating their face, then that same streetlight has to be the motivation behind the lighting for the background. Even though the Lighting Director (or you) is using a separate instrument for the background light, it has to look as though it is the same light as the one hitting your subject. This is called "motivated" lighting. To do this, you need to shape the background light the same way (by using barn doors, blackwrap, and flags) as you did for your key light. The lights don't necessarily have to come from the same position, but if shadows are being cast, they definitely need to be coming from the same direction. Look at Figure 5.12. Notice the shadows of the bushes?

They're definitely not caused by the house light. But you wouldn't have known without pausing it and looking closely. The key light is coming from roughly the same direction as the lamp, so viewers assume the lamp is lighting the subject. The light on the front of the door cannot be from the lamp. Yet, our brains assume it is because of the general direction of the shadows.

Lighting in Small Spaces

I remember learning how to do 3-point lighting in a wide-open TV studio, then going out to shoot my first interview and finding that the location wasn't ideal for that lighting scheme. It was in someone's office, and the space was so small I had to place my camera in the doorway just to be able to frame the shot wide enough. There was no way I was getting three lights in there, much less placing one of those lights behind the subject for a backlight. For film scenes, this isn't usually a problem because sets are constructed or locations are chosen purposefully. For news and documentary shooting, small spaces are often part of the challenge.

Each space will have a unique solution, but in these situations, I pretty much always have to bounce light or use reflectors for my fill and maybe even my backlight. I begin with my key light (I always begin with my key) and then try to figure out what I can do

Figure 5.12 A night scene. The house light appears to be lighting the subject's face, but in reality, we used a spot coming from the same direction so the highlights would be placed well. We also had a light inside the door rimming her hair to separate her from the background. The police officer is completely silhouetted because the house light didn't actually put off much light and because we used a flag to keep the spill off of him. He was just a shadowy figure delivering bad news.

from there. Sometimes, a white wall in an office creates just the bounce I need. I open up the barn doors and spill light intentionally onto the wall to get it to fill in the shadows. When I can get a light next to the key, I'll often aim it up at the white ceiling to bounce light down from there. For interviews, you have to be careful with this because it can cause darker shadows under the nose and chin. You can actually place the light down low, aim it at the ceiling, then position a white card so it catches just enough of the light before it goes to the ceiling, and bounce a little bit of the light into these shadows. I've also had to forego the backlight in some interviews because there's just no room to get it around behind. But in those situations, if I can, I place the subject closer to the wall to try to get some bounce off of it.

Although it's not typically an issue in narrative projects, the film shown in Figure 5.4 was shot in a tiny bedroom. Luckily, the closet doors were mirrors, so the light you see was actually bounced off a mirror. A white card would have diffused it too much. I used a very direct light placed almost next to the camera and aimed it at just the right angle to reflect directly onto the subject's face. I used the barn doors to control the spill onto the camera side of his face.

Lighting Outdoors

When shooting a scene outdoors with high-key lighting, it can be harder than you think. It's tempting (I've certainly made this mistake) to just go without lights or reflectors and let the sun light your scene. But the sun is a very bright, specular source of light. It's fairly direct and harsh, causing fast falloff and deep shadows. Shooting on a cloudy day can be so much better because the clouds actually diffuse the sunlight and soften it. As long as the clouds don't knock down the brightness too much, this is the ideal shooting situation outdoors. But if it's too overcast, the shot is ruined without bringing in generators or battery-powered lights and adding artificial lighting to the scene. If it's too dim outside, your subjects and backgrounds flatten out and colors turn gray.

Figure 5.13 This interview was shot in the journalist's home. We placed the camera in the kitchen and shot into the study. You can actually see the key light (the reflector umbrella) in the picture on the shelf. We had plenty of room for the fill, but we had to bounce the key onto the shoulder because we couldn't get a backlight behind him. The reflector is just outside the frame to the right.

Reflectors

Reflectors come in different shapes and sizes. Some are rigid or stretch into a rigid frame. When they're in a frame, a rigid reflector can easily be mounted on a C-stand. Some reflectors are soft, though. These are often easier to fold up and transport, but they almost always have to be held by hand (to "Hollywood" a reflector means to handhold it). In a C-stand, they're just too floppy to focus the reflection accurately enough. Reflectors also come in a variety of finishes. A mirror-like surface will reflect light in a hard bounce. This means that sunlight appears almost like a spot – very direct, very hard light. Some reflectors have a matte finish or something less glossy. These reflectors are a bit more like white cards. They diffuse the light slightly as they reflect it. These are typically the reflectors I use when shooting outdoors. If all I have is a mirrored reflector, I'll often pair it with diffusion gel to soften out the light. Why use a mirrored reflector at all then? When you want faster falloff on a daytime shoot – think Westerns, for example – and you need to essentially change the direction of the sun because it isn't oriented well to your background or subject, you can use a mirrored reflector to essentially move the sun. Of course, then you often have to use a flag or scrim on the actual sun to knock down the light from it. Otherwise, you end up with harsh shadows going two different directions. And on cloudy days, a mirrored reflector does a better job of maintaining brightness than a matte finish. Because the clouds already diffuse the light, the mirror appears less like a spot and more like a flood.

Flags

I discussed flags earlier, but I wanted to make a note here about their use outdoors. When you're shooting outdoors, flags need to be a lot bigger than the one in Figure 5.4. That one makes a decent courtesy-flag to shade the monitor and Cinematographer because you can place it really close, but it doesn't keep very much light from filling in around it when used to darken part of an outdoor scene. In a CU shot, it might be fine. But in an LS, you're either going to need a much bigger flag, or you'll need to get creative with your location. You might be able to use a building to cast a shadow, shoot under a tree (and bounce your key light in from outside the shade), or use something else opaque to block the light. A white card can bounce light, but it can also block light.

Diffusion

A slightly overcast day is the best shooting situation outdoors. The cloud cover can naturally diffuse the sunlight and create nice, soft light with slower falloff. Even though you still get shadows, they aren't as deep. When you don't have clouds, you need to bring large diffusion gels or silks to deal with the harshness of the sun. The gels will knock down a little bit of the brightness, but they will also scatter the light rays around and soften the shadows, slowing the falloff. Another option is to shoot in open shade. This is where your subject and background are actually in the shade, but sunlight bounces in from sidewalks, buildings, and other surfaces, and fills nicely – although you still might need reflectors to bring sunlight in or a key light to brighten up your subject. Open shade is great when your background doesn't necessarily matter. And as long as your background is slightly lower in brightness (luminance) than your subject, you can get a really nice shot. But anytime your background is bright, you need to compensate by raising the brightness on your subject. Otherwise, they'll be backlit, leading to a silhouette or a very

Figure 5.14 (left) The mirrored side of the Lowel Variflector. The mirrored bounce creates a hard, direct light.

Figure 5.15 (right) The matte side diffuses the bounce as it lights the subject. Either way, be sure to table the reflector (position it parallel to the ground so the wind blows across it) when it's not in use. And sandbag the stand it's mounted to.

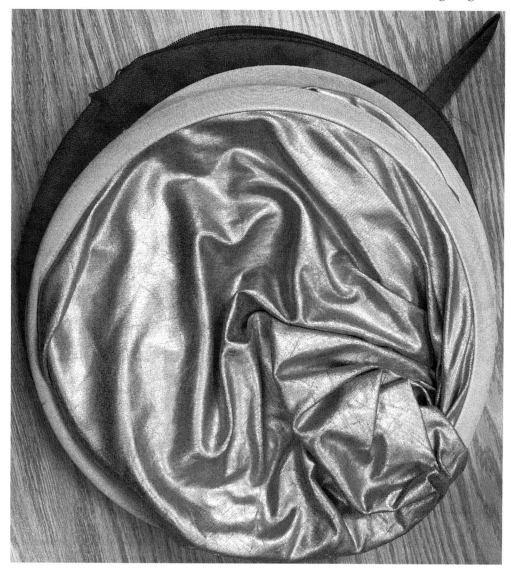

Figure 5.16 (left) A soft, flexible reflector. It folds up to be about the size of a large dinner plate.

flat subject. The same thing can happen in a studio, but it's much easier to control the amount of light in a studio than outdoors.

Using Light to Tell Your Story

In preproduction, you should plan out your lighting plots and storyboards to give your crew a good starting point. But once the lights are set, you'll often have to tweak them a bit. The goal isn't to set the lights where a textbook would tell you to put them. Or to use a Fresnel just because you know it's a light that professionals prefer. The goal with lighting should always be the way it helps you tell your story. I once lit a film scene using

Figure 5.17 (center) shows the matte reflector side of the same flexible reflector. Notice that it starts to fold up a bit when held in a C-stand. This kind of reflector really should be handheld.

nothing but flashlights. It wasn't professional. It wasn't what the textbooks told us to use. But it was certainly effective. And that experience helped me understand that the end result is always the most important thing. The process, knowledge, and techniques you learn as a student are essential to put you in the best spot to start producing something. But once you're setting up equipment, shooting, and eventually editing your footage, the story or message you're conveying to your viewers is the priority. Don't abuse that concept to cut corners or use poor process, but focusing on the story will always help you get the best shots you can. And it can keep you above any disagreements with crew members about the "right way" to do something. Especially in lighting, there are many ways to get the same result with your image. This isn't a comprehensive list of things to

Figure 5.18 (right) shows the same reflector, but the back side of it, which functions as a white card to bounce the light even softer and diffuse it even more than the silver matte side. White cards are most effective in CU shots when you can get closer to your talent with them.

look for when lighting a scene, but there are a few ways that lighting can help you tell your story.

Lighting the Focus

One of the main things lighting can do is direct your viewer's eyes. If one character is the focus, like in Figure 5.12, then they need to be the focus of the key light as well. That character needs to have highlights on their face. The other characters don't need to be poorly lit, but they shouldn't be the brightest part of the scene. In a conversation scene

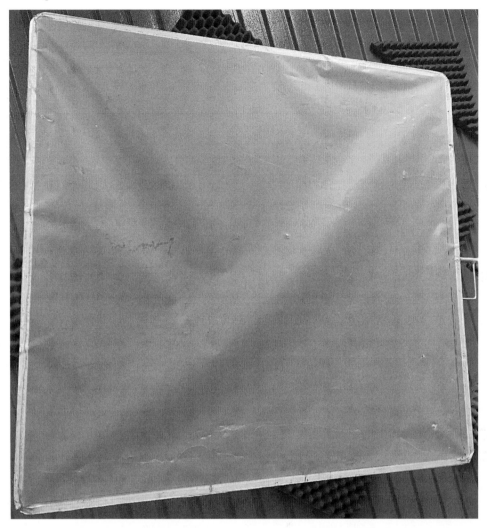

Figure 5.19 A 4×4 (4 feet by 4 feet) gel frame with diffusion gel mounted to it using snot tape. This is a fairly large diffusion gel, but it still seems small when we shoot outdoors and need to diffuse the sunlight across an entire scene. The gel itself is in pretty rough shape, but the nature of diffusion makes it so the wrinkles, marks, and tears don't really affect the way the light passes through it, or the image the camera captures.

where more than one character is the focus, be sure to light them both well. They should be brighter than the background and any other extras in the shot. This doesn't mean you should make the background dull and lifeless, but your lighting should reinforce what is the most important part of the scene.

Lighting as Metaphor

Another way to make sure your lighting is telling the story you want is to look at lighting as a metaphor. This means that you should make sure your light represents the inner feelings your character is experiencing, or that the lighting is consistent with the external

Figure 5.20 An interview from a short documentary film on the Wakonse College Teaching Conference. Even though this was a bright, sunny day on the beach in the background, I used a lighting kit to ensure that my subject stands out as the main focus of the shot. The sun still caused hard shadows (not to mention it made my subject squint), but the light kit filled in and raised the brightness. I was traveling light and didn't pack any diffusion tools unfortunately.

struggles they're trying to overcome. For example, in horror films, the backgrounds are often low-key. Falloff is fast, but the character may actually be fairly well lit. This places the focus on the character, but it also represents their struggle to see and understand what is going on around them. In reality, if you want to see details around you in a dark room, standing in the light is actually the worst place to be. But viewers don't think about the reality of the situation they're watching. They do, however subconsciously, think about the message the lighting conveys. Low-key lighting can also symbolize character duality, growth, sinister thoughts, etc. Figure 5.4 shows that the character is going through a very difficult breakup and having dark thoughts, but that he also has a good side still. Figure 5.12 shows a dark figure giving some bad news. This isn't a metaphor to say that the police officer is evil, but that the news he's delivering (that the woman's daughter has been murdered) is devastating.

High-key lighting can serve as a metaphor as well. My subject in Figure 5.20 has nothing to hide. The lighting reinforces that he is trustworthy and that the topic is heartwarming. When you want to convey trust, warmth, or happiness, high-key lighting should be your goal. Shadows hide things. Filling in those shadows illuminates what was previously hidden. Viewers don't often know why they read lighting in specific ways, but their minds most certainly see lighting as metaphor.

Lighting as Mood

I want to emphasize that lighting the focus, lighting as metaphor, and lighting as mood are not independent of each other. You should be making sure that you do all three as you look through the lens and decide how to light the shot. You should have all three in

Figure 5.21 A still from a full-length documentary I shot about a mental health institution. The lighting in this picture captures the current state of the institution – a dark past and uncertain future. The light in the shot comes in through the window, but it doesn't offer much hope. It simply serves as a reminder about what the building once was. The institution was once a busy and bustling place, but it has fallen into disrepair. The shadowy broom on the wall signifies that no one is there to care for the halls anymore, and the paint flaking off the wall casts hard shadows with fast falloff. The low-key lighting here isn't to mimic a horror film or equate this place with evil. But it does convey a sense of closure. It says that this building is at the end of its era (or maybe even past it).

mind as you storyboard and create your lighting plots. In addition to telling the viewer where to focus and using lighting to tell your story, lighting can also create a mood. The lighting in a scene should elicit an emotional response from your viewer. High-key lighting can make someone feel warm. It can send a message of safety. It can make a viewer feel nostalgia or remember a time when they were happy. We equate abundant lighting with abundant sunshine in a scene. And sunshine is heartfelt, joyful, hopeful, and safe.

We equate low-key lighting with the unknown. The shadows hide things, often making us feel cold, lonely, and scared. Deep shadows emphasize sadness and loss. Even when things are evenly lit, but overall dim, we feel certain emotions as we look on the scene. A gray scene – one that is overall too cloudy for quality lighting, although perhaps intentionally in this context – connotes sadness. Funeral scenes are almost always gray and dull. This makes the viewer see and feel the loss felt by the characters. It would be an inappropriate mood if we lit a funeral scene well with abundant sunshine or bright lights. We'll discuss color in another chapter, but lighting and color go hand in hand here. Even if the scene is evenly lit, using cooler colored (daylight balanced) lights will create a specific emotional response. Cooler colors tend to convey sadness, whereas warmer colors tend to convey happiness.

Figure 5.22 A sunset. The warm colors convey happiness and warmth, but the lighting itself creates a mood as well. The silhouetted boat, the reflections in swaths across the water, and the sun disappearing creates a sense of nostalgia. It's not sadness, but it is a day that is ending.

Figure 5.23 The exact same beach as Figure 5.22, with the same sun lighting the scene. This shot has a very different feel to it, though. This is overall bright (unlike the silhouetted boat), but the bolts of lightning convey energy, not nostalgia or warmth. The cloud cover causes the scene to be dull and gray, causing us to focus on the subject – the bolts of lightning.

Figure 5.24 A different beach, but many of the same elements as the two shots above. This time, the sun is very bright and streaks through the clouds. The trees are silhouetted, much like the boat. This lighting conveys hope and a promise, not nostalgia and longing. Three similar shots. Three very different emotional reactions because of the differences in the lighting.

Chapter 5: Lighting Main Points

- Lighting technology changes periodically. Knowing what type of lighting instrument you need and how to use it is important, but it shouldn't be the focus when you're learning how to light a scene.
- Light is either hard or soft. Highlights and shadows either fall off fast or slow. The quality of light the instrument produces will determine these factors. Spots create hard, direct light. Floods produce soft, diffused light.
- For most non-fiction, diffused light is preferred. Direct light with faster falloff creates hard shadows that are best suited for fiction.
- There are a number of tools available to shape your light. Flags, scrims, gels, silks, barn doors, and reflectors are common items on any set. Learning how to use them is important.
- Having said that, the most important thing about lighting is what it conveys to your viewers. Learning how to use lighting tools will also allow you to adapt and improvise to get the highlights and shadows to tell your story.

6   Sound

As a Cinematographer myself, I know that it's easy to focus on the image and forget that sound plays an important role in any video project as well. In many cases, sound can be even more important than the image. Think about it – you might listen to a podcast that doesn't have any video, but you probably wouldn't watch a TV show with the volume muted (and I'm not talking about a video with captions here). Our minds can easily fill in visual information. We have a much more difficult time imagining the sounds. Anyone who wants to produce video should have at least a basic knowledge of sound. In this chapter, you'll learn these basics. It's a difficult thing to remember to focus on both the image and the sound when you're producing a project. Specifically, this chapter will cover:

DOI: 10.4324/9781003010357-8

Microphones

Microphones (mics for short) are an essential piece of equipment on a production set. Sound is every bit as important as the video (or even more important at times), and knowing how to capture good, clean sound is a vital part of the production process. Mics come in a variety of shapes and sizes, and each captures sound in a slightly different way. So, even if you're mostly interested in cameras and the visual image, you need to take the time and effort to learn how to select and place a microphone to get the best audio possible. Mics are typically classified by their "type" (I refer to this as the "housing" at times), but even different types of mic housings can contain different pickup devices, have different pickup patterns, and have different frequency responses.

All microphones pick up vibrations in the air. These vibrations are caused by molecules in the air as they emanate out from a sound source as a sound wave (the molecules come together – compression – and then spread apart – rarefaction – as they travel in waves). The science of how sound works is very interesting, but a bit outside the scope of this book. There are a few things you should know, though, even as a video producer.

The first thing to know about sound waves is that they bounce around a room. A microphone picks up the direct waves coming from the sound source, but it also picks up the bounces. Harder surfaces bounce the sound waves more directly and crisply. Soft surfaces absorb some of the sound waves or even dissipate them at different angles so the mic doesn't pick the bounce up. Some bounce can be good (we call this "reverberation" or "reverb"), but too much bounce into a microphone can "muddy" the audio. This can be one of the worst things to happen to your audio. It's much easier to add reverb to audio that is too "dead" and make it sound more "live" than it is to remove reverb from your original recording. Most audio studios have a mixture of hard surfaces and soft ones to allow some reverb, but to keep it from bouncing uncontrollably.

The second thing to know about sound waves is that microphones simply pick up the vibration of the molecules. This means that a microphone will pick up any vibration and translate it into a sound recording. When holding a microphone, for example, if you shift your hands, the mic will pick that up as sound ("handling noise"). Or when the wind blows, a microphone will pick it up as sound because the air is moving and causing vibrations ("wind noise"). And when your scene has extra noise going on around you ("ambient noise"), there's no way for the mic to reject those vibrations while accepting others. So, it's important to limit these types of noise and be aware of them while recording your audio.

Lastly, and you probably already know this, but the speed of sound and the speed of light are very different. The speed at which sound waves travel (about 761 mph) is much slower than the speed at which light rays travel (over 670 million mph). If all of your equipment is fairly close to your talent, this doesn't usually create an issue. But when you shoot a long shot, it can be problematic. Or when you have a separate audio recorder, you might have a microphone at one distance and a camera at a completely different distance. I don't often run into issues syncing my audio to my video because of speed differences, but it can happen. And it's one of the many reasons that mounting a microphone on top of a camera to capture your audio is a bad idea.

Pickup Devices

A dynamic mic uses a metal coil inside to pick up vibrations. The metal coil is magnetized, and as it moves the microphone converts those movements into an electronic signal. The metal coils are more rugged than other types of pickup devices, making dynamic mics a good choice for drum sets, news reporters, and any other situations where the mic might take some abuse. Dynamic mics are better for loud sounds (the amplitude of a sound wave determines its loudness or volume) because a forceful sound wave won't damage the metal coil. Dynamic mics also don't require any additional power to boost the signal. It's strong enough as it is, so dynamics don't need internal batteries or external power provided through the XLR cable it's attached to (some cameras, audio recorders, and mixers can provide the mic with "phantom power" through the audio cable). All of these are great reasons to use a dynamic mic, but there is a downside. Dynamic mics are typically less crisp in the way they pick up sound waves. Softer sounds aren't as easy for the metal coil to pick up, and it's not as sensitive across all frequencies of sound waves (more on this later). So, for high-quality sound acquisition, you probably aren't grabbing a dynamic microphone. I have certainly used them, though. I find them especially useful when I have limited access to batteries and power, like when I shoot video at rustic camps. I also use dynamic mics on the drum set for our church's livestream.

It's more technical than this, but essentially a condenser mic uses a thin film inside to pick up vibrations. The film vibrates and the microphone turns this into a weak electronic signal that needs additional power to boost. The film is more sensitive across frequencies, so condenser mics typically record higher-quality sound than dynamics. Condenser mics require additional power and often have a battery compartment built in. They will also typically run off phantom power as well. When given the option, I always use a battery in my microphone. This helps me pinpoint problems faster and easier, but it also stretches my camera battery just a little bit further. Because the film inside the mic is fairly thin, condenser mics are also a bit more fragile than dynamic mics. They will overload a signal easier (we call this, "clipping" or "distortion"). And they're a bit more susceptible to handling noise and wind noise. Having said all that, condenser mics are by far the microphones I use the most. They're great for vocals, boom mics, radio shows, guitars, pianos, and almost anything else that produces sounds that aren't too loud.

Ribbon microphones are not very common. They're fairly expensive compared to condensers, and they're even more fragile. A ribbon inside is stretched fairly tight as the pickup device. This ribbon picks up vibrations and turns them into an electronic signal. Ribbon mics record a very smooth, warm sound, though, so there are certainly applications in video where you might want one. Voiceovers for commercials, narrations, animation voicework, or even some ADR (characters who re-do their dialogue in a recording studio and try to match it up to their lips in the visuals) might use ribbons. I've never had the opportunity to use one that I can remember. I do have a large-diaphragm condenser mic that records a nice, warm voice, though. These large diaphragm condensers have become increasingly popular and have replaced ribbon mics in a lot of applications.

Pickup Patterns

Microphones pick up sound from different directions, and they pick up sound waves as they bounce in multiple directions. Some mics are better than others at avoiding sounds coming from behind or from the side, though. In general, aiming a microphone so that the pickup device is "pointed" at the sound source is what you want to do. But when shooting video, it's also nice to have mics that will keep out some of the unwanted noise around you (ambient noise) as you record. This will keep your audio as clean as possible. There are really only two types of pickup patterns: omnidirectional (picks up well in all directions) and unidirectional (picks up better in one direction than others). Because sound waves bounce, using a uni (unidirectional) doesn't guarantee you won't pick up unwanted sounds, but it's a good start.

Omni (omnidirectional) mics are good for interviewing on the street and other applications where you might actually want to pick up sound equally well from different directions. Desk mics, some handheld mics, and many lavalier mics are omnidirectional. The lavalier mic was the one that surprised me the most – you would think a mic that was meant to create a very close sound would be unidirectional. But because the person talking isn't really projecting down into the mic, an omni lavalier keeps the sound levels more consistent, even when the speaker turns their head away, looks up, or otherwise changes the location of the sound. This is really what omnis are best at. If the sound source is going to move slightly off-axis, it will still pick up the sound at virtually the same volume level, so the talent won't sound like they're coming closer and backing away nearly as much.

Uni (unidirectional) mics are used for almost everything else in video. Unis reject sound coming from behind the microphone and often from the sides as well. There are several types of unidirectional patterns, though. A basic cardioid mic has a pickup pattern that still receives much of the sound coming from the sides, but rejects it from the back. Super cardioid and hyper cardioid mics do a much better job of rejecting sound waves from the sides. And a shotgun pattern is a variation on the hyper cardioid pickup pattern. Again, it's important to note that no pickup pattern can completely reject sound waves from any direction – sound bounces – but these unidirectional patterns certainly lower the amount of ambient sounds heard from off-axis.

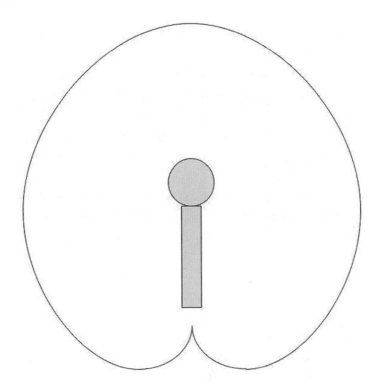

Figure 6.1 A cardioid microphone pickup pattern. It looks a bit like an upside-down heart in "polar response pattern" diagrams.

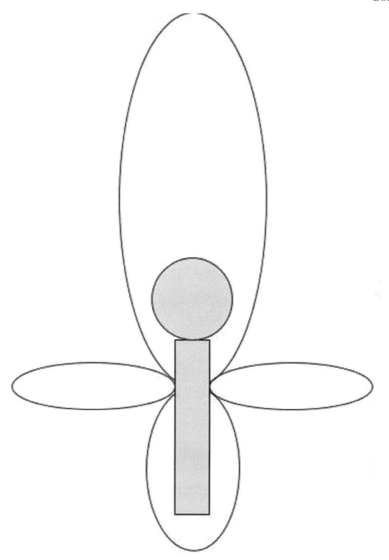

Figure 6.2 Even though Figure 6.1 and the shotgun pickup pattern here are fairly unidirectional, you can see that they both allow some sounds from the sides and from behind the mic. No microphone completely rejects sound from any direction.

Microphone "Types"

We often refer to a microphone based not on its pickup device or pattern, but on the housing that surrounds the device, for example, a "handheld" mic or a "lavalier" mic. Or, we might ask for a mic using its make and model number. A Shure SM-58, for example, is a fairly ubiquitous handheld mic with a dynamic pickup device and a cardioid pattern. Instead of saying it's a "handheld cardioid dynamic mic," we just say, "handheld" or "SM58." Even though calling something by its housing isn't the most specific thing (a model number is very specific, though), it usually gets you close enough that you can narrow it down from there if needed. And so, it's important to know the different "types" of microphone housings out there. The housings can often predict what kind of pickup pattern the mic has, but it's not always the case.

A handheld is a mic designed to be held. They usually have a bulbous part at one end where the pickup device is housed, and a handle attached to it. Handhelds can be dynamics or condensers, and they can have omni or cardioid pickup patterns (or sometimes even super or hyper cardioids). Some things we call handhelds are actually used mostly mounted on a mic stand, as would be the case in radio or with a ribbon mic for doing narrations. Handhelds that are seen in the shot have gone out of vogue in documentary films and even news reports recently, but sports broadcasters still use them all the time because it's an aesthetic the audience is accustomed to.

A shotgun mic (which describes the housing and the pickup pattern usually found with that type of housing) is long and skinny with ports that look like gills along the sides. I'm

Figure 6.3 A handheld mic. This one is a Shure SM58, a standard cardioid vocal mic. The metal bulb covering the dynamic pickup device inside is actually a foam windscreen to cut down on "plosives" (when air rushes in on "p" sounds and pops the mic's diaphragm).

Figure 6.4 An Audio Technica AT897 shotgun mic, my go-to mic for the end of my boom pole. Notice the battery compartment (I left it open to demonstrate) that indicates this one is a condenser mic.

also guilty of using the term "boom mic" when I really mean a "shotgun mic mounted on the end of a boom pole" (and often housed inside a zeppelin – a type of windscreen to keep the wind noise down). Shotgun mics are used when you want sound from one specific direction and you want to minimize sounds coming in from other directions. This means a lot of what we do in fictional film and video uses shotgun mics because we can use a boom pole to position the mic outside the shot, but still pick up audio fairly cleanly from the talent. In live TV, sometimes shotgun mics are hung from the ceiling grid to pick up dialogue.

Lavalier ("lav" for short) mics are very small and typically clip onto a collar or lapel (they're sometimes even called "lapel" mics). A lav will always have a small cable coming off the mic to send the signal, but many are attached to either a wireless transmitter or to a belt pack that houses the battery (for condensers). All mics will need either a transmitter or an XLR cable to carry the audio signal to your camera or audio recorder. Lavaliers are very useful mics because you don't have to worry about a boom operator or how to place the mic. The distance to the talent never changes. But lavs are pretty obvious when they're attached to someone, so they're typically only used in news and documentary when it doesn't break any illusions of reality when they're seen by the audience. There are ways to hide them, but it can be difficult to make them completely invisible.

A boundary mic usually has one side that is flat. It's designed to sit on top of a surface and pick up sound in a half-omni or hemispheric pattern (rejecting sound coming from the flat side of the mic). These are typically the kind of mic you'll see sitting on a conference table so people gathered around the table can all be heard equally on a group call. In narrative video, they come in handy because they can be hidden on the set behind props and other pieces, but still pick up sound from the talent.

Frequency Response

The frequency of a sound wave has to do with how fast the wave compresses and rarefacts (how quickly the molecules come together and move apart as the wave travels through the air). To simplify the science, frequency is what we hear as pitch. Humans hear frequencies from roughly 20 Hertz (Hz) to 20,000 Hz (20 kHz). The lower range up to about 250 or 300 Hz (there are surprising inconsistencies in the science here, so you may see different numbers) we hear as bass frequencies. Midrange frequencies go from around 250 Hz to about 5 kHz. Above that are the treble frequencies. Humans are more alert to frequencies in the midrange, which makes sense because that's where most speaking voices operate. So lower bass frequencies and higher treble frequencies sound softer, even at the same volume level (this is called the "equal loudness principle," even though it's actually un-equal).

Figure 6.5 A lavalier mic. This one is part of a Sony UWP D26 digital wireless system. Like many lavs, it's an omnidirectional mic so the speaker doesn't sound off-axis when they turn their head. This one also has an alligator clip attached. The clip is reversable so that shirts with buttons on either side can be used. Notice the thin cable coming off the mic. A standard XLR connector and cable would be much too large for a lavalier.

That's a lot to digest about the science of frequencies. There are two main takeaways here. First, humans are more attuned to human voices. When you structure your audio for your video, it's important to keep unwanted sounds and music out of that range or lower in volume when you also want your viewer to hear the dialogue. We "feel" the bass, but we "hear" the mids. Second, it's important to note that different microphones have different frequency responses. This means that they "color" the dialogue slightly – boosting some frequencies and lowering others. Most good vocal mics emphasize the midrange. Drum mics highlight the bass. When selecting your mic, be sure you choose one with the frequency response that best suits your needs.

Digital Audio Recorders

In video production, sometimes you use the camera's built-in audio recorder, and sometimes you use a separate recorder (this is called "dual-system" audio). Either way, you need to know how to choose the correct menu settings to get the audio quality you want. Digital audio recorders, like the camera's sensor, encode all of the frequencies and amplitudes of the sound waves they capture into binary code – computer code. We sometimes call this "ones and zeroes" (thus, the "binary" in the name), but it's more accurately either the presence of an electrical signal or the absence of one. Regardless, digital audio recorders use specific codecs, just like cameras do, to record audio files. And they can do it in a wide variety of quality settings as well.

Sampling Frequency

An audio recorder's sampling frequency is the rate at which it takes a sample of the sound waves. You can almost equate this to the lines of resolution of the camera's sensor. A higher sampling frequency will give you a clearer representation of the audio, just like more pixels will give you a clearer image. The more samples we take of the wave form, the more fidelity (likeness to the actual analog audio wave) it will have. The downside is that higher sampling frequencies lead to larger file sizes, which require more disk space and are slower to transfer – just like shooting in 4k creates larger video files. In audio for video, then, we tend to keep our sampling frequencies set to a rate that creates higher-quality, yet manageable, files. Digital video uses a sampling frequency of 48 kHz typically, although with hard drives getting larger and transfer times speeding up, I've started using 96 kHz as my standard. There isn't much need to go beyond this, as many television sound systems aren't going to have noticeably better quality above 96 kHz. While sampling frequency is related to the frequency of sound waves, they aren't the same thing.

Bit Depth

Bit depth (sometimes called "bit rate") is the number of ones and zeroes the codec uses to replicate a singular sound. There have to be enough possible combinations to make one sound unique compared to another. For example, let's say you have a bit depth of 2. Your possible unique identifiers are: 00, 01, 10, and 11. You only have 4 possible sounds (amplitudes and frequencies) you can replicate; and 4 bits gives you 16 possible sounds. In audio for video, the recorders are typically capable of 16 bits (65,536 unique identifiers) and sometimes even 24 bits (16,777,216 unique identifiers). Obviously, 24 bits allows the audio to sound fuller – it has the ability to differentiate between very slight differences in sounds – than 16-bit audio. But 24 bits takes up more disk space and slows transfer times down. Still, the same holds true for bit depth as it did for sampling frequency. With audio files today, it's probably worth it to record at the highest sampling frequency and bit depth that your camera or recorder is capable of – within reason – some recorders are capable of 192 kHz, 32-bit recordings, which is probably overkill. You can always transcode (compress the file and lose some of the binary information) down later, but you can't gain quality that wasn't there in your initial recording.

Codecs

Like video cameras, audio recorders use different codecs (languages) to record audio files. The two most popular ones right now are mp3 and wav. Mp3 files are compressed. The audio recorder purposefully leaves out some of the audio information to reduce the file size. Ideally, the mp3 codec removes information that isn't heard by the audience anyway (soft sounds are masked by loud ones at the same frequencies, so we don't hear them). Wav files are "uncompressed" in that the codec leaves in all of the audio information. Internet transfer speeds have come a long way since mp3s first came out, and wav files are small enough to fit on hard drives easily, so I always record in wav format. Most cameras are only capable of wav files, but audio recorders will often use both. There are a number of other codecs out there. For example, m4a, wma, and some proprietary ones used by specific software. All good audio hardware and software will be able to read and write wav files, so this is the only codec I use.

Microphone Use

The main purpose of good microphone technique is to get clean sound when you're recording audio. On location, that can be difficult. There are certain techniques to help eliminate background noises, ensure a clean signal, and keep the crew from tiring out as they hold a microphone, but the main goal is to get clean sound. Like lighting and camera movement, I've certainly gotten creative at times and ignored "good" technique as I focused on the end result. You can hide wireless mics in plants, hang mics from the ceiling, use a camera-mounted mic, or any number of other techniques in a pinch. In general, though, you'll get the best audio by doing it consistently and doing what's been done for years in the industry. In this section, I'm going to focus on these "proper" techniques for each type of mic.

Boom Microphones

Boom mics, or more accurately, shotgun mics mounted in a zeppelin on the end of a boom pole, are standard any time the mic needs to be completely hidden. In most fictional pieces, it would totally break the illusion that the scene is "real" if the audience could see the microphone attached to the actor. Imagine James Bond apprehending the bad guy with a wireless lapel mic clipped onto his tuxedo! Audiences are willing to suspend their disbelief that what they're watching isn't real, but seeing the mechanisms of production immediately breaks their willingness to imagine new realities. This is one of the reasons why good boom technique is so important: keeping the mic close enough to get good audio, but also out of the shot throughout the entire shot, is vital.

To boom properly, you need to either wrap the cable around the pole or have a pole with a cable built into the handle. I greatly prefer poles with the cable built-in, but you do have to be more careful as you expand the pole or collapse it. The internal cable is coiled and must be treated with care so it doesn't pinch or get uncoiled. When you expand or collapse the pole, you should never twist the entire pole. Just the connectors that screw tighter or looser to tighten the sections. This keeps the coiled cable inside at the same tightness and allows the sections to move freely. The other thing to note about poles with internal cables is that you'll want an elbow XLR cable or connector to attach to the end of the pole. This elbow allows you to rest the boom without breaking the cable when it's not in use. I typically set the elbow end down on my foot when resting – this softens the pressure on the cable, but it also helps me know exactly where the end of the pole is so I don't accidentally trip someone on set.

When you're booming, you should avoid wearing any kind of metal rings or jewelry. Anything that bumps up against the boom pole will create vibrations and handling noise. I do wear a silicone wedding ring, but it's soft and flexible and doesn't make any sound. My stainless-steel wedding ring, on the other hand, produces a lot of handling noise and metal clinking sounds. I've also known people who use tape on their wedding ring to dampen the sound (if you're not okay with taking it off, you've got to eliminate the issue

Figure 6.6 Proper boom operation. The front hand is open. The back hand pivots to rotate the mic and direct it. The back arm is higher than the front, elbows bent. An elbow XLR is on the end of the boom to avoid cable damage between takes. And I'm holding the slack so it doesn't pull or knock against the boom pole (avoiding handling noise). The wedding ring is silicone.

somehow). For the same reason, you should also hold up some slack in the cable that runs from your boom pole to the audio recorder or camera. I hold a small loop, or I'll hold right next to the elbow adapter connectors to keep them from clanking against the pole. Really good boom poles even have felt wrapped around them to limit your handling noise. You can also wear felt gloves if you find your touch isn't light enough.

A boom operator needs to hold the boom as comfortably as possible for a lengthy shot, and for a long day of shooting. Your arms tire out so quickly when you're holding a boom pole. The best position is to hold it with your arms up above your head, elbows bent slightly, hands a little more than shoulder-width apart. The hand closest to the mic should actually be lower than the other hand (to keep the pole from dipping into the corner of the shot). I also typically hold my hand closest to the cable all the way around the pole. My front hand (closest to the mic) is positioned more like a pool cue. The less friction here, the better. This is your "pivot hand" – the hand that supports the mic, but allows it to redirect without causing any gripping noise or vibrations. Your back hand will be the one directing the microphone and turning it slightly as you aim it from one talent to the other during a shot. In a single, a boom operator won't even need to worry about movement. In a 2-shot, it's common to boom both actors with one mic, moving it slowly and slightly so it is aimed at each person's mouth when they deliver their lines.

There's also a protocol on set for making sure your boom is up out of the shot. Especially as your arms get tired throughout the day, it's important for the boom operator to work with the Cinematographer to know where the edges of the frame are for the shot. To do this, start with the mic actually inside the shot. Then, as the boom operator lifts the mic slowly upwards out of the shot, the Cinematographer will alert them once the mic is no longer visible. At that point, the boom operator should raise the mic another inch or two (to account for tired arms) higher, then try to visualize where the edge of the frame is when the camera is rolling and stay just outside that. The boom operator will not be able to see the shot while they're booming, so it's up to the Cinematographer to alert the Director if the microphone drops down into the shot at any point (the Cinematographer should wait until the Director yells "Cut" before alerting them because parts of the take might still be viable). The boom operator should have a pair of headphones to listen to the sound perspective and keep the actors on-axis. Usually, the audio recorder or camera has a headphone output that can be split off and sent to the recordist and the boom operator (and possibly the Director too).

Lavalier Microphones

Lavs should be your microphone of choice for anything non-fiction. If there isn't any suspension of disbelief needed of the viewer, then it's okay if they see the mic in the shot. And lavs will give you the cleanest sound possible because of how close they can get to the sound source. Headset mics give an even closer sound, but they're reserved for live stage performances for the time being. I don't have a great rationale for that, but I can't imagine putting a headset mic onto a subject I'm interviewing for my next documentary film. It would just look out of place. So, lavalier mics are the next best sound and they're an acceptable aesthetic for news and documentaries. There are even uses for them on a film set as long as you can't see them or their transmitter packs.

When placing a lavalier mic on an interview subject, it's still better to make it look neat by running the cable attached to the mic up inside of the shirt. Ideally, your subject will be wearing a shirt with a button-up neck, where you can feed the cable through and clip the mic onto. You should always aim the mic upward toward the mouth and clip a loop of cable into the alligator clip on the lapel so that the cable doesn't pull on the mic directly. This would cause handling noise. The battery pack will usually have a belt clip on it, but it can also be placed in a pocket for convenience. The microphone itself should be about as close up to the mouth as possible. Since lavs are typically omnidirectional, you don't have to worry about redirecting the mic as they turn their heads. The things you want to avoid are letting your talent hold the pack in their hand or setting the pack down on a nearby table. I've seen too many people "walk off," forgetting that their microphone was attached. Or they fidget with the pack as they get into the interview if it's in their hands.

If your lavalier mic is hard-wired, you'll connect the XLR cable to the battery pack. If it's wireless, though, your battery pack will also double as your signal transmitter. In a live TV studio, I've often used wired lavalier mics, but when I shoot on location, my preference is most definitely wireless. Even in live TV, I've started shifting over. Signal interference used to be a big concern, so I would always have a wired backup or prefer wired mics. These days, though, digital systems are much better at maintaining a clean signal, so they've become my first choice. The placement for a wireless lav is the same as a wired one, but you won't have the XLR cable attached to the bottom of the battery pack running over to the recorder. However, you do have to figure out where to keep the wireless receiver on the other end. Cameras have hot shoes (that provide power) and cold shoes (that don't) for mounting accessories to. Wireless receivers often have a cold shoe adapter to mount it directly on the camera. And if you also need a shoe to mount a light, there are Y-adapters that allow you to mount both. Then, the receiver will have an XLR out that will allow you to run a short cable into the camera's input.

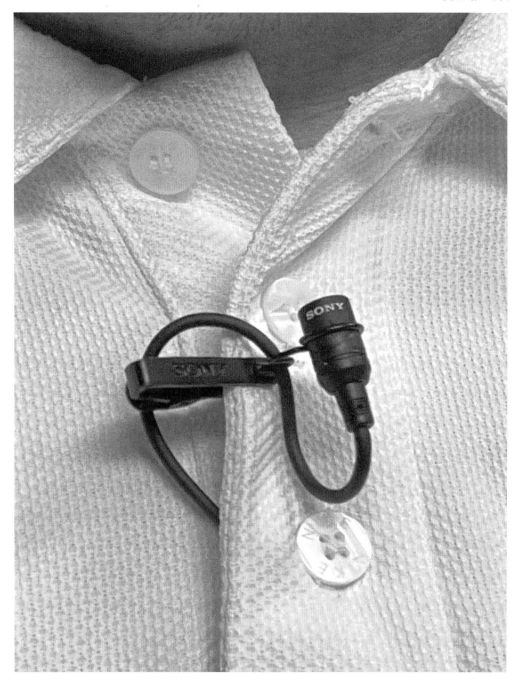

Figure 6.7 A lavalier mic is best when clipped onto a shirt with a collar. I've had to clip them to
T-shirts before, but it really looks sloppy. You should run the cable up through the shirt
and exit it below the button. Clip the mic below the top button that's done. This alligator clip has a place for the cable to loop up through. This is important to keep the cable
from pulling as the talent moves (avoiding handling noise). Even though lavs are usually
omnidirectional, you should still aim them at the talent's mouth.

The other option is to have a separate mixer bag for your audio recorder. Mixer bags typically have spots to clip on a wireless receiver and run cables through to the recorder/mixer. These are great for on-the-go recording, such as news or documentary. I've even used a bag on narrative film shoots when I'm running the mixer and booming at the same time. This requires practice and I wouldn't suggest trying to boom and mix at the same time as you're learning. But a bag that has a harness to hold the weight of the mixer is essential in those situations.

Wireless systems sometimes come with a transmitter pack that simply has an XLR connector as well. You typically see these in news packages where the reporter is "live on location" and handholding the mic. But these transmitters come in handy in other situations as well. I've mounted them onto the end of a boom pole instead of running an XLR cable to

Figure 6.8 A mixer bag. This one has a harness that I'm wearing on my shoulders. The SoundDevices 664 6-channel mixer in Figure 6.13 is inside the bag. With this rig, I can boom and mix at the same time, although it's extremely taxing. When I have the option, I unclip the bag and run sound separately from booming.

create a wireless boom. I've connected a transmitter to a short XLR and a boundary mic to create a wireless boundary mic (especially helpful in an LS where you would otherwise see the cable running across the floor). Digital wireless systems are starting to open up some creativity in on-set sound acquisition that proved difficult a few years ago. You do have to be careful, though, even with wireless systems. I've used transmitter and receiver pairs that operate on the same bandwidth as other pairs and canceled each other out. Even though you can program different frequencies within the band (and you should always make sure your transmitter and receiver are on the same frequency), sometimes the pair will only allow one set per band. There are systems designed to have more than one mic going at once, and these are much better if you're planning on using multiple mics at a time. You also can't typically use 2 transmitters and only one receiver, so even if your system comes with a wireless lav and a handheld XLR transmitter, you can't use both at the same time.

Other Microphones

There are wireless boundary mic systems that are used in narrative production, or when miking theater plays. They can go on the front of the stage or be hidden in the props and set pieces. They're usually designed with multiple microphones (the transmitter is

Figure 6.9 A wireless set. The receiver is on the left and has an XLR output for the camera or audio recorder. The wireless lavalier transmitter is on the right. The XLR transmitter is the middle. This is typically where you would plug in a handheld mic like the Shure SM58 I have connected. But you can get creative with these transmitters. I've plugged them directly on the end of a boom pole before to boom wirelessly (although I still need a cable for my headphones as I boom). With this set, you can only use one transmitter at a time or the signals cancel each other out.

built in) that all connect to a set of receivers. Each receiver has an XLR output, so these would require a mixer to record each in ISO (each mic would record onto its own track) or mixdown (where many inputs all mix down to a left and right stereo pair output). I've never used these wireless "puck" mics before, but I have used wired boundary mics and I can definitely see the potential.

For some livestreamed events, I use headset mics for the speaker. Every headset mic is slightly different with how it's worn and where to position the mic in relation to the speaker's mouth. I was recently surprised as I learned how to place a new headset mic on the pastor at our church. The specific mic actually worked best when only an inch or two in front of the wearer's ear, nowhere near their mouth. The previous headset mics had to be placed out in front of their mouths and occasionally picked up breath noise and wind noise as the pastor talked. These new mics sound way better and hardly have any of the issues the old mics had.

The last thing I'll admit to using here is an on-camera shotgun mic. This should be a last resort because anytime you use the on-camera mic, you can hear how far away they are. Even in a close up (CU) shot, if the mic is several feet away, the person will sound like they're several feet away (it's a hollow sound and they project differently if they have to compete with the ambient noises around them). So, here are a few tips if this is your only option. First off, don't ever use the built-in microphone unless you're positive you won't be using the audio from it. This records reference audio only (used to sync sound when using a separate recorder) and should never be your soundtrack. If you're going to use a camera mic, mount a shotgun onto the shoe and use that. They even make mics just for this purpose. In general, these mics are great at picking up ambient sounds and not so great at picking up dialogue, but at least they're fairly directional in their pickup pattern. I have used on-camera mics for weddings (although I still try to get a feed from the venue's mixer or place a wireless mic on the officiant). I've also used them for narrating short documentary films. When doing narration work, it is essential to pad the room with blankets to deaden the sound and find a nice, quiet place. Any noise the mic picks up will be almost impossible to remove later.

There are a few other specialty mics that are used in video production, but none that I've had the need for yet. Binaural mics can record 3-D sound that you need headphones to reproduce. I've used stereo pairs of mics before (where two mics are placed in a certain pattern to create a left/right separation), but I've never actually used a stereo mic (a special mic with a stereo pair of pickup devices built in). I've also never recorded a track with a surround sound mic (a special mic with five pickup devices all aimed in specific directions). I have mixed stereo sound and surround sound in post, but I've never recorded with these specialty mics. If you plan on doing something like this, you should seek out videos and tips on each.

Sound Acquisition on Set

The on-set protocols at the end of Chapter 4 (Shooting) include audio commands, so I won't rehash them here. The one thing those protocols don't cover is that you should test your microphone, headphones, and recorder ahead of time after running your cables or connecting your wireless systems. Your boom operator and your recordist should both have headphones. Some mixers cycle through stereo or mono (only right or only left) headphone outputs, so make sure that both audio people can hear in both ears. To test the mic, talk into it. You should never tap on a mic or blow into it. This can damage the pickup element. Better yet, position it about where you think it will be for the shot, and then have your actor say some of their lines in the delivery manner the scene calls for. That way, you can also adjust your mixer levels so they're not too high (clipping) or too low (in the mud – mixed in with too much ambient sound). Ideally, you want your VU meter to peak around −3 to −6dB. This allows a little bit of headroom before clipping – digital audio will cut out if the signal exceeds 0dB. If you record too low, you won't clip, but you'll need to boost the dialogue up in post, which will boost all of the background noise up as well.

If your mixer, recorder, or camera has "coarse gain" and "fine gain" controls, you'll want to adjust your coarse gain (also called "trim") as you do your mic check. The coarse gain will adjust in fairly drastic increments, so you'll notice a jump up or down as you move it. Setting this during your mic check will give you a good baseline for levels. During the recording, you'll want to make small adjustments with the fine gain controls. These controls will affect the audio more slowly and more delicately. On some recorders, you must first "arm" the recorder by pressing the record and play button at the same time (or the record and pause button if you don't want to roll). This is a holdover from recording on tape, and many modern recorders have abandoned the need to arm before you can monitor the incoming levels.

Single-system Sound

Single-system sound simply means recording the audio in-camera. Your microphones get fed directly to your camcorder (which ideally has XLR inputs). Usually, video cameras have two inputs. If you need more, you've got to look at either passthrough sound or dual-system sound (below). But if you only have one or two microphones, feeding the XLR cable from the mic directly into the camera isn't a horrible idea. We rarely do this when audio quality is important, though, because the audio recorders and options within cameras are fairly limited. They will most often only record wav format, stereo sound. And you typically can't EQ (raise or lower certain frequencies) them or roll off the bass (a bass rolloff cuts the lowest frequencies – usually this is where handling noise lives but not dialogue). But I've certainly used my camera's audio recorder many times – usually when shooting documentary or news interviews, occasionally for narration or instructional videos. The two main advantages of single-system sound are that it's less expensive than purchasing a separate mixer or recorder, and that it syncs the audio as it records, so you save time when you go to edit the footage.

I would never shoot audio single-system with a DSLR camera. The audio inputs are usually not XLR connectors, and there typically isn't a way to adjust or monitor your audio levels. This is by far the most limiting factor for shooting video with a DSLR. Even cheap camcorders usually have that ability, even if their options are limited. Cinema cameras often have XLR inputs and audio adjustments, but when shooting a narrative film, the audio usually needs to be higher quality. Cameras (of any kind) rarely record above 48 kHz 16-bit audio. I have used the built-in recorder on a DSLR to shoot event highlight videos. I'm usually setting them to music, so the music covers the fact that the audio is terrible. The only other time I've done it is when I shot interviews for a short documentary film and I had a high-quality wireless lavaliere mic that connected directly to the DSLR. Even then, the audio wasn't good enough for some distribution outlets.

The other issue with DSLR audio recorders is one you'll also experience with other cameras. Automatic Gain Control (AGC) is something you should avoid almost always.

AGC boosts the audio levels when the sound is low, and cuts the levels when they get loud. It seems like a useful feature, but many applications require a difference in volume level to convey the message properly. Imagine if two actors were whispering, but the AGC boosted it until it sounded like they were just as loud as the rest of the dialogue. Even though you should "ride the gain" and adjust levels throughout the shot, the AGC does it in fairly drastic increments. AGC also has a delay in how it reacts, so transients (loud sounds that occur suddenly) often clip still. It also boosts up all of the background noise when it raises the audio up. I've used it in situations where everyone got quiet and the AGC boosted the room tone to a deafening level because it was the only audio the camera could hear. If you haven't gotten the idea yet, AGC should mostly be avoided. The one time I use it is when I'm shooting weddings, events, or documentary footage where I don't know what is going to happen next with the audio (and if I'm doing the mixing single-system in the camera and don't have an extra hand to ride the gain). In those cases, AGC is better than letting the audio clip or get too low. But having a second person riding the levels and doing the mixing is a far better option.

Passthrough Sound

Passthrough sound still uses the camera's audio recorder, but the microphone(s) go through a mixer first. This means that the audio and video are recorded together, saving time in post syncing them, but it gives you the ability to use more than two microphones. A field mixer can have a number of inputs, and you can even use a large mixing console if you need more. The output from the mixer is stereo (left and right) and goes into input 1 and input 2 on the camera. I typically use a setup like this for live events. Weddings, concerts, public presentations, etc. often run multiple microphones into a house mixer.

Figure 6.10 A camcorder's audio controls are fairly limited. I can switch this from the internal mic to the XLR input. And I can put it on Auto (AGC) or Manual volume and adjust using the dial. That's pretty much it.

Figure 6.11 The same camcorder from 6.10 does offer phantom power to the XLR cable. This is necessary for the shotgun mic I currently have mounted and run into (XLR) input 1. This means the mic is a condenser mic, but that I don't have a battery inside to power it, or it's not capable of power by a battery. The other options are "mic" level or "line" level. These have to do with the power of the signal coming in. Any time you're attaching a microphone, this should be set to "mic" or "mic + 48V" (phantom power). "Line" would be for when you're pulling an audio feed from a house mixer or other device. I do this often when shooting weddings or other live venues so I don't have to mix the sound as I shoot.

Then I can take a feed from that mixer and put it into my camera to get higher quality sound that's mixed well, instead of using an on-camera mic. For documentary films, though, I rarely need multiple mics, so passthrough sound just adds an unnecessary layer of complication. And for narrative films, even if I need additional mics, the quality of the audio recorders inside cameras is just too limiting. So, for high-end projects, neither single-system nor passthrough sound is good enough. Instead, I'll use dual-system sound for those.

I have to admit to using passthrough sound occasionally when using my DSLR camera, though. DSLRs typically only have one input, and it's a mini plug, so most professional microphones aren't compatible. You can get around this, though, with an external mixer that's made for a DSLR. A mixer like this is built to make up for the DSLR's audio limitations (minus the quality of the internal audio recorder itself). It has XLR inputs, knobs for adjusting volume, a headphone output (which most DSLRs don't have), and an LED display for monitoring levels. Without this mixer, most DSLR cameras are limited to AGC and no monitoring of audio whatsoever. A mixer like the one in Figure 6.12 changes that. For documentaries, small commercial projects, instructional videos, and other lower-quality projects, this is a valuable tool for DSLR shooters. I still wouldn't rely on this for my live events (a camcorder is just so much easier and more adaptable) or narrative films (the audio quality will still be too low).

Dual-system Sound

Dual-system sound is slower all the way around, but it produces the highest quality sound. This is how movies record sound on set. With dual-system sound, you still record sound inside the camera for reference audio to sync the sound to the video in post (more on this later). But you also record a separate audio track for each take with an external audio recorder. These external recorders are usually capable of recording multiple codecs, high sampling rates, and large bit depths. They can also record more than two audio tracks (this is called "iso" recording) so you can later mix the tracks independently in post. When using a passthrough mixer to feed stereo sound into the camera, for example, you're limited to those two channels, so the mix is "baked into" the audio recordings. The audio from one mic cannot be lowered in post without lowering the other mics as well. In iso recordings, each track is isolated and independent from the others. So, you can record six mics onto six different tracks and raise and lower the volume of each one

Figure 6.12 A DSLR mixer. It's designed to be mounted to a tripod, then have the camera mounted to it. You still have to run cables to it and to the camera. This is an "active" mixer, meaning it takes batteries and it can actually boost the incoming signal. A "passive" mixer can only cut the signal. Notice the headphone output for monitoring audio, and the LED display to the left (nothing is lit because it's turned off right now) for monitoring levels. This one has 2 XLR inputs and one mini stereo plug output. I have another DSLR mixer that has all of these features plus a built-in audio recorder (for dual-system sound).

independently from the others in post. This can be a huge advantage on a film set with more than two mics (if you're only using two mics, you can assign one to the left channel and one to the right, keeping them independent).

The biggest disadvantage is that dual-system requires syncing sound in post. This means there are several extra steps required on set and when editing the clips. The first is that a sync slate is needed for every shot. This is also called a "clapboard." It's good practice to use one even with single-system so you slate your takes with pertinent info for each one, but it's essential if you're shooting dual-system. The clap of the slate produces a spike in the audio waveform that you can later line up with either the spike in the camera's reference audio, or the frame at which the sticks of the clapboard strike together. The second extra step with dual-system is that there are at least twice as many digital files to comb through, name properly, and organize into folders before you begin editing (the job of the Digital Imaging/Intermediate Technician – DIT). Finally, although software speeds up the syncing process in post, the software fails sometimes and manual methods still rely on the visual slate and are painstakingly slow. There are digital slates that jam timecode to the camera and the audio recorder, making computers much more accurate when they automatically sync audio to video. I've not had the budget to purchase and use one. I do have an audio recorder that is capable of jamming timecode into the camera, but I actually find the manual clapboard to be sufficient for short films these days. Most video editing software has automated audio syncing based on waveform matching, and they've gotten pretty accurate. If I were shooting a long-form narrative, though, jamming timecode would certainly help keep the metadata clean.

Sound Dampening

Soundwaves bounce all over a film set. Most rooms are designed for soundwaves to bounce at least a little so that spoken voices carry across them. This isn't ideal for recording clean audio, though, because those bounces come into the mic as echoes or unwanted reverb. Think about a classroom. Tile floors, acoustic dampening tiles on the ceiling, and concrete block walls. The floor and walls help sounds travel around the room so all students can hear the teacher. But recording audio in a classroom is a nightmare because of how "live" it is. When I've recorded film scenes in an actual classroom, I've placed sound-dampening blankets on the floors, the walls, and on table tops to absorb the soundwaves as they travel around the room. This helps keep the boom microphone

Figure 6.13 A six-channel field mixer. Each black knob controls the volume for each input. This one is capable of recording each channel in isolation, but it does actually have two XLR outputs to send passthrough audio to the camera. This seems redundant, but that passthrough audio can be much cleaner reference audio than using the camera's internal mic. The screen to the right allows the recordist to monitor levels, and there is a headphone output for them to listen to the audio and send a feed to the boom operator's headphones as well.

sounding nice and close, and keeps the dialogue easy to hear and understand. On a soundstage, the set pieces are built so they're missing at least one wall. This allows the camera to record easily, but it also decreases the soundwave bounce. Sets are also usually missing their ceiling, so even if soundwaves bounce off the floor, you only get one reflection and not a series of back-and-forth waves. Even then, I still prefer carpet as part of the set design to deaden the bounce from the floor.

You can purchase a set of special sound blankets, but in reality, any heavy wool blanket or similar material will work. I've actually had great luck with a cheap set of moving blankets on a narrative web series I did sound for. On one of the sets, we shot in a wine cellar with concrete floors, stone walls, and stone ceiling going down a long corridor. The bounce was actually the worst I've ever dealt with, but the moving blankets (placed pretty much everywhere we could put them without getting them in the shot) did a great job dampening the soundwaves. Having four or so of these on a film shoot is definitely worth it. You can see the "egg crate" foam in Figures 6.6 and 6.8. This is our radio talk show studio and the foam works great to deaden the sound and allow the voices to be heard clearly. But those walls would make a terrible backdrop for a fictional film shoot. Still, you can find egg crate foam in various places and it can be handy on a film shoot if that's what you've got.

Room Tone

It might seem counterintuitive to collect room tone as part of the audio process. Essentially, after all shots are done in one location (for each day), the sound crew should record somewhere between 30 and 120 seconds of silence. Only, it's not actually silent; it's the ambient sounds of the room. Air conditioners, lights, fans, and other things make noise, and those sounds are mixed together in the room as the soundwaves bounce around. Room tone should be done right after the final take, when all the crew and equipment are still on set. Everything should be left on (lights, camera, refrigerators, etc.) because all of these things affect the ambient sounds and therefore the room tone.

The idea is to later use the room tone to mask any unwanted sounds in post. By laying down (and looping if needed) a room tone track underneath the dialogue, the sounds remain constant. Our brains filter out constant noise a lot easier than transient sounds, so the room tone actually helps viewers ignore the hum of the air conditioning or other noises. This doesn't mean you can record bad sound and make it better. On the shoot where the coffee shop foot traffic was too loud on the floor above us, no amount of room tone would have covered up those sounds. Room tone is best when it's subtle. But it can mask sounds up to a point.

Whenever possible, you should also remove unwanted sounds. In the interview with Andy Miller (Figure 5.13), we had to unplug his refrigerator because it was too loud. When shooting commercials in a grocery store one time, the manager allowed us to unplug all of the freezers for a certain amount of time. This helped tremendously. Even though constant noise is easier to filter out, it's still noise. Viewers' ears still pick up on it. And they notice when the next scene begins and the noise is suddenly gone. Room tone can also give you a sound profile to help you remove unwanted noise. This can be very time consuming, but software can analyze the frequencies of the noise and remove them. I've had to do this on videos we shot live in our studio because our dimmer packs for the lighting instruments produce a 60 Hz hum.

Principles of Sound

There are a few principles for structuring sound that are important to think about in the sound acquisition phase. Some of these also apply to the way you structure sound in post, but Chapter 8 will cover those in more detail. The three to keep in mind when recording are sound perspective, balance, and the figure-ground principle. For each of these, you'll want to listen in your headphones to ensure you're capturing the audio correctly. Your VU meters won't tell you anything except whether or not the sound recording is at a good volume level.

Sound Perspective, Stereo Sound, and Surround Sound

Sound perspective is the principle that says audio should sound like it's coming from the location that audiences expect it to. When recording stereo sound, this means that when a car or other sound-producing set piece is to the left, we would expect the sound of the engine to come out of the left speaker more than the right. Sound perspective is the foundation for surround sound experiences – sound comes from the left, right, behind, and all around you. It's one of the main reasons we enjoy going to movie theaters to experience a film instead of simply watching in our homes. Sound perspective is certainly important for stereo and surround sound films and TV shows. For other projects, though, you're probably okay mixing in mono (where sound comes equally from all directions). Even in narrative films, there are a few exceptions.

The first exception is that dialogue always comes from the center channel in surround sound. In stereo systems, it comes from the phantom center (there isn't a true center speaker in right/left stereo, but by placing dialogue equally into both, it appears to come from between them). It would be too disorienting for audiences for dialogue to jump around between the speakers. We tend to focus our eyes and attention to where sound is "located," so if that were to change with every line back and forth, it would really tax our ability to focus. So, when recording dialogue on set, it's always firmly in one channel that can be placed in the center when editing. Dialogue isn't recorded with surround sound or stereo microphones with few exceptions.

The second exception is that sound perspective includes how far away the characters are perceived to be located. For instance, in an XLS (extreme long shot), we might expect the characters to sound far away. This means placing the mic further away so it collects more room tone and reverb from the scene as the sound waves take longer before the mic picks them up. If someone is behind a glass door, we might expect them to sound muffled and distant, so we would place the microphone on the other side of the door from the character. Sound perspective means that we place the mic(s) in an appropriate location to approximate that location to the audience. However, the figure-ground principle (see below) overrides this principle, so placing the mic further away or behind doors is only done in special circumstances and for effect.

Figure-Ground Principle

The figure-ground principle in audio is the same as in video. Audiences perceive that there is a primary figure or subject, and a background behind them that is usually less important. When we structure a shot, we keep this in mind and try to minimize the distractions in the background so the focus can stay on the subject. In audio, the concept is the same – we want the subject to stand out above any background noises so the audience focuses on them. Typically, this means that we want the dialogue to be the loudest part of the soundtrack. Any ambient sounds, music, or sound effects need to be "underneath" the dialogue. And those things typically need to be a lot lower than you might think. Dialogue should be clearly heard and everything else should be placed underneath it, then brought back up, if necessary, once the voices are done. In a 30-second TV commercial, we typically "envelope" a music bed under the voice: the music starts loud, then lowers as the voice comes in, then raises back up at the end once the voice is done. This helps the viewer transition from one commercial to another, it helps the voice actor deliver their lines in a way that doesn't have to be precisely 30 seconds, and it both introduces the product and leaves the listener at the end with the catchy tune. In film recordings, this is done as well. The dramatic scene with the sweeping music still fades away at times to allow the characters' dialogue to be heard clearly. Fight scenes have massive sound effects, but those effects die down when the characters talk.

This is also important to keep in mind when recording, and it's the main reason we try to eliminate as much background noise from the dialogue as possible. If the ambient sounds are part of the dialogue recording, when we raise or lower the volume of the dialogue, the background raises and lowers with it. The figure-ground ratio is baked into the recording. Instead, we want to record the dialogue as cleanly as possible, then record the room tone separately and add it in at the level we desire. We can bring the ambience up when necessary (outdoors at night, for example, you might hear crickets loudly at times) and back down when the characters are talking.

Balance

Balance means that the energy we see on screen should match the energy we hear. Energy is a difficult principle to measure – you can speak forcefully even when you whisper, for example – but when you're placing a microphone, it's very important to capture the character's energy appropriately. If a character is yelling, the microphone should be a bit further away, not only to avoid overloading, but also to allow the force of the voice to reach the mic with the appropriate amount of energy. This seems counterintuitive, but when singers really belt out their notes, you'll see them back away from the mic a bit for the same reason. When they sing softer, they're very close to the mic. This helps them control volume to a certain extent, but they also know the person mixing their levels will make adjustments. So, this is mostly done to convey the appropriate amount of energy for the delivery. If a character is whispering, get the mic closer. It creates an intimate, hushed feeling. If a character is talking in a normal voice, a normal distance is appropriate. If they're yelling, back off just a bit. A matter of inches can make a big difference in the energy of the recording.

Case Study: *Kip and Brin* Short Narrative Film

At the University of Central Missouri, we teach a course in narrative filmmaking where one class writes, shoots, and edits a short film. A different class records audio for the films, creates music and sound effects, and does the audio postproduction on the films. *Kip and Brin* was a short film completed in cooperation between these two classes. Directed by my colleague, Mark von Schlemmer, it's a simple one-act film that takes place in

Figure 6.14 The slate for the project right before the clapboards are clapped together. This is Scene 1, Shot E, Take 2. We actually ran two cameras on this shot, so where it says "CAM," it lists both operators. Notice the FPS (frames per second) is 24. The date is on here, as well as the indication that this is an interior (INT or indoors) shot, a NITE shot, and SYNC (to indicate that there is a corresponding audio track on the audio recorder, as opposed to MOS/without sound).

Figure 6.15 This project was shot in the ProRes 422 HQ codec on a Blackmagic Design URSA Mini Pro 4.6k cinema camera. The frame rate was 24fps, 1920×1080 resolution, progressively scanned. The shutter angle was 180 degrees. The ISO was 800. The f-stop was 4.0. The white balance (WB) was set to 3200 kelvins, as were the lighting instruments. For this shot, I believe we used a 35mm prime lens (cinema lens by Rokinon). You'll notice this shot looks normal distanced and focused compared to the next (Figure 6.16) where I'm pretty sure we used a 50mm lens. The lens info is the only thing not captured by the camera's metadata, so I'm going with my best guess on these. It's possible that 6.15 was a 50mm and 6.16 was an 85mm, but an 85mm in our studio gets awfully tight.

Figure 6.16 The lighting instruments were set to 3200K to match the lamp in the background and not "color" anything. The walls were actually gray, as were the blanket and our actress's shirt. The practical (the lamp) in the background is a great "source" of light for the viewer to draw on, but it's clearly not the source that's lighting her face in either Figure 6.15 or this figure. In this figure, it's a nice reminder that it's a dimly lit motel room and that this is a "shady" character. We used LED light panels for much of the background, and had them a bit too hot for Figure 6.15. For the faster falloff shot here, we used a Fresnel on the talent and a scrim to block the side of her face where the shadows are.

Figure 6.17 The lighting in this shot is also clearly not coming from the lamp, although it's made to look like it. In reality, if the practical were the only source of light, these hands would be silhouetted. Instead, a Fresnel was used to "rake across" the arm on the right and catch the money. These lines lead the viewers' eyes straight to the center of the shot, which is where the focus is supposed to be. The arms, fingers, and lighting all tell the viewer where to look.

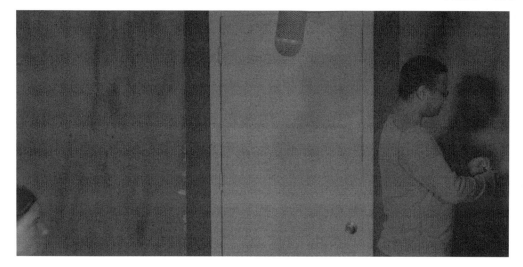

Figure 6.18 The microphone dipped into the shot here. You can see that we were using a boom pole with a zeppelin on the end to house the shotgun mic. Part of the problem with using two cameras is getting in close on the LS cam. Audio was wav codec, 24-bit, 48 kHz, 2-channel stereo. We got much cleaner sound on the close ups and had less concern about dipping in.

a dim motel room. We shot it in our studio, so the set design allowed for an open wall to shoot video and get audio easily. In this case study, I'll walk you through our production decisions and show you stills from the set to illustrate the concepts.

Chapter 6: Sound Main Points

- Microphones have three different types of pickup devices: condenser mics, dynamic mics, and ribbon mics. Dynamics are rugged and don't require power, but they're not as sensitive. Condensers are typically what you'll use when recording audio for video, but they need either battery or phantom power. Ribbon mics are typically only found in recording studios.
- Microphones can record all around (omnidirectional) or in one direction (unidirectional/cardioid, hypercardioid, and supercardioid).
- Microphones are often referred to by their "type" (handheld, shotgun, lavalier, etc.), but it can be helpful instead to call them by their make and model number (Shure SM58, for example).
- Digital audio recorders allow you to record in different codecs, sampling frequencies, and bit depths. For video, you should always use the wav (Linear PCM) codec and a minimum of 16-bit, 48 kHz audio. For higher quality sound, use 24-bit, 96 kHz audio.
- Operating a boom mic requires strength, stamina, and proper technique to get good audio over a long day of shooting.
- When operating a boom, be sure you know the protocols for keeping the mic close but out of the shot. When operating the audio recorder, be sure you know Director's commands and set procedures.
- When shooting video, single-system sound (running mics directly into the camera and using the camera's built-in recorder) will save time but give you the lowest quality.

- Using passthrough sound (using an external mixer but running the outputs from it directly into the camera) will increase the quality, but will take more time to set up and more crew to run. Typically, this is done during live events where someone is already running the sound board and you can just pull a feed off of it.
- Using double-system audio (recording to a separate audio recorder) will give you the highest quality sound. But it will require meticulous slating for each take, it will create separate audio files, and those files will have to be synced to the video in post. All of this takes more time.
- Always take 30–120 seconds of room tone for each location (and potentially throughout the day if the ambience changes). This allows you to mask or remove unwanted sounds.
- There are three principles of sound to pay attention to during production: sound perspective, figure-ground principle, and balance. Keep in mind which one is the most important for each take and adjust your mic technique to match.

Part III

Postproduction (Chapters 7–9)

Postproduction, or "post" for short, is where the story finally comes together. We often think of this as simply "editing," but there's a lot more that goes into shaping the final version of your story. Hopefully you recorded good, clean dialogue on set, but there's still a lot of work on the audio side in post. And in modern production, you'll need to know how to do color correction and color grading to make things look consistent between shots, or to use color to help shape your message and story. Post can be the most rewarding phase because you really start to see all of your hard work come together.

DOI: 10.4324/9781003010357-9

7 Editing

Editing is where your ideas finally take shape. Up to this point, you've actually only been planning your project. Even when you shoot the video, you're only collecting elements that may or may not be used to tell your story. Editing is a technical process, and you have to know how a non-linear editor (NLE) works. But you also need to remain focused on telling your story and making good choices in ways that enhance your viewer's understanding of your storylines and message(s).

DOI: 10.4324/9781003010357-10

The Process of Postproduction

Postproduction (often simplified to "post") is what happens after the footage has been shot (although some re-shoots may still be needed), the audio has been recorded (although some audio may still need to be recorded), and the project is ready for editing. For almost all video projects, postproduction follows these basic steps:

1. Import all of the footage into the computer.
2. Organize the files, name the files, and back the files up on the computer.
3. Import the files into your non-linear editing system (NLE) software.
4. Sync the audio and video together if you shot double-system.
5. Cut the clips and place them in the order you want them in on a timeline.
6. Add transitions, graphics, and any other effects.
7. Color grade.
8. Export the timeline in the preferred codec for distribution.

There are some differences between editing a fictional video and non-fiction. When putting something fictional together in post, you've already storyboarded it, and you have a good idea of how the narrative should flow. Music videos, commercials, and movies are all pretty well planned out, so cutting clips and putting them in the correct order isn't nearly as time-consuming. With non-fiction, the time involved can vary greatly. The full-length documentary I just finished took my editor over a year to put together because they were literally writing the story as they went. They had no blueprint. Just 30+ hours of interviews, b-roll, still images, and research. It was interesting working with an editor, because the story they put together was so different than the one I imagined in my head. But I'm also very happy with the story they told, and it turned out better because it wasn't the one I had imagined. News packages and other non-fiction projects are definitely easier. With a news package, you have a basic idea of the flow when you script your interview questions and plan out your b-roll shots. Plus, most news packages follow the same basic flow (more on this in Chapter 14). With instructional videos, they're much more like fiction – you script everything out ahead of time. Importing footage into your computer is different depending on your computer's operating system. For most, though, you insert an SD Card, C-Fast Card, or other medium, then drag and drop the files from the card over to your computer. After that, every genre follows the process outlined above.

File Naming and Organization

In post, this is one of the places I see students take costly shortcuts all the time, only to regret it later when their files become lost or disconnected. It's so tempting to save time and just go with the file name the camera gave each clip, or to name the clips after importing them into your NLE, but it is absolutely essential to develop a consistent naming convention for all of your projects and take the time to implement it for each and every clip you ever shoot. Even if this is your first project, you'll want to keep it and the raw footage, so you'll end up with more and more clips as you complete more and more projects. And cameras name things weirdly – like "CN87354D" or other complete nonsense that will mean nothing to you later on. Finding take 3 of scene 4, shot G later on will be virtually impossible if your clip is named, "CN87354D." And I'm telling you from experience that computers and NLEs sometimes lose the connections to files and you have to go find it and reconnect it again.

Instead, I use a system for scripted projects where each and every file is named for the project, the act, the scene, the shot, and the take. This leaves me with video files named, for example, "KipandBrin_1_5_B_1" (the Kip and Brin Project, Act 1, Scene 5, Shot B, Take 1). My audio files are named the exact same thing, but they'll have a.wav extension instead of.mov, so it will be easy enough to keep them separate. If it's a short project (short film, commercial, instructional video, or music video), I'll put everything into one project folder and then have separate folders inside that named:

1. Raw Video Clips (unaltered clips after they're renamed)
2. Raw Audio Clips (unaltered clips after they're renamed)
3. Production Stills and Graphics (video files created after shooting)
4. Music, Sound Effects, and Narration (audio files recorded after shooting)
5. The saved project file itself (not a folder, just a file)

For a long project, I'll do the same thing, but inside of each folder, I'll put additional folders for each act, or possibly even each scene. If you break it down too finely, it takes longer to bring everything into your NLE and navigate through the folders. If you don't break things down finely enough, you'll have so many files to scroll through in your NLE that it will take more time.

For an unscripted project, I still name it with the project name and then some identifying info, but I don't know what shots will make up each part of the story when I'm naming them, so it's slightly different. For example, the documentary I just finished about Central State Hospital used names like "CentralStateProject_PowellBuilding_Shot1." You won't have multiple takes for non-fiction, but you might have multiple shots, especially when shooting b-roll. You might not even have a concrete name for the project (we didn't) when you're organizing the files. So instead, you group them by common themes. In our case, building names, interviews, and events were the ways we kept things organized. That way, when the editor went to put the story together, he at least knew what he would be looking at before he even opened the file. And we actually put the stills of the buildings and grounds of the hospital into those folders instead of the Production Stills folder because otherwise the photos and videos would have been separated. The project relied heavily on graphics, though, so the Graphics folder was still quite full.

Sometimes, you'll have video clips without audio clips. Usually, these MOS clips are inserts or cutaways. I name these based on the scene they fit into, for example, "KipandBrin_1_5_Insert_Notebook," or "KipandBrin_1_5_Cutaway_Clock." Sometimes, you'll have audio clips without video clips. These are called "wild" audio clips, and they're usually the room tone clips, sound effects captured on set, or similar things. Otherwise, when you're shooting dual-system, you should have an audio file and a video file for every take. I'll go into detail in the next chapter, but naming them identically will help later when you go to sync them, because most NLEs allow you to sort files alphabetically, so the video and audio clips will be next to each other if you name them correctly.

Ingesting/Importing and Metadata

Ingesting is the process of capturing something from tape or card into a computer. When cameras shot on tape, they had to play back the clips in real time while the computer recorded each frame of information and put it into a digital file. "Ingesting" is rarely used these days. Instead, we simply say we "import" the footage from the card into the computer. As mentioned above, this usually means just dragging and dropping the files from the card into the Raw Video Clips folder for the project. Don't forget to place the audio files into the Raw Audio Clips folder if you're shooting dual-system.

This is a good place to remind you to back everything up. There's a saying in film: "if you don't have at least 2 copies of something, you might as well not have it." I could give you numerous horror stories (both my own and many of my students) to illustrate my point, but hopefully you can simply take my word for it. Back up all of your files. I usually do this after renaming and organizing them, otherwise I have to do that step twice. If it's a really important project, I'll back up everything immediately, then create a backup of the named files (leaving me three copies), then I delete the unnamed, unorganized files. This way, I don't leave any gap where my originals are the only copies in existence. And you should always back things up on a separate hard drive. If your original and your backups are on the same drive, you risk the drive failing and losing everything. I personally have a RAID array of disks that creates an immediate duplicate of all files. This array has four 8TB hard drives. But instead of 32TB worth of space, I only have 16TB because the other 16TB are an exact duplicate. This is the ideal way to back things up. If one disk fails, you simply replace the disk and the RAID writes the duplicate files back onto the disk. The one downside here is that human error can still cause havoc. If I delete a file from the RAID, it doesn't have a previous copy I can return to. Since it's an external drive, though, I rarely work directly from it. When I'm currently working on a project (I'm doing this right now with this book I'm writing), I'll have my working copy on my computer's hard drive. Then every day or at least once a week, I copy that file over to the RAID and replace the previous versions. For this book, I'm also backing up a copy of everything once a week onto my cloud storage space. I probably wouldn't do this for video projects, though, because some clouds actually compress your video files when you upload them. It also takes a long time to upload and download video files. You're much better off having an external drive to back things up.

I've already mentioned metadata a few times in this book, but this is a good spot to go into more detail. Metadata is the information (data) about all of your files (data). It's the data about your data. For video files, this means knowing and keeping track of these things for each clip:

1. Field of view (CU, MS, LS, etc.)
2. Act
3. Scene
4. Shot
5. Take
6. Whether or not this is a usable ("good") take
7. Iris/Aperture setting
8. Shutter speed/Shutter angle setting
9. Gain/ISO setting
10. Focal length of your lens
11. White balance setting
12. If you used a filter, and if so, which one(s)

For a scripted project, you should write each of these things down for each take as you shoot. On a film set, this is the job of the First Assistant Camera (AC). This allows you to re-create the shot later on, if you need to re-shoot it. For non-scripted projects, keeping track of this much metadata is probably unnecessary. Newer cameras will usually record some of this metadata with the clip, but some won't. And very few cameras record focal length and filter information. Again, skipping this step seems like an easy way to speed up the process, but it's important to make sure that you keep track of metadata for each clip and input it into your NLE to keep everything organized and more efficient later on. Another exciting way I'm using metadata these days is to use tag words. As a filmmaker and freelance videographer, when I shoot a clip of a sunset for a project, I can tag it with the keyword "sunset." Then, when I'm working on another project later on, I can search for all the clips on my computer or RAID with the "sunset" tag. Even though I didn't shoot that clip specifically for the project I'm working on, it still might work out just fine. And that will save me time going out and shooting (or re-shooting) a sunset.

Most NLEs allow you to type in this metadata for each clip. In fact, they usually give you about a hundred additional fields you can input as well. You can even color-code your clips. You can (and should) play around with metadata fields and see what you find useful and what you find excessive. I don't typically color-code my clips or go beyond the 12 things I listed above, and I'm only starting to tag my clips with keywords. But I'm also not a professional editor, even if I do know how.

Editing

I'll go into much more detail below about how to edit using an NLE. As I overview the process here, I'll keep it simple. The actual editing part of postproduction comes after importing and organizing all of your clips into bins – essentially folders inside of your NLE that allow you to organize things differently than the way you have them on your hard drive – and the process varies based on which software you're using to edit. Most NLEs allow you to open a clip and watch it or listen to it inside a clip viewer. Once you find the clip you want, you can trim it inside the clip viewer or else drag it down to the timeline without trimming it. You can view your timeline in the main viewer (sometimes called the "program viewer"). Once on the timeline, you're still able to trim the parts off the beginning or end of the clip that you don't want. This part of the process entails laying down all of the parts of all of the clips you want, in the order you want them, on your timeline. Once you've put everything together in order, then you add any transitions (cuts, fades, cross-dissolves, wipes, etc.), color grade, and you're ready to export.

Exporting

When your project is complete, color-graded, and ready to go, you're ready to export. Each NLE handles this a bit differently. There are a lot of tutorial videos out there for each. In general, though, the most difficult thing about exporting is making sure your codecs and settings are what you want them to be. When exporting, you can often change the frame rate, the lines of resolution, the file type, and many other things. The good news here is that as long as you save the files and the project, you can always come back and export again with different settings. In fact, I generally export a high-resolution version for my archives regardless of the distribution outlet requirements. These days, I'm often shooting videos that are designed for distribution on the web. The best codecs here are h.264 or h.265 video, at 1080i. These are the ones YouTube prefers, and YouTube videos are really easy to embed into websites. But I will usually export an.mov version as well where I rewrap the timeline settings.

This means that I will generally set the codecs and settings on the timeline to be the same codecs and settings that I shot in. You cannot actually gain quality above what you shot your footage in (unless you send your footage through specialized upscaling software), regardless of how you set your timeline or your export settings. For example, if you shoot in 1080i, you gain nothing by editing or exporting in 1080p or 4k. You gain nothing by editing in 1080i and trying to export in 4k. This will increase the file size, but without any additional pixel information, so the actual resolution doesn't get any sharper. It can work the opposite way, though. I can shoot in 4k, edit in 4k, and then export in 1080p and have a nice looking 1080p project. So, it's always better to shoot and edit in the same resolution, and it's not a bad idea to shoot and edit in a higher resolution than the one you might be exporting.

Non-linear Editing Systems

Non-linear editing systems (NLEs) are software programs that allow you to import, edit, and export clips. These days, there are a range of programs out there. Avid Media Composer is still preferred by some, especially in filmmaking. I used Apple Final Cut Pro 3, 4, 5, 6, and 7 for years, but I never picked up Final Cut Pro X when it came out. I do know some that prefer it after they get used to the different interface, though. I primarily use

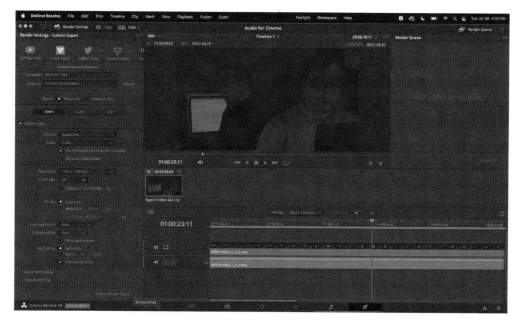

Figure 7.1 The exporting interface in DaVinci Resolve. The settings can all be adjusted in the lefthand panel. The timeline and viewer are still part of this interface, allowing you to do a quick check that you've selected the correct timeline for export. Notice the automatic presets for YouTube, Vimeo, Twitter, and Dropbox up in the upper-left corner. These will automatically adjust your settings for these popular distribution outlets so you don't have to manually set everything. In DaVinci and others, you have to "queue" up your project, then render it upon export. I often forget this is a two-step process and wonder why nothing is happening after I click "Add to Render Queue."

Adobe Premiere and DaVinci Resolve for the projects I work on these days. DaVinci has a free version that comes with most of the high-end features enabled. It's a great program to download and edit videos on. Apple iMovie comes installed on Mac computers and is easy to use when you're getting started, but it operates very differentky from more professional and robust editing systems. Same thing with web-based programs like Shotcut, ClipChamp, WeVideo, or the editors built into Vimeo and YouTube. These are good for quick, easy edits, but they lack the features of more professional software. It's still true that you'll need a fairly good computer running professional software to really have all of the features you need for professional video projects. Even the professional NLEs have differences between them, and it's certainly worth watching tutorial videos on the one you choose to dive into to learn all of the features and how to use them. Here, I'll overview some of the basics and things that are common to all NLEs.

Bins

As mentioned above, bins are how NLEs organize all of your assets (audio files, video files, timelines, graphics, stills, etc.). Even though you've already organized your raw footage into folders on your computer, you may want to organize things differently in your NLE. For example, you might decide to keep everything in one raw video clips folder on your computer, but in your NLE you might choose to have one bin for each scene that contains both audio files and video files. Or you might be re-using graphics across multiple sections in the project, so you might create a template graphic plate, then have a bin to keep all of the graphics you make from that template. Keeping them separate will prevent you from messing up your template.

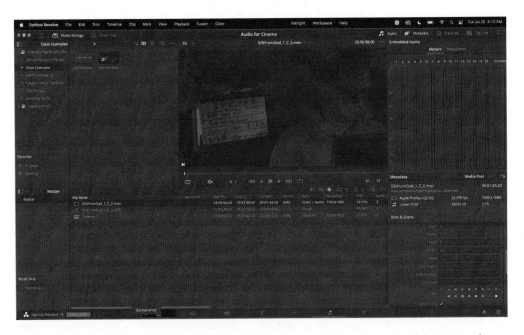

Figure 7.2 In DaVinci Resolve, you create bins in the media management tab of the NLE software. This is where you import files, tag them with metadata, and put them into folders.

Clip Viewer

The clip viewer is next to the program viewer, typically to the left. It's the small box that allows you to preview each clip before bringing it down and placing it on the timeline. The clip viewer allows you to make sure you're selecting the clip you want, but it can also trim clips, add effects to clips, view audio waveforms, and add audio effects. The changes you make in the clip viewer don't necessarily apply to a clip on your project's timeline – changes you make affect whatever clip you have selected at the time. For example, if you place a clip into your project by dragging it down to the timeline, but then select that same clip in your bin, when you make changes in the clip viewer, you're affecting the clip in your bin, but not the clip that's already on your timeline. Instead, you have to make the changes before bringing the clip onto the timeline, or you have to select the clip in the timeline before you begin making adjustments. I prefer the second method.

Program Viewer

The program viewer shows the clips on your timeline in the order you place them and cut them. It's the box in the upper right, typically. You can see in Figure 7.3 that the program viewer is not showing the same part of the clip as the clip viewer. Above the box, it even says "Timeline 1" to indicate what you're seeing in the viewer. The clip viewer says "GiftFromGod_1_C_2.mov" to indicate which clip I have selected.

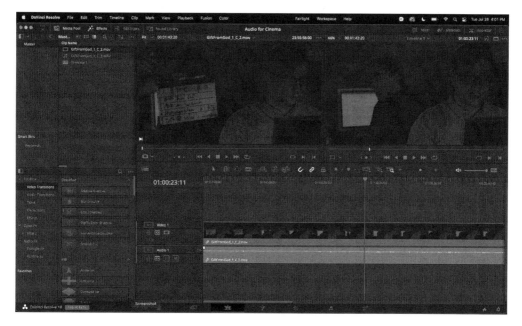

Figure 7.3 The editing tab layout in DaVinci Resolve. This layout is similar to other NLEs. In the upper left is the bin(s). The lower left shows the effects I can place onto the clips in the timeline. The timeline runs across the bottom, with timecode to show how long everything is (because you can compress or expand the timeline view). The timeline shows the video track and the audio track (because you can separate them and remove one or the other) for the clip. Above that are the clip viewer and program viewer.

Timeline

The timeline is where you build the narrative structure for your project. You take clips and put them in the order you want them. You can also trim them down and remove parts of the clips you don't want on the timeline. This is where you add transitions, effects, adjustment layers for color grading, and anything else to create your project.

The timeline in Figure 7.3 only shows one clip, but you can layer multiple video clips. You generally only see the clip that is "on top" of the others, based on the highest video track number – for example, if I had a clip in Video 1 and a clip in Video 2 that were layered at the same time code, you would only see the clip in the Video 2 track. So, why do this? Sometimes it makes editing faster because we don't have to cut clips down, but usually we do it because layering tracks allows us to do more with effects. If we want to do a split-screen, for example, or a super-imposition (where you see traces of both images on the screen at the same time), we need both clips to be on tracks at the same point in the time code. Generally, though, when I'm editing, I condense tracks down before they get out of control. But I have to be careful when doing this, because the audio clips in the timeline move up or down on the track numbers along with the video clip because they're connected.

Audio tracks in your timeline operate a bit differently than video. The audio clip in Figure 7.3 only has one track, but if you bring in a stereo clip, it will occupy one video track and two audio tracks. One audio track will be panned (routed to) the left speaker channel, and one will be panned to the right. As you move the video clip, the audio clips will move around the timeline and match it. To manipulate the audio clip separately from the video clip, you have to "unlink" them. Then you can delete the video (or audio), move a clip earlier or later in the timeline without the others following, or move the audio or video up or down the track layers without the others moving as well. For example, say I have 2 video tracks with 2 clips on them and 4 corresponding stereo audio tracks. If I want to hear one set of audio (narration) but delete the video track, I can unlink them, then delete the video. Now, I only see the video in track 1. But I still hear both sets of audio, so I need to unlink the b-roll video clip from its audio and delete those audio clips. Then, I can also move those audio clips up to audio tracks 1 and 2 instead of leaving them on 3 and 4.

Tools

Tools are where NLEs can be very different from each other. There are a few basic tools, and they're generally found to the left of the timeline, or above it. In Figure 7.3, the tools are immediately above the timeline. The arrow (red indicates that the arrow is currently the tool I have selected) is the "selection tool." This means I can select a clip on the timeline. Sometimes, the selection tool also allows you to grab the beginning or end of the clip and "stretch it" or "shrink it," manipulating where the clip begins, where it ends, and the clip's duration. Most NLEs will also have a "blade tool." The blade tool allows you to go to a specific frame within the clip and "cut" the clip, creating a new beginning point and end point for the two parts of the clip. With the selection tool, you can then select part of the clip you cut off and delete it, or you can select the beginning or end of the part and stretch it or shrink it. Aside from the selection and blade tools, almost nothing else is standard. Each NLE has unique tools. Some allow you to "ripple delete" blank spots between clips as you cut them. Some allow you to slide a clip (it keeps the beginning and end timecode points but allows you to manipulate which frame starts the clip and where it ends). Depending on your NLE, you should watch some tutorial videos on the various tools and how they're used. For my purposes, I rarely go beyond the basic selection tool and blade tool. The rest are designed for efficiency, and if I were editing video on a daily basis, I would certainly take the time to get more familiar with all the tools available to me.

Non-linear Editing Process

In the first part of the chapter, I gave a general overview of the entire postproduction process. Here, I want to outline the basic nuts-and-bolts of using an NLE. I also want to specify that this is the way I edit video. Like driving across town to the gas station, there are about a dozen different ways to get where I want to go. None are "right" or "wrong." Some save more time, but only if the stoplights are in my favor. With editing, I would encourage you to experiment with different approaches. Watch tutorial videos online, learn the tools designed to make you more efficient, and know that something that works for one person may not work as well for you.

I/O Editing

"I/O" stands for "inpoint/outpoint" editing. This is how I learned to edit, but not how I currently do it. Essentially, in I/O editing, you mark a frame as your start point (your "in" point) on the clip in the clip viewer. Then you mark a frame as your end point (your "out" point) on the same clip in the clip viewer. From there, when you click and drag the clip from the clip viewer and place it on your timeline, you're only bringing down the part of the clip you specified. If you don't mark an inpoint and outpoint before bringing the clip down, it will start when you first hit record on the camera and end when you pressed the button to stop rolling. This means that the slate and Director's commands will be part of the clip placed on the timeline (the unwanted part of the clip at the beginning is called the "head" and at the end it's called the "tail") unless you cut them off first. Many editors prefer to I/O edit their clips down before bringing them down to the timeline. Even when you do this, you still have the option (and typically end up needing) to adjust the start and end point of the clip by trimming it later. The alternative is bringing the clips down whole and then trimming them.

Trimming Clips

I find it easier these days to bring the clips down whole and simply trim them immediately on the timeline. So, I first preview my clip in the clip viewer, but instead of taking the time to mark inpoints and outpoints, I just drag the clip down to an unused video track (make sure the audio isn't replacing audio on a track below), then hover the mouse over the front edge of the clip in the timeline and grab it and shrink it down to remove the head of the clip. As I shrink, the program viewer shows the frame I'm on, so I can select the exact frame where I want the clip to start (and I can always adjust this later, if needed). Then, I do the same with the tail of the clip. If it's a really long clip, I use my blade tool to cut where I want, discard the unwanted half of the clip, then stretch or shrink the head and tail until the clip is the length and content I want. From there, I move on to the next clip and do the same thing. Neither I/O Editing or Trimming whole clips is right or wrong. Just two ways to get to the same goal. You might find you prefer one way or the other, or that one way is faster for you.

Transitions

The majority of transitions in a video project should be cuts. This means putting one clip immediately after the one before it (make sure there isn't a single frame gap in between, which happens to me sometimes) on the timeline. If you need to do a dissolve (where one clip gradually replaces the other) or a wipe (where one clips pushes the other off the screen in some pre-set pattern), you have to allow for "handles" on each of the clips. This means that the viewer will see a little bit after the ending frame of the first clip (they'll see some of the tail) and a bit before the start point of the next clip (they'll see some of the head). It is impossible for a computer to extrapolate the pixels if they're not there, so you can't do a dissolve or wipe if the end of the clip itself is your endpoint on the timeline – if you don't have any handles on the clips. So if you want transitions, you need to start the camera rolling 5–10 seconds before the action and leave it rolling 5–10 seconds after the action before yelling, "cut!"

On most NLEs, inserting a transition is as easy as grabbing one from the "effects" list and dropping it on the cut point between two clips. The hard part is deciding which transition to use. You can see in Figure 7.3 that there are 6 different types of dissolves. The "Cross Dissolve" is the most common one I use, but there are times when the others might work better. This is where you need to experiment with different looks as you're learning to edit so you know which to use when. There are also many different types of wipes (DaVinci Resolve calls these "Iris" transitions), and experimenting with these can be humorous and potentially rewarding. Wipes have very much fallen out of style. They're often used in sports to transition between a replay and the live shot – this works because wipes are jarring and call attention to themselves, so it helps the viewer differentiate between the shots). They're also used occasionally in comedies for visual transitions. The one serious film franchise that has used them to great stylistic effect is Star Wars. But very few projects I've done really needed wipes. And when I've tried to use them, they just seemed cheesy. Trust me, when I first started using an NLE, I thought they were the coolest and I tried to put them in everywhere. Now, when I look back at those projects, I'm embarrassed.

Another type of transition is a "dip to black" or "dip to white." You rarely see any other color. These can be effective to indicate the passage of time. A dissolve can do the same thing, but doesn't transition as completely as a dip to black. Dipping to black can be done using the "dip to color dissolve" transition in Figure 7.3, but it's also possible without handles. Doing a dissolve to a blank frame in between clips allows the timeline to fade to black. Then doing a second dissolve up from that black frame to the next clip fades that clip in. The end result is a dip to black, but one that didn't require handles on each clip. Dips to black are still acceptable stylistically because they don't draw much attention to themselves. This leaves the viewer believing in the world you've created for them (they're still willing to suspend their disbelief), unlike a wipe, which seems mechanical and draws attention to the editing itself.

Keyframes

Keyframes allow you to automate any number of editing functions. When using keyframes, you set a frame (the "key" frame) for a value change to begin, then scrub forward through your clip to the frame where you want the value change to end. You set the second keyframe. Then, you set the ending value for the frame that you want to change.

The computer will extrapolate all of the values in between and make incremental changes in each frame, starting with the first keyframe and ending with the second. You can even set multiple keyframes throughout a clip for a specific value, and set different keyframes for other aspects of the clip that you want to automate.

I realize what I just said is probably sounding very technical and complicated, so let me give you an example. In Figure 7.4, you can see that I've set a different value for the "Zoom." The beginning "Zoom" of the clip was set to 0, meaning that the clip I shot is framed the way I shot it. Pixels haven't been enlarged to digitally zoom into the shot. I set a keyframe for that zero value on "Zoom" earlier in the timeline by clicking on the diamond icon to the right of the "Zoom" function. If I wanted to set a keyframe for "Pitch" or "Yaw," I could have done that here as well. After setting the first keyframe, I played through the clip until the frame that I wanted the zoom to end on, and set a second keyframe there. There must always be at least two keyframes – one to start the value change and one to end it. After clicking the diamond icon to set the second keyframe, then I make the value adjustment. In this case, I digitally zoomed in about 3x. When I play back through the clip now, it starts with normal framing, but then zooms in slowly and smoothly until the second keyframe at time code 01:01:08:02. The computer has extrapolated all of the "zoom" values for each and every frame in-between the two keyframes.

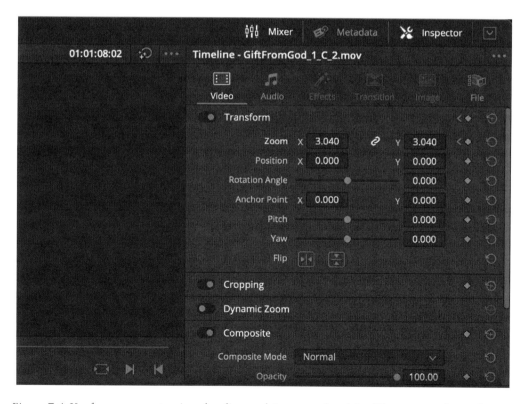

Figure 7.4 Keyframes are set using the diamond icons to the right. There must always be two keyframes – one to set the initial value for the change, and one to end the value. You can also add keyframes in between if you want the changes to speed up or slow down.

Editing Audio

Editing the audio clips in an NLE is very similar to editing the video clip(s). When you mark inpoints or outpoints, the audio clip is marked as well. In fact, using I/O editing, you can even drag down just the audio clip or the video clip to the timeline. If you don't mark in- or outpoints, you can also just trim the ends of an audio clip on the timeline by grabbing and dragging them. Some editing systems will even add a cross fade audio transition automatically (where one clip gets softer as the next clip replaces it by getting louder) when you drop a cross-dissolve transition onto the corresponding video clip. If not, you can add cross fades to the audio transitions by dragging and dropping them onto your clip edit points. Like video clips, you have to have handles in your audio clips for this to work, and you might hear a bit of the head or tail, so you need your edit points to be tight before dropping the transition onto them. Like a video transition, you can grab the end of an audio transition and stretch or shrink the transition itself, which speeds up or slows down the cross fade. I even find it beneficial at times to put very short (3 or 4 frames) cross fades into my audio track, even when I'm using basic cuts in my video track. This just helps to smooth out the audio cuts.

In order to do that, though, you'll probably need to unlink the audio and video tracks. If you leave them linked, most NLEs will adjust both the audio and the video whenever you make any adjustments to either. For example, if I add a cross dissolve to the video track and it automatically places a cross fade onto the audio track, I can't shorten the cross fade without also shortening the cross dissolve. If I stretch the video clip to make it longer, it will also make the audio longer. So, I have to "unlink" the video from the audio if I want to manipulate either of them separately. After putting the transition in, stretching the clip, etc., you can always re-link them if you want them to move together later. The next chapter goes into a lot more detail about postproduction for audio, but these are the basics for editing your audio clips.

Editing for Continuity

There are entire books that cover the theory of editing and how to best put a project together. I want to give a summary of approaches you can take when editing, but the following pages are far from comprehensive. Much of what is taught in film theory classes is the narrative structure – the editing decisions that were made to tell the story. And even though the script, storyboards, and production clips determine the raw materials, the editing is where the story truly comes to life. This is true across a number of projects, including documentary films, commercials, and music videos. Even instructional videos have to flow well and keep their audiences interested. Editing for continuity means that you structure your story in a way that flows well and makes easy sense for the viewer from shot to shot. For example, in the first clip on our timeline, we see a person opening a car door. Then for the next clip, we place one that shows that person sitting down in the car and closing the door behind them. The next clip might be the person starting the car, then a clip of them driving away. This flows well, and the viewer doesn't have to think to figure out what pieces they missed in between the clips. The camera could even reposition from outside the car in the first shot/clip to inside the car for the next few clips, and the viewer wouldn't be disoriented or wonder how they went from outside the car to inside. Continuity also means keeping movements flowing from one shot to the next (if someone is walking toward the left side of the screen in one shot, they should continue walking in that direction in the next), and positioning things in a similar way from shot to shot. We see a lot of "Continuity Error" videos online these days, and most of them focus on continuity of props. This obviously happens during shooting, and this is why you need a good script supervisor on complicated films. But there are a lot of other things to think about when you're editing in order to maintain continuity. Specifically, here I'm going to talk about how to keep your lines and movement continuous, how to maintain the 180-degree rule, and how to edit using what Herb Zettl calls a "deductive approach" in his landmark book, *Sight, Sound, Motion*. Although the 180-degree rule should be applied while shooting, and the flow of your edits might already be spelled out in your storyboards, there are certainly instances where you'll be editing something together that did not adhere to these rules during shooting. This means as you edit, you need to make sure you're using clips and editing them in ways that maintain continuity (assuming this is the approach you're taking to the editing and you're not intentionally trying to confuse the viewer).

Lines

There are different types of lines in video projects, but in general, we want to maintain continuity with them from shot to shot. Eyelines are especially important to think about from one shot to the next. If we see an actor's eyes in one shot, we assume that what we see in the next shot is the person or thing they were looking at. So, their eyes should be directed toward the person, and in the next shot, the second person's eyes should be looking back.

Horizons and other lines are equally important to maintain continuity. When shooting, it's important to mark your monitor or viewfinder where the horizon line is (I use a small strip of painter's tape on my monitor), so you can maintain that line from shot to shot and help your editor out. An editor can crop or reframe the shot slightly, if needed,

Figure 7.5 The actor in one shot is looking to the right.

Figure 7.6 The actress is "looking back" at the actor in Figure 7.5 in the next shot, even though these two shots were taken at very different times on set (we shot this scene using the Master Scene Method described in Chapter 4). The shots aren't framed identically, but notice that the eyes are the same height in the frame in each, and both are sitting on the intersections of the thirds (rule of thirds).

but it's better if the person shooting keeps lines in mind as they shoot. The viewer's gaze is naturally drawn along those lines, so inconsistencies are noticeable.

Movement

The same thing goes for movement. It's the editor's job to make sure that movements are consistent across cuts, and that the scene maintains continuity of movement. Like maintaining continuity with your lines, this begins in preproduction and shooting correctly helps the editor out. If a character or object is moving in a direction in one shot, the movement should continue in the next. For example, if a person is walking on a sidewalk and crossing the screen from left to right, the next shot should continue the movement from left to right (even if it's a slightly different angle). If the movement changes direction, you're implying to the viewer that the person turned around. Seems simple enough, but when you're shooting scenes and shots out of order, it can actually be difficult to keep track of lines and movements. That's why it's a good idea for someone to take notes for each shot on the script.

It's also a bad idea to cut at the beginning or end of the movement exactly. If someone is walking from left to right in one shot, then standing completely still in the next, it can be jarring to the viewer, who assumes they missed something. Instead, if you're going to cut during movement, it should continue from one shot to the next, with the last shot holding until the movement ends. Instead of cutting from the shot of the person walking to one of them standing still, you should cut to the shot where they stop walking and reach the standing position. During shooting, you should always have your actors "rock in" to a shot if the shot needs to maintain movement. This means having them shift their weight onto their back foot. Then when the Director calls "action," they shift the weight onto their front foot and begin walking. This gives the impression from the very start of the action that they were moving, and it helps your editor maintain continuity of movement.

180-degree Rule

Both eyelines and movement can be maintained by adhering to the 180-degree rule. This is a rule you need to keep in mind while shooting, but since Chapter 4 didn't really cover these continuity tips, I'm putting it here in the editing chapter. The 180-degree rule (also called "axis of action," "180 line," or simply "The Line") stipulates that you should always keep the camera on one side of the action.

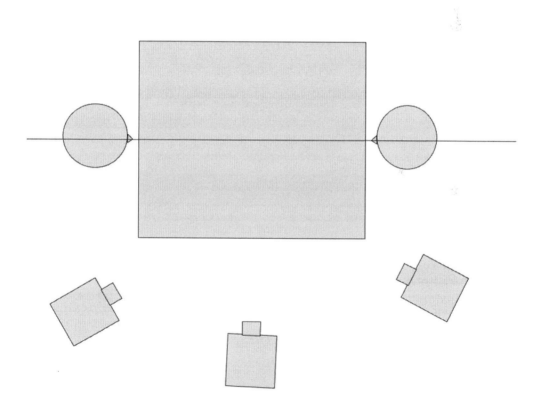

Figure 7.7 The line created by the axis of action runs in between the two actors (determined by their eyelines). The camera to the left is cross-shooting the actor on the right for their single. The camera in the middle would be for the 2-shot master. All three cameras are on the same side of the 180 line, otherwise the actors would switch positions or their eyelines would change.

In Figure 7.7, the actor on the left is looking to the right in all three camera shots. If we were to break the rule and place a camera on the other side of the 180 line, their eyeline would now be looking off to the left, which would break continuity. In the 2-shot, if we crossed the 180 line with that camera, the actors would switch places and their eyelines would swap. The 180 line works with movement as well. As long as you stay on one side of the line, then the thing in motion will stay continuous from shot to shot. If there are no eyelines, then the movement itself creates the 180 line, and you don't want to cross the direction of the movement, or the subject will appear to switch directions.

The 180 rule gets a bit more complicated when there are more than two actors in a scene. The eyelines of the main actors create the 180 line, but you may find yourself in a situation where there are multiple lines you don't want to cross. Thinking through each shot and paying special attention to eyelines and screen positions is important in those situations. You might even want to look over your location sketches and figure out the locations of the 180 lines before deciding where to place your camera locations.

Deductive Approach

A "deductive approach" (Zettl) to structuring a scene in editing means that you start with the wider shots and work your way into the detailed close ups. For example, in a conversation scene, you might begin with a shot that shows the outside of the building, or a shot of the location that shows the viewer where the conversation is taking place – an "establishing shot." The next shot may be a longer 2-shot that shows both of the people before the conversation begins, followed by a closer 2-shot as the characters start to speak. From there, we can cut into the back-and-forth singles of each character as they say their lines and react to what is being said. This approach leads the viewer gently into a scene and gives them ample clues about what is going on. Most scenes are structured this way because it's less jarring to viewers. And it's also important to note that you can start with an establishing shot and then quickly get into the close ups. You don't have to stick with formulas; you just have to have intentionality when choosing how to put your shots in order and guide your viewers through the scene. Sometimes, an editor has a really detailed storyboard to work from, but sometimes after shooting, you'll find that things need to be structured differently. Perhaps time didn't allow for some of the planned shots. Or perhaps some of the shots didn't turn out as well as they were planned. There are many reasons to give your editor some latitude to use the shots they think are best and to put those shots in the order they think is best. From there, the Director and producer can always work with the editor to make sure the story is being told well.

Sometimes, you'll have a fantastic idea and plan an entire scene around it. Then, you'll spend a lot of time during production to make sure you get the shot. And then you'll get to editing and you'll try to force the shot into the timeline, even if it doesn't really work. It's always better to have someone else who isn't as invested in that shot or scene watch the project and give their honest opinion. And then you'll have to be open to listening to them and removing the shot that you worked so hard on. Hollywood calls this "killing your babies." I'm not a huge fan of the term, but the point is that you shouldn't get so invested in an idea that you're not willing to abandon it if test audiences don't think it works. For the first music video I ever shot, we storyboarded a really cool concept with parallel cuts (where one storyline's shots visually match another storyline's shots and you cut back and forth between the two storylines). When I tested the video on an audience, there was major confusion about a plot point between the two storylines, and the audience read a connection that would have flipped the narrative we were telling. I was too immersed in the concept to see the problem, but when my test audience pointed it out, I realized that the parallel cuts would have to go – they were the reason the audience made connections that were counter-productive. After rearranging the shots (and making the video way less cool), a second test audience followed the narrative easily and understood the message the video was sending. It was a more effective video when I abandoned the concept that we had worked so hard to create and shoot.

Montage

Montage is a term used by the Soviet filmmaker Sergei Eisenstein to describe editing techniques that combine a series of images to tell a story. Montage would not necessarily be deductive, although it could be. Instead, when Eisenstein edited his film, *Battleship Potemkin* (1925), he used cuts from one part of the scene to a different part to jar the viewer and force them to think about all of the different pieces they were seeing and what the filmmaker was trying to say. For example, the "Odessa Steps" scene in the film cuts back and forth between soldiers shooting, a crowd on the steps running and being shot, a baby carriage rolling down the steps, and close ups of the baby inside. Deductively, the scene is laid out in fairly chronological order. But it doesn't take a huge leap to understand that the baby carriage and the passenger inside are a metaphor for the innocence being taken away in that scene. By juxtaposing the imagery in a montage, Eisenstein is producing a message about the two images and their contradictory nature. Essentially, this is what montage is. When you structure your scene and put shots together, montage allows you to put two shots that might be unrelated together to create an overall message for your viewer.

Inductive Approach

Zettl uses the term "inductive approach" to describe scenes that don't lead the viewer into the action gently like a deductive approach does. In an inductively structured scene, the first few shots would be pieces of a puzzle that the viewer needed to put together in their mind to get a sense of what was happening in the scene. Inductive approaches often have an establishing shot at the end to show the viewer the actual layout of the scene, but the sequences of shots don't have to have that payoff shot. For example, I could start a commercial with extreme close ups of a car, cut together in a way that the viewer only sees colors and shapes, but not a definite idea of what the product was or how the shots lined up to make the whole. Perhaps a shot of the seat, the dashboard, the headlight, the tire, or other parts of the car. Then, after several of these close up shots, I cut in a long shot of the car so the viewer can see it in its entirety. After that, I might end the commercial with more long shots showing the car performing on curvy roads or driving through the city. You get the idea. This inductive series of shots is structured so that the viewer gets clues about what they're seeing, but isn't given the payoff until they've had ample time to wonder about it and build up suspense.

Montages can be edited deductively or inductively. And it's important to note that not everything is montage. The car commercial example above isn't montage because it isn't using metaphors. The shots strung together in the beginning of the commercial are all very similar and could stand alone and still convey the message and emotions. For something to be montage, the editing typically operates at a metaphorical level as well as a visual one. Going back to the car commercial example, if the opening shots were close ups of the car, intercut with racehorses running down the track, this would be a montage. It would still be inductive because we're holding back the payoff shot from the viewer still. But the metaphor would be the similarities between the car and the thoroughbred horses speeding down the track. The strength of the horses, their speed, all the things we associate with their races – the viewer understands that by juxtaposing those images with the car, we are transposing those qualities onto the car itself.

Intensifying Energy

We primarily increase the energy in a scene by camera movement and by creating a feeling of movement through our editing. A chase scene can be intense because of the camera movements (pans, dollies, car-mounted shots), but it also needs to be edited together with fast-paced cuts to intensify the event. Even slower scenes without movement can become more intense when the editing is quick and crisp. Perhaps it's a scene where two roommates are sharing a bowl of popcorn, and when there's only one piece left the editing speeds up to show the tension and add energy to what started out as a pretty slow scene. Maybe we see more close ups of the roommates as they look down to see the last kernel, then at each other, then back down at the kernel. A scene like this might start deductively, with a long shot of the two roommates. The pacing might be slower – 5 or 10 seconds between cuts – until the realization that there's only one piece left. At that point, the scene turns into an inductive montage, where the kernel is a metaphor for greed, or competition. The close ups help the viewer ignore the rest of the scenery and narrative to focus on the immediate nature of the fight over the final kernel. The pacing has to increase to match the tension – 1 second or less between cuts.

You can, of course, also slow down the pacing to add a sense of balance or to allow your viewer to slow down and take everything in. Even action movies have to give their viewers a break throughout the narrative. Humorous scenes, love-interest scenes, or just scenes where the characters slow down to regroup, are all necessary for the audience to avoid action fatigue. Think of some action movies that have been criticized for being nothing but explosions and special effects. Critics aren't saying that they don't appreciate the artistry of the special effects. They're saying that they're fatigued by the lack of opportunities to slow down and soak in the narrative and character arcs. If a storyline feels too thin in an action movie, it's probably because the film is missing the scenes where the characters just sit around and talk about what they're going through. These scenes are necessary for the audience to really absorb everything that's happening. The pacing here has to be slow and deliberate. Instead of intensifying the energy of the scene, you can slow down your cuts to help the audience slow down. Instead of 5 seconds between cuts, a scene like this might need 10 or 15 seconds in between edit points.

Intensifying Emotion

The same thing can be said for emotions. Montages can express emotion by operating on a metaphorical level, and the pacing of the cuts needs to match the mood. One of the primary ways to heighten the viewer's emotional reaction is to add music to a scene. Music hits viewers at an emotional level in a way that dialogue and most visuals can't (except for sweeping landscapes). Think about it. When you're feeling nostalgic, you listen to music that brings up memories. Those memories have feelings associated with them. When you're at the gym and want to get energized, you listen to music that gives you adrenaline and makes you feel motivated. When we juxtapose music with visuals, we can convey these emotions. Even when the song isn't well known, you can use music to affect your audience. Major chords are typically associated with happiness. Minor chords with sadness or suspense.

You can also intensify emotions by cutting inward from long shots to close ups, or by slowly zooming in on a shot. When you edit, you're telling the viewer what to focus on and how to read the storyline. I can intensify emotions by cutting away at just the right time to something that evokes memories or feelings. For example, if I have a long shot of someone walking along the beach, I can add emotion to the scene by cutting to a close up of their smiling face. Or I could cut in a shot of the sun reflecting off the water – viewers would associate the sunlight and water with a warm, sunny day and feel happy. Or you can cut a different metaphor in. When shooting a western scene, perhaps you emphasize how dry and thirsty the characters are by cutting in a shot of the sun overhead and vultures flying. Without any dialogue or graphics, you're telling the viewer that the characters' lives are in danger.

Comparing and Contrasting

Montage editing also helps you compare similar things or contrast things in a way that causes your viewers to think about the message you're conveying. When you compare similar things, it can be similarly framed shots, similar subjects, similar lighting situations, similar movements, or anything else that highlights how one shot is parallel to the next one they see. For example, I could have a shot of the sun setting over my house, and cut to a shot of the sun setting over the ocean. This would convey that my house is a serene, peaceful place where I relax at the end of the day. Or, I could cut from a close up of a book to a closeup of someone reading on a tablet to highlight the rapid changes in technology in the last 20 years.

I can also use editing to contrast two different ideas in a way that creates an alternative message to either one. Zettl calls this a "Collision" montage. These things can be framed in similar ways or have common elements, but taken by themselves they typically convey something different. For example, if I cut a shot of a bonfire with flashback shots of a burning house from a character's childhood, these are similar shots in many ways. But the message is very different. In the shot of the bonfire, we would think of s'mores, warmth on a cold day, Fall campouts, and other "fun" memories. A bonfire would typically be read as something positive. But the flashback of the house fire would be a negative. The contrasting messages here would highlight the fact that for the character who experienced the house fire, a bonfire might not be the happy memory it is for everyone else – a separate meaning altogether from the actual images.

You can also compare or contrast music from the visuals and have the same effect. The "Baptism" scene in *The Godfather* is a great example of this. The organ music from the church clashes with the visuals of violence and blood. The music by itself conveys a message, and the violence conveys a separate message. But when you juxtapose the two, you get an entirely different message – that Michael Corleone is being baptized in the blood of his enemies and not exactly renouncing Satan like the dialogue is telling us.

You can also use music to heighten emotions consistent to the visuals. For example, the "Training" montage in *Rocky III* uses Survivor's "Eye of the Tiger" in a way that conveys the energy and determination Rocky experiences when training and fighting, preparing for the ultimate showdown against Clubber Lang. In fact, the music became so synonymous with Rocky's underdog persona that it was an inspiration and motivation for an entire generation of kids.

Rhythmic Editing

Rhythmic editing means that you place cuts (and any other transitions) in a way that helps the visuals flow together from one to the next, and it is an important concept no matter what approach you're taking to editing. In a music video, for example, you might put the cuts on the beat – not every beat (or it would get too repetitive), but when you do cut, it helps to cut on the beat instead of just before or after. It conveys movement and a feel for the music. I've edited highlight videos for events where the dialogue is less important than the music and movement of the audio track. Even though the videos are long (around 30 minutes each), cutting on the beat of the music bed helps me structure the visuals and provides a good sense of movement – instead of feeling as though the visuals are repetitive, which they are, the music and cuts help keep the viewers interested and highlights the fact that the photos and video clips are moving in chronological order and following the conference's daily events for the most part.

You should also consider dialogue and narration to have "beats" and cut to them when you edit. A simple conversation scene in a film might consist of two characters talking back and forth. After one character speaks, the other one delivers their lines. There is typically a pause in between, or a pause between one character's lines where it makes sense to cut. Cutting in the middle of a line is rarely done because it disrupts the rhythm of the conversation and draws attention to the editing. This doesn't keep you from cutting to reaction shots or cutaways, but even those shots should come when there is a natural "beat" in the conversation or the narration.

Rhythmic editing can also be done on the "beat" of character movement or camera movement. As one character moves, there will be a natural point at which their glance, their hands, their legs, or something else will dictate the need for a cut. Perhaps they turn their head to look at something. Cutting too soon or waiting too long to show the viewers what they are looking at will disrupt the flow. Developing a rhythm to these types of cuts is just as important in narrative filmmaking as it is in commercials and other video projects. Ideally, these cutaways (where you show what the character is looking at) or shot reverse-shot cuts (where you cut between the close ups of the two characters as they speak to each other) have a rhythm that also relates to objective (clock) time as well. If it's a simple conversation, it will bore viewers or seem odd if one character is on screen for a long time and the other is hardly there at all. This is when the reaction shots (from the single where a character is listening to the other character as they speak from off-screen) come in handy to give both characters enough screen time.

Metric montage is a similar concept, but instead of using the audio or movement, Eisenstein uses clock time to establish the rhythm of the cuts. In other words, you might have a cut every 2 seconds. Or every 12 frames. Typically, metric montage is used when there isn't necessarily something else (movement, conversation, music) to motivate the cut. I've used metric montage as a way of structuring visuals in experimental films, but I've also used it for b-roll in documentaries, where the visuals simply need to be shown, and then at some point get replaced by the next visual. In my recent documentary on a mental healthcare institution, I had a lot of pictures and video clips of buildings. If I cut to the beat of the music or dialogue, it's possible that one picture might be up there for a short amount of time compared to other pictures. Instead, using metric montage here makes sense and still provides a sense of rhythm and flow, even though the pictures aren't necessarily following the beat of the music bed.

Inserts and Cutaways

I've actually seen these terms used in slightly different ways, but both refer to a shot that isn't necessarily one of the main shots in the scene, but that allow the editor additional coverage. For example, my master shot might be a 2-shot of two characters talking. When I shoot the scene using the Master Scene Method, I would shoot the 2-shot, then a close up of each character (the singles). But I would want additional coverage so those 3 shots aren't the only ones my editor can use for the scene. I might shoot a character's hands as they fidget. Or I might shoot the door of the room from the outside, or a poster on the wall. These shots give additional depth and texture to a scene. They also allow some space for the editor to cover up camera mistakes or continuity errors. Putting additional coverage into a scene can also help change the rhythm and slow things down.

I think of inserts as anything that can only really go into one spot within the scene. This is a bit narrower than most people think of inserts – an insert can really be anything from within the scene established in the master shot, including the singles – but it helps simplify the concept to think of an insert as needing to be inserted at one specific point within the scene. For instance, when a character pulls out a pen to sign a document, the CU of the pen scrawling across the paper is an insert shot. The shot of the pen wouldn't make sense anywhere else in the scene. The point of an insert (using this definition) is to add details to the scene at the moment the audience needs those additional details. Even though inserts are fairly easy to remember because the dialogue or the script will determine the need for one, sometimes they get overlooked while shooting. This is because they're usually shot after the master and the singles. At that point, it's easy to get nervous about the shooting schedule and skip the inserts. This is definitely a mistake. Inserts should be part of your shot list and shooting schedule.

A cutaway is different from an insert. Again, my explanation here might be slightly different from other sources, but a cutaway shot can really be inserted into the scene at any point without causing a continuity error. An insert is always part of the scene shown in the master shot, but a cutaway can be something from outside the scene. For example, in a conversation scene in a teenager's bedroom, we might cut away to a shot of a poster on the wall. Unless the characters are talking specifically about that poster, this cut would be a cutaway – it isn't part of the scene or the action, but it still isn't completely out of place, and it won't jar the viewer visually. The shot of the poster could most likely be used anywhere within the scene (while still paying attention to the rhythm) to cover up a continuity error, to slow down the pacing, or just to add some visual interest to the scene. When editing, cutaway shots are very valuable and add flexibility. Insert shots don't necessarily do that because they generally only fit one specific spot within the scene. The problem with cutaways is really in the shooting. They're hard to remember to fit into the shooting schedule, and they're often difficult to anticipate in your shot list and shooting schedule. The script will rarely contain cutaway recommendations. It's easy for the Director and crew to focus on shooting the master and the shots that focus on the main action within the scene. It's important for a Director to look around when shooting a scene and notice opportunities for cutaway shots.

Chapter 7: Editing Main Points

- Editing begins with organization. Maintaining a consistent file naming scheme and organizational structure is an important first step in any project and throughout your career.
- he editing process starts with downloading and organizing files into bins, then editing, adding transitions and effects, sweetening audio, coloring, and then exporting.
- When shooting and editing for continuity, paying attention to lines and movement is important, as is the 180-degree rule.
- Montage is not the opposite of continuity or a deductive approach. Montage is the juxtaposition of two clips in a way that conveys something beyond the subject matter of those two clips.
- Editing theory is important to know. Conceptualizing how to put video and audio clips together to tell the story or convey the message is just as important as knowing how to use a specific software program.
- Software will change over time, and sometimes rapidly. Knowing the basics of what an NLE can do is more important than knowing exactly which tool or button does what.

8 Audio Post

Putting video clips in the right order and adding transitions is only part of the postproduction process. Audio is at least as important as the visuals, and even if you acquire great sound when you're on set, you still have a bit of work to do in post to make the soundtrack as impressive as your image. During audio post, you'll need to edit, add transitions, EQ, sweeten, and sometimes add music and sound effects.

DOI: 10.4324/9781003010357-11

Postproduction Workflow for Audio

Working with the audio you recorded on set is an important, and often overlooked, part of the postproduction process. Audio is at least as important as the video, and in some cases it's more important. The process is fairly similar to editing video – it begins with file organization, then moves on to importing and editing the clips – but the process has to run ahead or behind the video editing at times. For example, files need to be synced before they can be edited if they were shot dual-system. For single-system sound, many of the following sections don't necessarily apply. For single-system audio, it will already be synced with the video and you'll only need to worry about editing and then sweetening the sound.

Audio sweetening mostly occurs after the video is picture-locked (meaning that the timing of clips won't change) so you don't waste a lot of time working on audio that won't be used in the final cut of the project. But some things can run parallel. You can edit the audio clips along with the video clips and add transitions to both as you go. You can work on the perspective and pan sounds into the center channel or in stereo as you work. In this chapter, I'll go through the basics and some intermediate concepts when it comes to audio postproduction. I teach a class on Audio for Digital Cinema where we go a bit beyond these basics, and there are great books out there where audio for video is the main focus of the entire book. In this chapter, though, I think it's important to go through a few intermediate techniques, however briefly.

File Naming and Organization

The naming structures outlined in Chapter 7 apply to audio as well. I name each audio clip based on the project name, act, scene, shot, and take. So, my video clip named "KipandBrin_1_5_B_1" (The Kip and Brin Project, Act 1, Scene 5, Shot B, Take 1) will have a corresponding audio clip named the exact same thing. The difference will be in the file extension. The video clip will have a.mov extension (or some other video codec extension) and the audio clip will have a.wav extension (you should definitely not be recording.mp3 or any other compressed audio codec with your dual-system audio recorder). This way, you can sort by the names of files in your finder window or NLE bin and have the audio and video clips next to each other, which will allow you to sync them a lot faster (more on this below). You'll also have some wild soundtracks (ones that don't have a matching video clip) that need to be labeled as such, for example, "KipandBrin_1_5_B_SFX_Bell." This would be an audio clip from Kip and Brin, Act 1, Scene 5 where the audio crew collected some sound effects for the scene or shot while they were on set. You might also end up with some narration tracks ("KipandBrin_1_5_ Narration," for example) or some ADR tracks (more on this later, but you might name the track "KipandBrin_1_5_B_ADR_Kip" or "KipandBrin_1_5_B_ADR_Brin"). If the wild sound, narration, or ADR goes with a specific shot, then you would include the shot letter. If it goes underneath multiple shots within the scene, you could leave it at the scene number. Either way, when you sort by name, it will fall into place with the other tracks from the scene or the shot and allow you to find anything quickly.

Ingesting/Importing and Metadata

Audio clips are imported exactly the same way as the video clips into your NLE. The one thing I'll add in this section is that you should also take the time and tag your audio clips with metadata. Dialogue tracks should be tagged with Act, Scene, Shot, and Take.

You could tag your tracks with the Sampling Frequency and Bit Depth, but that info should already be in the metadata somewhere. The really important thing to note here is that you should always tag your sound effects tracks with keywords. Those keywords, like the "SFXBell," should also be in the name of the clip, but tagging that info in some NLEs and programs like Adobe's Bridge media management software will allow you to access that clip from even outside the project. In other words, I can go into the project folder and do a search for a file name with the word "bell" in it, but if I tag the bell sound effects clips across all of my projects with the keyword "SFXBell," I can search across multiple folders and projects instantaneously and see if I've ever recorded a bell sound effect before that might work for my current project as well. For dialogue tracks, the audio clips will only really be usable for the current project. But sound effects tracks will build up a library over time that can be used again and again. Taking the time to tag the sound effects audio clips now will save you a lot of time looking for them in the future.

Syncing Sound to Image

There are a few different ways to sync the sound to the image when you're working with audio you recorded dual-system on a shoot. As mentioned in Chapters 4 and 6, when you record a shot, you should always slate your take by holding the clapboard in front of it when you start rolling the camera. Then, you should verbally slate the shot info and then clap the board to produce a spike in the audio waveform. You should also roll sound on the camera when shooting dual-system to give your video clip "reference audio." This will help your NLE automatically sync the audio waveforms together, ultimately syncing up the high-quality audio to the video clips. These clips need to have audio synced and the reference audio replaced even before the editor begins putting everything down onto a timeline in the NLE. Sometimes this is done by the assistant editor, but on smaller projects, the editor might be the one syncing the clips. Either way, don't fall into the mental trap

Figure 8.1 DaVinci Resolve allows you to tag audio and video assets with keywords inside of the Media Management tab. Even though the clip is named in a way to make it easy to find, tagging it within the NLE will allow for "Smart Bin" searches where the NLE will collect all files tagged with those keywords. This allows you to build up a library of sound effects for future projects, without having to duplicate the file and take up storage space on your hard drive.

of trying to sync the clips as you edit, or editing first, then syncing. It might seem like a shortcut since you won't use all of the takes in your final project (and therefore you'll have synced tracks you don't end up using), but it will actually take longer. You'll end up putting clips down on your timeline where the audio might not actually be as good as a different clip, and you'll waste valuable time second-guessing whether you have the best audio and video combinations available. You'll only be editing with part of the puzzle pieces. Once you've gotten everything in the NLE bins named and synced, you'll be ready to edit.

Editing

When it comes to audio, the actual editing is similar to editing video. In fact, your audio clips will be connected to your video clips as you put both down on the timeline. It's important to break beyond that mindset, though. Just because you use a visual doesn't mean you have to use the audio connected to it. For example, if you have a CU shot of the back of someone's head as they're looking out into the distance, the audience isn't going to know if you use the audio from a different take because it was cleaner. The viewers don't even see the actor's face. Even if they can see faces, as long as the lips match the sound the audience hears, you can use any combination of audio and video clips you want.

When shooting a basic conversation scene, you typically get the best audio during the close up singles than you get from the 2-shot because the boom will be able to get much closer to the actor's mouth. Luckily, editors don't usually leave a 2-shot up for long because they're boring and static. Instead, the singles offer a more interesting way to show a conversation, after the scene has been established with the 2-shot. So, the audio from the singles is going to get used most. But there are times when editors show reaction shots of the character who isn't speaking. This means there are many opportunities to cut in the best audio, regardless of which angle or take it's from.

Once the audio clips have been placed in the right order and the timing is right, then any narration or ADR (dialogue recorded in post and essentially dubbed in) is recorded and added, as are the sound effects and music. For the editor to get a feel for what the music might add to the tone, a temp track might be placed. This gives the editor something to cut to, and gives a good starting point to convey ideas to a composer if the music will be an original score (you typically score the music after the edit is mostly done so the timing works out between the composition and the visuals). After all the elements are in place, then the audio is "sweetened," meaning the volume levels, frequencies, balance, and perspective are adjusted in small ways to smooth everything out and make it match the visuals and allow the viewer to become immersed in what they're watching.

Syncing

There are really only two general ways to sync audio and video together when you've shot dual-system. You can either do it manually by making adjustments to each clip and each audio track, or you can do it automatically by letting your NLE analyze aspects of the clip and the track and then sync them. Syncing automatically saves a lot of time in post, but it requires a little bit of planning up front and discipline when shooting video and recording audio. And sometimes, the NLE just can't automatically sync a track for some reason, so it's good to know other ways to sync the audio to the video. Recently, I livestreamed an event where the audio didn't stream for some reason. Luckily, I made a recording of the stream, so I was able to sync the audio from that and match it up with the video that was streamed later on. But I had to do it manually because there wasn't anything the NLE could pull from the video to sync automatically.

The first step to syncing audio to video is to sort the bin in your NLE according to name. Now is when the tedious work of naming each file pays off. When you sort the bin by name, each video clip will be right next to the audio clip it corresponds to (or if more than one camera was used on set, all of the video clips should be next to the audio clip they correspond to).

Auto Sync with Timecode

By far the easiest and most accurate way to sync the audio clips to the video tracks is using timecode, but this only applies if the timecode was "jammed" during shooting. Some higher-end audio recorders allow the recorder to send timecode to the cinema camera through a cable (or wirelessly). The camera has to also allow timecode to be fed, so this option for syncing is often unavailable on lower-budget shoots. Another option is a smart slate that jams timecode to both the audio recorder and the camera. These slates have a digital readout, so when each take is slated, the timecode is actually continuously rolling and can be seen in the shot.

To automatically sync using timecode, you simply select both the video clip and corresponding audio track (on a Mac computer, you use the command key to select multiple items at the same time; on a PC, it's the control key), right-click on them, and select, "sync based on timecode." The NLE will automatically analyze the timecode addresses for each frame of audio and video and sync them together. If you shot with multiple cameras, they should all have the same timecode, so you can sync the audio track to each one (one at a time) automatically based on timecode.

The other automatic option that uses timecode to sync audio to video is when you set an inpoint or outpoint on the audio track and the video track. To do this, first open up the video clip in the clip viewer, without placing it on your timeline. Then mark an inpoint (using the "I" key shortcut or the button in the clip viewer). Then open the audio track in the clip viewer and do the same thing. Ideally, you're setting the inpoint of the video clip to be the frame where the clapboard comes together as it's clapped. The inpoint of the audio clip will be the spike in the waveform as the clapboard hits together as it's clapped. For hopefully obvious reasons, this method is rarely used anymore. It's more time-consuming to do this than it is to have the NLE analyze the waveforms and automatically sync everything based on comparing the reference audio from the video clip to the high-quality audio track from the recorder. Even if you have to sync things manually, there are faster ways to do it than this. DaVinci Resolve doesn't even have an automatic option for syncing based on inpoints anymore, but Adobe Premiere does.

Auto Sync with Waveforms

For all of my projects these days, I'm not jamming timecode. It would be nice, but it's easy enough to automatically sync audio in post using the waveform analysis tools in NLEs that I usually don't take the time on set to run the timecode cables, or I'm using equipment that won't do it. Instead, the NLE will analyze the waveform peaks and valleys and match the reference audio from the camera to the audio from the dual-system recorder. I've found that this method is pretty reliable as long as you're getting a good clap from the clapboard in the beginning of the clip. If you're using softsticks (clapping

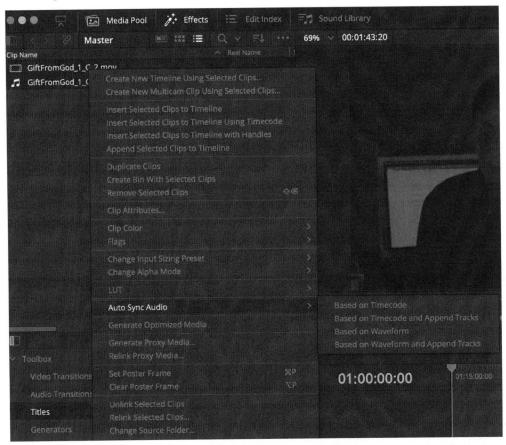

Figure 8.2 DaVinci Resolve will "Auto Sync Audio" based on timecode or based on waveform. Simply select both the audio clip and the video track, then right-click and scroll down to the "Auto Sync Audio" options. Choosing the options that "append tracks" leaves the reference audio as one of the audio tracks on the clip. The other options remove the reference audio. I always go ahead and remove the reference track. Even if there is an error, you can always go back to the original files and sync them again.

softer when you're close to the talent's face), or forget to clap, it can cause issues with matching up the waveforms automatically.

In DaVinci Resolve, when you auto sync based on waveforms, the clip in your bin simply replaces the reference audio with the dual-system audio from then on, allowing you to drag it over to the timeline and edit like you normally would. In Premiere Pro, automatically syncing creates a new video clip with dual-system audio included (Premiere calls this a "merged" clip). I actually prefer Premiere for this reason when I'm shooting dual-system, but each NLE has advantages.

Manual Sync with Clapboard

Manually syncing using the clapboard is just what it sounds like. If your NLE can't automatically sync your video clips to the corresponding audio for any reason, you have to drag the video clip onto the timeline, drag the audio track onto the timeline, and then

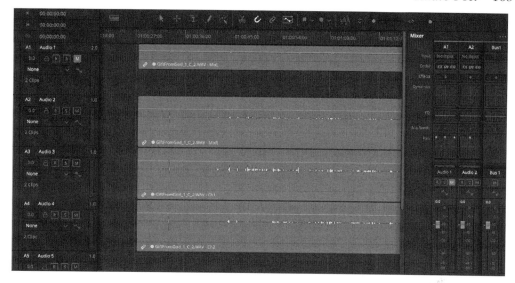

Figure 8.3 The waveforms of the reference audio (MixL and MixR) and the dual-system audio. Notice that the spikes/peaks match up, even if they're different amplitudes (different heights). You can see the spike at the front of the track where the clapboard hit.

manually move one until it's in sync with the other. The clapboard is essential here. Using this first manual method, you're lining up the spike in the dual-system audio waveform with the frame where the clapboard first strikes together. This is the method I use when no reference audio was recorded. If the only audio you have is the dual-system track, this is your only choice. And you'll figure out quickly how important it is to record sound on your video clips even when you're recording sound externally as well.

Occasionally, the audio spike falls in between frames. When this happens, I usually try first to have the spike hit on the frame break after the clapboard comes together. But sometimes I find that the lips match up better if I put the spike on the frame break right before the clapboard hits. Either way, this gets you really close, and you can shift by a frame or two until things look pretty natural.

A tip here: I usually place both the video clip and the audio track a few seconds into the timeline. This allows me to slide either one forward or backward as I sync them. After placing both on the timeline, I put a marker on the frame where the clapboard hits. Then I click on the waveform on the exact spot where the audio spikes from the clapboard and I drag the clip until my mouse pointer is lined up with the marker I placed. This gets me really close. Then, I zoom in on the timeline until I see each frame and I slide the audio until the spike lines up with the clap frame.

If you (or the film crew) forgot to clap or to record reference audio on the video clips, you're essentially just using trial and error until you get things synced up. I've had to do this many times, and it is extremely time-consuming, relies heavily on just getting lucky to get things close enough to have a starting point, and is often not accurate.

Manual Sync with Waveforms

This option is similar to using the clapboard to visually sync the clips, but you've got the additional reference audio waveform to help you. I find it much easier to use the waveforms, but sometimes they aren't exactly in sync. This usually happens when your camera is a bit further away from the action (recall that light travels faster than sound). It's not a problem, but sometimes it means you have to shift the audio by a frame or two after you match the two waveforms visually in order for the lips to look right. When shooting, you can keep this from happening by feeding audio from the recorder to the camera. You can even use a wireless transmitter and receiver to avoid having cables running everywhere. The audio quality feeding the recorder doesn't have to be great, just usable for syncing in post. But by feeding the audio to the camera's audio inputs, you ensure that the waveform on the recorder and the waveform on the reference audio from the camera are identical and easy to sync automatically or manually by waveform.

Sync Drift and Back Sync

If you're shooting clips that are long in duration, the sync between the audio and the video can actually drift. Drift happens when the audio and video are in sync at the beginning, but by the end of the clip, it's off by a few frames or more. I've only had sync drift when editing clips that are around 60 minutes or longer, like when I shoot a long documentary interview session, or I'm recording a live event. It's always a good idea to back slate when shooting these kinds of clips. To back slate, you simply bring the clapboard back out, walk into the frame with the clapboard upside down (to visually indicate quickly that it's a back slate), and clap it again. I don't usually verbally slate when I do this because the verbal slate is helpful for naming and organizing things, and the front slate can serve that purpose.

If you experience sync drift, you have a couple options. If you need the clip in its entirety, you'll have to go through the clip and try to figure out where it drifts. At those points, remove or add a frame of audio. Don't adjust the video track or the viewers will notice. But a frame out of the audio track won't be noticed if you add or remove it during a silent part. The other option is to cut the clip up into smaller clips and sync each one separately. When you do this, the clips should be small enough that the audio won't drift away from the video. For a documentary interview, it's much easier to break a long clip up into shorter ones (your editor will probably do this anyway because one interview will cover multiple topics and will be edited into the film in pieces). For a live event, it's much more likely that you'll need to keep the entire clip intact from start to finish.

The other reason to back slate is if you forget to slate the beginning, or if it wasn't possible to slate. For example, I've shot both live events and documentary footage where I wasn't planning on shooting, but something started happening, so I grabbed my camera and started rolling. When this happens, it's good practice to keep rolling even after the event and back slating the shot (using the procedure outlined above) after the fact. Having the slate information is still helpful, and the clap is still important to sync up the audio to the video. When I'm shooting single system, I usually skip this step.

Editing

Editing audio is a lot like editing video. In most NLEs, you can grab the ends of the clip on the timeline and stretch it out or shrink it until you get the sound bites (a sound bite is a brief audio clip that has the phrase you're trying to convey) you want to keep in the video. If the video clip has an audio clip attached, either because you shot single-system or because you merged the dual-system audio clip, you'll need to unlink the audio from the video if you want to trim one down without affecting the other. The other option is to lock the track (usually the video track) you want to avoid moving or trimming, then moving or trimming the other. It doesn't hurt to re-link them after you're done. Then they will move together if you time-shift the clip on the timeline.

Heads and Tails

In general, you want to cut the heads and tails off of all audio clips. A head is the beginning of the clip up until the dialogue or soundbite you want to keep. A tail is everything that comes after the soundbite. If you're using a dialogue clip or any other voicework where there are multiple lines you want to keep, the head would be the space before the first line and the tail would be the space after the last line. You wouldn't want to trim down everything in between the lines, or you'd risk drawing attention to the way the background drops out every time.

We cut off the heads and tails because usually they contain unwanted noise that can be distracting. We do the same for video, but often we want the audience to see something even if they don't hear the audio that was captured with it. For instance, in a western stand-off, there's probably wind noise, people talking in the distance, perhaps the sound from the power generators on set, and a bunch of other things that might distract the audience from what they're seeing. Instead, we'll replace those sounds with music or ambience. The wind noise might stay, but we'll want something that helps the viewer focus on the action.

Transitions

I cannot stress enough how important transitions are for audio. On the video track, cuts are simple enough, and because they mimic how our eyes blink, we barely notice them. Cuts are preferred for video transitions. But audio is something that is constant for us. In every room, everywhere we go, there is always ambient sound around us. Close your eyes and listen. Even when we blink, the audio is still there. Because of this, audio tracks require smooth transitions between the clips. My preference is a very quick cross fade where the volume isn't amplified (often noted by a "Cross fade +0dB" in the audio transition options). The transition has to be quick – only 5–10 frames usually – or you risk audio from one clip bleeding into the audio from the other clip. But those 5–10 frames will keep the audio from dropping out and then coming back in abruptly. Our ears notice those dropouts and become attuned to the clicks that come with them. Later, we'll add room tone to the audio tracks to help smooth everything out, but it's totally worth taking the time in editing to add these cross fades in between every audio clip on a track. If there is a time gap in between the audio clips, then put a cross fade on the end of the first clip and another one at the beginning of the second clip.

Matching Sound to Image

Everything in this chapter to this point has been technical – a guide for how to edit audio. After getting your audio tracks laid out on your timeline and putting in transitions, you also have to make the audio sound good. This is where choices can become a bit subjective. For example, there are movies where the sound drops away completely to show you the panic felt by the main character, or the sound of a car overwhelms everything else so that the viewer focuses on that sound. We strive to maintain a good balance, energy, and perspective with the audio.

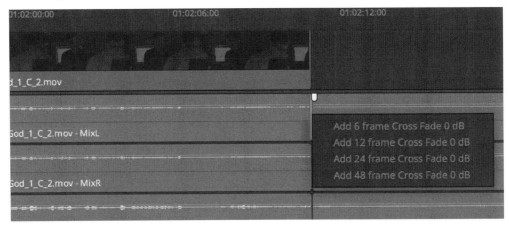

Figure 8.4 When you right-click on a transition point in between two audio clips on the timeline, you typically get a few limited options for transitions. In this case, I usually choose a 6- or 12-frame cross fade with 0dB added. This smooths out the transition point and helps keep the audience from noticing.

Figure 8.5 If there is a gap between the two audio clips, you should put a quick cross fade at the end of the first one and the beginning of the second. This happens sometimes if you're shooting a reaction shot and the actor who is talking is off-screen. You might want to add a pause that wasn't actually there when shooting. This allows you to hang on the reaction, but not hear the dialogue in between the two sound bites you're wanting to hear. Anytime you leave a gap like this, it means complete silence – a total absence of noise. Our ears and brains are actually a bit unnerved when this happens. So, we'll add room tone later to put ambient sound back in.

Perspective

Sound perspective is essentially the direction of the sound. If the sound is only coming out of one speaker (many TVs are designed this way), then the sound is mono and not stereo. With mono sound, you cannot manipulate the direction of the sound. Even a soundbar has multiple speakers inside of it to simulate stereo or surround sound. For playback systems with more than one speaker, you can make decisions about how loud the sound should be in one speaker vs another. This causes the sounds to seem like they're coming from a specific direction. When you watch a movie in the theater, there are many speakers all around you, so it's easy to make a spaceship sound like it's coming from behind you and flying around you until it's in front. This is done by manipulating the perspective – how loud the sound is in one speaker vs others.

To simplify it a little bit, imagine you see a car driving across the screen from right to left. We would start with the sound of the car louder in the right speaker. It would be heard a little bit in the left, then as the car moves across the screen, we would increase the volume in the left speaker and decrease it in the right speaker until the car is mostly

Figure 8.6 The audio channel in DaVinci Resolve's Fairlight Audio DAW allows spatial panning. The square represents the surround sound location the audience will hear, with the two circles showing the left/right relationship. In this example, the audio track here will sound as if it's slightly to the left and almost to the side (even across the front and rear speakers). To reproduce this effect, it will take at least 5.1 surround sound – right and left front speakers, a center front speaker, and right and left rear speakers (the .1 stands for the subwoofer, which is not directional) – two-speaker setups make it so the sound always comes from the front.

in the left speaker as it ends up on that side of the screen. Luckily, your NLE or DAW (Digital Audio Workstation) does the mathematical calculations for you. They allow you to simply "pan" audio into one speaker or the other, and the sound will automatically get louder in one side and quieter in the other. And you can set it to automate – putting it in the right speaker at one point on the timeline, then setting another point where it's in the left, and letting the computer pan across the screen at a smooth rate.

Perspective also means that sounds that are far away should sound far away. If the car in our example is in the background of the shot, it shouldn't be louder than the sounds in the foreground. If the car is in the foreground, it should be louder. Distance perspective isn't done in post, though. It's done when recording the sounds on set or when doing Foley sound effects (more on Foley later). To get good distance perspective, you should place the microphone closer or farther away to make it sound closer or further away. In post, you can add reverb to try to make it sound farther away, but it rarely works well.

For sound effects and music, perspective generally matches the visual location of the object the audience hears. Mixing in stereo in post is usually enough, unless you're working on a fictional film for theatrical distribution. It's also important to use perspective in subtle ways, or the sound will draw too much attention to itself. Instructional videos, commercials, news packages, etc., rarely mix in surround sound.

At times, you'll want dialogue to sound closer or further away. But almost without exception, dialogue and narration are placed in the center channel or the mono speaker. This is a convention that audiences have grown so accustomed to, that it feels weird and draws attention when dialogue is actually moved to the left or right to match the image. Surround sound speakers have center channels that are dedicated to reproducing dialogue as well, so the sound is clearer. If a stereo system only has right and left speakers, the dialogue can still be panned to the center. When the two speakers reproduce sound equally, they create a "phantom center" – the sound will appear to be coming from the middle of the screen, right where a center channel speaker would be.

Energy Balance

Similar to perspective, the audio should match the energy of the visuals. If there are explosions, fast-paced cuts, and lots of action, you would expect the music, sound effects, and dialogue to be louder and more noticeable. You would want to normalize those audio tracks (amplify the volume on them) until the peaks of the waveforms are around 0dB on the peak audio meter. If the visuals are slow and somber, the dialogue might be at a whisper. The music might be softer. There are certainly exceptions to this, such as when a character is overwhelmed by the chaos around them and the sound drops out completely, or when the character's senses are focusing on one specific sound and the other sounds drop out. But as a general rule of thumb, the feeling the audio conveys should match that of the visuals.

Figure-Ground

The figure-ground principle is the same with audio as it is with video. There is a foreground, a middle-ground, and a background. This principle overrides the previous two (perspective and balance), meaning that we almost always put dialogue or other sounds that we want the viewer to focus on in the foreground. The music and sound effects are most often in the middle-ground or background. Even if the characters are far away in a long shot, we should still hear their words clearly. Even if the music is setting a nice tone for the scene, it should still drop into the background when people are talking. When you listen to a commercial, for instance, there might be a music bed underneath the narration that's talking about how great the product is. The music might start out loud, but it envelopes underneath once the narrator begins their lines. It starts in the foreground to capture the audience's attention, but then it quickly moves to the background so that the voice can be placed in the foreground. And even if it's an action scene with lots of explosions, we lower the volume on those sound effects when there is dialogue for the audience to hear, even if the characters are whispering to each other.

Recording Audio in Post

Like re-shoots of visuals, it's not uncommon to have to record some of your audio in post. Oftentimes, music and sound effects need to be customized for the project you're working on. Using canned sound effects or prerecorded music just might not fit. And sometimes when you're on set, it's just impossible to get good audio, so you need to record some dialogue in post.

ADR (Automatic Dialogue Replacement)

I'm not really sure why it's called "automatic" because this is actually a very manual process of replacing the dialogue from the set with dialogue recorded in a sound booth in post. When recording ADR, you will want the same actors you used in the shot (this sounds obvious, but I wanted to be clear), and they should really be in the same mindset and physical condition. If the dialogue is being replaced because you recorded the dialogue as the actor ran through a bootcamp obstacle course and you couldn't really follow them with a boom mic, then in ADR, they should be fairly out of breath and maybe even seem like they're in a bit of pain. If you're recording ADR because it was just too windy that day, then the important thing is to have the actor deliver their lines at the same pace and tone as when you shot the visuals. Sound perspective is also very important here. In a studio, you can record audio as close to the mic as you want. But if the character is a bit further away in the shot, you should have them further from the microphone in the studio as well. Essentially, you should reproduce as much of the original scene as you can so that it mimics the rest of the audio from the scene (you might only need to replace one line out of an entire scene). The room tone you recorded on set will be inserted under the ADR tracks to help them blend in as well.

In the cases where the ADR is pretty tight – where we actually see the actor's lips move – pacing and tone are extremely important so that when you place the ADR track onto the timeline in post, you won't have to do too much work to get the dialogue to match the lips. You can do a time remap on it to stretch it out a little or speed it up a little, but too much of that will be pretty obvious to the viewer. I'm fortunate to have an audio studio with a separate control room, and I'd suggest this for doing ADR. If you're recording in a cramped room where you're running the sound board right next to the actor delivering their lines, it's much harder for them to get into character. If you do have a control room, the talkback system will be important so you can direct the actor or voice talent in between takes. You should have a script handy as well so they can mark notes on it (speed up, slow down, louder, emphasize this line, etc.) as you direct them. I've also found it helpful with professionals to have a video monitor there for them to see the lips as they deliver their lines. For students and amateurs, the visuals might be too distracting.

Once you've recorded the lines, you can cut them down and insert them into the timeline just like the dialogue recorded on set. Ideally, they'll fit fairly seamlessly. If not, you can speed up or slow down some phrases or even some words to get it to fit, as long as you're not throwing off the cadence (the pace of the delivery of phrases) too much. And if lips aren't seen in the shot, you can really just leave things as they are. This happens with long shots as well. The audience can see the person, but can't really make out their lips, so they can't tell if the dialogue was recorded on set or in ADR.

Music Beds

Even for short films, there isn't anything wrong with using prerecorded music. There's some high-quality stuff out there across many genres and moods, and a lot of it is licensed for free use through Creative Commons or other such artist-sharing programs. But for my latest film, I hired a composer and it was some of the best money I've spent. They were able to match the mood I wanted and also hit all of the major transitions in the film with the tempo of their music. My editor and I used some filler music when putting together the picture-locked version of the film. This is common, and sometimes that music fits so well that a producer will go ahead and pay for the rights to it. But most of the time, as was my case, we sent the picture-locked film to the composer with that music in it. The composer then matched the tone and tempo of the piece, but put together entirely original melodies and sequences. They were even able to use their original melodies and put variations together for other parts of the film. That way, we had a recurring theme, but with slightly different music each time.

A cautionary tale about using prerecorded music: I produced a commercial once and we used a licensed box set of music (music beds designed for commercials that are sold in limited quantities). Years later, I heard the exact same song used in a commercial for dryer sheets. Even though it's unlikely that my audience would hear and remember that music, you risk your product or film being associated closely with another when you use a music track that others might also have the right to use. Likewise, when you use popular music, viewers will have things they associate that song with already. Sometimes, songs evoke positive emotions. Sometimes, they will already have negative feelings tied to them. Perhaps the viewer's deceased father liked that song a lot. Perhaps their mother used to sing it to them as a child. Whatever the case, the filmmaker has very little control over how the viewer will react to music they've heard before. Popular music can also be very expensive to license, and you should never use copyrighted music in your projects illegally (if you intend to show them publicly, which, I assume you would want to do – or else why are you making it?).

I've also composed my own music for some of my projects. It's surprisingly simple, and it can be very rewarding. I worked on a film where the producer didn't even know how to play the cello, but he borrowed mine, learned a few notes, and played them in a somber way to lay down the musical tone for the entire film. Three notes was all it took. And it was a beautiful film. I've also used programs like Apple's GarageBand to compose original pieces. GarageBand lets you lay down premade loops and layer them on top of each other in original ways. This can help you compose music even if you know nothing about music theory or playing instruments.

Foley and Other Sound Effects

I try to get sound effects recorded on set whenever possible. Usually, I do this by getting someone to re-create the sounds of the props in between shots and recording each sound effect on its own track. That way, I have the ability to mix volume levels for the effect separately from any dialogue I recorded during the scene. But there are many times that I don't know I need something until the project gets into post. Or maybe the effect I recorded on set just doesn't sound right or have the impact I'm going for. At that point, the only option is to create the effect and record it. In post, these are called Foley sound effects (named after a person famous for recording sound effects for films). Essentially, when we say "Foley," we mean we're re-creating the effect using things that aren't necessarily the actual source of the sound. For a punch, I might drop a sack of flour on the floor and get a mic in close to record the impact. Foley is all about getting creative. Once you have these sound effects recorded, whether from the shoot or Foley, then it's just a matter of putting them down on a separate track, editing the heads and tails off, mixing the volume level and perspective to match the visual, and making sure the dialogue can still be heard.

Sweetening

Sweetening is a rather generic term for all of the things you do to audio in post to make it sound better. Sweetening doesn't include trimming the audio clips, or laying down a music bed. It does include mixing levels so that the appropriate sound is in the foreground. It also includes equalization of different frequencies of sound and normalization of levels (amplification of levels so that they are consistent during playback). I'm going to include how to use room tone here, although I don't consider it to be part of sweetening. Room tone does get laid down during this part of your audio post, though, while you're mixing layers of sounds together.

EQ (Equalization)

Equalization means raising or lowering the volume for certain frequencies. This is often done on dialogue to accentuate certain aspects of a voice, or to cut out unwanted background sounds. If there was a little bit of wind noise or handling noise, lowering the bass frequencies (80–100 Hz and below) will usually not change the sound of the voice, but it will often lessen the wind or handling noise. Raising the midrange frequencies will often help clarity in the dialogue (but not too much, or it will sound a bit thin). And rolling off (lowering) the highs will help cut down on unwanted sibilance (when the sounds whistle a bit).

For a while in our television studio, we were having issues with the dimmer packs for our lights. The fans that cooled the dimmer packs created a fairly noticeable hum. This made it difficult to use footage shot in the studio without using an EQ on it first. In that situation, removing the 60 Hz frequency (or rolling off the bass below about 80 Hz) usually did the trick. Using EQ to lower the volume substantially on a narrow band of frequencies is called a notch filter, as you're filtering out one specific sound.

Normalization

Most video and audio editing software has an effect you can place on audio clips that will automatically normalize the levels for you. Just like adding an EQ, you find the effects group in your NLE, and you can add an effect to the clip you want. Some NLEs will allow you to add an effect to the entire track, including all of the audio clips that are on that track. Be careful doing this, as there will be some clips that you'll want to

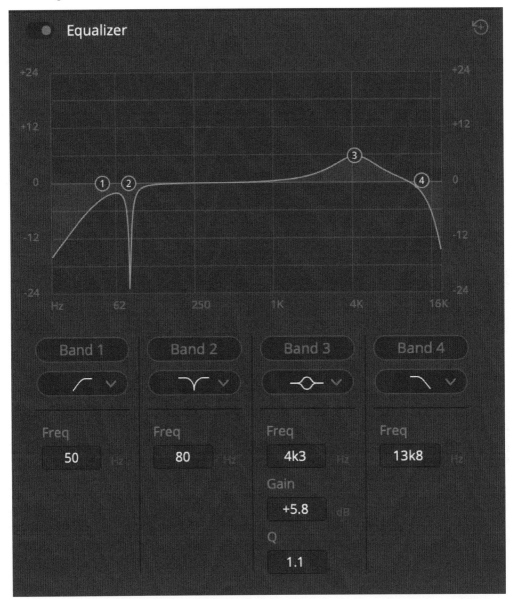

Figure 8.7 An equalizer applied to an audio clip. To do this, you typically go to a list of effects, drag it onto the clip, then double-click the clip to get information about it, including effects that have been applied. Then you can manipulate the EQ for that specific clip. In this case, I've rolled off the bass frequencies at 50 Hz and below. I created a notch filter at 80 Hz. Around 4,300 Hz (4.3 kHz), I boosted the gain by 5.8dB to accentuate the dialogue. The Q value represents how many frequencies around 4.3 kHz are affected by this. In this case, a Q of 1.1 should allow frequencies on either side of the 4.3 kHz to lower in a gradual slope. A higher Q value will lead to a narrower band being affected (a narrower spike). In this picture, I've also lowered the high frequencies starting around 13,800 Hz (13.8 kHz).

increase the volume on more than others. I often amplify (increasing the volume – also an effect you can add) each clip prior to normalizing an entire track. You can also use a compressor/limiter to set a floor and a ceiling for the volume instead of normalizing, or at least prior to normalizing. This will boost the levels of the quiet dialogue up to a certain volume, and also keep the loud dialogue from clipping (getting so loud it distorts). Needless to say, there are several approaches to getting your volume levels where you want them. During this normalization phase of audio post, the main thing is that the volume levels keep the dialogue understandable, while also keeping them from overloading the playback signal and clipping.

It's a common mistake to think that if an actor was whispering their dialogue, that it should be kept very low and quiet. If you record a whisper at low volumes and try to amplify it in post, it will boost a lot of background noise. Instead, the whisper should be recorded at the same peak level as a shout (usually about –3 to –6dB on a peak volume meter). The energy conveyed by a whisper or a shout comes from the delivery, not the overall volume level. If a line of dialogue is whispered, but it peaks at 0dB, it will still sound like a whisper. If a line of dialogue is shouted, but we record it (or amplify it in post) so that it peaks at 0dB, the speakers will actually re-create these two sounds at the same volume level. But the audience will feel the energy being delivered by the actors in two very different ways. When I normalize levels, I keep my mix of everything together at 0dB so nothing is distorting or clipping when I export. This means that I normalize my dialogue slightly lower so that when my room tone, music, and sound effects are added together, they don't peak out together and go over 0dB (this is called constructive interference – when sounds occur at the same time and the same frequency, they actually amplify that frequency – and two sounds that don't clip alone can clip when they're layered one on top of the other).

Using Room Tone

Remember when we recorded sound on set and we made sure to get 30–60 seconds of room tone after the scene was done? This is the point where those room tone clips become useful. After normalizing and making sure all of our volume levels are where we want them on the dialogue track(s), we lay down room tone over the entire scene. Each room tone audio clip should be labeled by scene, so we know which one to use under each set of dialogue. If the scene is longer in duration than your room tone clip, there is a clever process you need to follow to make it sound smooth under the dialogue: start by laying down the clip onto a blank audio track in your NLE. Next, copy that clip and paste it immediately after the first one. Then, right-click and select "change clip speed" (in DaVinci Resolve – other NLEs might call it something different) and click on "reverse speed" or set the speed to –100%.

By reverse looping the clip, you're creating a seamless and consistent background noise instead of having something that resets every 30 seconds. Imagine that your room tone clip had some wind rustling the trees in it. If the clip simply cut off at 30 seconds and started over again, the sounds at the end of the clip would cut out and be replaced by the sounds at the beginning of the clip, which might be different. A viewer will easily hear this reset point and it will draw attention away from the dialogue. Reverse looping takes out these seams. But it only works for room tone, not any discernable sounds, since

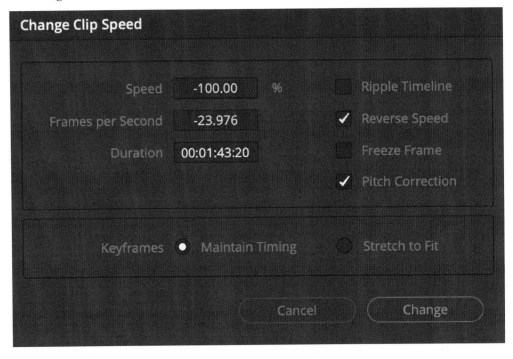

Figure 8.8 In DaVinci Resolve, there is a handy feature to reverse-loop an audio clip. This causes the second audio clip you just laid down to play backwards. Since the clip is just room tone, this means that any sounds at the end of the first clip will continue through the second one and the room tone won't reset to what was heard at the beginning of the first clip.

those sounds will be played backwards. Finally, after you've laid down a clip, then laid down and reversed another, you can copy and paste those two room tone clips together on the track as many times as you need room tone for the scene. For example, a 5-minute scene will need ten total 30-second room tone clips (five sets of clip and reverse clip) copy and pasted under it.

After laying down the room tone, you'll still need to mix the levels to make sure the room tone is barely heard and that the dialogue is still very prominent and understandable. The point of the room tone is to mask unwanted sounds (cars driving by, people talking, etc.) by creating a consistent bed of sound underneath the dialogue. When the sound is constant, our brains actually ignore it much easier than if the sound comes and goes. When we lay down clips recorded on set and increase the volume on some of them, the background noise in those clips gets louder as well, creating an inconsistent level of noise. The room tone track has to be at a volume level where it also masks the inconsistent background sounds in the clips, smoothing out the ambience.

DME Stems

On a film production, you might hear the term DME stems (dialogue, music, sound effects). Typically, only narrative films do this. This means that when you edit the audio in post, you're producing one track for dialogue (this includes the room tone you just laid down under it, although I have worked on films where the editor wanted a separate room tone track), one track for music, and one track for sound effects. Having each of these tracks mixed down into one simplifies the audio portion of the NLE for the editor, but still allows them to mix volume levels differently when desired. Perhaps the editor or Director wants the sound effects to be lower in a specific part. Even though the sound designer mixed them a specific way, the effects can still be lowered in that part without affecting the level of the dialogue or the music.

To create stems, you need to place a countdown leader (sometimes called a "two-pop" because there is an audio spike that lines up with the frame of the video leader when the number two first appears) at the front of each track. Ideally, the picture-locked video track has its own leader on it, and you can just copy the audio portion of the leader and paste it on each of the three stems. This countdown leader allows the video editor to ensure everything is in sync easily, as the spike in all three waveforms should line up with the number 2. Once the DME stems are finalized, the audio is sent back to the editor for the finishing touches. If you're not working on a film project, it's likely that you're mixing your dialogue, music, sound effects, and room tone together on your timeline as you go, and you're exporting the entire project once you're satisfied with the way everything plays on your timeline.

Chapter 8: Audio Post Main Points

- Editing begins with organization. Maintaining a consistent file naming scheme and organizational structure is an important first step in any project and throughout your career.
- There are automatic ways to sync audio to video, as well as manual ways. You still need to know how to sync manually for those times when the auto sync functions fail.
- When editing audio, you can use almost any combination of video clip and dialogue audio, as long as the visuals match the audio when it's noticeable, like when an actor's lips are moving as they talk.
- The figure-ground principle in audio overrides the need for any other preferences about perspective and energy balance. Dialogue is almost always in the foreground, with music, effects, and ambience being placed in the middle ground or background.
- When you're editing audio, there is often a need to re-record dialogue. You should also plan on recording or somehow producing original music and sound effects for your project in this phase. While there are prerecorded music and effects out there, you won't want your projects to sound the same as others.
- Sweetening is the process of equalizing frequencies and adjusting volumes until dialogue is understandable and the levels are consistent. This is an important part of the process, and it takes a lot of patience to get things right instead of rushing to export.

9 Coloring

Color grading is a necessity for many forms of production these days. There are entire textbooks that cover the technical aspects of it (and it does get very technical!) and a lot of videos online that can help you with the software programs that allow you to color grade. My hope with this chapter is to give you some basic terminology and enough of an understanding about coloring to get you started.

Luminance (Brightness and Contrast)

Luminance refers to the light values (sometimes called "grayscale") of an image. If you were to shoot something in color, then convert it to a black and white image, you'd be left with a grayscale image composed only of luminance values. While luminance has a range of gradients (hundreds of small differences between each different gray pixel), when you're color grading, you primarily focus on the extremes of those values – the shadows and the highlights.

DOI: 10.4324/9781003010357-12

Shadows

When shooting, I don't always black balance my camera. Many of the cameras I shoot with don't even have this option (DSLRs, for example). One of the basic functions of color grading is to make sure your shadows are black, or at least as dark as you want them to be. Perhaps your exposure was set a little too high and the shadows have some detail you want to get rid of, or they appear gray instead of black. Most NLEs have a "brightness" effect you can drag and drop onto a clip, but this just raises or lowers all of the luminance values at the same time. So, if you lowered the brightness in the shadows, the highlights would also get darker, which dulls your image. Instead, working on the luminance values when color grading allows you to lower the blacks in the shadows without affecting the highlights, and only slightly affecting the mid-tones (the middle gray values).

Highlights

The highlights are the parts where the luminance values are the closest to white. In other words, if you removed the color from the image, the highlights would be the brightest parts. If the image was overexposed, the highlights would be solid areas, where details were lost. I rarely overexpose my images except for extreme highlights (like when the sun is seen in the background of a shot) because I'm always paying close attention to my exposure values and meters. It's more likely that I slightly underexpose my image in an effort to stay within the dynamic range of the camera (the range of data it can store for luminance values, typically measured in the number of f-stops the camera allows between the most open aperture to the most closed). When I color grade, I can push those white values up a little bit to make the highlights pop, but without clipping the image and losing details.

The difference between the shadows and the highlights is called the contrast. Contrast is something that you can manipulate with a contrast effect or a brightness/contrast

Figures 9.1 and 9.2 These figures show an image that was shot underexposed and the same image after changing the luminance values. The image on the right brought out details in the faces and shirts that weren't seen. This doesn't necessarily save the image – it would have been much better to light it well and get the exposure right when shooting than to try to fix it in post. But it does show just how much you can boost up highlights when color grading. In this shot, I didn't use a simple brightness/contrast effect, so it kept the shadows down in the black without messing up the midtones.

effect in an NLE, but you rarely want to use those crude tools. Before color grading was integrated into NLEs, I would often use a brightness/contrast effect on my clips to push the shadows down and boost the highlights up, but usually the image suffered in quality. Those effects would often make the blacks feel a bit artificial, and things that should have been kept in the middle luminance values were pushed towards one of the extremes. Skin tones and shadows on faces suffered the most. I say this because you might be tempted to use one of these effects because they're quick and easy to understand. But there are much better ways to change luminance values that I'll explain later in this chapter.

Waveform Monitor

Some cameras, some screens, and most NLEs have waveform monitors built into them. These monitors are really great for showing luminance values. They read left to right across the image and, like an audio waveform, they show peaks where the brightest values are and valleys where the blackest values are. Different monitors have different numbering systems, so it can be confusing, but basically the lowest values are 0% luminance (total black) up to 100% luminance (total white). The midtones are in-between.

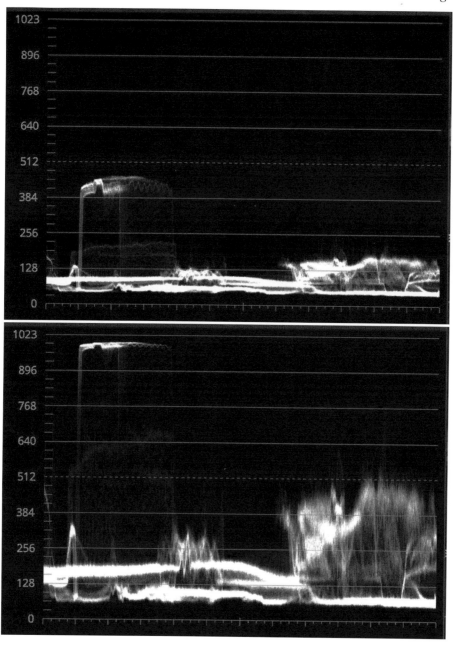

Figures 9.3 and 9.4 These figures show the waveform monitors for Figures 9.1 and 9.2. The one on the left has a very solid line down near 0%, indicating that most of the gray values are almost black. The peak over to the left is where the computer screen is seen in the shot. The waveform on the right shows the image after I've increased the brightness and expanded the dynamic range. The blacks are still sitting down near 0%, but the midtones and highlights have stretched out. In fact, the screen is now clipping at 100% – see how the wave has flattened? I'm okay with that tradeoff because the midtones are more spaced out now around 50%. Still, if I had lit and shot the image properly to begin with, those midtones would be much more vibrant and spaced further apart. The actor's shirt on the left is where you really notice the lack of contrast, even after color grading.

Chrominance (Colors)

Chrominance refers to the colors in the shot. Specifically, the amount of red, blue, and green within each pixel. Red, green, and blue (RGB) are the primary colors when light is projected. That means that every color we see on a screen is made up of some amount of each color, with a corresponding luminance value underneath (luminance is usually indicated by the letter "Y"). If a pixel is yellow (a secondary color), that means it has equal parts of green and red, and no blue value. The other secondary colors are magenta (equal parts red and blue) and cyan (equal parts blue and green). Black is the absence of all projected light (no colors firing within the pixel). White is the presence of all three colors firing at equal intensity all at the same time within the pixel.

Chrominance is an important concept when talking about color grading. Getting the correct mix of colors in your image is important. Even though we sometimes want a

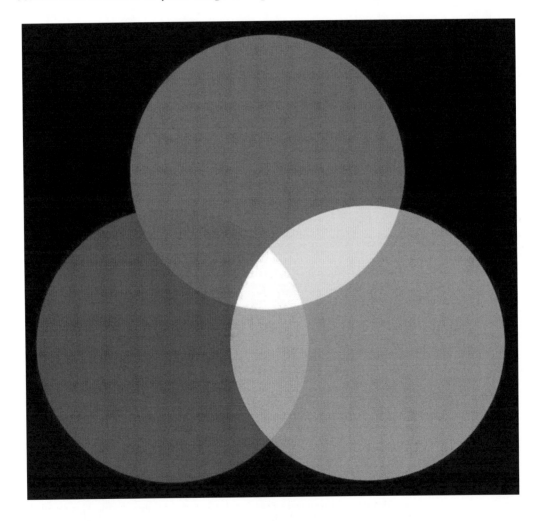

Figure 9.5 A color diagram. Red is on top, blue to the left, and green to the right. Red and blue combine to form magenta, red and green make yellow, and green and blue make cyan. All three colors together make white. The absence of any color is black (around the outside of the circles).

stylized look based on colors, most often we're color grading in order to make the image more like what we're used to seeing in real life.

Saturation

Saturation describes the intensity of the color. The more saturated the blue is in a shirt, the purer it will look. "Boldness," "pureness," and "intensity" are all words we use to describe how saturated a color is, but the concept is difficult to explain. When I teach color theory in my basic courses, I typically say, "saturation is how much color is in the color." A highly saturated color will be easy to spot because it will be a great example of that specific color. In technical terms, there are monitors and scopes we can look at to determine just how saturated our colors are. More on this below.

Color Temperature

Chapter 5 talks about color temperature with regard to lighting equipment and camera settings. You white balance a camera so the camera can adjust to the color temperature of the light coming into the sensor. As Figure 9.5 shows, when you mix all three primary colors together at equal intensities, you get white light. So, when you put a white balance card in front of a camera, the camera can accurately read all three colors by white balancing. When those three colors are accurate, then all colors recorded by the camera should be accurate as well.

These days, I do my best to white balance on set to get accurate colors, but I have more confidence that I can make adjustments in post to correct this if I'm off. For example, when I'm shooting later in the day or earlier in the morning, the color temperature of the sunlight actually changes as the sun rises or sets. In post, I might need to make adjustments as I cut from one shot to another because the color temperature might be slightly

Figure 9.6 An image and the vectorscope monitor for that image. The square targets on the scope are R (red), G (green), B (blue), M (magenta), C (cyan), and Y (yellow, not to be confused with luminance, which a vectorscope doesn't show). In this image, you can see that the sky isn't actually blue. It's somewhere between blue and cyan. But it is very saturated – the length of the reading on the blue/cyan is fairly long compared to the other colors. You can also see the green grass, which is actually almost directly pointing to the green target, but is not very saturated, since the spike on the scope isn't that long. The rest of the colors are grouped in the center, which means that they're pretty close to being white. This is the building, which is white or gray (which will read as white on a vectorscope since gray isn't an actual hue – it's a shade of white).

different. On a set with lighting instruments, I shouldn't need to make these adjustments in post unless my entire scene is slightly off. It doesn't happen often, but I have certainly shot footage where I forgot to pay attention to my white balance and I ended up with blue-ish or red-ish tinted video clips. There are settings in color grading software now that automatically adjust from one color temperature to another.

Vectorscope and Parade Monitors

A vectorscope is a monitor that shows how saturated the colors are. There are targets on the scope for each primary color and each secondary color, and the scope shows the hue where it points towards these targets, and the saturation where the length of the image on the scope demonstrates how saturated the color is.

A parade monitor is a lot like a waveform monitor. It shows the brightness of each color in the shadows, the midtones, and the highlights. The red, green, and blue values are sometimes separated out, sometimes overlayed. And there are also monitors that show the colors overlayed with a luminance waveform as well. If the colors are separated out, as they are in Figure 9.7, then you read each color as its own waveform. The left side of the color (red, then green, then blue) represents the left side of the shot. The right side of only that color represents the other side of the frame in the shot. Then the middle color, green, has its own starting point that represents the left side of the shot.

Waveform monitors, vectorscopes, and parade monitors all tell us valuable information and are useful in both shooting and in color grading. It's actually not often that I'm on a set where monitors are readily available, although larger budget productions should have them. Instead, lower budget projects often have to make due with tools like zebra stripes, manual white balancing (and white balance cards) to get as accurate as possible with their colors. They use these tools to guide them as they stretch the dynamic range of the camera out in the luminance values so they capture details in both the highlights and the shadows.

I find these scopes to be invaluable when I color grade, though. Every video screen is different, and even though good screens can be calibrated, having scopes gives you a visual representation of what you're actually doing with the colors when you grade

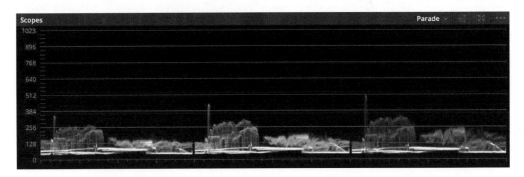

Figure 9.7 The RGB parade monitor shown here gives us information about the red, green, and blue values of the image – the shot in Figure 9.1, in fact. You can see that the color values are present, but much of the image is too dark and the colors rest mostly down in the shadows. In fact, the brightest part of the image is represented by the peak over to the left side of the waveform, and it isn't even close to clipping, or bright enough for proper exposure.

them or correct them. Every professional NLE has all of these monitors built into them, and you need to use them as you grade in post. You can't trust your eyes. Really, it's the screens you shouldn't trust.

LUTs (Look Up Tables)

LUTs allow us to load a preset "look" into a screen to see what an image could look like after color grading is done in post. In other words, a LUT allows us to see an image that looks very different than what the camera is actually recording. Cinema cameras especially shoot a "flat" image – one where the dynamic range isn't all that broad and a lot of color information is missing. When a Director looks at the image on these cameras, they are often underwhelmed and have trouble making decisions about backgrounds and camera placement because they don't know if colors might interfere or be distracting. By installing a LUT on a screen for viewing, the camera can still shoot the flatter image (technically speaking, a Log-encoded image) which is better for capturing the data in the scene, but the Director can look at a screen that has all of the color information reproduced.

What Is a LUT?

Technically speaking, a LUT is a mathematical matrix. The LUT gives the screen information that basically says, "replace this color value with this other, more saturated one." There are 1-dimensional LUTs (where there is only an x-axis and a y-axis in the matrix) and there are 3-dimensional LUTs (where there is also a z-axis in the mathematical matrix). A 3-D LUT gives you more vibrant options.

We use LUTs in a number of ways. The first one, as I mentioned above, is so that the Director can look at a screen and see colors that aren't actually there on the recorded footage, but that will be added back in post. The second way is as a starting point for color correction and color grading in post. You can actually load a LUT into your NLE, and it will use the mathematical matrix to automatically adjust most or all of your colors to match the color space you want. For instance, you might have a "Canon Log to Rec.709" LUT that will transform the footage from the color space it was shot on (Canon Log) into a video color space (Rec.709) – more on color spaces below. It will make all of those decisions automatically, and your color work in post is fairly simple.

The third way to use LUTs is a bit more creative. There are a lot of LUTs out there that are essentially creative color grades that have been packaged to create a "look." For instance, I have a LUT that makes my Log-encoded Blackmagic URSA 4.6k "film" footage look bright and warm, where the oranges and reds are a bit more saturated than the other colors. I have another LUT that makes the same footage feel cold and dreary, where all the colors are less saturated, and the blues and grays dominate the overall color scheme. These are "creative LUTs," as opposed to the "color transform" or "color correction" LUTs mentioned above.

Color Spaces

Many cinema cameras come with a LUT built in, although they just call it "video color space" (vs "cinema color space"). This means the camera actually has a Rec.709 LUT built into its screens. Rec.709 is what video cameras and camcorders use for their color spaces. But video cameras usually shoot natively in that color space, meaning that you don't need to do any color correcting in post. A cinema camera screen with a Rec.709 LUT will show an image that is colored a lot like what you're used to shooting with your phone, DSLR, or camcorder.

Technically speaking, a color space is what defines the limits of the colors you can use in your footage. Rec.709 is a very popular color space because it keeps the red, green, and blue values confined to the range that most TV screens are capable of reproducing. Cinema cameras are capable of recording values outside of that color space, and most NLEs will allow you to edit and color grade beyond that space as well, so you have to make some choices about where your project will play and what those capabilities are. Unless you're a colorist or you want to learn more about color grading, you probably don't need to know much more about color spaces than this. But you should be aware that they exist and that you might need to transform your footage from one color space to a different one from time to time.

How to Apply a LUT

Every screen is different, so you'll want to watch a video tutorial or read the manual for your specific model. It's important to note, though, that the LUTs aren't typically loaded into the camera itself. During production, LUTs are loaded into the Director's monitor screen directly, as they are the person responsible for final decisions about framing and composition. The exception is the cameras that have Rec.709 LUTs installed as a default. Be careful with this because some of these cameras allow you to apply the LUT to the recording as well as the monitor output. Don't do this, or the colors will be "baked in" to the footage in a way that makes it more difficult to color grade in post.

In post NLEs, each one applies LUTs in slightly different ways. For instance, in Da-Vinci Resolve, the LUT is applied to a color grading node. Nodes are a bit harder to wrap my head around than the effects rack system that Adobe Premiere Pro uses in its Lumetri color plugin. Nodes are fairly useful, though, once you get the hang of them. Whether it's a node or a rack function, you can apply a LUT to one part of the color grading process in a way that allows you to do color correcting separate from color grading (more on how those things are different is written below). Nodes and rack effects even allow you to separate out your color grade for one color from the color grade for another color, or to separate out each decision about color you're making in post, so that you can easily toggle that specific adjustment being turned on or off without affecting the other decisions you're making. In other words, if you layer all of your color decisions on top of each other, to remove one, you have to press the "undo" button and remove all of the decisions you made after the one you're removing. With nodes or racks, you can isolate each decision and play around with each one until you achieve your vision.

Grading

Color correction is the first step in coloring your footage in post. Following that, color grading is when you use the color tools to make creative decisions. Even though one flows directly into the other, the language and subtle difference between the two is important. When you're correcting, you're taking the first step towards bringing your values within the safe ranges of the color space, but you're not creating a distinct "look" that will set your images apart from others. Correction involves making decisions on brightness and contrast, and generally broad decisions on color spaces. For instance, applying a LUT to transform footage from Log into Rec.709 is a correction. Applying a LUT on the next node that brings out the blue values and desaturates the reds would be a color grade. Outside of using a LUT, you might make initial color changes using curves or wheels to correct white balance and bring your image "right" on the vectorscope and waveform monitor. But after that, you might make adjustments to the curves that give your footage a distinct look.

Curves

If you've ever worked in Photoshop, chances are you're familiar with using curves to change colors. The thing I like about curves is that they can work specifically in any of the three primary colors, specifically in the luminance, and specifically within the shadows, highlights, or midtones. In Figure 9.8, I raised the midtones in the greens. You can see on the parade waveform that the greens are mostly balanced. The effect of raising the greens in the midtone values was that the grass is now a little greener. The downside is that the windows of the building and the roof are now also a little more green. Making color adjustments like this applies to the entire image. You would have to mask out a small section, like the grass, and color correct only that section if you didn't want to change the green values of the entire image. When you look at the parade waveform, you can see that green (the middle waveform) is grouped more toward the middle. This shows that the midtones are where the green values were raised.

You can also see in Figure 9.8 that I increased the red values in the highlights. On the parade waveform, this is shown by the concentration of values toward the top in the reds (the one on the left) near 100%. Especially compared to the greens, the reds are both in

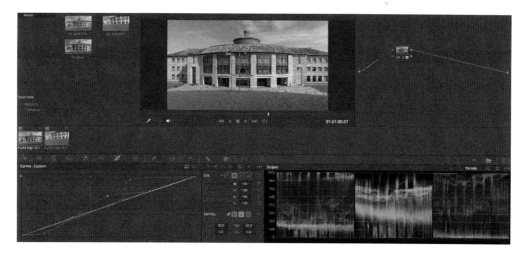

Figure 9.8 Curves. In this example, I also brought the blue values down in the shadows. The parade waveform now shows a pretty solid blue line (the one on the right) down around 0%. The shadows of the building now have less blue in them than they did before. Also note that I haven't touched the luminance. The "Y" button next to the "Edit" function in the middle of the figure allows you to manipulate just the luminance curve (next to the "R," "G," and "B" buttons to control those curves).

the shadows and the highlights, but not a lot in the midtones. The visual effect this has is that the clouds now have a reddish tint to them in the shot.

Wheels

When I first started coloring footage, curves weren't part of NLE systems and the only option was color wheels. With wheels, the effects are slightly different, so there is some benefit to using both curves and wheels. In other words, they're not exactly just two different interfaces for the same outcomes. Wheels are often labeled different things, but the idea is that you have one wheel for the shadows, one for the midtones, and one for the highlights. In Figure 9.9, these are called "Lift" (shadows), "Gamma" (midtones), and "Gain" (highlights). The "offset" is a global adjustment that changes colors across all luminance values. At the bottom of the wheels, you'll see "Shadows," "Highlights," and "Saturation." The shadows adjustment will lighten or deepen the blacks. The highlights adjustment will do the same for the whites. These are luminance adjustments and don't affect the saturation of the colors.

To use the color wheels, you use your mouse to click and grab the white dot in the center of the wheel you want to adjust. When you drag that dot towards one of the colors on the outside of the wheel, the tones you're adjusting will become tinted toward that color. For instance, if you want the sky in this image to be a deeper blue, you might drag the gamma or the gain toward the blue a little bit. The only problem there, much like with the curves, is that it affects the entire image. The building tones also tint toward blue. This is a bit advanced, but this would require us to create a mask that moves with the camera shot and adjust the colors only within that masked area; or, to create a color effect that changes exact color values and not others, even if they are close on the color wheel to the one you're adjusting.

Figure 9.9 Color wheels in DaVinci Resolve. Dragging the dot in the center of the wheel towards a color places more of that color in the shadows, mids, or highlights and removes some of the color in the opposite direction.

(Sort of) Automatic Methods

Most NLEs have some user-friendly ways of color grading. In Figure 9.9, there is a very small "A" in a circle just above and to the left of the lift wheel. When you click on this in DaVinci Resolve, the NLE uses analysis algorithms to identify where and how to automatically correct the image. Essentially, the computer aims to color correct everything into a Rec.709 color space when you press this button. The "dropper" icon next to the Auto function is a white balance tool. When you click on this tool, your mouse turns into a dropper. When you click on something that should be white in your image, the NLE will adjust all of the colors accordingly, effectively automatically adjusting your white balance as if you shot it that way.

There are other really excellent coloring tools in NLEs today, and they continue to get better. DaVinci's "Color Warper" is a way to shift things within a color space. The "HSL" adjustment tool provides the ability to change hue, saturation, and luminance values in subtle but important ways. Probably one of the most interesting things I've seen added to NLE systems is the "Color Match" tool that lines up with color cards that shooters now use. When beginning a scene (no need to do it for every shot, just every location and/or lighting setup in that location), the camera will roll while shooting a color card, a gray card, and a white balance card. Some cards have all of those things combined into one card. Then in post, the colorist can use automatic methods to adjust the colors of the footage to what the colors on the card should look like. By adjusting these colors, the whites, the blacks, and the grays, we can automatically get everything corrected quickly.

This is a pretty short summary of coloring techniques. The technology is also evolving rapidly. I would encourage you to scour the internet for videos and other tutorials that can help guide you on the processes that your NLE uses. It seems like the last few DaVinci Resolve updates have brought in a new coloring tool almost every year. To keep up, there are a few YouTube channels I subscribe to regularly to learn how to use those tools and the new processes that colorists are using.

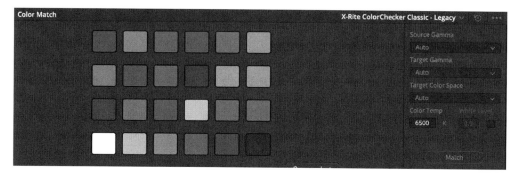

Figure 9.10 The X-Rite ColorChecker Classic card in DaVinci Resolve allows you to overlay this grid onto the one that was shot. Once the color blocks are lined up, you click on the "Match" button to automatically adjust all 24 colors. You can see the grayscale at the bottom going from white to black. There are also colors that represent different skin tones that can be matched up as well.

Case Study: *Backseat*, a Short Student Film

I teach a class in audio for cinema techniques. Each semester, the class partners up with students in a film production class to make a short film. A few years ago, a group of students between the classes produced an award-winning film titled *Backseat*. It can be found here: https://www.youtube.com/watch?v=1BVK2HFSkro or by searching for "Backseat" by Brendan Wade. Special thanks to Brendan (Producer, Writer, Director), Tre'Von Wilson-Wade (Cinematographer), Brandon Williams (Editor), Isaac Barkley (Sound Designer), and Elhanan Pete Grigsby (Music Composer) for letting me use their film as the case study for this section of the book.

The film opens with a shot of the main character's eyes in the rearview mirror, and the music comes in during that shot to really set the stage. The edits are well timed with the music, and tell the story of a young man who is struggling to work and attend college at the same time. He's a hard-working person scraping to get by, behind on his rent and tuition payments. He moves into the backseat of his car, and is faced with a choice to stay in school or to give up.

The students wrote the treatment for this film first. In our Narrative class, every student writes a treatment, and then the class votes on the three or four films they will break into groups and produce. Brendan's concept was selected, at which point he got started on the script. While he wrote the script, the Art Director storyboarded the scenes and the producer began working on the crew roles, audition dates and recruiting for the actors, and an overall shooting schedule. Once locations are scripted, the producer also secured the locations for the shooting dates. For about the first half of the semester, preproduction was the main focus. Once actors, locations, schedules, and the script were complete (or at least the first few days were nailed down), production started.

During preproduction, the audio crew focused on their role with the script. They began talking to the Director about the music that would be needed, as well as locations and how they were going to mic the actors to get good dialogue. For *Backseat*, they also identified some ADR work that wouldn't need to wait for post – the phone calls. Finally, they identified natural sound effects that they needed to focus on capturing while on set.

Once shooting began, everyone already knew their roles and what needed to get done. Some of the shots in the film are simple, like the shots where the main character is watching the train. Many of the shots are a bit more complicated, like the push-in while the main character takes a test in the classroom, or the shot of his eyes in the rearview mirror inside the car. The focus for the Director was getting quality acting performances, camera movement that adds to the narrative and keeps the audience interested, and presenting the shots from interesting perspectives. The Cinematographer was focused on the visuals, the movements, and working with the Director to make sure every shot helped tell the story. The Cinematographer was the chief technician on this set, so they also directed the Grips on how to set the lighting. The audio crew captured the little bits of dialogue and the sound effects, like the train passing during the shoots. To be honest, my audio students expressed a bit of frustration in the moment because there wasn't a lot of dialogue to capture in this film. But once they understood the Director's vision, they embraced their role in creating the ambience for each scene. And the music they composed fit perfectly for the story.

In post, which is the focus of this section of the book, the editing followed the blueprint put together in preproduction (with some changes along the way). The editor for the project worked with the Director to use the visuals, the ambiance, and the music to tell an effective story of someone who struggles with homelessness and working toward a better life. Some of the scenes were shot with blue gels on the lights, but the colorist also cleaned them up in post. Each shot is well lit, and the low-light shots still use the dynamic range of the camera to create fast falloff and show the deep shadows that fill the life of the main character. The blue shows how he's struggling, both internally and externally, to stay in school and find work and housing. The day scenes are overall bright, but aren't highly saturated, because the main character is struggling. Vibrant colors convey happiness. Desaturated colors convey sadness, bleakness, hopelessness. As the main character stares at the train, he's daydreaming about a better life, but the lack of bright colors shows that he doesn't fully believe it's possible.

The music carries the audio track in this film. In many films, the dialogue is edited into the scene first, and music is put in after editing, or at least a temporary track is used to help the editor find the rhythm for the shots while the music compositions are being recorded. In this case, the editor really needed the actual tracks to be laid down first. The dialogue was done in ADR, probably after the scenes were laid down on the timeline. To convey that these recordings were phone messages, the audio crew cut the low end (bass frequencies) completely and added a slight echo effect. There are also effects you can add in post that essentially do those things and make audio sound like a phone call. Overall, the audio crew was much more heavily involved in post during this project than is typical. Outside of the music, the room tone and sound effects they acquired were also essential to the story. Instead of sweetening the dialogue in post, they spent a lot of time sweetening the atmospheres. It should also be noted that when they recorded the room tone, they needed much longer tracks and treated them like the dialogue during production. Because there isn't much dialogue, the atmospheres were more important than typical room tone.

Overall, the story in *Backseat* took careful planning and beautiful shooting, but really came together in post through the editing, coloring, and sound design. Without the proper planning, the story wouldn't be as effective. But without the music and atmospheres, the story also wouldn't be effective. It's rare that good editing can save bad shooting. But it's equally rare that bad editing and sound design can still tell a good story.

Chapter 9: Coloring Main Points

- Luminance refers to the brightness of the image. It's the greyscale behind the image if all the color is stripped away.
- Contrast refers to the difference between the bright areas. Cameras have a dynamic range. If anything falls outside of the dynamic range, that part of the image is either overexposed (digitally clipped) or underexposed (falls into the shadows). If the camera captured luminance values inside of the dynamic range, they can be expanded in post. If not, color grading can help brighten or darken the image, but it can't bring back details that weren't captured in the first place.
- Chrominance refers to the color values and amount of saturation. Specifically, you can measure the values of the reds, greens, and blues, which are the primary colors cameras record. All other colors are created by mixing the three primary colors together.
- Waveform monitors tell you the luminance information about the shot. Vectorscopes tell you the chrominance information. Other scopes show variations of chrominance and luminance, and scopes are invaluable when color grading.

- Look Up Tables (LUTs) are computer matrices that transform colors in a shot. They typically transform the color information the camera recorded into a different shade, saturation, or variation on that color. LUTs are great to use on set so the Director can see an approximation of what the final color grade might look like and shoot more effectively. But they can also be used to transform the image from one color space to another during post.
- Different cameras shoot in different color spaces, typically with a "flat" image being recorded. LUTs can transform those flat images into something with a much broader color space in post, and can be a good place to start color grading.
- At this point, NLEs also have the ability to do "transforms" from one color space to another as the footage is imported instead of using LUTs. This is an intriguing way to speed up the color grading workflow. There are a few videos online about beginning color grading this way. One word of caution: if you use the transform function, it's better not to let the NLE automate it because then it's done "under the hood" in a way that isn't easily recognized in the clip effects data.

Part IV

Producing Fiction (Chapters 10–12)

We often think of fictional video projects as short films, but there are a variety of genres that include an element of fiction. Making commercials, music videos, short films, feature-length films, experimental films, and some short reels all have elements of fiction in them. The main distinction between producing fiction and producing non-fiction is the amount of scripting you do in a general sense. In a fictional film, commercial, or music video, you write out and draw out what the audience will see ahead of time. The actors on set are delivering lines that were written out for them and memorized. The performances in a commercial are shaped by the Director who is on set and controlling the visuals and dialogue. In non-fiction, you can plan things out, but you can't dictate what will happen in front of the camera. This is the primary distinction I'm drawing here.

DOI: 10.4324/9781003010357-13

10 Narrative Films and Series

Many of the examples I've already used in the book are from fictional projects I've been involved with over the years. Chapters 10–12 will take this one step further and discuss how films, commercials, and music videos differ in their production process and techniques. Chapter 10 will focus on fictional films and series. Chapter 11 will cover commercials. And Chapter 12 will highlight the differences in process when making a music video. Until now, I've tried to present concepts and workflows in a general way that applies to all genres of single-camera production. I'll try my best not to review too much of what's already been said, but some overlap is inevitable. In the rest of the book, I'm going to break it down and go through specific differences when you're shooting different genres. For Narrative Films and Series, I'll show you how to take things from preproduction through post. And then I'll do the same for other genres.

DOI: 10.4324/9781003010357-14

Preproduction

I've taught video production for years. Often, the classes combine learning about single-camera techniques alongside multicamera techniques, even though the two modes of production are very different. The other option that seems to be out there teaches single-camera techniques, but almost always focused entirely on one mode of production – typically either news packages, fictional films, or documentary film production. And so, dedicating just a single chapter on narrative filmmaking seems condensed. There are some great books out there that go into some depth on how to make movies. Here, I'll try to give a quick overview of the process.

The Pitch

The first thing you'll need for a fictional film of any length is a treatment. The general outline of the narrative will guide everything that comes after it, so it's an important place to start. The treatment should include the characters, locations, and major plot points. It should outline everything that happens in the film, including the climax and the resolution. For movies, the treatment doesn't usually focus on the audience or the overall message, just the characters and their story arcs. From there, you're ready to pitch the treatment to potential funding sources and writers (if you're not writing the script yourself).

I often find a misperception out there that a treatment should end with a cliffhanger, but this is definitely not the case. For example, you don't pitch a treatment and say, "Will the main character overcome this obstacle? Fund my movie and I'll make it and you can find out." No one would take you seriously. Instead, the treatment needs to include all of the details, even the ending. You can bet that the people who financially backed *The Sixth Sense* knew the plot twist at the end.

You really need two separate pitches. The "elevator pitch" is a super-brief, 30-second summary of everything. This is the pitch you need to have memorized and bring out any time someone asks you what your film is about. The elevator pitch is the conversation starter when it comes to funding and finding a writer and/or producer. The second pitch is the one you'll need to be more formal with. Have slides, "look" comparisons, potential actors and crew you're going to go after, possible locations, and an ideal budget needed to make the film. This formal pitch should last about 30 minutes and should include a full synopsis and visuals to help potential funding sources understand what the final product will look like. If you have a track record for returns on previous investments in films, this is very helpful to include as well.

Funding

The funding should match the project. If you're shooting a short film, you shouldn't need 30 million dollars to get started. Knowing your budget is important, even though you don't have actors, crew, or locations lined up when you're pitching the idea to potential investors. As you go through your treatment, create a breakdown of what it will cost to rent equipment, hire crew, secure locations, and pay for licensing. If you're in school and shooting a student film, then most likely you have very few of these costs. It's not a bad exercise, though, to think about how much time it will take and what it would have cost you if you needed to fund the film outside of your classes.

Most of the short films I've seen in academic festivals max out around $25k–$30k in their budgets. Many are done with almost no money at all, but some MFA degrees require fundraising as part of the thesis film process. Since these films aren't likely to be financially successful in their returns to investors, funding is often crowd-sourced online. Family and friends often chip in money just to help get the film made.

A very successful producer I know recently told me that she never asks people to invest more than they can afford to lose. And yet, she's raised millions of dollars for big-budget movies by asking the right people and by having the right connections. And you can bet that she has a very polished treatment to pitch her upcoming film going into production this summer. I've seen the packet and it's an impressive set of actors, crew, locations, and budget numbers.

In my world, I'm also writing grants or finding potential sponsors to fund our films. Students and faculty at universities often have access to grants that the general public do not have access to. I've received thousands of dollars for equipment over the years to produce my films and other projects. Outside the university setting, there are also funding sources available through public grants (especially if you're shooting a documentary or something that a foundation might be interested in funding). Tax breaks are also available in many states. Missouri just passed one. Georgia's tax breaks are what shifted a large part of the film industry from LA to Atlanta. Tax breaks are probably only going to help if you're producing a film with a fairly large budget, but I'm trying to at least mention the possible ways films are funded in this section.

Script

The scripts for fictional films are always written in the single-column dramatic style detailed in Chapter 1. It's really important to do this so that your actors and crew are familiar with the format and can easily read the information they need for each scene. For a film script, the general rule of thumb is that each page of script will occupy about a minute of the film. So, if your script is 15 pages, you should end up with about a 15-minute film.

I've seen two different trains of thought when figuring out how much detail to write into the script. Imsdb.com (the Internet Movie Script Database) has a huge archive of Hollywood movies, many of which you'll recognize. As you look through them, you'll see that they're all formatted the same way. But some will have more details in their scene descriptions and some will have almost none. For example, a detailed description might say, "We start with a CU of the main character looking down at their watch, then pan across the scene until we see a CU of the antagonist staring intently at them through the open window." A less detailed version might just read, "The antagonist stares through the open window at the main character." One style attempts to tell the Director and Cinematographer how to set up the shot. The other style allows a lot more freedom for how to shoot it. Neither way is right or wrong, but you'll want to be consistent with the amount of description you give to your crew so they know what to expect.

Storyboards

Storyboards are an important part of the fictional film process. In my experience, they're at the same level as the script and the shooting schedule. Storyboards help everyone visualize each scene and possibly each shot before anyone shows up on location. Storyboards help everyone visualize the flow of the film during the entire preproduction process, but they're also important for being on the same page during production. Going through the storyboards that correspond to the daily schedule is important for the Director, Cinematographer, lighting Director, and actors. The script can guide the specifics and the details, but the storyboards convey the overall emotions and look.

I also find that the storyboards are often the place where students decide to try and save time, then wish they hadn't later on. For instance, I've seen student films that were hastily storyboarded using the template in Figure 1.9 in Chapter 1. The drawings often depict an entire scene, and the written descriptions are just a sentence with little detail – often something like, "Scene 5: The main character talks about their plans." Without any specific shots being drawn out, the Director and crew might waste a significant amount of time on set deciding where to the put cameras, what lenses to use, which shot should be done first, second, etc. A good, detailed storyboard plan, along with a detailed shooting schedule, will guide the crew through their day and keep things moving efficiently. The Director still has the latitude to change a shot or to add some coverage if something at the location works better. But they'll have a better starting point if storyboards are detailed, like the example in Figure 1.10 in Chapter 1.

Actors

Casting the right actors is a very important part of the process for films. A good performance can make or break a film (when it comes to the main characters at least). Ideally, you'll find actors who have some training in acting for the screen, and who will take direction well. If you have to choose, I would cast someone who can take direction well over someone who is trained. You should absolutely avoid casting someone just because it's convenient unless they're the right person for the part. When I shot and helped produce the film *King of Hearts* with Mark von Schlemmer (the film used as a case study at the end of this chapter), we were struggling to cast the male lead. We opened auditions and had several people read for the part. Incidentally, one of the crew members sat and read opposite some of the young women who came to read for that lead, and we liked the crew member's performance so well that we ended up casting him in the part. This was convenient, but it was also intentional. What I see in many student films is that crew members are cast in parts simply because little effort was put into recruiting actors. And most often, you can tell that those people aren't really actors.

The first step in recruiting actors is to figure out how you want the part played. Having someone read for a part might be futile if they don't have any direction from you in how to play it. If someone reads through the script and thinks the part should be played in a southern accent, they might throw the Director off and lose the part, even though they might have been able to do a perfect west-coast accent. Just an example, but my point is that the Director leading the auditions should be able to give a few basic directions to lead the actors through the tryouts. Doing so will also give an indication of how well the actors will take directions. If someone doesn't seem able to shift gears from how they planned to play the part, they likely won't be able to shift gears when shooting a scene if the Director asks them to.

Once you know how you want the part played, reach out to people you know who might fit the part. In Hollywood films, the leads are actually targeted and sought out to play the parts. For smaller-budget films, you should at least try to do the same. For *King of Hearts*, the female lead was cast without an audition. She was a talented actress out of

Kansas City, and the Director knew her work and reached out to her specifically to play the part. And she really set the bar for the other actors when we were shooting on the set. If you can't recruit people specifically, or those connections just don't pan out (or honestly, even while you're trying to recruit specific people and regardless of the outcome), you should set up a series of auditions and then get word out as broadly as possible. At a university, post fliers, connect with faculty members in the Theater Department, reach out to local community theater groups, and talk to your peers who have worked on other films to see if they can recommend someone.

When directing actors, be kind, but give guidance for how to play a scene. I've seen many Directors as they work on set, and the best ones focus more on the actors than the crew. They huddle up with the actors while the crew is setting up the cameras, lights, and backgrounds and discuss what's going on in the scene, how they'll approach each shot and the overall timeline for the location, and what they expect from the actors. After that huddle, the Director will eventually work their way to the camera shot and the lighting and give some direction there. An inefficient Director will focus on the crew – micromanaging where to put the camera and lights, what lens to use, and how to set everything up. The problem with this is that the actors sit around waiting while setup happens, and then the crew sits around waiting while the Director works with the actors. Or worse, the Director calls for the first take and the actors are left to play the scene without direction. This is inefficient because the actors almost always shoot several takes before the Director gets frustrated and tells the crew to "take 5" while they take the actors aside and walk them through the scene like they should have done in the first place.

A note on intimacy training: regardless of the subject of your film, the requirements for your actors, or the speed of your shooting schedules, you should *always* prepare your actors for the film in its entirety and for each scene before they show up on set for the day. For *King of Hearts*, we did an entire evening of table reads with the actors before shooting even began. The film did not have any situations that might have made our actors uncomfortable, but these table reads helped expose any potential issues. You never know what might bring up past traumas. Words and situations in a film might make one of your actors uncomfortable, and if you run into those things while you're shooting, it can lead to disaster. Actors have been known to back out of projects because the Director put them in a situation that made them uncomfortable. I worked on a film once where one of the actresses tried out for a role, got the part, showed up on set, and was told that it was a nude scene. The Director actually had a really good reason for this, and it fit the genre, but she immediately left and withdrew from the film. Actors should never be kept in the dark about things that could potentially make them uncomfortable. They might be willing to push their limits, but it should always be discussed before shooting even begins. If the film has a high probability to push actors, you should even consider bringing in a counselor, or someone trained to discuss intimacy and other psychological issues with the cast and crew.

Locations

The best locations are the ones that help tell your story. Again, settling for things that are convenient is most likely going to hinder your film. Shooting a scene in a dorm room looks like, well, shooting something in a dorm room. If that's the story you're trying to tell, this is absolutely appropriate. If you're trying to make that dorm room feel like a hotel room, it won't. It won't substitute for a room in the house you grew up in either. If you're shooting a scene about a middle-aged couple in their house, you need an actual

Figure 10.1 A still from *The Computer Lab*. This set design already existed and required very little work. The hardest part was asking the homeowner for permission.

house. Or at least a studio set that looks like an actual house. By the way, you also need to cast a middle-aged couple and not your college student classmates.

Lining up locations is usually a lot easier than you might anticipate. We shot a unique web series, *The Computer Lab*, recently that needed a unique location. We found a house in town with a walk-in wine cellar and vault. The bars in Figure 10.1 are real, as is the brick-lined arched ceiling. I produced another shoot where we used similar jail-cell bars in a studio, but these looked better and they were easier to set up. The producer for this web series knew about the house and simply asked the owner if we could use it. The owner was happy to help, and the scene turned out amazing.

The main takeaway is that when it comes to fictional films, there really isn't a substitute for the real thing. The point is to transport your audience to the world of the film. And if you're cutting corners on locations, the audience has a harder time suspending their disbelief and immersing themselves in the narrative. The only other option is to rewrite the script to better match the locations you have available. If you're a student and you're writing a murder mystery, set the film at a university. Then when you use a dorm room as the setting, it's entirely appropriate. For lower-budget films, this is actually a necessity. You won't have the budget to build elaborate sets, and you won't have access to exotic locations. One of the most brilliant films I've seen lately was shot on a college campus (*Publish or Perish*, by David Liban), using the locations and actors readily available to the filmmaker, who is also a professor. It can be done when you acknowledge the limits of your locations, when you do your research and ask around for the best locations, and especially when you don't try to pretend that a location might pass for something else if your audience just squints a little.

Crew

For narrative films and series, you will want to have a hierarchy and plan out who will fill each role. When you're on set, it slows things down too much to shoot a film by democracy. That's not to say that you can't take opinions into consideration when shooting a film, but

Figure 10.2 The Director is in charge of everything on the set. This is a picture from the set of our film, *King of Hearts*. The Director, Mark von Schlemmer, has already discussed the scene with the actors. In this picture, he's working with me, the DP, to discuss the shot – the framing, lighting, and composition. I'm bouncing the light off the ceiling in the back to diffuse it.

someone needs to fill the Director's role and someone needs to be the producer. When decisions are made, the producer almost always has the final say, but the Director is in charge on the set. Even in low-budget and student films, this hierarchy is necessary to help things move along efficiently. Having said that, as a Cinematographer, I really appreciate when the Director gives me some freedom to set shots the way I think they should be set. And I appreciate when a Director looks my way and asks what I think about the lighting or the approach to the scene. Just because the Director is in charge doesn't mean they can't be collaborative. It just means that after they seek input, they make the decision and everyone moves on.

For a small film, you might need a producer, Director, Director of Photography (a DP usually handles cinematography and also lighting), a First Assistant Camera (AC), and an Audio Engineer. In a smaller production, people might wear multiple hats, like the DP. The producer might double as the script supervisor for continuity as well. It's best to let the Director and Cinematographer stay focused on their tasks, though. I've seen many productions lose track of prop continuity or blow past times on their shooting schedules when the Director is trying to keep script notes on top of directing the actors and crew.

Equipment and Props Checklists

As mentioned in Chapter 3, for scripted films and series, I like to have two lists for equipment and two lists for props. The first equipment list helps me line up the items

I need for the entire project. The first prop list is similar – it tells me what I need to track down for the entire film. The other lists are part of my daily schedule. This is my checklist as I pack everything for the location I'm heading to. In fact, for narrative projects where I'm mostly shooting out of order, it's essential to have this daily breakdown by scene and/or shot to make sure I don't forget anything I need for the shoot. And if I'm shooting at multiple locations on the same day, the equipment and prop lists might be different from one location to another. If possible, I try to group shoots together so I'm shooting entirely indoors one day and outdoors another day. That way, I don't have to pack around twice as much equipment. On a larger shoot, you'll have access to a Grip truck or trailer that will already have much of the equipment packed, so your equipment doesn't determine your shooting schedule quite as much.

Shooting Schedules

A well-planned schedule is essential for a narrative shoot. Because you'll probably shoot things out of order and group scenes together on certain days based on actor availability, equipment needs, location availability, or any number of other things, making sure your daily schedules have all the information you need is really important. One of the best examples is the movie *Castaway*, in which Tom Hanks shot the first part and the last part of the film at one point, then took a year off to lose weight and mentally prepare himself for the scenes of the film where he was stranded on an island by himself. A lot happens over the course of a year, but most of the film was planned out before the first scenes were even shot. On a large project, this will be done using specialized software that will cross-reference equipment lists, props, call sheets, and shot lists. Producers have access to the database and can easily pull specific information for each day.

Craft Services and a Word of Advice

When working as part of a crew on a nationally syndicated reality show, I learned a valuable lesson: crews need to be rested and well fed to be at their best. On film shoots, long days are often part of the process. Scenes happen early in the morning and late at night. Locations might only be available at specific times. Actors might have projects coming up and have a limited number of days to shoot. Ten or twelve-hour days are unavoidable for some projects. It's important to schedule breaks for cast and crew. Craft Services is what we call catering on a film set. Large productions will hire a catering service to make sure everyone on set gets fed throughout the day. Smaller projects might just get takeout or a stack of pizzas to feed everyone. During *The Computer Lab* series shooting, we actually got a local pizza place to sponsor the series and provide pizza for one of the days. For *King of Hearts*, we used the back room of a different pizza place, so we all ate there and the producer paid for the meal to show the owner our appreciation. Planning meals and breaks is important. I've seen the effects on morale and energy when the shoot gets behind schedule and the producer decides to work through a break or take a quicker lunch than planned. I suggest setting aside 15–30 minutes for a break every hour or two – between shooting scenes or shots, not as an inflexible time mark. And for lunch and dinner, an hour allows everyone to eat and let their stomachs settle before getting back to work. If you're working with actors or crew who are members of a union, there are specific rules about breaks that you'll need to plan for.

Production

Production on a film set is a major production, even on smaller projects. You're often shooting multiple scenes in a day, and even with just a few actors and crew members, there can be a lot of moving parts to keep track of. Add a B camera or a C camera to the mix and it can be a nightmare to plan and shoot.

Cameras

My preference is to shoot films single-camera. That's what this book is about, and what my focus has been. For single-camera shoots, planning your lighting, lens choice, and movement for each shot is pretty straightforward. The shot can be seen on the storyboard and the script can specify pretty much where the focus needs to be and what needs to be in the background.

Now that cameras have come way down in price and films aren't shot on actual celluloid, many narrative projects are done with more than one camera. Especially when starting out making movies, I'd encourage you to keep it simple. When you use multiple cameras, you have to block all of the movement, set all of the lights, and get different camera angles all at the same time. I've seen this take more time to set up than it would have taken to shoot out one side and then just move everything to shoot the other. And I've also seen things shot with multiple cameras, only to find that in the editing room the angles won't actually cut together well without getting awkward cuts or continuity errors.

Having said that, there are times when I absolutely would shoot with more than one camera. If you're shooting a choreographed dance, fight, or something else that is very difficult to replicate in terms of the exact movements and placements for each take, you might consider using more than one camera. Getting a great performance from an actor falls into this category for production crews that are experienced in multiple-camera shoots. When you have a special effect, like an explosion or fire, you might also consider using more than one camera. Those kinds of things are expensive and hard to replicate. And if you can't replicate the action, it's a continuity error waiting to happen.

Lighting

If you're lighting for a single camera, lighting is much easier. Trying to figure out how to light for multiple cameras is hard primarily because lights cast shadows and it's easier to hide those shadows when you only have one angle to worry about. In narrative productions, though, it's not just as easy as setting a key, fill, and backlight. In fact, 3-point lighting is probably the last thing you want. For more dramatic shots in movies, we usually want the light to be motivated in some way. Often, this means setting up a key light that puts highlights on the actors that look like they're being cast by the light coming from a window or desk lamp in the scene. And if the light is coming from that

Figure 10.3 In this short film, *Gone Fishin'*, there is a window directly behind the subject. He's not silhouetted, but we used a key light to mimic the motivated lighting. Both the key and the fill are positioned almost behind the actor. The end result is that the key light is the one brushing the side of the actor's face on the camera side. It's a bit harder than the back light that fills in on the other side because it's less diffused. The impact on the scene, though, is that the light looks like it's coming in through the window and wrapping around the actor's face.

motivated source, there should be corresponding shadows that aren't filled in directly by a fill light. Instead, the light often rims the side of the actor's face so that there are some shadows.

Sound

There are three different ways I've acquired sound on a film set. The first is to use a shotgun mic mounted on the end of a boom. I almost always put the mic inside of a zeppelin like the one in Figure 6.6 in Chapter 6. The zeppelin acts as a windscreen and cuts down on any air movement reaching the mic. It also has a shock mount built into it that helps cut down on handling noise. On very windy days outdoors, I'll also put a windsock on the outside of the zeppelin (most zeppelins come with a custom fit windsock). From there, it's just a matter of aiming the mic at the actor's mouth and getting as close as possible without dipping down into the shot. There are two modifications on this – you can mount the boom onto a C-stand to maintain distance and free up a crew member to do something else, and/or you can hang shotgun mics from the ceiling grid with special cables that help keep them aimed in a specific direction.

The second way I do sound on a film set is with a wireless lav. The key here is to make sure the viewers can't tell there's a mic there, or it will disrupt their suspension of disbelief. I like to use gaff tape and make two inside-out triangles with it (we used to

Figure 10.4 The mic itself is sandwiched between two footballs, then stuck between two shirts. This variation also has a loop that's secured with gaffer tape. If there's stress on the cable, the loop will tighten and release the stress without pulling directly on the mic.

call them "footballs" in elementary school). The mic clip is removed and the mic itself is sandwiched between the two footballs as they're stuck to each other. Then the outsides of the two footballs are stuck between the outer shirt and the undershirt the actor wears. This keeps the mic from rubbing and creates a fairly low profile that goes unnoticed. If the actor is only wearing one shirt, I'll use moleskin and stick the mic to the inside of it, then stick the moleskin onto the actor's skin. Don't stick it to the outer shirt or it will swing and move around as the actor moves.

The last way I do sound on a film set is with boundary mics. A boundary mic has a hemispherical pickup pattern that is fairly broad. They can be hidden around the film set behind set pieces like desks, plants, lamps, etc. As long as you don't see them in the shot, they can be almost anywhere. Sometimes the wireless versions of boundary mics are called "pucks," because you can hide a bunch of them on set and pick up sound in long shots where a boom can't reach. The good thing about these mics is that they pick up dialogue and ambience pretty well. The bad thing is that it's hard to isolate the background noise from the dialogue.

I'll often run two different ways at the same time on a film set, giving me options in post. For a recent short film, *The Other Cheek*, I did a combination of a wireless lav and boom mics. The boom mics were supposed to be the main source of dialogue, but one actor was moving enough in long shots that I put a wireless lav on them. I was actually happier with the wireless lav than the boom, as the sound was just closer and cleaner. But then I tried to mic both my talent with wireless lavs for *Gone Fishin'*, and there was noise on all of the frequencies. It took a lot more time in post to remove the noise.

You also need a good set of headphones to monitor the sound while you're shooting. Listening to make sure the track is clean and the dialogue can easily be heard is important. Monitoring the levels on the recording device is equally important. I've seen many student films where the dialogue was clean, but the levels were so low that they had to be boosted in post. And, of course, when you boost the dialogue levels in post, the levels of the background noise come up with it. And even though there are some good tools to isolate and clean up dialogue, this takes time and effort.

Directing

Directing a film or series pretty much follows the procedures laid out in Chapter 4. The only difficult thing is being able to visualize how the pieces might fit together when a film is shot out of order, and making sure your actors are giving you the appropriate performance for the scene. Being familiar with the entire story, each scene, and how everything will look when edited together is a very important skill for a Director. I've noticed that people new to directing often focus too much on the technical aspects of the shot they're getting in the moment, instead of looking at the larger picture – what the camera is capturing and how it will fit in and help tell the story. That's why good Directors lean on their crew to work out the technical details, while they focus on the actors and how they will play the scene being shot.

DIT and Workflow

This is probably one of the biggest differences I've noticed between narrative films and other types of single-camera productions. Meticulous organization is essential for postproduction in narrative films. Because they're most often shot out of order, each take needs to be labeled and backed up immediately. And since you're probably shooting in a higher resolution than you might with other projects, you'll fill the cards up quickly and need a designated DIT and DIT cart to offload them in order to continue shooting throughout the day. Having large drives with lots of space is important so you have room for original files and backups. And if you're shooting over a series of days, it's worthwhile to screen your dailies in the evening so you can learn from any mistakes you're making and fix them before you start the next day. You might also catch something and be able to reshoot it the next day instead of waiting until post and realizing that you need to get the cast and crew back together.

Post

Postproduction on a film follows the workflow outlined in Chapter 7. The DIT organizes the files as they're shot. After that, the assistant editor will sync everything and create a bin for each scene. Then, the editor will put the scenes together and create the overall timeline for the film. For a short film, everything might be done in one bin and a single timeline. From there, once the length of each shot is locked in, that picture-locked track will be sent to the colorist and the sound designer for sweetening, music, and sound effects. At the end, there are almost always test screenings with audiences before the final festival release or theatrical release. For series, the process might be a bit different, as the crew might be shooting multiple episodes while the post team is working on those same episodes.

Picture Lock

Picture lock refers to the point in the process where the editor has the visuals locked in enough that the timing of the cuts won't change. The film can still be color graded, special effects and transitions added, and graphics or anything else, as long as the visuals match the dialogue that's being handed off to the audio team – which means that when you edit a film together, the first step is to work toward picture lock by putting the clips in the order you want them and cutting them down to the correct length. Once the rhythm of the cuts is established and they're in the right spot on the timeline, the visuals and the synced dialogue are exported out to the audio team.

There are multiple ways to do this. One is to save the project file alongside the clip files and copy the entire folder onto a hard drive for the audio team. The downside of this is that the audio team is stuck starting out using the same NLE as the editor. For example, if the editor used Adobe Premiere, the Audio team must first open the project in Premiere before exporting out to a DAW (Digital Audio Workstation) to do the audio tracks. In DaVinci Resolve, this might work okay since Fairlight Audio is now embedded in the NLE, but many sound teams are using Avid ProTools for their sound design. So, the other way to export out the picture-locked video and audio tracks is to export as an XML, OMF, or AAF file. In theory, these files package up the timeline editing decisions you've made along with the source files and put everything into one file. From there, you open that file in an NLE or DAW and it should unpackage everything out into your timeline. In practice, I've gotten those file types to work sometimes, but sometimes errors happen. It's always best to communicate and coordinate between the editor and audio team until the files are open and working in the DAW.

Once the audio team sweetens the dialogue, normalizes the levels, and creates the DME stems completely, they add a countdown leader to each audio stem and export them, typically as.wav files unless they're working in a software program that easily transfers back to the NLE that the editor is using. Each stem should be mixed down. The main reason for this is so that the editor doesn't have a lot of work to do and there's no possibility of accidentally deleting any dialogue clips or shifting things. On a large project, the editor and audio teams might work together in the same editing studio. These studios often have large screens, great sound systems, and specialized interfaces to run the software. In these settings, the audio mixer might be running as the picture plays on the screen and the Director is giving feedback in real time.

Color Grading

Coloring is much more intricate in a film project. Making sure that colors match the overall scheme and tell the story can take a lot of time during postproduction. In other single-camera projects, the timeline isn't as long, so coloring isn't quite as intricate. For example, even though a commercial probably needs to use a LUT to correct the color space, that might be the extent of the coloring. Maybe a commercial needs to be on the happy side, so things are shifted to a warmer tone. Or maybe some shots need to be brightened so the exposure levels match. But in a film, each shot needs to match the other shots in the scene, and then the overall color schemes need to be thought out and applied. When I color a film scene, I end up spending a lot more time on it than when I color anything else.

Screening

For film projects, it's really important to screen the film with a test audience prior to releasing it. Sometimes this is done informally – the film is posted privately to YouTube or Vimeo and the link is sent to people you know for their feedback. Sometimes, the screening is more formal. A friend of mine shot a feature-length film and recruited an audience of about 30 people to watch it in an actual theater. It was so fun to get a sneak peek of the film, and the Director had some specific questions about some parts and general questions about the whole storyline. Without getting too specific, there were a few scenes that needed to be re-cut to make better sense for the audience.

For one of my recent films, *Central State Hospital: An Oral History*, I sent the feature-length version out to a few friends for their feedback and we were able to make a few changes before sending it off to festivals. But the feedback we got from the festivals actually helped guide us to the final version, which ended up being only 42 minutes instead of 90. The key here is to take the feedback and make the changes, but then finalize the project and move on. Getting feedback is very helpful, but at some point, the film needs to be done. I don't know any filmmakers who finish a project and are 100% satisfied with it. Just look at how George Lucas released the "Special Edition" of *Star Wars* in 1997, 20 years after the film was initially released and added things to the film that weren't there in the original.

Case Study: *King of Hearts*

King of Hearts is an award-winning short film written and directed by my colleague, Mark von Schlemmer. I've used it as an example already throughout the book, but I'll outline the entire process for the film here. The working title for the film was, *Heads Up*, so some of the preproduction still has that title on it. You can view the film here: https://www.youtube.com/watch?v=nhHul6lq6B8.

All of these documents were available in a cloud drive for the entire cast and crew to prepare for each day of shooting. The script, location stills, costuming ideas, release forms, raw footage, rough cuts, character backstories, financials for the film, and the final version of the film are in the folder as well. That way, things are archived and also available for everyone involved to access.

Other examples from *King of Hearts* can be seen in Figures 1.12, 2.6, 4.9, 5.4, 7.5, and 7.6.

Camera Gear
URSA
V-mount Batteries
V-mount Charger
Lens Kit
Filter Kits
Lens wipes
Vinten Tripod
Slider
C-stands for slider

Lighting Gear
Both Arri Kits
Litepanels Kit
V-mount Batteries
Both Softboxes
All 4 Road Rags
8 C-stands
Blackwrap
Gaff Tape
6 Extension Power Cords
*China Ball light
*Slate and extra dry erase markers and wipes

Audio Gear
Sound Devices Mixer
AA Batteries
4 x XLR Cables
2 x XLR Elbows
2 x Wireless Mic Kits
2 x Boom poles
2 x AT897 mics
2 x windscreens

Figures 10.5 and 10.6 The overall equipment list and the breakdown sheet for the film. Notice that the breakdown sheet is only one page, but has links to other documents, like the still photos for location design, equipment lists, prop lists, wardrobe, call list, and even the daily schedule for scenes 1, 3, 5, and 7. These were the scenes shot at the first location. On day 2, we shot scenes 2, 4, and 6 (the flashback scenes) at a second location.

BREAKDOWN SHEET

SHOW __Heads Up__   BREAKDOWN PAGE#1

LOCATION __Mazzio's backroom__   PROD# _____

☐ STAGE   ✔ LOCAL LOCATION   ☐ DISTANT LOCATION   DATE __12/14//2017__

SCENE #s	DESCRIPTION ✔ INT.☐ EXT. Dining room turned poker room	STORY DAY ☐ DAY ✔ NIGHT ☐ DAWN ☐ DUSK	#OF PAGES
1	"Setting the Stage" = 9pm		4/8
3	"Peter Probes" = 9:30pm		2 pages
5	"A Different Love" = 9:45pm		1 page
7	"A Change of Heart" = 10:30pm		4 & 6/8 pages
		TOTAL PAGES	8 & 2/8

NO.	CAST	ATMOSPHERE	PROPS / SET DRESSING
	Peter (Alex Hutcherson)	View in Drive.	Framed picture of Ashley (On set)
	Sidney (Michael Miller)		**Mark** Poker chips
	Brianna (Jennifer Seward)		Playing cards Corner table
			Shannon Sofa table

WARDROBE		CAMERA	Trim Outlet plates
Peter: Solid muted color tee with flannel, faded jeans			Curtain rod Curtains
Sidney: Casual dress shirt w/ sweater vest (fall palette), dark jeans/slacks		View in Drive. Nick is bringing to set up(Price will bring blue duffle bag items.)	2 wooden chairs Table
Brianna: Casual shirt, cheery, nice jeans.			**Jacque** Shelf with knick knacks Glasses

MAKEUP / HAIR		DIT EQUIPMENT	
Makeup Kit (Jennifer) Make-up "Artist" (Jacque)		View in Drive. Grab spare 32 GB SD Card for audio (Mark)	

Special Notes	ELECTRIC / GRIP / CRANES	SOUND / MUSIC	
- Shannon set dress at Mazzio's @ 6 - Extra white table (Price) - 4x4 Diffuser gel (Price/Nick?)	View in Drive.	View in Drive. Zach has equipment.	

Figures 10.5 and 10.6 (Continued)

		Production Title: *Heads Up - SHOT LIST*				***Sheet #*** *1 of 2*		
		Director: *von Schlemmer*				***Date:*** *2/14/2017*		
		Locations: *Mazzio's*				***Scenes #*** *1-3-5-7*		

Scene #	Shot #	subjects	Shot Size	Movement	Lens	Notes	Takes	Sound
1	A	3-SHOT	Long Shot/MLS	Dolly In		Master Shot - of scene 1 (shoot entire action/dialog)		
1	B	Brianna	CU/MS	Dolly Out		CU on Queen of Hearts, TILT UP/PULL OUT to Brianna (first line)		
1	C/D	Sidney	MS	TILT Down		MS on Sidney, stepping into shot, putting out hand, TILT as he sits, smiles, looks at chips, looks dopey		
1	E/F	Peter	MS/MCU	Dolly In		MS on Peter, shakes hands, TILT as he sits, looks wary, looks at chips		
1	pickups		CU	PAN		CU on chip stacks, PAN from one to other, Bri shuffling cards, dealing cards		
3	A	3-SHOT	MLS	Tracking Right		Master Shot - of scene 3 (shoot entire action/dialog), TRACKING slight right		
3	B	Sidney	MCU			MCU on Sidney as he wins a pot (frame for photo behind him maybe?)		
3	BB	Sidney& Photo	MS or CU			Peter POV shot of photo or Sidney and photo, or PAN over to photo		
3	C	Peter	MCU	Dolly In?		MCU Peter for several lines, push in maybe on "interesting" (2nd line)		
3	D	Peter	CU			Closer on Peter for reaction to Sidney's lines, Peter noticing photo behindSid		
3	E	Brianna	MCU	TILT Down		MCU on Brianna, suspicious look, TILT Down to shuffling cards and dealing		
3	F	Brianna	CU	-		Brianna smiles at Sidney, turns looking suspicious at Peter		
3	G	Brianna/Peter	MLS			MLS 2-shot of Brianna and Peter as she stomps on his toe/kicks him under table		
3	H	Peter	CU			Peter slamming cards on table as he folds		
3	pickups		CU			Chips on table, new stacks favoring Sidney 800/400; CU of Sidney's full house hand and him sweeping chips; Ashley photo CUs		
5	A	3-SHOT	MLS	3/4 Push in/Track Right		Master Shot of scene 5, slight PUSH IN and TRACK RIGHT to foreground Sidney		
5	B	Brianna	MCU	TRACK RIGHT		TRACK RIGHT as Brianna refers to hubby watching TV elsewhere		
5	C	Sidney	MCU	TRACK RIGHT		TRACK RIGHT from Peter's POV as he gets distracted by photo behind Sidney		
5	D	Sidney	MCU	DOLLY IN		PUSH IN on Sidney's big "this love is different" line		
5	E	Peter	MCU			Peter (matches with end of scene 4 shot maybe?) talking to Sid then to Brianna		
5	F	Peter	CU			Peter CU reacting to photo as much as Sidney's lines, ends with Peter looking down to his cards		
5	G	Peter	XCU			Peter's hands CU as he tosses cards in to the middle, cards leave frame to cut to next scene		

Figure 10.7   This has the shot list for scenes 1, 3, 5, and 7. Even though the breakdown sheet has a timeline for each scene, the shot list goes into a lot of detail about each shot, the lines from the script, the character and camera movements, and how to frame the shot.

Production Title: *Heads Up - SHOT LIST*

Director: *von Schlemmer*

Locations: *Mazzio's*

Sheet # *1 of 2*

Date: *2/14/2017*

Scenes # *1-3-5-7*

Scene #	Shot #	subjects	Shot Size	Movement	Lens	Notes	Takes	Sound
5	pickups		CU			Chips on table, new stacks favoring Sidney 900/300; Sidney playing with chips while he muses		
7-1	A	3-SHOT	MLS			Master Shot of Scene 7 up through "something significant" line		
7-1	B	Brianna/Peter	MLS			Mini-master of Brianna and Peter, pickup on Sidney's "Ash" line and take through "I told you so look"		
7-1	C	Brianna	MS			Shufflinbg cards, giving looks to Sid and Peter, run through Peter's Line "no, it doesn't make sense"		
7-1	D	Brianna	CU			Brianna smiles warmly at Sid after "because she is happy" line		
7-1	E	Sidney	MS/CU	Dolly In		MS on Sidney for first couple shots, then push in as he's "thinking about Ashley", in for CU by "I mean I think . . . "		
7-1	F	Sidney	MS			Reset to MS for Betting shots of Sidney		
7-1	G	Peter	MS/CU	Dolly In		MS on Peter for his first couple shots, then move in for "Focus on Poker, Sid" line, and CU on him for "How, how is it different" and reactions		
7-1	H	Peter	MCU			Backlooser on Peter for back to poker shots		
7-1	Pickups		CU			Card dropping on table as Sid folds; Sid neatening his stack PAN to Peter's chips; Ashley photo POV; Brianna trying to Kick peter		
7-2	A	3-SHOT	MLS			Master part 2: Start on pg 13 - betting . . . throught o the end		
7-2	B	Sid/Bri	MLS			Toward end, Bri and Sid on her congratulating him		
7-2	C	Brianna/Peter	MLS	TILT DOWN		Toward end, Bri & Peter Standing up & walking off, possible TILT DOWN to K&Q on table for final shot		
7-2	D	Brianna	CU			Brianna reacts to Peter looking troubled . . . few other reactions to cards . . . then concerned at Peter's all in, then skeptical of Peter		
7-2	E	Sidney	MCU			Sidney MCU pondering his cards, then pushes chips all in, then shows his cards and looks to Peter		
7-2	F	Sidney	CU			Sidney CU - Various reactions ending with Peter mucking and Joyful win smile		
7-2	G	Peter	CU			CU on Peter as he checks his cards, looks at pot, glancing to Sidney, photo and away, then to Brianna, finall the All in Call		
7-2	H	Peter	MS			Peter MS calls all in and pushes chips in . . . mucks his cards . . . ending.		
7-2	PU1		XCU			Peter's cards XCU to see two black Queens		
7-2	PU2	table	CU			CU of cards on table - 4 community cards: Ad Ks, 8h 5c . . . Then CU as 2d is added . . . hold on community cards		
7-2	PU3	Sidney	CU			Sidney pushes all his chips in		
7-2	PU4	table	CU			XCU of Sidney's cards King and Queen of hearts - first shown, then for end shot		

Figure 10.7 (Continued)

Scene by Scene Notes:

<u>Scene 1:</u>
Chips Position A –Chips stacks should be: Peter 700, Sid 500 (1200 in chips in play total)
      Chip values: White = 1, Red = 5, blue = 10, green = 25
Pick up shots:
          1. PAN of chips.
          2. Hands stacking chips
          3. Bri shuffling cards and dealing.

<u>Scene 3:</u>
Chip Position B: Peter 400, Sid 800 (approximately)
Work in Ashley Photo shots from Peter's POV

<u>Scene 5:</u>
Chip Position C: Peter 300, Side 900 (approximately)
More Ashley photo shots (only need to shoot once)

<u>Scene 7:</u>
Chip Position D: Peter 500, Sid 700
7-1 = 11, 12, 13.5 for first half of scene - shoot this out with MS and CU, then move back for 7-2
PU shots are cards or hands XCU

Figure 10.8 This shows the Director's notes as we were shooting. These were taken by the script supervisor while we were on set shooting. Many of the notes were dictated by the Director as we went.

Chapter 10: Narrative Films and Series Main Points

- Producing a narrative film or series follows the process laid out in the book: pre-production, production, post. But films need to be meticulously planned out because they're often shot out of order.
- In preproduction, having a detailed daily schedule, called a "breakdown sheet," is important. So is having a detailed shot list.
- During production, it's important to shoot everything in a way that conveys the emotions and messages the story needs. Dialogue needs to be clean and lighting needs to be motivated by the scene.
- During production, it's also important to maintain continuity and do things in a way that allows the audience to believe the events truly happened. Superman doesn't exist. But we watch the movies because we want to believe it's possible.
- For films and series, postproduction is often way more involved than other single-camera modes of production. Color grading and audio sweetening are often done by people who are specialists. So are graphics and effects.
- It's important to screen your projects before sending them off to festivals or for distribution. Test audiences will tell you if there are continuity errors, or if the storyline is confusing. It can be difficult to hear, but re-shooting or re-editing something is worthwhile – you've spent so much time on the film already, take the time to make sure it works.

11 Commercials

Some commercials are shot more like short films, but many are done quickly and with an abbreviated process. Commercials often steal some things from live studio techniques, like the script format and shooting styles. And post is often done on a shorter timeline so the commercial can be done in time to get it on air in a timely manner. The process can vary widely based on who is producing it. Many local commercials are/were produced by local TV stations who worked primarily in live studio TV. And national commercials often hire film Directors to actually come in and shoot them, so those typically follow the process outlined in Chapter 10. In this chapter, I'll try to cover all the different things you might see when working on commercials, but to be honest, there's a wide range of possibilities.

Preproduction

Unlike a film project, most of the time you're producing a commercial, you're doing it for someone else. That client has a specific goal in mind, but they may not have an idea of how to accomplish that goal. Your job as a commercial producer is to figure out how

DOI: 10.4324/9781003010357-15

to reach the audience your client wants to target, and then sell them on the product or idea. Sometimes, the commercials that really get your attention aren't actually the most effective ones. If the ultimate goal is to sell an audience on a product or idea, then that's the measure of success (and not producing something that looks cool, even though the audience may not remember the company name or product). Of course, the best commercials leave a lasting impression and also sell the audience.

Funding

Commercials almost always begin with the goal in mind and go from there. Whether you're a freelance producer, working for an advertising agency, or a student working on a video for a university program's website, the good news is that you don't have to do the fundraising yourself. Your client should cover your expenses for equipment, locations, actors, crew, and catering. Commercials rarely cost as much to produce as a narrative film project, but they can be expensive if you're using film-quality gear and recognizable actors. Figuring out a budget with your client is actually an important conversation to have at the start of the process so you know what constraints you're operating under when you start to plan out your project. I've produced commercials for almost nothing, and I've also seen ad campaigns that cost major companies several million dollars.

Audience Research

Once you know your budget, you need to figure out how to best reach your audience. Doing research is an important part of the process, although your client might have actually hired a marketing firm to do that part for you. If not, you should discuss the target audience with your client. Perhaps they're asking you to market a new line of tennis shoes to teenagers. The shoes themselves should appeal to teenagers, but the commercials need to as well. You might think you know what will catch a teenager's attention, but actually talking to some or sending out a survey might surprise you with some of the findings. Perhaps when you were a teen, neon laces were cool (they were!). But now, maybe not so much. Or maybe they're back in style! I honestly can't keep up. Which is why it's important to do some research. Look at other advertisements for shoes and see what they're doing to draw a teenage audience. Or ask a focus group of teenagers what catches their attention when they see ads with shoes in them. That helps you craft the message and use visuals that will catch their attention and connect with them.

Storyboards

For commercial projects, the storyboards need to come immediately after the funding conversation and audience research. Allowing your client to visualize the final product is essential. Otherwise, you risk a final product that they're not happy with and you've already spent their money. These storyboards need to be neat, look good visually, and clearly convey what the commercial will look and sound like. They also shouldn't cost a lot of money to produce, the way previsualization for some film projects might. Using digital photos or rough computer graphics is probably fine. Hand drawing pictures should be avoided unless you're an artist or you hire one.

S1/S1   S1/S2   S1/S3

Silence Ch.1 (left) foot is bouncing   Intense staring   Intense staring

Figure 11.1 A rough computer graphic storyboard. It looks professional, doesn't take a lot of time to produce, and conveys the information to the client well.

Pitch

Before you do anything else after storyboarding, pitch the idea back to your client. A script is probably not necessary yet – you'll want the client to agree to the concept before you put any more work into it, and unless they're film people, they probably won't be able to visualize the project based on the script anyway. So, storyboarding is enough to get together for the pitch. During the pitch, talk through the concept with your client and help them visualize the flow of the shots. Unlike the shooting schedule storyboards in Chapter 1, the ones you present to the client should be simple and not contain information on equipment, props, or crew. The simple one-line explanation you see in Figure 11.1 is about all you need. Once your client is on board with the concept, then move on to the rest of the preproduction for the commercial.

Script

I've used two different types of scripts for commercials. A single-column script like the one in Figure 1.2 in Chapter 1 works well if the commercial is mostly visual. This way, you can use poetic language and focus a lot on the emotions the visuals need to convey. The script may or may not specify the lens choice and framing, but it will give the Director the idea behind the commercial. Since film crews are used to working from single-column scripts, this is also the kind I would use if I know I'm going to be hiring a crew that usually works on films.

A two-column script like the one in Figure 1.3 is a lot more technical. It gives the crew pretty specific instructions, but not in a way that is overly descriptive, or the script would be too long and more difficult to read. I use a two-column script for commercials where the location and background are simpler. I also use it when the timing of the visuals or words is really important because the timing column allows me to line visuals up to words pretty precisely. Since TV stations are used to working from two-column scripts, I also use this kind when working with people who usually work in live television. And if it doesn't matter what kind of script I use, I typically use a two-column script just because I prefer to know exactly how the timing of the script should flow.

There are many ways to structure a commercial, but you should always begin with something that gets the audience's attention. Especially in today's world of streaming and YouTube, viewers aren't willing to sit through a commercial that doesn't grab their attention. They will skip through it or tune it out. Think about your favorite commercial and how it got your attention. Or watch the next Super Bowl, where companies spend millions of dollars to air their commercials. All of them are designed to grab attention immediately. This can be something funny, something dramatic, something weird, or someone famous telling them to listen.

After getting their attention, good commercials create an interest in the product or company, then persuade the viewer that they have a need that the product would satisfy. Or perhaps the commercial is simply a brand-enhancing pitch. For example, well-known companies don't necessarily need to make the audience aware of their products, but they might want to be associated with something. A soft drink might produce a commercial where people are on the beach, having fun, and drinking the soda to quench their thirst. In this way, a viewer might be heading to work and thinking, "man, I wish I was on the beach right now. Maybe I'll grab a soda."

Actors

Depending on the goals of your commercial, you should be very intentional with your selection of talent. If you're trying to appeal to the "average person," then you should cast someone who looks similar to your audience. If you're trying to sell someone the idea that their life could be better if they bought this product, you might use a more recognizable actor or someone who looks like the person the target audience wants to become. There are a few important concepts here.

When a commercial uses an "average person" to sell their idea or product, we call this a "testimonial." The goal here is to make the viewer believe that this person is like them, actually uses the product, and believes it works for them. For example, if I were cast in a commercial where I discussed how much I like chocolate chip cookies, it would be a testimonial. I'm sure I could sell the product because I really do like chocolate chip cookies, but it only works if people think, "hey, if that random person likes them, I might too."

If I cast a celebrity or recognizable person in the ad, it would be an "endorsement." With endorsements, people look up to their favorite singer, the local news anchor, or another celebrity. If those people use the product, it must be good, right? Perhaps my favorite example of this is the Taylor Swift ad where she's working out on a treadmill and using Apple Music. The implied message here is that Taylor uses Apple Music, so if you're a fan of hers, you might like it too.

Average people or celebrities can become a "spokesperson" for the company or product as well. This happens across a series of commercials where we see the same person endorsing it, for example, "Jake" from State Farm or "Flo" from Progressive. Neither "Jake" nor "Flo" was famous before becoming the spokesperson, but after being in a series of commercials, they became household names. There are perhaps variations on the testimonial, the endorsement, or the spokesperson, but for the most part, when you cast someone in a commercial, it needs to be intentional and connect with the audience.

Locations

Some commercials are shot in a studio or a set that is constructed just for the commercial. If the location doesn't matter too much, this can make securing a location faster and easier. Unlike my advice about film locations, I've mostly used locations that were simply convenient when I shot commercials. If the commercial needs to be set in an office or a kitchen, then finding one that is nearby and available is fine. I did an advertisement for a local animal rescue foundation (search "Have a Heart Save a Life" on my YouTube channel) and needed a park setting to show someone walking two dogs down the street. The opening shot of the commercial is effective and grabs attention. But the two dogs are actually mine, the woman walking them is my wife, and the sidewalk is right outside my old office. It was easy to schedule everything. The sidewalk was a public space and didn't need any permits. And the location is just fine. I'm not trying to create a suspension of disbelief the way I need to in a film project. I'm just trying to quickly convey a simple idea: these dogs are happy now.

On the other hand, you may need a very specific location and it might take some work to make it happen. If you're shooting an advertisement that is set near the Golden Gate Bridge, then you need to get a permit, schedule a time when the lighting is what you want, transport your equipment and crew, and get the shot. However, if another bridge conveys the same idea in the commercial, you might consider using it instead. In a film project, it might be essential to convey that the story takes place in San Francisco, necessitating the Golden Gate Bridge as a backdrop. Commercials don't always have those needs because the ideas are conveyed so rapidly. And you don't necessarily need to connect shots and scenes together in a commercial, so locations are fleeting.

Virtual sets are also used in commercials, but typically bigger-budget ones. It takes time and expertise to do greenscreen or an entire virtual set with screens behind the actors, the way *The Mandalorian* was shot. If you're using virtual sets, it can definitely allow you to script out lots of exotic locations and still keep on schedule. But it comes with a price tag to do the greenscreen backdrops in post. The opposite of this is the TV studio with a black curtain or simply background. I've shot PSAs before where the background is just a color wash or black curtain. The lack of background gives more power to the words the talent is saying, and allows the viewer to focus entirely on the message without distraction. Unless you work at a TV station, a studio might actually be difficult to come by, but many cities have ones you can rent out. Or there might be a public access TV station that has a space.

Schedules

Scheduling a commercial project is usually a lot easier than scheduling an entire film. Shooting can usually be done in a few days or a week. For studio commercials, most of the shooting happens in one day because you don't have to transport people and gear to multiple locations. Even when you're on location, if only one background is needed, the shooting can often happen all in the same day. As a cliché, a local car lot commercial probably doesn't need anything more than a few hours: the salesman talking about all the great cars on the lot, giving the tagline, and then collecting b-roll of all the cars he just talked about. On the other end of the spectrum, a national car ad for a new model might take weeks to shoot: a series of helicopter shots of the car driving through the mountains and deserts, a shot of the hero driver pulling up to the restaurant in his tuxedo, a shot of the crowd reaction as he tosses the keys to the valet. Then b-roll of the factory or whatever else needs to go in the commercial. You might have multiple locations and actors to schedule out ahead of time. This is still easier than a film project, but commercials can become complex, especially when they need to look like a film with action, heroes, and epic shots.

Production

Like film projects, once everything is planned out, production should be simply a matter of executing the plan. Usually, though, commercials have a smaller crew and don't have as many moving parts to keep track of. The producer is often the Director on the set. And the Cinematographer might be the Lighting Director. Even though there is often money to be made up front in commercials when a client or company hires you, you're still going to have to stay within budget and keep costs down – probably even more than when you shoot a film.

Cameras

I've mostly used camcorders and studio cameras for the commercials I've shot. It really comes down to the overall schedule and how important sound is to the project. Many higher-end camcorders have good audio components and some ENG (Electronic News Gathering) cameras have the ability to house a wireless mic receiver. On these cameras, sound is high-quality and synced immediately. This cuts down on the time spent in post. There are some major advantages to using camcorders for commercials.

Figure 11.2 We used a high-end camcorder for this commercial. It used high-quality lenses with a high dynamic range. Even though we had a boom operator, the audio was done single-system and fed directly into the audio inputs on the camera, so it synced as we were shooting.

Figure 11.3 A student of mine using a DSLR camera to shoot a commercial for the local distillery. The camera allows her to be nimble and get many different angles easily and quickly. The visual quality of these cameras is really good, but the audio is terrible. For this commercial, though, the voicework will be recorded separately and added in post.

On the other hand, DSLR cameras and cinema cameras can provide higher-quality visuals. When shooting a postcard-type commercial or promo video, where the location or amenities are the highlight, using a camera with higher-quality lenses, shallower depth of field, and greater dynamic range will provide the high-end visuals your client will want to show off for their potential customer. In these instances, the sound is often a voiceover or not as important as the visuals. It's okay if the narration is added in post, or if the location sound is not as clean as it could be otherwise. However, if you do choose to use a DSLR, expect to spend more time in post doing color grading and audio sweetening.

The middle option these days might be a lower-end cinema camera. Many of the pro-sumer range models have XLR inputs and allow for wireless mics or boom mics to feed directly into the camera. This will still allow for high dynamic range lenses to be used, but will also sync the audio during shooting to cut down on time spent in post. For example, Blackmagic Design's cinema cameras (like the one in Figure 10.2 in Chapter 10) have XLR inputs and places to mount wireless receivers. It seems designed to record single-system audio while producing the highest quality visuals. Here's a word of caution, though: I've had a lot of signal interference when shooting with wireless mics with these cameras. With boom mics, I've hardly had any issues. But with wireless, I've had both good luck and bad. Monitor the audio closely in the headphones during the shoot, regardless of what type of camera you're using. And always have a backup plan if you're going to do single-system audio with a cinema camera or DSLR.

Lighting

Typically, lighting for a commercial is high-key lighting with few shadows and softer, slower falloff. For the most part, we want the audience to see the talent and focus on what they're saying. The backgrounds should be well lit and not give an air of mystery, or the viewer will be distracted from the message. With only 30 seconds (or less these days!), a commercial has to focus on conveying its message immediately. Usually, this means I'm setting up 3-point lighting on my subject and washing the backgrounds with even lighting. In a studio, lighting is often set for this – a flood of light on the talent and the background. Many of the ads you find on television and online are lit high-key and convey a sense of humor, normalcy, hope, fun, or other upbeat tone. The lighting fits the message. But it's also much easier to light this way because the multitude of lighting instruments cuts down on the shadows, so exact placement is less important. Just set up your 3-point lighting, diffuse it, and then aim a bunch of lights at the background and diffuse them.

The exception here is if you're trying to tell a story and give your commercial a "film" look. For example, there's a Starbucks commercial titled "Every Table Has a Story" where the actors have shadows on their faces. The light is motivated by sunlight pouring in through a storefront window, or by the overhead lights during the evening shots. The point here isn't to convey mystery, but to convey realism. It's a contrast to the advertisements I'm talking about in the paragraph above. Instead of focusing on a message of hope, normalcy, humor, etc., this lighting tells the viewer to hold tight until the story unfolds itself. The message of perseverance and overcoming obstacles doesn't come until the end. The company logo is there in the background the entire time, subtly, and the commercial connects this hope to the coffee company. The realistic lighting and shadows are integral to this connection because it conveys the duality of the commercial – rejection and hope.

Sound

I talked a lot about sound acquisition on set above in my discussion about cameras. Here, I wanted to add how important music and sound effects can be to a commercial track. When you need to catch attention immediately, or set the mood, or convey a tone, music can be an extremely effective way to do that. Popular music that already exists in the world can bring attention the way a famous celebrity can. Ominous orchestral music can set the tone for a big reveal in the commercial. Whimsical music can help lighten the comedic tone. Music affects us at a subconscious level, so it can change the audience's mood immediately and without thinking about it.

Using popular music can be great. When I hear a song from my childhood, I immediately become nostalgic for those times. Hearing Guns N' Roses or U2 in the background automatically puts me in a better mood. At a conscious level, I assume those bands probably allowed for their music to be used, so the product must be trustworthy. Of course, this isn't always the case. In the case study at the end of this chapter, I wanted to use a popular song. Even though my client was the State of California, and the commercial was for a very worthy cause, the record label that owned the song wanted the same rate they would have charged anyone to use it. I didn't have the budget to purchase the rights to the song for the ad, so we used the track you hear on it instead. The music still fits, but I think the commercial would have been better if we had been able to secure the song we envisioned. More on that later.

Using popular music can also be a terrible idea. Commercials often have the budget to purchase song rights, but choose not to. This is because the song may already be connected to other ideas or products. If the Green Day song in the ad is the same one they played at my friend's funeral, that product association is now ruined for me. Instead of wanting to purchase the product, I'm going to avoid it. An example of this, for me at least, was the Sarah McLachlan ASPCA commercial where she sang, "Angel." The ad is extremely slow and depressing when considering that these dogs and cats are victims of abuse. After seeing that ad many times, I can't hear the song on the radio without being sad and wanting to change the station. The song did its job too well in the commercial, and now the association is lasting. This can be bad for the product or idea conveyed in the commercial. It can also have a negative impact on the artist's career if their song is hijacked and given a negative association.

There are a few other ways to get music beds for your commercials. You can hire a composer. Sometimes this is more expensive than other options, but it will give you a completely unique song to associate your product with. You can also layer your own loops together in GarageBand or Logic. These programs have instrumental loops that you can layer on top of each other to create your own unique compositions. I'm certainly no composer, but when I lay down a drum track with a specific beat, then find a guitar riff with the same beat and lay it on top, it starts to sound like something. Add some horns that are in the same key as the guitar, or piano, or whatever else you like, and you can create a layered song that can easily set the mood. I've found that the key here is playing around with it until I hear something that clicks with the tone I'm trying to set. Once you get the tone, you can adjust the timing. The guitar might start first, then the drums come in later, or vice-versa. Horns or piano might only happen for a few beats here and there. Do your best to line those things up with the natural transitions in the narrative voiceover or the visuals, and it can help you with the timing of your edits later.

The "old" way of doing music beds in commercials is still valid as well. When I first started producing commercials, TV and radio stations would actually license a music library that was exclusive to their region. The library of CDs would contain hundreds of different music beds. Some would be 30 seconds; some would be 60 or longer. There would be an entire CD of "happy" music, and another CD of "dramatic" music. There were many different songs for each tone because your visuals might require a specific tone or specific timing for the edits. Something with a faster beat might not work, but the same tone in a slightly slower beat might be perfect. These libraries are fairly expensive because they used to be sold exclusively to one station in a given market. That way, it was unlikely that viewers would hear the same song for two different commercials or on two different stations. It helped solidify the association between the product and the song. These libraries are still available, but they're much harder to find because of the loops option mentioned above and the next option: purchasing single music beds from an online library.

There are several online libraries of music beds out there. I used bensound.com for one of the promo videos I produced recently. In fact, I even paid the small fee for the song; I think it was about $5. I don't have exclusive rights to the song, so it can be used anytime by someone else. But because there are plenty of free songs on bensound.com, I'm fairly confident it won't be used that much. There are some great songs on the site. They vary in length, and aren't just 30 seconds or 60 seconds, because many promo videos and web videos are different lengths. The only reason 30 and 60 are "magic" numbers is because that's the length commercials need to be for broadcast stations and linear channels on cable. These stations only have 24 hours in a day and can't go 5 seconds over or the next program won't start on time. For online distribution and streaming, though, your commercial can be any length of time – although, I wouldn't go much beyond 30 seconds these days. The online viewer's attention span isn't that long.

Another word of caution here: when you use the free songs online, just remember that other students and people on very limited budgets are using the same songs. If you're hired to produce a commercial, it's worth searching for the perfect song – and one that won't be heard too often elsewhere – and paying a little bit of money for it. I've seen many student projects over the years that use the exact same song, and I can't help but associate it with the previous times I've heard it. On demo reels especially, if you're applying for a job and you're using the same soundtrack as another candidate for your demo reels, you'll probably both lose out on the job. It reads as a lack of creativity.

Directing

Directing a commercial can be a lot like directing a film, but it's much easier to shoot with the end in mind. Getting the right visuals is often easy enough – many of the commercials I've shot are nothing but b-roll underneath, a collage of visuals of the product or of the event. When directing these shots, because there isn't any sound to go with it, I can direct the talent and crew as we shoot. It's really easy to forget to slate your takes when shooting like this, but I would caution against it. Your editor will really appreciate it if you slate each take instead of continuously rolling. If you're going to be the editor, then do whatever works for you.

If you need the actor to say lines, then you should definitely slate each take and record high-quality audio. In one of the California EBT commercials I produced (one that ended up not airing because it didn't come out like I had hoped), we had our actress look into the camera and read lines as a direct address to the audience. We had to spend a lot more time setting up the lighting and audio for these shots than we did for the rest of the b-roll shots that are seen in the commercial over the VO (short for "voiceover"). And because of the hum of the refrigerators at the grocery store we shot at, the audio didn't turn out as well as I had hoped, and this commercial ended up being the weakest of the three that we produced. I was the Director for this shoot as well, and we did multiple takes. The actress memorized the script because we didn't have a portable teleprompter, and each take had small changes in the lines. Instead of trying for continuity, we wanted the actress to sound completely natural. So, as long as she got the main points across, I wanted her to simply talk to the camera. The result is far more natural than if I had tried to hold her to specific words. Unlike a film, I'm not shooting multiple angles of the direct address, so continuity didn't really matter. However, getting a good, solid take, all the way through mattered a lot. Sometimes you can lay b-roll over a cut in the narration, but you shouldn't assume that you can cut together voicework in a commercial and have it sound natural. If I'm directing, I just go for a solid take through the entire script.

I've also done promo videos and commercials where I shot them documentary style. This means conducting interviews or recording off-the-cuff testimonials first, then shooting the b-roll visuals that support what was said in those sound bites. In these cases, you'll use the storyboards to pitch back to your client, but the visuals might actually change in the final project. In this style of directing, I'm not doing multiple takes because I want honest answers and trustworthy deliveries. So here, I'm asking multiple questions, sometimes the same question in different ways, and I'm looking for very short sound bites – one or two sentences – that convey the exact thought that I'd script out for an actor anyway. Asking open-ended questions that are easy to answer quickly is the key. Don't say, "tell me about the last time you used this product," or you'll get a long, drawn-out answer. Say, "in one sentence, tell me what your favorite thing is about this product."

There's a concept from audio work that's relevant here: vox pop (vox populi, or "voice of the people"). A vox pop happens when you ask a series of people the exact same question and you get a series of sound bites that can be edited together to show that everyone feels the same way. If I asked a bunch of people what their favorite thing is about the product, I don't even have to have them repeat the question in their answer. The viewer will understand, and I can even use fragments of sentences to convey the idea. I'll get answers like, "it's easy to use," "it's affordable," "it does such a good job," etc. that can edit together and show the multiple benefits. Vox pop is an effective technique if your goal is to show that everyday people use the product and so should your audience.

Post

Editing a commercial or promo video is generally a straightforward process. Unlike a film, though, you probably won't follow the storyboards. If you're presenting a montage of visuals over a compelling audio track, they can often go in any order as long as the general flow is maintained. Timing the visuals is important, but either the music or the voicework will give you the rhythm to help you time out when to cut between shots. And especially if you shot single-system sound and used a Rec.709 color space when shooting, there won't be a lot of time spent syncing audio or color grading, although those things can sometimes be worth the time spent on them, even if your production schedule is fairly tight.

Workflow

Like a film, I start out by labeling my files with something descriptive. In this case, I may not have scene numbers and shot letters to assign, but calling the b-roll a name that matches up with the visual is important. And don't forget to start the file name with the name of the project. This makes it much easier to search for those shots later on if things get lost. For example, I might call a file "calebtcommercial_cardswipe_1" for take 1 of the shot where my talent was swiping the debit card in the California EBT commercial spot. In fact, this shot was used across all three of the commercials I produced, so it would have been impossible to name the file based on scene and shot. For audio files, the same thing goes: if you need to sync the files, name them the exact same thing as the corresponding video.

Once you sync the files, you might consider exporting the merged file as a distinct video file for use in future projects or related projects. As an example, I regularly produce highlight videos and promo videos for the Wakonse Conference on College Teaching. I've been able to reuse some shots across multiple videos, so after syncing audio for these shots, if I export them, I have the synced file later on. That way, I don't have to sync it again when I open up a new project. It's also worth mentioning here that there are programs like Adobe Bridge where you can tag video clips with keywords and search for them more easily in the future. This comes in handy if you're working at a production house or somewhere that b-roll shots might be used across multiple projects. In my Wakonse videos, I regularly show shots of sunsets. One year I shot video for the conference, I did a time lapse of the sun setting. Instead of shooting this shot and doing post work on it each year, I've occasionally reused the shot. I have about 100 different shots tagged with the keyword "sunset" just for this reason. And they wouldn't necessarily be limited to the Wakonse Conference if I had another project where it was an appropriate shot to use. A wedding video, for example, might need a transition shot where a sunset would be perfect.

Editing

After labeling the files, I import them into my NLE and go about editing. Unless the commercial tells a story like a film, I usually lay down the audio track first. I often start with the music bed and then lay down the sound bites. If you do the music first, you can develop a rhythm to your cuts a lot faster and pace out the spacing between the sound bites or the lines of narration a lot easier. If the narration is one continuous track, you might lay it down first and then put the music underneath it. Either way, you'll want some space before any lines are spoken to let the music establish the mood. When you do it this way, you want the music to be normalized to 0 decibels when it first comes in, but then envelope it down underneath the voicework. In fact, my music beds are often peaking around –50dB when they're under the narration because I want the words to be completely understandable and I don't want the music to be a distraction. At the end of the commercial or during a long space in the sound bites, I might envelope the music back up to leave the viewer with something that will stick in their heads longer than the words. To envelope the audio track, you need to set keyframes in the audio clip where you want the volume adjustments to occur. You'll need one keyframe for the beginning of the fade, and another keyframe at the end of the fade. Keep the first keyframe at 0 dB, but lower the second one down to –50dB or wherever you think the mix between the music and voicework sounds good. At the end of the commercial, place two more keyframes and raise the second one back up to 0 to have the music envelope back up.

Once the audio track is laid down, you'll place the visuals and graphics, then add transitions. Graphics can be any number of things, but you'll definitely want to have text that displays the call to action – the name of the product, the website to go to for more information, the company's tagline, and whatever other information the consumer might need to act on the message in the commercial. Sometimes those graphics are done by a digital artist in a separate software program, or sometimes you'll have to create the graphics. I'm not much of an artist (remember my stick figure storyboards?), so anything beyond basic fonts or shapes and I have to go hire someone. As with music, it's worth doing this instead of using a template because you want the graphic elements to be unique to your commercial or the product. When I do commercials and promos, I'm often lucky enough that my client already has the logos I need to use in the project.

For transitions, you'll mostly use cuts, but you might decide for something a little more stylistic. Some commercials use wipes or dip-to-colors, something that makes the viewer take notice because they're not used to seeing it. If you can develop a unique style in the editing, graphics, or transitions that viewers can associate with the company or product, it makes future commercials easier to make and more effective because the viewer will remember. If you look at the three California EBT Card commercials on my YouTube channel, you'll see that I was not consistent across them with the graphics or transitions. All three have a different feel, and that's most likely why my client decided that only one of them would air. Quite frankly, if I could go back and redo them, I'd make them look and sound even more similar.

Screening

After you've edited the commercial, you'll want to screen it. Much like a film project, you'll want to get ideas from a test audience on what works and what doesn't. Or, given a timeline that doesn't allow for this, you'll be screening it with your client to get their feedback. If you followed the ideas laid out in your pitch, this shouldn't be a problem – your client should know what to expect. I would certainly talk to them about finding a test audience, though, to see how actual viewers will interpret the message and the appeal you're using to sell them on the idea or the product. If there are things that need fixing, it's much better to do it before paying for distribution. And in my experience, it usually just means going back to the project in your NLE and making a few tweaks. It's rare in a 30- or 60-second commercial to need re-shoots.

Case Study: California EBT

On my YouTube channel (@steveprice1599), you'll find the "EBT Then and Now" commercial. You can find it here as well: https://youtu.be/oAmpt7Icigw. Ignore the credits at the end. I'll walk you through the project from pre through post here and talk candidly about what went well and what I learned from doing it. I've done many commercials and promo videos since this one, but I learned so much from this one that I wanted to use it as my case study – even though it's about 20 years old at this point.

To begin with, I produced this commercial for the State of California while I was an MA student at San Francisco State University. We had a team of people working on the project, and I was the producer and Director. I oversaw the team from preproduction through the pitch, shooting, editing, and the final screening. The first step was hearing from our client about what their needs were. At the time, California was launching a new EBT card that would replace physical food stamps and benefits checks. The card was called the "Golden State Advantage." Because people using the services didn't need to be convinced, our client's goal was to help the transition go as smoothly as possible.

From there, our marketing team did an audience research analysis. They surveyed a sample of people who used benefits programs in California and collected data that would help us shape the messages of our commercials. We found that consumers were nervous about the change and were afraid that it would make things more complicated for them. So, our message became, "Golden State Advantage. Benefits Made Easy." Once we had the tagline and the audience analysis, we began to storyboard. We decided on three different TV commercials and one radio ad. The first commercial was a direct address to the viewer. We decided that a user testimonial would be the most effective way to gain the trust of the audience and convince them that this change was for the better. The second commercial had a series of graphics to describe the benefits of the change from physical coupons and checks to a debit card. It contained a lot of nuts and bolts about the card. We decided this was the best way to teach users how to use the card. The final commercial was more of an emotional appeal. It put images of the "old" system intercut with images of the new card and how it was an improvement. We honestly thought this commercial would be the weakest of the three, and we thought the testimonial would be the most effective.

Once we had storyboards, we pitched the ideas back to our client. They agreed with us on the three concepts and gave us the greenlight to move forward. They had a few minor changes, especially with the tagline. I believe our first one was something like "Making Your Life Easier," and they pointed out that this was probably an overreach for what the card might do. So, we settled on "Benefits Made Easy" and went to work. We wrote the four scripts, recruited talent, secured locations, and rented equipment based on our shooting schedule.

Our talent recruitment was an interesting process. The internet was in its infancy, but there were already a few websites where creatives were connecting with other people interested in working with them. We could have taken the easy route and cast ourselves in the commercial, but we wanted to aim as high as we could. We went online and screened a number of actresses until we found one we liked for the part. Storm Cattoche was an actress and luckily also a flight attendant. She flew up from LA for each of our shoots, so we scheduled everything around her availability. She performed the direct address in the first commercial, did voicework for narration in another commercial, and acted in a bunch of the b-roll we used across the entire set of ads. Everyone else in the ads was recruited out of convenience. Since no one else had lines, we were okay working with non-professionals for those roles.

Once we had Storm's availability, we needed locations. We reached out to several grocery stores to do the direct address ad. We wanted the backdrop to be somewhere natural and relatable. An apartment wouldn't do, because it didn't have a lot to do with the changing EBT Card system. Rainbow Grocery, a local store in the Mission District, agreed to let us use their store after hours when there wouldn't be any customers and we could better control the setting. This meant that most of our shots were done between 10pm and about 2am. We rented our equipment, but we also used my personal Canon XL1 camcorder as the main camera. At this point, I was already doing other freelance work and had purchased a professional broadcast-quality camera. It's the one you see in Figure 11.2.

We also recorded a series of other shots. One was at a CalWorks office, so our client helped us secure that one. Another was at an ATM on campus, so we contacted the campus authorities and the bank that ran the ATM and got their permissions. All the other scenes were shot in a studio. But the big shoot was at Rainbow Grocery. We put together a shot list for that night and headed out. When we got there, we started unpacking. As the Director, I didn't set anything up myself. Instead, I trusted my crew to get things done and I simply told everyone which shot we were doing. While they set up lights, audio, and camera, I went through the shot list with my talent.

The first issue came up when we realized that the rental house only gave us one power cord for six lights. To this day, I use this as an example in my teaching. Always check

Figure 11.4 Shooting the ATM was relatively simple since there wasn't any dialogue. We did use the lights to brighten up our talent, even though we were outdoors on a fairly sunny day.

your equipment before you walk out. Since it was 10pm, the rental house was closed. There was nothing we could do. And since a single hard light would have cast too many shadows, I think we decided not to use it at all (although it's possible we diffused it heavily and used it to just brighten up the scene a bit). Needless to say, the lighting isn't great in the commercial we did, titled "EBT Coming Soon," where Storm directly addresses the viewer. The shadows are harsh and distracting. The background is bright and distracting. She's not exactly silhouetted, but the overhead lights from the store ceiling aren't what I would have used intentionally. We also wanted the address to seem natural, so we avoided using a lavalier mic that would be seen in the shot. The boom mic worked well, except when the refrigeration units in the store kicked on. We were able to unplug some of them, and that helped. But ultimately, we had a lot of work to do in audio sweetening to get viable dialogue.

Regardless, we shot the b-roll of Storm and her "daughter" shopping, the shot of her swiping the card, and the shot of them leaving the store that were used across the three ads. Shooting the ATM shot, the waiting line, and the phone call to customer support took way less time because there weren't any lines to be spoken. In all, the grocery store shoot took several hours for all the shots. The ATM took maybe an hour, including setup time and getting different angles and takes. The waiting line at the Self Sufficiency Center took a while because we had to drive over an hour to get there. Once we were there, it probably took about 2 hours for the two shots, just because we needed the reverse shot for one of the ads. Lighting is what took the longest during setup. During all of these shots, I could simply yell out directions because we weren't collecting audio on any of these sets.

In post, I spent a lot of time. First, I edited the "Coming Soon" ad with the direct address. That was the one we spent most of our time on during preproduction and production. We just knew it would be the best one. Editing was easy. I just followed the script and put the best takes of each shot in the order they were needed. We had the b-roll to cover over the specific things Storm talked about in her direct address and I used cuts to keep the viewer's attention on what was being said. The thing I spent the most time and effort on was the tagline at the end, but since it ended up being the tagline for the other two commercials, it was worth it. The problem was, though, that the visuals weren't good enough to carry the ad. The idea was great. The research was solid. The message was very clear. But the ad didn't really catch anyone's attention.

The second ad, "EBT It's Easy," was easy enough to create. We just laid down the music, recorded the narration with another actress, and put in our b-roll shots to match the copy she's reading. It's a very informative commercial, but it also didn't really do anything to catch the viewer's attention. I tried to use eye-catching words in graphics to reinforce the main ideas – "Simple," "Secure," and "Support" – but there's just too much information in this one, and I don't think it's as effective as either of the other two ads because of it.

The third one, "Then and Now," changed dramatically in post. Our original plan was to show an "old" way, then cut to a shot of the new, better way. Then back to the old way. Then the new way, etc. But when I did that, the ad was a bit underwhelming. We certainly didn't think this was our best ad of the three, but the shots were easy enough to get while we were shooting everything else, and we simply recorded the voicework for this when we recorded it for the second ad. Once someone had the idea to actually put the shots next to each other on the same screen, everything clicked and this ad really came together. Putting the "old" shot in black and white helped emphasize our point in a shortcut. (Remember how color information can hit at an emotional level? Black and white footage conveys "old" and "outdated.") The music helps carry the ad along – it was from a music library and I've heard it in other advertisements since this one – and the narration is solid and conveys easy-to-understand concepts about security, simplicity, and support. By asking questions and by creating compelling visuals, we catch the viewer's attention. We create a need and satisfy that need. We call to action – contact your public assistance office – both in the voiceover and in the graphics. We didn't think this was going to be the strongest of the three ads, but it's pretty clear to see why our client chose this one to air all over the state instead of the other two.

After screening all three ads to our client, they chose the most effective one. The radio ad also aired, and it went through some dramatic changes as well. Most notably, the radio ad was supposed to have bus sound effects, as if the two women were waiting at the bus stop. But the sound effects were distracting and unnecessary, so the very simple dialogue in the ad is what we decided would be most effective.

Chapter 11: Commercials Main Points

- Commercials and promo videos almost always start with a client. Because of this, the process is slightly different and requires research before coming up with the rest of your plan.
- Storyboards for commercials need to be done well so the client can visualize what the spot will look like. Once they're on board with the idea, message, and concept, then you can move on with the rest of the preproduction planning.

- During production, shooting a commercial might feel like shooting a film. Or it might feel more like a news package or a documentary. As a Director, you need to know when to coach your actors to deliver lines, and when to coach them to answer questions honestly and sincerely. Always focus on the message and tone you're trying to convey.
- You can never have enough b-roll/coverage for a commercial. Get multiple shots of the product from lots of different angles. It won't take that much longer, and your editor will thank you.
- In post, spend some time getting the music right. It should immediately convey the intended tone and emotion, and it shouldn't be something that will become associated with another product, company, or emotion. It's worth paying money or composing an original song for the music bed.
- The same thing goes for graphics and transitions. It's worth hiring someone to do the graphics for you if you're not up for it. Or get premade graphics that your client already uses in other settings. Make sure the style isn't something the audience will associate with a different product or idea.

12 Music Videos

Music videos are a lot of fun to produce. Along with films, music videos are where you can really let your creativity shine. Looking back at some of the most memorable music videos, all of them have some things in common. Many of them tell a story or have a message or idea they're conveying. Most of them have strong visuals and are very cinematic. And all of them highlight the artist. The main goal of any music video is to promote the song and the artist. When MTV and VH1 still played music videos, the job of the video was to get people interested in the song and the artist so they would go buy the album (thus, making money for the record label and the musician). These days, most music videos are watched on YouTube, but the goal is still the same: to promote the song and the artist so you want to go to Spotify, Apple Music, or wherever you stream your tunes and listen to that specific song.

Preproduction

Preproduction for music videos is a bit of a cross between planning for films and planning for commercials. They're visually more like short films, but since you're working for the musician or record label, the process is a bit more like producing a commercial.

DOI: 10.4324/9781003010357-16

You'll want to begin by meeting with your client and discussing what they want to see and what they would like to accomplish with the video. You'll also want to discuss their budget, locations, and any actors or extras you'll need up front.

Funding

I've worked on many music videos where the budget was non-existent. To be fair, I've only ever worked directly with the artist, and not with a record label. But my point is this: it's easy to lose money making a music video if you don't discuss everything up front with your band or artist. I would highly recommend discussing who will pay for equipment rental, crew rates, catering, location fees, actor rates, etc. ahead of time and writing out an estimated budget for everything. Ideally, you'll be able to keep everything to a workable budget. For many of your crew, they might do it just for the experience and to have something cool in their portfolio. You should look for people who might be Grips or production assistants on film sets who are looking to get some experience as a Cinematographer or First Assistant Camera (AC). For actors and actresses, it can also be a way for them to get some experience and get work for their demo reels. A-list actors don't often do music videos, but you can certainly get professionals who are doing work as extras and who want to be the next star. And the great news for equipment is that music videos are being shot with all kinds of cameras these days. DSLR shooting is very common, as is lighting with natural light, LEDs, flashlights, and whatever else you can get your hands on. Because it doesn't have to have a realistic "look," you can get artistic and creative. And since location sound isn't an issue, you won't even need to worry about audio gear and syncing in post if you use a DSLR or cinema camera.

Treatment

The main goal of writing a treatment for the music video is to get all your thoughts down on paper so everyone is on the same page. This will help tremendously before you even do your storyboards or flesh out your visuals. You'll want to know who the intended audience for the video is and what the concept will be.

Your audience will be the people your client wants to reach with the video. They probably already know who listens to their music and whether the song you're making the video for will reach that audience or if they're trying to broaden their appeal. Figure out what you know about that audience first. What kinds of TV shows are popular with that demographic? What other bands do they listen to? What do they watch on TikTok or what kinds of visuals grab their eye? Perhaps your video needs to have a plotline – if the band appeals to people my age, then using visuals and ideas from '80s music videos like Michael Jackson's "Thriller" would be a great idea. If the audience is much younger, then they won't likely sit through an almost 15-minute-long short film, even if Vincent Price lends his voice to it.

Once you know who your audience is, you'll be able to develop a concept that will reach them. When I say a "concept," I mean how will you put together visuals that keep the audience hooked on the video, but also focused on the music.

A music video that just shows the band playing would be pretty boring after a while. You absolutely want artist shots in the video – it's to promote them – and you'll want to mix it up a bit as well. Good videos either insert the artist into some sort of storyline, or they show the artist in a variety of settings playing the song. Perhaps it's a live venue, or perhaps it's a studio recording. Maybe you insert the band playing in the different locations you see in the rest of the video. It's difficult to have an entire video where all you see is the band playing, though, even if you do it with a variety of backdrops. There are certainly many music videos like this out there, but they're not very creative, and I doubt if you remember them once the song loses its popularity.

Instead, I coach my students to produce music videos that either tell a story, or have parallel imagery to the lyrics in a way that keeps the viewer watching and interested in seeing what will come next. As an example, OK Go's "Here It Goes Again" video shows the band the entire time. It's an in-one where the band does a choreographed dance on a series of treadmills. It's very entertaining and the viewer watches just to see the stunts the band continues to pull off. But after a while, the video loses its novelty and the viewer becomes bored. Contrast that with the same band's video for "This Too Shall Pass," and you'll see an in-one that takes you through an entire Rube Goldberg machine (think of a series of dominos set up and being knocked over, but with things like bowling balls and television sets getting smashed). Their second video does a lot more to keep the viewer interested, even though it doesn't tell a story. The band is inserted into the video in a way that promotes them, but it also adds visual interest for the viewer.

Not every video needs to be that elaborate, but my point is that you'll want some imagery or a traditional film storyline to keep the viewer's attention. It's an old example at this point, but if you google "No More Victims Music Video" (https://www.youtube.com/watch?v=O_nkgQUovIo), you'll be taken to a music video I produced for the Missouri Department of Corrections. The artist, Johnny Williams, was actually in prison at the time, and the video was done to promote his song, which was being used as the theme song for a program called "Restorative Justice." You'll see parallel imagery in the video, but not an actual storyline. You get elements of one: the perpetrator being arrested, the victim's mother mourning, the reconciliation panel, but you don't get enough points to connect all the dots necessarily. And you'll see the artist in a variety of shots inserted throughout the video: walking through the prison, singing in a dark room with a spotlight on his head, singing with other offenders in the room as his backup. These shots are as important as the imagery shots, and both things work together. The treatment is where you lay out the artist shots and locations, and where you piece together the other shots that make up the entire video. The treatment should be a paragraph or two that details the types of shots you'll see in the video, as well as the general flow. In editing, you won't necessarily be locked into any of it, but it will give your artist a good idea of what the video will convey, both emotionally and cognitively.

Pitch

Before you create storyboards, you'll want to pitch your treatment back to the artist or client and make sure they're on board with the video. There's a music video by The Fray that I like to show in class because it's a good example of when the record company wanted one thing and the band wanted something else. In the first video for their song "How to Save a Life," the storyline shots show a young couple running through the woods, as if they've snuck out of the house to go make out in the forest. The story is intercut with shots of the band in a house with a weird poster of trees all lit up behind them. The video is perfectly fine. There's great cinematography and lighting; some slow-motion shots add some cool effects; and it shows off the band in a cool way. After this video came out, though, the band wasn't really happy with it. They decided to re-shoot and the second "official" video doesn't have any kind of storyline, but it visually highlights young people who are struggling with various things in life. The result is a very powerful message about how to help peers and young people who are experiencing loss, bullying, depression, and other things that lead to those struggles. The song lyrics are about how to help people, and this video does so much more to promote the band and give the song meaning in a way that makes you want to hear it again and again.

When you pitch your treatment, be sure that you get the artist's buy-in. Making a music video is a very cooperative process. When you pitch your treatment, be open to input from the band. Often, they know the meaning behind the lyrics when it's not completely clear to everyone else listening. They might even have specific images or ideas they want to incorporate. Because of this, I would spend some time developing the treatment and brainstorming with the artist before you even storyboard.

Storyboards

Unlike storyboards for a film or commercial, music videos don't necessarily follow a linear pattern; they may be edited in a way that doesn't follow the storyboards. So, your storyboards are there to help you plan your shots out and to help your client visualize the structure, but things might change. Because you're most likely working with artists, having well-drawn images, or even using photographs or screen shots from other videos is a good idea. My stick figure drawings might be okay to convey the idea, but it wouldn't take very much longer to throw something better together so the client gets the idea. When you storyboard the band shots, you probably just need to do it once for each location. You'll end up shooting the band with multiple cameras, most likely, and this is the one time when I won't go into a lot of detail on my storyboard. When I'm shooting or directing the band shots, I find it much better to let the music guide me in my shots. You will want more detailed storyline shots on your storyboard, though. Knowing what to shoot in a CU or MS ahead of time is beneficial and helps save time once you're on the set.

A note here about scripts for music videos: I rarely use them. Since there usually isn't any dialogue or lines to read through and memorize, a music video script just becomes a page of shot descriptions. Since your storyboards should already contain that information, I find scripts to be redundant for music videos. However, you might have a client who wants one anyway. If you do, you'll probably be using single-column script formatting. If you're setting up a filmic intro to your video (like the "Thriller" video), then you'll definitely want a script for your actors to work from.

I have found some use in two-column scripts for music videos, but I usually use them strictly internally as I'm planning shots. The benefit of the two-column script is that it has a timing column and an audio column. As you listen through the song, you can pick out transition points and write the set of lines from the song into the audio column. From there, you can brainstorm ideas for each line or set of lines in the song and write out a description for the corresponding visual. You can also do this on the storyboard, but if you're like me, a two-column script is a bit cleaner since it can fit on relatively few pages. Be careful about using the two-column script, though, until you get a feel for your client, crew, and actors. Since two-column scripts are mostly used in live television, you may lose credibility as a filmmaker/artist if you use them on set to guide the shooting. Many music videos are made by film Directors and producers, and the two-column script is a bit foreign in that world.

Actors

Like commercials, I've had great luck casting my main actors and then using people who are convenient for the rest of the background characters. But like films, you really do need to put some thought into who will play your main roles. Occasionally, you'll be making a music video for a musician who is also a good actor and can carry one of the main roles. But often, you'll want the musician to stay in the artist shots and find a professional to play the main roles.

As I've mentioned earlier, looking at people who do work as extras, looking at theater programs at your school or local theater groups, and putting out casting calls through regional online forums will be your best bet to find actors. If you already have a network you can work through, then you might have better luck recruiting people who already have a reputation, but it's likely that your music video will be seen as more of a breakout opportunity, not a lucrative role for an established actor or actress.

You'll also want to avoid the trap of thinking that since there aren't any lines, you can throw anyone into the part. It's actually the opposite – because the emotions and storyline need to be conveyed without words, you need actors who are adept at playing emotions with their non-verbals. They need to be able to show sadness, heartbreak, happiness, loneliness, etc. with their eyes and their faces. Their body language needs to be able to convey lust, nervousness, joy, etc. without any words. I've seen many student-made music videos where classmates were cast, and they often fall flat because the people in the video aren't good at acting. It probably goes without saying, but if dancing is part of the video, you need to recruit people who can dance – not just dancers, but people who can take direction and choreography and stay in rhythm with all the other dancers.

Not every music video needs actors, though. I've also seen many music videos like the ones from OK Go where the artist(s) are the only characters in the video. This can especially be effective if the song is personal to their journey. If you search for a band called "Biscuits and Gravy," you'll find a song called "Shootin' Deer" where the lead singer is also the main character of the story. It gives the video a fairly personal feel, even though it's a silly story and a tongue-in-cheek kind of video. It's also a style at this point for the band. Their song "Kiss You Goodnight" also stars the lead singer as the lead actor. This can be really effective if you want the viewer to relate to the band as actual people. Just be careful to show the band members as the heroes of the story. The last thing you'll want is for listeners to have negative thoughts about the musicians and turn them off. Remember, your job is to promote the song and the band.

Locations

Since music videos are often done with much lower budgets than films, it's easiest to find convenient locations that still work to tell the story or give you the visual imagery you're looking for. You won't be able to construct a set inside a studio, most likely, so you'll need to find the next best thing. Luckily, the locations in most music videos don't matter too much. A coffee shop, a local bus station, a forest, or other places that are easy to access will probably do the trick. I've seen artist shots from the top of a parking garage, and they conveyed the gritty, urban feel the band was going for in the video. There's a local park with a lake that my students love to use in their videos because when sunlight reflects off the water, it conveys nostalgia, happiness, and other warm emotions. There's a train station in town as well, which is the one seen in the "Kiss You Goodnight" video mentioned above. The train gives the viewer the sense of transience – the singers are headed out and can't easily return.

As with films, I highly recommend working to get permissions before shooting at a location. The park may be a public space, but reaching out to the city government that oversees the park is a good idea. If nothing else, you might actually get some buy-in from them and some help. If you need a ball field at night, perhaps they're willing to turn the lights on for you. I've had great luck, especially working locally and on very small budgets, getting businesses and agencies to support productions I've worked on. Many will agree as long as they're given thanks in the credits, or as long as you work their business sign into the video somehow. And unlike films, you'll only be using the location as a backdrop for the artist or the storyline shots, so they won't be on screen long and you probably won't need access on multiple days.

Having said all of that, I also recommend making sure the location at least works for your video instead of forcing it. In the "Kiss You Goodnight" video, the scene opens in a kitchen. Or maybe a dining room? It's very hard to tell. The scene is very serious – the singer is telling his girlfriend that he's leaving, but he'll be back and he'll miss her. She's sad that he has to go. It's very touching. But the background is extremely distracting and hurts the seriousness of the situation. There are newspaper clippings on the wall. A shelf full of boxed food. In the reverse shot of the girlfriend, there are clothes on the floor and piled up in a chair. This might be intentional – it would convey the chaos of their lives and their relationship – but it's still distracting. And as the camera tilts up and pans to follow the singer out the door, there is a framed painting of Kramer from *Seinfeld*. The painting is ironic and totally ruins the serious mood of the video. The location actually isn't too bad, but the students who produced the video didn't provide basic props and set dressings to make it seem more real. Instead, it looks like a college apartment and not a house or apartment where a couple lives that pays bills and makes grown-up decisions like going out on the road as a singer. If you're going to use convenient locations, do your best to make them look the part.

Production

Music video production is a bit like shooting a film, but the artist shots can really be done any time it works out in the schedule. When you shoot the artist shots, you'll want them to play through the song in its entirety. These become your "bail out" shots in editing – when the storyline shots don't work out, or the edit would be awkward, just cut to one of the artist shots and then cut back to the storyline or imagery. Don't make the mistake of shooting parts of the song in different locations and leaving it short. You might not plan on cutting back to the shot of the band on top of the parking garage in the second half of the video, but I've seen it happen many times where the shots that were planned for that spot didn't work out, and the parking garage shot covered it up. For the storyline shots or visual imagery, you can shoot them like a film. They can be done in any order that works out for your actor's schedule, the location availability, or the equipment needs for the day.

Cameras

As I said above, many music videos are being shot with DSLR cameras and other less-expensive gear these days. If you're producing one for a record label, you'll probably have a bigger budget and you'll want a more cinematic look. But for local, independent artists, you'll want to look for gear that gives you the best bang for the buck. This is typically DSLR cameras or something like the Blackmagic Pocket Cinema Camera. The shallow depth of field and quality resolution that DSLRs offer is great for music videos, and since sound isn't really an issue, you get very few downsides. I would recommend, however, using a full-frame DSLR or mirrorless camera if you go that route. A cropped sensor (Canon calls this an APS-C sensor), micro 4/3 sensor, or even a super-35 sensor won't give you quite the same look.

A good tripod is still a must. I've seen students crash and burn at their shoots when they think their video needs to have a "handheld" look. Handholding a DSLR especially is nearly impossible. Even a shoulder-mounted camcorder is difficult to hold still when you're walking around or moving. Most of your shots should be from a tripod, although that doesn't mean you can't add movement. Pans, tilts, even dolly shots add some energy to the video and can greatly enhance the shots. When you're shooting like this, I would suggest doing at least two takes: one that's static and one that moves. That way, you have options in editing. Or, you might want to shoot with multiple cameras.

Especially since DSLR shooting is relatively inexpensive, I would actually encourage shooting with multiple cameras for music videos. Unlike film shooting, you don't have to worry as much about lighting, microphones, and other elements that might destroy the illusion of realism. As long as your subject isn't moving, or you can rehearse the movement with all of the cameras ahead of time, shooting with more than one camera shouldn't be an issue. And for the artist shots, shooting with multiple cameras can save a

Figure 12.1 A shoulder-mounted DSLR camera rig with counterweights on the back. The weight rests entirely on the shoulder so the camera operator's arms don't get as tired. This rig really helps steady the camera, but if you're walking or moving a lot, it will be too shaky.

Figure 12.2 This 3-axis gimbal can hold a heavier camera than a handheld gimbal, but still puts the weight of the camera entirely on the camera operator's arms. All gimbals have motors inside and gyroscopes that work at very fast speeds to counteract sudden movements. This allows the camera to float as if it's being held by hand, but smooths things out so the viewer doesn't get motion sick.

lot of time. For example, if you have a band with a singer, guitar player, drum player, and bass, I would recommend using five cameras if you have them available: one for a wide shot, and four others for close up shots and "handheld" shots that have movement. This way, the band only needs to play through the song a few times at each location instead of 10–15 times to get all of the shots.

I would also highly recommend using a gimbal. If you want to add a "handheld" look, use a Steadicam rig or a gimbal to add the movement. Steadicams use counterweights and springs to let the camera "float" on an arm in front of the camera operator. They take some practice to get good at, and I wouldn't recommend just renting one for a video if you haven't ever used one before. Steadicams can hold a much heavier camera, though, so if you're using cinema gear, you'll probably want to go that route instead of a gimbal. Gimbals come in a variety of shapes and sizes. Some look like sticks with a camera mount on top (handheld gimbals) and some have handles and even attach to a vest to help distribute the weight load from the camera operator's arms to their shoulders. If you're using a DSLR, a 3-axis gimbal or a handheld gimbal is probably fine. For a music video, you don't need to worry about sound, so just using the internal microphone on the camera to sync is fine.

My experience with gimbals is that they're very easy to use, once you get them balanced. Balancing them can be a nightmare, though. You'll want to set up the camera with the lens you're planning to use, take the lens cap off, and get everything exactly how you're going to shoot. Then, I would recommend watching through a video on how to balance your specific model of gimbal. And make sure you balance every single axis. Missing even one will make things seem like they might work, but then the gimbal will just shut down before the motors overload. It can be a difficult, frustrating process, but the movement you can get with one is worth spending some time to get it right.

Lighting

As with cameras, you'll want lights for music videos, but you'll want to look for lights that give you good quality for a lower price. I've had good luck with LED panel lights for a softer, more diffused look, and the newer designed LED lights, like the open-faced light in Figure 5.2. These LED lights can give you a hard light, but they often come with many accessories to soften the light, diffuse the light, and shape it in other ways. For a music video, you'll often want broader light on the band, even if it's hard and creates shadows. You'll want all of the band members to be lit well and be seen. If you're going for a more dramatic video, I'd suggest using several hard lights for the band, and highly selective lighting for your other shots. If you're going upbeat, then broad, diffused light will be best. You'll still probably want several lighting instruments with diffusion gel on each one. Either way, you'll want to put the lights up in locations where the cameras can move around them to get the shots.

A Note on Sound

Even though you don't need to record dialogue on set, you'll want to do a couple things when it comes to sound. The first is that you'll want to have a decent set of speakers to play back the song you're doing the video for. Anytime the band is playing, people are singing, or anything else needs to happen to the beat of the song, the people on set will need to hear it. And it has to be louder than any sounds they're making. For example, you might want to put pillows inside the drums to deaden them some. You'll want the guitar player to turn their amplifier down quite a bit. They need to play as hard as they do in the song so the visuals match the energy in the song, but you want to lower the volume as much as possible so they can hear the master track being played back. Oh, and by the way, they will need to have the master recording completely done before you start shooting. Anything they change after you shoot on the track will throw off the sync and the timing. For my videos, I typically bring a small portable PA system. A phone just won't cut it, but some Bluetooth speakers that connect to the phone might be loud enough. You won't want your musicians wearing headphones or Bluetooth earbuds, though. It ruins the illusion that they're actually playing the song the viewers are watching and listening to.

The second recommendation on sound is that I would go ahead and record reference audio. This can help you sync up the visuals to the lips and guitar strumming easier in post. Just because there isn't any dialogue doesn't mean you won't need to hear what happened while you were shooting. Obviously, you'll get rid of the audio tracks once you've lined everything up in post, but recording audio in-camera on set can be very helpful.

Directing

The nice thing about directing a music video is that you have more attention to spend on the camera shots. Since you're not necessarily spending time with actors on their lines, you can float between the different cameras and give the operators directions about what you want them to focus on. If there's a specific part of the song where the drums are prominent, then direct one of the cameras to focus on it. In shots where there are actors or dancers, or band members that need rehearsal, it's still your job as the Director to prepare them and get quality takes. But directing a music video can allow you to really flex some creative muscle. Like a film, the ultimate goal on set is to get the visuals that your editor needs. They can then take those visuals and put together a piece that flows well and conveys the emotion and the message the song requires.

While you can talk through the shot, you may not want to. Especially for the musicians, you'll want them to get into the zone as much as possible. They'll already need a little time to acclimate to their drums being muffled and the guitars being turned down. Interrupting them during their shoot will feel even more artificial to them. It's better to just let them play through the entire song and give them directions in between takes. For the storyline shots, feel free to direct it like a film. Give your actors directions before the first take and in between takes. Trust your crew to set up the shots while you focus on the actors, then come together before the first take to get everyone on the same page. For visual imagery types of shots, just shoot them MOS like inserts or cutaways. If you just need a shot of clouds passing through the sky, no need to overcomplicate it. Just set up the camera, slate the shot, and shoot it. If you've got a camera operator for the shot, talk them through it.

Post

Like a documentary film, the structure of a music video really takes shape during postproduction. You should have an idea of how the video will flow in general before you shoot, but you probably haven't planned out exactly where the artist shots or visual imagery will fit into the video yet. And that's okay. The post on a music video extends the creativity you flexed in the planning and shooting. And often, the producer or Director will also be the editor, so you'll be intimately familiar with all of the shots and the raw footage you have to work with. The actual workflow uses elements from narrative film postproduction, commercials, and documentary films.

Workflow

As always, start out by labeling and backing up all of your footage. Begin editing by laying down your music track first, and then placing your visuals on the timeline. Once you get things in the order you want them, work on your transitions and any effects and color grading. Color can be especially important to convey the appropriate tone to match the music. Since colors and music both hit us at an emotional level, they should match in tone and feeling. An upbeat song that's happy and hopeful should have warmer colors. A sad song should have cooler colors. Some epic songs, like Disturbed's "The Sound of Silence" (a Simon and Garfunkel remake) are phenomenal in black and white with all of the depth of contrast in the grayscale. The deep blacks in the video really reinforce the impact of the lyrics and the powerful singing.

After editing, you'll want to screen your video with a test audience. Like a commercial, you'll also want to make sure your client is happy with the video and screen it for them as well. Distribution these days is either handled by the artist, typically on their YouTube channel, or by the record label. You'll probably need to export in different codecs for each purpose – a higher resolution video for archives, a broadcast version in case it makes it on cable or streaming, and a YouTube or Vimeo compressed version.

Editing

As mentioned above, the first thing I do when editing a music video is to lay down the master track of the song in the audio track of the NLE. This is by far the best way to figure out where the edit points need to be. Some software can analyze the beat of the music and put markers in. You can also look at the audio waveform and just cut your video clips around the peaks. Or, you can do what editors have done for years: click on the "marker" tool in your NLE instead of your selection tool, blade tool, etc. The marker tool will add an invisible mark every time you tap a key or the mouse button. As you listen to the song, just tap along to the beat. If you're off a bit, you can grab the markers you placed and move them. With the markers in place, you can lay down the video clips and cut them to the marks (with snapping enabled, the edit points will "snap" to the markers). This leaves your cuts pretty clean and with a good rhythm to them that matches the tempo and beat of the music. You won't want a cut on every single beat, so feel free to stretch out some video clips longer than one or two markers. You also won't want every single cut to land right on the beat, or it will lull your audience to sleep a bit because they'll start to expect it.

As you lay down your visuals, I would also suggest starting with the storyline shots or any shots that need to happen in a specific order. From there, cut in the visual imagery, and then the artist shots. Sometimes I lay down the visuals in a linear fashion from the start of the timeline to the end, but most often I'm figuring out the story first, then filling in with other shots. Figuring out how to place the artist shots might require moving other things around at times, so you'll want to plan these out a bit. For instance, if you have artist shots of the band in a warehouse and the storyline uses the warehouse as a backdrop for the first few shots, but not anything after, you'll have to decide whether you want to show the artist warehouse shots only in the first part of the video, or if you want to come back to the warehouse periodically throughout the video. Either way might be fine, but you'll want a plan as you lay everything out. And it should be done with a purpose – to convey an emotion or a message, or to focus back on specific words in the song or melodies. For example, maybe every time the song comes back to the chorus, you might have a shot of the artist in the same location. Then when a new verse begins, show them at a different location.

After laying down the visuals, I typically do color grading and effects. "Effects" is a really broad word to mean greenscreen chromakey, graphic elements, words, overlays, keyframing movements, or anything else that alters the original shots. Adding movement to a shot in post, putting a sharpening overlay, and things like that can create a stylistic element that makes your video stand out. But less is typically more. With films, it's definitely true. With music videos, because they're a bit more of an art form than a storytelling form, you can certainly get more creative and stylistic. But if you go too far, then the video will look dated or risk being too obscure for the viewer to relate to. Your test audiences will let you know if you've gone too far.

After effects, I'll work on my transitions. Cuts are still the main transitions in a music video, but you can get away more with dips to black, transitions, and even wipes. Again, it's more artistic and creative, so viewers often give music videos more latitude in the area. As with effects, less is often more. Even though I use transitions that aren't cuts in music videos, I still use them sparingly. You don't want to take the focus away from the lyrics or the visual elements. You should also be consistent with the transitions you use.

If you dip to black, don't also use dissolves. If you use a wipe, use the same wipe pattern each time you wipe. The viewer should be able to expect what's coming, otherwise their focus will shift to the wipe itself and not the content.

Screening

As with commercials, you'll probably want to screen your video with a test audience before you screen it with your musician (as long as they're okay with it – some musicians and artists definitely want to be the first ones to see it). Unlike commercials, this can simply mean showing it to friends and family members to get their reactions. You don't necessarily need a representative sample of the target audience to see if the video is effective. You just need to make sure the flow, structure, and emotional impact are what you intended. For example, if the song is a sad ballad, and your audience gets comedy vibes from your video, that might mean you need to make some changes before showing it to your client. If the song is a biting breakup song, it shouldn't make the relationship shown in the video too nostalgic. You just want to make sure the audience feels the way the artist wants them to feel when they listen to the song. And you want to make sure everything flows well and makes sense. I screened a music video to my family once and they made a story connection that actually wasn't there and it hurt the story I was trying to convey. After a bit more editing, the story flowed a lot more logically.

Case Study: "Faded" Music Video

If you go to YouTube and look for the Clay Clear Band's channel, you'll see the video for their song, "Faded" (or just search for "Clay Clear Band Faded"). Students in my Cinematography class produced the music video from start to finish. With their permission, and permission from the band, I'm using the video as the case study for this chapter.

At the start, my students, Abbey Daniel, Laura Jacobs, Caroline Smith, and Kelsey Vestal connected with the Clay Clear Band and discussed the idea of doing a music video for them. The band decided on "Faded," and the students met with them to figure out what kinds of images and storylines the band wanted for the song. The idea of hitch-hiking and the "will play for Booze" sign continue the tone set by the lyrics. As the lead singer connects with the rest of the band in the back of the truck, they start playing the song together. Then, we see the band up on stage in a venue together. These venue shots intercut with the band playing out in a field as they drink beer and play the song. The song ends with the band walking away and passing out on the ground. Finally, the lead singer wakes up, closes his guitar case and seems to move on. This was all storyboarded by my students and then pitched back to the band. With a few tweaks and additions, the story was approved and the students began working on schedules, props, and locations.

Scheduling was tough. The band was touring and playing concerts, so it was important to line up the days they could shoot. Since most of the shots had at least one band member in them, and no additional actors were used in the storyline shots, the schedule had to line up with the band's availability. Luckily, the only location that was difficult to secure was the theater venue, and it was available on one of the days the band had open. The students lined up the schedule, then rented their equipment for the shooting days, found a truck they could use for the shots, rounded up beer cans and bottles, connected with the band about their instruments, and got to work.

The only additional thing to mention here is that around the 2:14 mark in the video, you'll see a really cool transition where the camera tilts down suddenly as if it were being dropped. The tilt begins with the band outdoors and concludes with a similarly framed shot on the stage inside the venue. This transition is brilliant. It adds motion and creates a dynamic feel, but it also connects the band's reality (playing out in a field) to its ambition (inside the venue). This kind of transition has to be planned out ahead of time, and I imagine the students shot the field images first, and then used a screen of some kind to review the footage and match it when they shot the video inside the venue on the other side of the cut. It needed meticulous planning, otherwise this transition wouldn't have worked.

During production, I believe they shot over the course of two days. I honestly don't remember if they were able to shoot the outdoor scenes roughly in order, or if the band's schedule required them to shoot out of order, but the sun's position in the sky and shadows don't cause any continuity errors, so the story flows well either way. The band shots in the field were done at the same time, using a tripod and a gimbal. I don't remember if they used multiple cameras or a single camera, but there is a good variety of close up shots and long shots of all the band members throughout the song. I'm sure the band played through the entire song many times while they shot the field performance and the venue performance. For the shots during the storyline where the singer is singing and the band is playing, I'm thinking they probably didn't play through the entire song. Because the truck is moving, the camera is moving, the singer is moving, and it would have been difficult to keep everything choreographed just right, I would have shot these opening shots in pieces, knowing that I would edit them later anyway. For some of the shots, if I remember correctly, the truck was driving very slowly while someone walked behind it and shot the band using a gimbal to steady everything. Logistically, these shots are very complex and took a lot of planning to capture the movement of the truck and the playfulness of the band.

The shots inside the theater venue are much easier, by contrast. Creating spotlight effects by placing the lights out in the seats and shooting from behind the band is easy. It also masks the fact that no one is in the seats (although it really doesn't matter for the video). The band is on stage and there are tripod static shots and handheld gimbal shots, much like there were when the band was playing in the field. Since these shots were inside, power was readily available for lights. For the outdoor shots, the students had to schedule times of day where the sun could provide most or all of their lighting. Luckily for those shots, the shadows fit the western-movie theme of the band and the song, so it worked well.

In post, the students had a good idea of how they wanted to edit everything together based on the storyboards. But the video is complex enough and moves quickly enough that I'm sure they had to edit many of the opening shots together by feel. The shots flow well, but the choice of one shot over another, and how long to keep a shot on the screen, is often something that is figured out in post. The editor laid the music down first, and many of the cuts hit on or around the beat. The tilting transition happens right as the song transitions and matches the tone perfectly. Many of the cutaway shots are used, like the shot of the guitar case full of beer cans, at places that further the story, but also just add an additional shot to make the video feel full and well covered. Even for music videos, your editor would prefer to have too much coverage than not enough. Because the student producers got so much coverage, the video doesn't have to hang on a shot too long or cut to a shot that doesn't quite fit with the storyline. There are plenty of shots of the band to choose from at every point in the song, for both the venue and the outdoor shots.

After putting the storyline together and inserting the band shots (some of which are also storyline shots), the rough cut was done. At this point, it's a good idea to watch the video and time out the cuts. The shots in this video aren't too long. None of them linger, so the story flows and the viewer feels like they're getting somewhere. But none of them are too short, either. You don't want a viewer to watch the video and pause it just to see what happened in the shot. This makes the song choppy and works against your goal of promoting the band and the song.

Lastly, the students color graded the video. They applied an almost sepia color to make it feel like an older western movie. The band's jackets help reinforce this, as does the dirt road and the pickup truck. But there are splashes of red and pink throughout. The red truck, the beer cans, and the lead guitar all pop out against the sepia background. The greens are muted, but the reds are enhanced. This coloring is continued inside the venue as well, so the video has a consistent look and feel for the audience.

If I remember correctly, the band was brought in after the color grading and shown the video. They loved it and the students didn't have any changes to make. As the executive producer for the video, I reviewed the preproduction before allowing the students to begin shooting. Their storyboards, shooting schedules, location permissions, and prop lists were all ready to go before they rented their equipment and shot the video. After shooting, I reviewed the raw footage and gave them advice on the editing. As a class, we also screened the final cut of the video and gave them feedback on it. From there, the video was given to the band to do what they wanted with it. Although no money changed hands, music videos are usually done for the band or the record company, so the producer isn't usually the one distributing it. In the case of "Faded," the band decided to distribute it through their YouTube channel and website.

Chapter 12: Music Videos Main Points

- Music videos are a lot like commercials – you're shooting them to promote a product (the band, the song) and you're working for someone else while doing it. It's important to collaborate with your client and the musician(s) so you reach the right audience and land the right tone.
- When planning out a music video, you should storyboard out your shots in a way that will keep the viewer interested and help the video flow. This can mean an actual storyline, but it can also just mean that you're planning out the flow of everything ahead of time. Music videos are rarely captivating if they're just a montage of random shots of the band.
- Music videos don't need a script, but they do require a lot of planning.
- When shooting, be sure to bring a sound system to play back the master track of the song so everyone stays in sync with it. You should shoot multiple angles and frame the shots multiple ways while shooting the band performances. And they should perform the entire song at least once in every location. These are your insert shots that are invaluable in post and give your editor a lot of options at any point in the song.

- For the artist or band shots, I would highly recommend using more than one camera. That way, you can knock out multiple angles and shots in one time through the song. This will help keep your musicians and crew fresh.
- In editing, lay down the song first, then cut your shots close to the beats in a way that enhances the rhythm of the song. Not too much, but if you're close to the beats on many of your edits, it will help the visuals flow as well.
- Music videos are most often low-budget, artistic endeavors. They can be a lot of fun, but few people exclusively make music videos.

Part V
Producing Non-fiction (Chapters 13–15)

We tend to think of non-fiction as documentary filmmaking, but it encompasses a lot more than that. When I make an instructional video for my classes, I'm creating non-fiction (although I do loosely script them out, I often don't know exactly how they will end up until I put them together in post). I've shot many weddings and other live events, and every one of them is slightly different. I can plan how things will go, but in the moment, I have to rely on my instincts to react to new shot possibilities and sounds to record.

DOI: 10.4324/9781003010357-17

13 Documentary Films

For Chapters 13–15, I'm going to focus on non-fiction modes of production. For documentary films, news packages, and an array of corporate and freelance productions, the workflow is quite different. The biggest difference is that you won't script out your entire project, even though you should do a significant amount of planning before you shoot. These types of projects feel like they might not need as much planning, but I'll outline what you absolutely need to do before going out and shooting a non-fiction project. Like the chapters on fiction genres, there will be some overlap between these chapters and the rest of the book, but I'll try to keep it to a minimum. For the non-fiction chapters, I'll go through preproduction planning, shooting, and post. I'll highlight the ways that these genres are the same and different from what the book has already covered. For documentary films, this chapter will cover:

DOI: 10.4324/9781003010357-18

Preproduction

Preproduction for documentary films is unlike almost anything else. For my films, I've done a lot of research, scripted out questions, made a lot of phone calls and networking connections, and planned a million details. But I've never had a complete plan for the entire film before I started production. It's not impossible to have everything planned out, but I've found that making a good documentary film usually requires you to be open to new directions and ideas, and to be flexible with your goals. You'll start with a solid idea and approach – this is necessary to get funding, crew, locations, participants, and everything else you'll need – but often you'll end up going deeper, finding the need to limit how broad you go, going in new directions when new information comes to light through interviews or research, or just being open-minded in general.

I'll talk in more detail in the case study later, but when I produced the documentary film on Central State Hospital, a mental health institution in Milledgeville, Georgia, I was asked many times whether I thought institutionalization of individuals was a good thing or a bad thing. To this day, I don't have a stance. I have a deep and passionate understanding of all of the issues on either side, but I never came down on one side or the other. And I think the film is better because of that. I could have made a film that argued for or against it, but I stayed open-minded and heard people on both sides, and I think the film helps viewers understand the complexity of the mental health crisis in America.

Funding

Every mode of production costs money. Documentary films are often very low-budget, but you still have to figure out how to pay your crew, feed your crew, rent or buy equipment, and cover travel costs. I've funded most of my documentary projects through grants, but I've also purchased cameras and gear out of my own personal funds. I'm lucky enough to work at a university, where I have access to grants and equipment. I've also taught classes where students crewed for me as part of their class credit.

Outside of the university setting, you can either fund your film yourself, or you can get money from somewhere else. If you choose to fund it yourself, there are fundraising sites out there specifically for documentary films and other creative projects. Indiegogo has been a crowdsourcing site for filmmakers for years. There are many others out there. You can offer swag, credits, a return on investment, or a number of other incentives. Or, you can simply ask for help getting your film made. There are people out there who are passionate about certain topics and just want to help make people more aware. Unlike fictional films, people who invest in documentaries rarely expect them to make a return on their investment. You can also ask businesses or people to sponsor you directly. If a local pizza shop is willing to donate pizzas so you can feed your crew, that's money you don't have to spend out of your own pocket. And there are associations out there that might be willing to fund your project as well.

Just be careful that you are ethical when you accept donations from individuals, companies, or organizations. Even if your opinions are not swayed by their donations, you don't want to open yourself up to that criticism. For example, if the documentary film I produced on Andalusia Farm (the birthplace of the author Flannery O'Connor, and a tourist attraction) had been funded by the farm itself, it would have been seen even more as propaganda than a documentary film. It already feels a lot like propaganda (which is actually a legitimate purpose for documentaries, so I'm not using the term derogatorily) because there isn't really another "side" to the film.

There are grant programs out there through PBS, the US government, and private foundations like the W.K. Kellogg Foundation and the MacArthur Foundation. For these, you need to do a lot of research, develop a treatment, and work out your logistics. You'll also need to have access to locations and participants lined up to show that you can actually complete the film. What I've found is that grants most often ask for specific things in very specific language. To even have a shot, you must have a complete application that addresses everything required. And to be competitive, you'll want to use the exact same language in your request that the grant parameters use. For example, if the grant says to submit location release forms, be sure you have the forms, they're filled out completely, and you don't call them "permissions" instead of "location release forms."

The other way of funding projects is through networks or broadcasting companies directly. I've never done this, and typically these are filmmakers with a proven track record of success. Places like PBS, ITVS, and Netflix work with established filmmakers who already have distributors lined up for future films. While they do have funds available for emerging artists, these are highly competitive. It certainly doesn't hurt to try any and all of these sources of funding, especially if you've got a lot of travel expenses. I recently watched a documentary series on trains, and the travel alone cost the producers quite a bit. I'm sure they had distribution lined up before they even began production.

Treatment

A treatment for a documentary is quite different from a fictional film treatment. Since you don't necessarily know the structure of the film or the stance(s) the film might take, you can't really lay everything out and tell people what the film will look like. You can, however, show any potential funders, crew, or participants that you know everything you possibly can about the subject. Your treatment should show that you've done significant research on the topic(s) you're covering in the film. It should describe the issues, identify specific people you plan on interviewing, give layouts of locations and the importance to your film, and any other details you can include to show people that you have a solid plan. You should know who your audience is going to be, how the film will connect with them, and potential distribution outlets that will reach them. You should also identify specific festivals you want to target with the film once it's complete. For documentary films, this is very important. Film festivals can bring attention to your film, and awards can lead to broader distribution. Your treatment should have a logline, just like a fictional film. And you should have an elevator pitch ready for any potential investors you run into. But your treatment should be very thorough.

Scripting What You Can

Your treatment will be your guide, but you can script parts of your film before you begin shooting. Unlike a fictional film where you storyboard out exact shots, locations, and actions, your treatment will guide you to places, people, and topics. It won't tell you how to frame the shots – you'll most likely have to figure that out on the fly – but it should have enough information that you know who you need to talk to and what kind of b-roll you need. When I shoot documentaries, I don't write narration until after I'm done shooting and I'm beginning the edit. I never know exact timing, and often I don't even know how pieces of one interview might connect to pieces of another interview until I begin editing. So, when I'm scripting, I focus only on the background information and the questions I'm going to ask my participants. I spend time researching the person and why they're important to the film. I work on open-ended questions that will ideally elicit profound sound bites that can edit together with sound bites from other participants.

It's a good idea to practice your questions on someone before doing your first interview or two. Even if the person you're practicing on has no knowledge of the topics, they'll be able to tell you if the question is phrased well and if they think it will get an appropriately long answer. The goal is to write questions that can't be answered with one word, but that are contained enough that someone won't ramble in their answer. For example, don't script out "Does the university have a plan for additional housing?" That would easily be met with a "yes" or a "no," giving you no options in your edit except including the interviewer asking the question to give the audience context. If you ask, "What are the university's plans for additional housing," you'll be met with a long, complex answer that has been rehearsed many times, which will also be difficult to cut into a short sound bite for the film. Instead, script your open-ended question sufficiently to get a sentence or two for each answer. For example, "What is the first priority the university has for increasing housing?"

Besides questions, the only other thing you might script ahead of time for a documentary film is any reenactments you plan on shooting for it. If you're doing a film about the civil war, there's no way to go back in time to film the actual event. It's accepted practice to reenact something from a diary, eyewitness accounts, or other research. It's not ethical in a documentary film to simply make up details that have no historical basis. These scenes are always scripted, actors are hired, locations are scheduled, and production happens much like a fictional film. You might know which scenes need to be re-created before you begin, but you might also find the need for some of these scenes after completing interviews. If one of your participants discusses a certain event, and you didn't have the details of that event during preproduction, you might have to go back into preproduction for those scenes.

Participants

In a documentary film, you only call people "actors" if they are acting out the scripted reenactments. Otherwise, the interviewees and other people in your film are "participants." It is unethical to pay these people to be in the film, but often filmmakers will cover all expenses incurred by their participants for food, travel, lodging, etc. This ethical line is there because it would give the appearance that they were being coerced into saying specific things that the filmmaker wanted them to say if they were being paid. Additionally, if someone who was originally part of the scene that is being reenacted appears in it, they are still a participant, and not a hired actor. For instance, if you have someone who spent time in college housing, and you're staging a scene where they're sitting in a dorm room, they still wouldn't be considered an "actor," and it would still be unethical to pay them.

Finding participants can be the most difficult part of the process. The film about Central State Hospital would have been a better film if I had been able to talk to more people on camera who had mental health challenges. But many people in that population require a guardian's signature to participate in something like a filmed interview, so this was extremely difficult. While making the film, we found that the participants snowballed – that is, we did the research on who to interview as we got started, but as we interviewed one person, they would tell us about someone else to contact. When we interviewed that additional contact, they knew of someone else. Eventually, we interviewed a lot of people with a lot of different perspectives. Only a few of those interviews were ones we initially lined up in our preproduction. So, the goal of lining up participants in the planning phase is to do as much as you can to figure out who to talk to, but then to be open to exploring new avenues as you learn about them.

Many times, it's also nice to have a participant who walks the audience through the film. By this I mean someone who was part of the original events you're showing or ideas you're presenting. This is one style of documentary, but it can give a personal touch to the film and connect with the audience in a different way than hiring a narrator to do voicework. For instance, one idea we had when creating the *Central State Hospital* film was to have my partner on the film, Daniel McDonald, serve as the narrator. Daniel had worked for the local newspaper and wrote about the hospital and had experienced the recent history of the institution. He would have been able to talk about why he's passionate about the topic and what led him to making the film. It would have given a personal touch and explained things in a first-person kind of way. But I ended up moving away before we could script out and record these narrations. Instead, we decided to exclusively use sound bites from the interviews we conducted to tell the story of the hospital. Because the sound bites weren't seamless, we used graphics to transition between them and to add more information we had researched that didn't come up in the interviews. It's still a personal approach, but not quite as intimate as one person's (Daniel's) exploration of the history of Central State Hospital would have been.

Locations

Your locations will, of course, depend on the story you're telling. A documentary might be about the location itself, like the film about Andalusia Farm I referenced earlier. Or the location might play a significant part in the story, like the film I did about the Indian occupation of Alcatraz Island. For those two films, we really only had one location. The interviews we conducted were done at those locations because they provided the necessary backdrop to set the tone. Shooting the interviews at Andalusia helped us make connections between the farm and the sound bites we used in the film. Even the actor we hired to do a standup and narration we filmed at the location (a standup is where the actor reads the script in direct address to the audience, like a news reporter).

The opposite end of this is that sometimes locations don't matter at all. When we interviewed a journalist for the *Atlanta Journal-Constitution* newspaper about Central State Hospital, it would have taken a lot more coordination to bring him to the hospital or interview him at the newspaper offices. It was much easier to simply interview him inside his own home. We got there early, discussed the best place in the house for sound, lights, and background settings, and ended up shooting the interview in his home office. There is a nice set of books on a shelf behind him that lend him credibility as an expert, and the interview went very well. He had a lot of great answers and history to discuss, and we had the added benefit of him being relaxed. Since he was in his own home and didn't have to drive 5 hours roundtrip that day, he was fresh for the camera. Given that we ended up editing together one version of the film that was 105 minutes long, it would also have been monotonous if every single interview had the hospital as the backdrop. In fact, only two of the many interviews were actually done at Central State.

The middle ground is to conduct interviews in locations that aren't immediately tied to your subject, but are still important and give credibility. For instance, for the *Central State Hospital* film, we interviewed the local sheriff in his office. This makes even more sense than interviewing him at the hospital because our discussion with him really centered more on how the local law enforcement communities are strained when an institution the size of Central State Hospital shuts down. Unless I specifically want my interviewees to have the location as a backdrop, I generally make contact with them and then work out the best location. If it's obvious that travel might be difficult, or that I'll get better information from them in a familiar setting, I plan on taking my equipment and crew to them. If it truly doesn't matter what the backdrop is, I'll just ask them where they would like to shoot the interview and see if it works for my needs. If the location is important to have as the backdrop, I'll figure out a way to get them there if at all possible.

Don't forget to get release forms from all participants and all locations. Unlike shooting a fictional film, when I shoot a documentary, I carry a folder around with me that has blank release forms in it. This way, if I show up at a location and decide to also shoot the house next door as part of my story, I'm ready. If the person I'm interviewing suddenly says, "my friend here has something to say as well," I'm ready. Because non-fiction is inherently less predictable, it's always good to be prepared and to be flexible. In the *Central State Hospital* film, we went to Atlanta Legal Aid to interview a lawyer who successfully argued in front of the Supreme Court in a pivotal case on mental healthcare. When we got there, she felt strongly that her colleague should be part of the interview. Even though it wasn't ideal, I had a second microphone (as a backup). We shifted gears with our interview questions and drafted some extra questions. Visually, the location and framing aren't as nice with both participants in the frame, but we managed and we got some excellent background information to include in the film. I had extra release forms and extra equipment, so we easily accommodated the request.

Crew

I've been fortunate to work with some amazing crew members on my films who were often there just because they were passionate about the project. The editor for the Central State film, Joe Windish, took on the project because he was very interested in the subject matter. On other projects, I had crew members whom I had done work for, so they worked for me in exchange. For several projects, I've been lucky enough to be teaching a class in documentary production and have had students who were willing to crew for me in exchange for course credit and credits in the film. On a low-budget film, which most docs are, you'll have to get creative when securing your crew. If you end up paying anyone, it should probably be a good Cinematographer and a good sound person. In post, you might want to hire an editor. The images and sounds will end up telling the story, and having people who are used to shooting non-fiction will help when you need to make adjustments on the fly. Most likely, you'll be the person directing. You'll have the best information available to make the decisions along the way.

For most of my documentary films, I've been one of the producers, the Director, and the Cinematographer. It's not uncommon for people in the crew to serve multiple roles. I would highly recommend, though, that you take a minute during preproduction or when you arrive at a location to develop a gameplan for who is going to do what. I've seen many chaotic sets where the producer is afraid of upsetting a volunteer crew member. In those cases, the producer/Director often fails to give adequate instructions to everyone, and people end up sitting around and wasting valuable time. It can cause frustration, even with volunteers, if people don't know what their responsibilities are.

I often run with very small crews when shooting documentaries. I've been on locations shooting b-roll by myself. I've done interviews where it was just me. I've done interviews where I set up the lights and the mics, then ran the camera while someone else asked the questions. I would highly recommend doing it this way (with someone else asking questions) if at all possible. During the interviews where I asked questions from behind the camera, I often found myself paying more attention to the shot and the audio levels instead of following along with what the participant was saying. If you do this too much, the participants can get distracted and think you're not paying enough attention. They also have a difficult time figuring out where to look while they're talking.

I've also shot interviews with crews of ten or more. In those situations, I've prepped everyone for what their role was ahead of time: one person to place microphone(s), one person to set up the audio recorder or test the in-camera audio; two people to set up the camera and tripod; three or more people on lights – one for each light is ideal as you move them around to get the best lighting; one person coordinating electrical to the lights (when I'm interviewing someone inside their home, I always try to spread the lighting load around to different circuits in the house so I don't trip a breaker); one Director (usually me); and one interviewer or producer who can work with the interviewee and prep them for the questions and the structure we're looking for in their answers. You don't want to give them the questions ahead of time (unless they specifically ask for them) because you want their answers to sound unrehearsed, but they should have an idea of the topics you're planning on discussing so they can adequately prepare to talk about them. I've also used extra crew members to take notes for important sound bites during the interview. And these days, many interviews are shot with multiple cameras, so if you have extra crew and the ability to set up extra shots, you can get multiple angles during the same interview and provide your editor with options in post.

Equipment

One of the great things about shooting a documentary film is that viewers are much more forgiving when it comes to the aesthetics. You can often get away with a shaky camera, poor lighting, and other things that would completely ruin a fictional film. Because documentaries are unrehearsed and it would be unethical to do multiple takes of a spontaneous event, viewers understand that the crew might have to shoot images on the fly. Natural images are better than fake ones every time in a non-fiction film.

Over the years, though, low-budget equipment has gotten better and better. DSLR cameras shoot high-quality video, cost a fraction of the cost of cinema cameras, and are used more and more in documentary films. When I first began shooting docs, I used video camcorders. Their ability to get good sound and decent images on the fly was paramount. Today, I usually shoot with a DSLR or cinema camera. A DSLR is portable and has acceptable in-camera audio. Even though DSLR audio isn't good enough for a fictional film, it's usable for a documentary. If I'm sitting down for an interview, it doesn't take a lot of extra time to set up a cinema rig instead of a camcorder. I can feed microphones into a separate audio recorder or directly into the camera.

When I shot the Central State film, I used a shoulder-mounted camcorder. It was a very expensive ENG (Electronic News Gathering) camera that produced great images and high-quality sound. We used it for interviews and for our b-roll as we roamed the halls of abandoned buildings on the hospital's campus. Having said that, if I were to shoot it again today, I'd use a cinema camera for the interviews and a DSLR on a tripod or on a gimbal for my b-roll. The footage I shot with the camcorder is a bit too shaky and at times is unusable because it bounces as I walked. A gimbal would have smoothed out the movement. There is enough usable b-roll because we shot for hours, but I look over the raw footage today and know it could have been better if I had had access to the gear I use now. And the gear I have now costs a fraction of what that camcorder cost.

For microphones, I always bring a minimum of two – one wireless and one wired. Unfortunately, when I shoot documentaries, I don't always have the ability to scout out a location ahead of time. I usually try to make time to look at the places I want to shoot b-roll, but when I'm going to someone's house to do an interview, it feels awkward to ask if I can come and scope out their house before coming in with all my gear and shooting. Because of this, I always over-plan on my gear. I was a Boy Scout, and I still appreciate their motto: "Be Prepared." As a filmmaker, especially doing documentaries, it's great advice. You should bring at least three lights, but probably bring a second three-light kit you don't plan on using. When I ended up shooting the double-interview with the Atlanta Legal Aid lawyers, I found myself needing more than the three lights I had planned on using. I've also been places where I needed extra stingers (extension power cords) to reach additional circuits in a house. And I've certainly been places where I couldn't get a clean signal on the wireless mic and I've had to switch to the wired one.

Schedules

For my documentaries, I always do my best to schedule as much as I can before shooting begins. Depending on the timeline for your film, you might be able to add more days to the schedule, but you might not. Sometimes I have to plan the schedule around the participants I line up initially. Sometimes it's the locations that have the most restrictions and I end up planning around that. For the Andalusia film, we found out that the farm was hosting a bluegrass concert and decided to schedule a shoot and record songs from the concert for the soundtrack. For the Central State film, we spent over a year shooting, so we scheduled our first round of interviews and hospital shoots, then we regrouped and planned out a second round. Once we thought we were finished, word had gotten out about our film, and several people contacted us with their stories, so we decided to set up another round of interviews as well. The schedule was ongoing and fluid. But it was never done without a plan.

Production

I've covered a lot of information in the previous section on preproduction, but there are a few things to highlight when it comes to the actual shooting of a documentary film. In this section, I want to get into the specifics of how to set up your gear and the aesthetics of modern documentary films. While audiences are more forgiving with non-fiction, good aesthetics still convey the message better and with fewer distractions.

A Note on Ethics

I've alluded to some of the ethical decisions you'll make as a non-fiction filmmaker already, but one of the first things you'll need to do as a documentary filmmaker is think about where you draw your lines. Would you ask someone a "gotcha" question in order to further the film's main point? When you interview someone you may not agree with, can you do it with an open mind? When you're shooting b-roll and you see something you know would help your film, but that your participants or location owners might not want in it, do you shoot it anyway?

I'll give you a concrete example. When we shot the *Central State Hospital* film, the hospital's Public Relations Director was invaluable. She set up all of our access to the hospital and helped set up interviews with hospital staff. When we were shooting on the campus and security guards pulled up, we had a signed release form from her that explained our permission to be there. She even agreed to wear a microphone while we shot b-roll. She signed a release form for this, and agreed to have her voice in the film if we needed it, but we also knew that her preference was that we would only use her voice as research. The stories she told as we walked through abandoned hallways would give us context to produce graphics or ask other participants about those hallways. When we got to postproduction, our editor wanted to use a sound bite from her. Daniel and I felt that even though we had permission, we would be violating our own ethical lines to include her in the film. We wanted to honor the spirit of our original agreement – even though the film was arguably better with the sound bite.

During shooting, we also had ideas of shots that would have gone against the spirit of the institution. Shooting at night to give it a ghostly feel, going inside buildings that were deteriorating and we were not given permission to enter, and a few other similar ideas were tempting, but would have definitely crossed our ethical lines. Central State was extremely open with their access and one of the things I struggled with making the film was deciding whether to show the institution's dark history. Ultimately, we decided to walk the middle path – showing the positives and negatives of mental health institutions in America. You can't think of every possible hypothetical situation you might encounter, but thinking through some of the decisions you'll face ahead of time will help guide you as you launch into production.

Cameras

I've already talked about the range of cameras that are acceptable to use in documentary films today. A good tripod, gimbal, or Steadicam rig is essential, even though you can probably point to many historical films that are a little bit shaky. When I shoot b-roll these days, I like to use a gimbal (like the one in Figure 12.2 in Chapter 12) or a shoulder rig (like the one in Figure 12.1). The shoulder rig helps steady the shot like a tripod but is way more mobile. Sometimes I'll even set up the tripod with the rig mounted to it. This gives me the ability to pop the rig off the tripod and shoulder-mount the camera very quickly if the situation changes while I'm shooting. A gimbal is harder to control when it's mounted on a tripod, but some have that capability. The gimbal smooths out my movement if I'm walking around while the camera is rolling, though, so it's my preference if I'm shooting while moving.

When setting up an interview, you'll want the main camera in front of the participant and framed in a waist-up or head-and-shoulders medium shot. This should be a fairly standard-looking shot that you can fit a lower-thirds graphic underneath in post, like the ones later in this chapter in Figures 13.1 and 13.2. When I shoot single-camera interviews, I used to slowly zoom in during a very profound answer or when the interview gets more in-depth. These days, I just shoot the interview in 4k or even HD and just zoom in slightly in post. When I zoomed in while shooting, I occasionally found that I would need a sound bite when the shot was awkwardly framed for a lower-third graphic. Zooming digitally in post makes it so you can always use the wider shot when you need it. Just be careful – zooming in too much in post will pixelate your image.

With that main camera, you'll want the camera lens to be eye level to the interviewee or a bit higher if they're sitting down. The interviewer (the person asking the questions) should also be about lens high and slightly off to the side. This way, when the participant is talking, their eyeline remains consistent and they're not looking directly into the camera (which would make it look like they were awkwardly talking directly to the viewer). Figures 13.1 and 13.2 illustrate the eyelines you want – about eye level and looking slightly to the side of the lens, not directly into it.

If you have more than one camera, the general rule is that the shots need to be at least 30% different – either at a different angle with similar framing, or at the same angle with different framing, or both. It's common in documentaries these days to see a side-shot of the interviewee. If you're doing a sit-down interview where the interviewer is seen sitting across from the interviewee, then a standard three-camera dialogue scene setup is needed – a 2-shot LS, a CU of the interviewer, and a CU of the interviewee. I've also seen films lately where there is an LS coming from roughly the same angle as the main camera. That LS shows the entire set, including some lights. I think the purpose here is to show that things aren't being staged or faked; the interview isn't artificially produced (AI) or edited together from other speech excerpts.

I'm certainly not against giving your editor these types of options in post, but I really want to caution you to avoid using these secondary shots in place of good visuals. If you can get b-roll of the things the interviewee is talking about, you absolutely should. If you can put graphics into the film to help the viewer process the concepts being talked about, you should. Don't overuse visually interesting camera angles just because you're too lazy to get better visuals. Talking heads can be boring for sure, and sometimes it's important to just see the person's body language when they're talking, but good b-roll can help a viewer visualize the context for the words they're hearing. One of the limitations of the *Central State Hospital* film is that I didn't have any archival footage from when the hospital was at full capacity. Because the population is highly protected, that kind of footage just doesn't exist. My b-roll was all recent shots of the hospital decaying, and my editor ended up needing to use a lot of graphics for illustration.

Lighting

For b-roll, I rarely need lights, because I prefer to show the actuality as it is. If a location is too dark, you should absolutely use lights, but I find that I mainly use my lights for interviews. A standard interview kit for me will have 4 soft lights, either LED panels, or softboxes. I've shot with hard lights many times, and it's a lot more difficult to soften and remove shadows. For documentary work, your goal is almost always soft, even lighting with very few shadows. Shadows will convey that the interviewee is hiding something, which would actually be a bit unethical to do on purpose as a filmmaker. I place a key, fill, and backlight, and do my best to wash the background with my fourth light. I also regularly leave the room lights on and try to match the color temperature with my light kit. The room lights often fill in shadows a bit as well. I usually try to bring an extra three- or four-light kit as backup or for when I suddenly have two people to interview instead of one.

Sound

As mentioned, I usually bring a wireless mic or two as my "plan A" and a wired mic or two as backup. For both, I also bring several XLR cables. For the wired mics, they'll be essential. For the wireless, it's sometimes helpful to put the receiver somewhere else and run a cable to the camera. Sometimes this helps with wireless interference. Sometimes it's just easier, especially if the camera isn't moving and the mic receiver doesn't attach to the camera easily. I always try to run the microphones to the same audio recorder or to the same camera. If I have more than two microphones, I'll need more than two audio channels. In those cases, I will either run all of the mics into a mixer and then to the camera, or I'll rent a separate audio recorder and sync the sound later. Running one mic to one camera and another mic to a different camera is a recipe for disaster when you get to post and try to sync everything up.

Directing

Directing a documentary is very different from directing a fictional film. Documentary sets tend to be a bit more collaborative, and Directors should be open to input from Lighting Directors, Cinematographers, and audio crew members. When I direct, I'm often running camera as well, but ideally I have a camera operator who will set everything up and frame the shot(s) the way they think is best. Then, I come along and talk the shot through with them. If it's b-roll, we just keep shooting different angles at the locations to give the editor options in post. If it's an interview, there are some standard-looking shots that will be expected by the audience, and then extra shots where we can get a bit more creative. As the Director, it's also my job to talk to the participants and actively prep them for the interview. This usually means having them spell out their name and title once the camera is rolling – this helps ensure that lower-thirds graphics are accurate – and then either repeating the question or including enough of the question in their answer that the viewers will understand the context of what they're saying. If your interviewees don't repeat the question or give enough context, your only option in post will be to include the voice of the interviewer asking the question, which is very awkward and disruptive.

Early on in my career, I was doing a film on the erosion of the cliffs near Pacifica, California where I lived. For b-roll, I wanted to get shots of the beach, the cliffs, the houses sitting on top of the cliffs, the sunset over the ocean, and a number of other shots. It was a short film, and I only had one interview to carry the story. The interview went really well. The b-roll was a disaster. Until that point, I had mostly worked in TV news, where b-roll consisted of pretty quick shots and cuts that lasted only a few seconds (news packages are typically only a few minutes long or less). I ran down to the beach with my camera and shot b-roll. My shots almost all had movement (pans, tilts, zooms) that was too quick and didn't sustain at the beginning or end. When I went to edit, I realized that I could hardly use any of it for the longer cuts needed in my film. I learned very quickly on b-roll to start the camera, let it roll in the static shot for a count to 10, then begin a slow, steady movement that only goes in one direction. When I get to the end of my shot,

I sustain a static shot for another 10 seconds before either ending the shot or moving in a different direction. I'd suggest doing the same 10-second counts for zooms as well. When shooting a documentary, your adrenaline will be pumping at times, especially if the action unfolding in front of you isn't something you'll witness again. But you have to take time and slow down to make sure your shots are usable.

I rarely slate my takes for a documentary film, but it is essential if you're shooting dual-system audio and syncing the audio and video in post. Or you should at least clap loudly and sharply on camera to give a spike in the audio waveform to sync with the frame of video where your hands come together. If you're not doing dual-system, I would simply suggest having your interviewees spell out their names and titles. I would also suggest that you develop a good naming system for your raw footage files so you can find everything later. For the Central State film, we ended up with over 30 hours of footage. We named each clip with the name of the film and a descriptor of what was in the shot, for example, "CentralStateFilm_Chapel_Hallway_1," where the number at the end told me which take it was. Since documentaries aren't storyboarded or scripted, I can't name files according to scene number and shot letter like I do for fictional films. Because of that, it's also difficult to slate the different takes. And sometimes action happens suddenly and there isn't time to slate. In those instances, you should slate at the end (this is called a "backslate") if you're shooting dual-system.

Post

For documentary films, postproduction can be the most difficult part. I've made a few short documentaries where things were pretty straightforward and flowed in chronological order. But most of the time, I find that I have a bunch of interviews and b-roll and I have no idea how I'm going to edit it together to tell the story. When I started the *Central State Hospital* film, I assumed I would be the one editing it. I'm fully capable, but every time I sat down to work on it, I quickly became overwhelmed by the amount of footage and the range of topics and ideas we could highlight.

For this reason, one of the first things you'll want to do with your footage is to sit down and organize it into groups. You'll want to decide if you're going to present the film in chronological order, transition from one theme to the next, have a section for each topic, or any other way you choose to present it. Then, work on grouping your visuals and interviews into those themes or into that order. When I edit the Wakonse College Teaching Conference videos, which are non-fiction, it's really easy. The events at the conference happen in chronological order, and the viewers probably appreciate seeing the highlights from the conference in the same order. For the Alcatraz film, I had to figure out the themes and how to transition. I chose to use Native American poems to highlight the issues and to transition from one idea to the next. Then, I grouped the visuals accordingly.

Workflow

Like a fictional film, the first thing to do is to label your clips and back them up. After that, organizing them into folders based on themes or timelines is a good idea. Once you have your themes grouped, you should think about how to transition between them. Maybe you'll use a narrator, graphics, or music. Maybe you'll get very lucky and the sound bites will actually lead from one to the next. Once you've got an idea for how everything will flow, open up your NLE and get started. If you're doing a short film, you can probably just keep everything in one bin and on one timeline. If you're doing a feature-length film, it might be best to start out with a bin and timeline for each topic or theme, then put the timelines together later into a master timeline (that contains the entire film). This way, you can shuffle the order of your themes if you need to. Once you've got everything in order, create a lower-third graphics template. Keep your graphics consistent throughout the film so the viewer is focused on what the interviewees are saying and not why the graphics are different. Finally, add any other graphics and transitions, do audio sweetening, add credits and a title, and then export.

Editing

I already talked about the process, so here I'll give a few pointers on how to choose specific shots to include in your film. As much as possible, when an interviewee starts talking, we should see them and see a graphic over them. After we've seen them on screen once and seen the graphic with their name and title, it's okay not to show them as much. At that point, put b-roll that directly correlates with their words on the screen as much as possible. If they're talking about living in a dorm room, show the dorm room. If you have additional shots of the interviewee as they talk, you can edit these in at natural breaks in the audio. When a person pauses or shifts to a different aspect of the topic, it's a good place to cut to b-roll or another camera angle. If you're transitioning from one person talking to a different one (vox pop style), you'll want a transitionary device in between. I will sometimes use a dip-to-black here, or a graphical transition, even though the audio continues seamlessly. Ideally, you'll have b-roll at the end of the first person speaking, so when the next person speaks on camera, you can cut to them directly without it jarring the viewer.

Graphics

For anyone talking, you'll want to establish their credibility with the viewer as quickly as possible. The easiest way to do this is with a lower-third graphic. It's called a lower-third because when you divide the screen into the rule of thirds, these graphics fall entirely within the lower third of the screen. Figure 13.1 shows an example of a fairly plain lower-third graphic. I did this quickly within my NLE – all of them have standard templates for lower-thirds – and it contains the person's name and their title. The title gives viewers the context and credibility for why the person is speaking on the topic.

Figure 13.1 A simple lower-third graphic from an NLE template. Most of the time, you can choose your font type and size from the template options. You can also choose a background color and shape, as well as the opacity/transparency of the color background. I used a dropper to match the color of the sky for symmetry.

Figure 13.2 This lower-third graphic contains the person's name and title. When we interviewed Sheriff Massee for the film, he was a wealth of knowledge because he grew up in the area around the hospital and because he was the sheriff who had to respond to calls when people with mental health issues were in crisis out in the community. Thus, two separate titles.

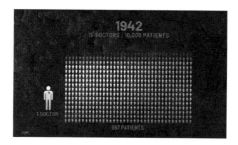

Figure 13.3 A fairly complex graphic that helps illustrate the points made by the interviewees. Problems happened at Central State because the hospital was severely understaffed at times and not because of an uncaring staff. Graphics like this should be easy to read and understand quickly.

You might also need to do graphics in a separate program and not your NLE. The lower-third in Figure 13.2 and the graphics done in Figure 13.3 are not standard templates in any NLE. My editor for the *Central State Hospital* film created these graphics by hand in a separate program. Notice that the font types are consistent. The image of the hospital building in the lower-third graphic ties the interviews to the film's topic.

It should be obvious, but your title screen in the beginning of your film and the credits at the end of your film should match the text style developed in the graphics throughout your film. There are few good options inside the NLE for title graphics at the beginning, but there are many different credit roll templates for the end of your film.

Distribution

Once your film is finished, you'll want to send it out to festivals, screen it for interested audiences, and hopefully house it online or somewhere people can watch it. As with other genres, it doesn't hurt to test it out on an audience or two to see if it flows well and elicits interest in the topic. You might have to do some tweaks in editing, but a word of caution here: a documentary film can feel like something that is never quite finished. Because they're often done as side projects, on low budgets, and without hard deadlines, it's easy to keep tweaking your film indefinitely. Set yourself a festival deadline and get it done. Once there, do your best to love it and move on. When looking for festivals, do a little research and target specific ones at first. Some festivals are only open to debut entries, or they have special awards if this is the first festival the film will screen at. So, before you send it out to a large number of festivals, target a few that seem to be good shots to be interested in your film and your topic. After that, a website like filmfreeway can help you get your film out there to festivals around the country and around the world. Today, many of these festivals are virtual or don't require you to attend in person. For the *Central State Hospital* film, I targeted four very specific festivals. It didn't get into the first three, but it did get screened at the fourth. From there, I put it on filmfreeway and won awards at two more festivals. Now, the film is available online, and it's on permanent display at the University of Georgia state archives, as well as the museum on the grounds of the former Central State Hospital.

Case Study: *Central State Hospital: An Oral History*

Search online for "Central State Hospital: An Oral History (festival version)" or go to https://www.youtube.com/watch?v=Y31Alp-fpWA and you'll find the version of the film that we entered into most of the festivals. The feature-length version was our first attempt, and once we entered it into the first festival, we got feedback that it was too slow in places. The festival version settled in at around 43 minutes, which is under the 45-minute cutoff of some festivals, but well over the 30-minute cutoff to be considered a "short" film at other festivals. We debated trying to produce different length versions to match some of the festival parameters, but ultimately those versions didn't feel complete.

I've already used the film as an example for much of this chapter. We began the process by doing a ton of research. I read books on mental health and mental healthcare. I read newspaper articles about the hospital itself. I had students compile all of this research and write up synopses of the different topics we could explore. Together, we developed a treatment that settled on an initial round of interviews and shots of the hospital buildings and grounds as they were currently. We hoped to find historical photos and videos to include, but struggled to do so once we began. What visual materials the hospital had weren't organized very well at the time, and we abandoned that route. Once we had done the research, we started off with a few interviews. We interviewed Andy Miller, the reporter from the *Atlanta Journal-Constitution*, which reported on the hospital and several deaths that had occurred, as well as the Supreme Court Decision in the Olmstead case. Olmstead determined that individuals need to be cared for in the least restrictive environment possible. It didn't ban institutionalization, but it required states to move people into community-based care whenever possible. We explored the decision a bit in the film, and eventually connected with the lawyers from Atlanta Legal Aid who argued the Olmstead case. But since it was only part of the history of the hospital, we had other avenues to explore.

After the first round of interviews with some of the hospital staff, a representative from NAMI (the National Alliance on Mental Illness) who used to work at the hospital, and the Director of a local non-profit that taught art and music classes to people in the community, we regrouped. We listed out other people we wanted to interview, like the son of a former Director of the hospital, and Goldie Marks, a former client of Central State Hospital who had since moved out and lived independently. This round of interviews led us to other people, like Betty Vandiver, the former first lady of Georgia, whose husband was the governor when the Chapel of All Faiths was built on the campus. As we interviewed someone, they often told us about someone else they thought we should contact. They would even help us reach out and set everything up. I found that all of these participants were eager to tell their stories, and it was actually difficult to start figuring out which ones to pursue and which ones to let go of. I haven't reached that point of saturation with other films I've done, but for this one our reputation began to spread within the community, and we had more people willing to do interviews than we had time to do them. We ended up talking to some notable people, and we made sure we had at least one person who could speak with authority about each aspect of the hospital and mental illness in general.

We also toured around the hospital and made notes of the different buildings we wanted to go inside and what shots we thought would be good from the outside for our b-roll. Going inside of the old maximum-security building for the criminally insane felt important at the time, so we put it on our list. Going inside the new building also seemed important at the time, but none of that footage actually made it into the film. It ended up looking just like any other modern building, and of course we didn't have access to places where clients were actually housed. Sometimes shots will work out great, and sometimes they won't even make it in your film. When people talked about specifics, like when Betty Vandiver remembered the porches and how clients would sit on them in rocking chairs, we felt that it was important to get shots of those porches. Again, I'm not sure those shots even made it into the film, but this gave our editor the option of including visuals to illustrate the sound bites. Of course, we didn't know we needed these shots until after that interview, so we ended up going out to the hospital grounds during and after each round of interviews.

In the end, we had over 30 hours of raw footage. About two-thirds of that (or maybe more) was interviews, and the rest was b-roll. We also shot about 500 still images with a DSLR camera. We didn't end up using them, but for some of the graphics and the film's poster, they still turned out to be valuable. Daniel ended up conducting two more interviews after we had already entered post-production. I moved away from Milledgeville before completing the project, but I attempted to edit it myself at first. Because the footage called for something longer form than we had originally planned, I had trouble figuring out how to tell the story. I hired our first editor a couple years after shooting wrapped. That editor cut together a 90-minute version where the sound bites flowed from one topic to another really well. It was entirely talking heads, though, and we had a disagreement on whether the b-roll and stills we shot were usable. It was the same sort of argument that I heard from festival judges later – we needed historical footage and images of clients in their daily lives at the institution to illustrate the words. Since this footage just didn't exist, that editor left the project on good terms, but incomplete. A few years after that, Joe approached me about editing the project.

I purchased a hard drive, filled it with the 30 hours of footage and previous project files (keeping everything backed up on my own drives), and shipped it to Joe. We had several Zoom calls during the beginning of post with Joe, Daniel, and I to decide on the direction(s) we wanted to go. We decided to start from scratch instead of using the 90-minute version that the first editor had done. After getting a good idea of the vision together, Joe set about editing. Later, we discussed using a good number of graphics to help illustrate the sound bites and transition between topics. Joe's first cut was the feature-length version at 105 minutes. I really like this version, and it tells the most complete story of the hospital, but when we sent it off to festivals, we got some valuable feedback. That version didn't make it into any festivals. We used the feedback to tighten up the film and make it move a little faster from one topic to the next. We ended up with a 45-minute version that we sent off to another festival, but we felt like that one wasn't quite right. Finally, Joe cut the 43-minute festival version and told me he felt really good about it. Daniel and I watched it and we loved it.

All three of us felt like we could have kept going and produced another version, but quite frankly, we were all starting to feel like we should be done with the project and we were getting burned out and ready to move on to other things. Especially for the editor, a documentary film can always be a work in progress. Unlike a fictional film where the story was outlined in preproduction, documentaries can take on many different forms and tell many different stories with the same footage.

I learned a lot from the experience. In total, we worked on the film for over ten years. At times, I gave up on completing it. I had classes to teach, weddings to shoot, TV shows to produce, and many other projects that took precedence. Many documentary films are done as side projects, and this one wasn't any different. I also learned that the documentary impulse to simply explore a topic is a powerful one. We didn't know what the story would be when we started the project. We didn't even know what the story would be while we were in production. So, it was easy to follow all of our leads and shoot anything we were interested in. The downside of that approach is that we stalled out during editing. If we had developed our topics and stories in preproduction, or even while we were shooting, post would have been a lot easier. But we also would have had an incomplete film that didn't explore the complexity of the topics we presented. Lastly, I learned that it helps to be passionate or to develop a passion for the topic. Joe was only able to take the film across the finish line because it was a topic he cared deeply about.

Chapter 13: Documentary Films Main Points

- Producing a documentary is a lot different than fictional films and scripted formats. It's best to plan out everything you can ahead of time, but you have to be flexible and open to new directions.
- During preproduction, you need to do a lot of research and develop a detailed treatment to guide you as you begin exploring the topic with your cameras and microphones.
- You should line up your first round of interviews during preproduction, but keep a schedule open for additional interviews as they snowball. One participant will lead you to additional participants.
- Always treat people, locations, and topics ethically. Your reputation will precede you as you dive into a community that is intimately familiar with the film's topic. It's important to treat everyone with respect and integrity.
- Postproduction is where the story will come together. It's worth taking the time to look through all of your footage and get everything organized before you sit down to edit. Develop a plan first, as if you're back in preproduction and scripting everything.
- Making a documentary is full of highs and lows. It's easy to get discouraged, but stick with it. Reach out to others who have an interest in the topic when you need fresh eyes or help.
- Getting your film out there for people to see can also be discouraging. Find festivals where the film will fit in. When you're done entering festivals, look for distribution outlets. Finally, put your film online or in archives for people to access.

14 News Packages

The timelines for news packages are usually incredibly tight, and often within hours of learning about the topic. Like documentaries, doing as much research as possible helps, but there is a balance between getting to the scene or event quickly and knowing about the topic before you get there. At times, you might have months to do research and collect interviews and b-roll, but other times, you might have mere hours between the time you get assigned to the story and the time you need to have the package shot and edited. For example, if you're coving a typical election cycle, you'll know who the candidates are and what they stand for prior to covering a debate or other event. But if you're covering a car accident where a politician was injured, you might know quite a bit about the person and absolutely nothing about the situation. Good news producers develop formulas for their production process so they can be as efficient as possible when heading into unknown situations.

Preproduction

When I worked for a local news station, we were often covering breaking news and planned events. Preparation for the two was pretty different, but in both cases things happened quickly. The station had a number of ENG (Electronic News Gathering) sets of gear ready to go at any moment. This means the batteries are put on chargers the minute the camera is returned to the station so it could go out at a moment's notice. It also

DOI: 10.4324/9781003010357-19

meant that the cameras, microphones, and lighting gear were standardized and people were trained on how to use them.

Often, a reporter would go out and cover an event or breaking story by themselves. This is the MMJ (Multimedia Journalist) model, where the reporter is responsible for a number of things. In the MMJ model, the reporter gets the call on a story, grabs the gear, and travels to the location. Once there, the MMJ quickly assesses the situation and lines up interviews. If people are busy dealing with the situation and there isn't a spokesperson on the scene yet, then the MMJ sets up the camera and records b-roll of the developing situation. If there is a person willing to give interviews, then the MMJ sets up the tripod, camera, lights, and mics, and conducts the interview first. After the interview(s), the MMJ will then shoot b-roll and a standup. A standup is when you see the reporter live on the scene, standing in front of the camera, talking directly to the audience or the anchors back in the newsroom.

An example of the MMJ model would be a story on a local house fire. The reporter would hear the call go out on the scanner, grab the gear, and head to the location of the fire. They probably won't know many details, and won't know exactly how they're going to cover the story. There isn't any time for planning or preproduction, but the MMJ relies on a standardized workflow to help guide them. They arrive on the scene and look around to see if there is anyone to talk to. If the firefighters are still battling the blaze, then the MMJ will switch gears and shoot b-roll with the camera. After things settle down a bit, someone from the fire department will likely be available to give interviews. At that point, the MMJ will set up the tripod, mount the camera to it, put batteries in the wireless mics, set up the lights (or use an on-camera light), and quickly draft some questions to ask during the interview. These interviews are usually not as polished as a documentary film interview, and there is almost never a second camera to get side shots. But the goal is the same: to get succinct sound bites that can be cut into a news package and help tell the story. After everything has been shot, the MMJ will be able to script out an intro, outro, and transitions for the news package and record these in their standup. If this sounds like very little preproduction, it's because it is. If an MMJ takes the time to research who lives in the house, how the call came in, and other details before arriving at the scene of the fire, they might not get the same footage, or other news stations might already have the story covered. Speed is important in news.

There are also times when news reporters cover scheduled events. A press conference by the governor, for example, is usually planned days, weeks, or months in advance. The News Director at a station would have plenty of notice to assign a reporter and a photog (short for "photographer," even though it means the person who shoots the video) to the event. When I worked in news, these were the types of news packages where the production assistants got to go out and shoot. Otherwise, my job mostly consisted of cutting together b-roll that came in over satellite feeds for national stories, and running a camera or other equipment during the live studio news show. When I did get to go out and shoot in the field as a photog, it was a welcome change to my normal routine. For something scheduled, a reporter was assigned in advance. They would do the research on the event and make phone calls to set up interviews ahead of time. They would even sometimes go and shoot b-roll ahead of time, or recall old footage from previous news stories that could be related to the current event. For example, if the governor's press conference was scheduled to introduce a new funding package for road improvements, the reporter could go out and shoot b-roll of roads ahead of time. Or, they could go through archival footage and find old stories of road repairs and look for b-roll that might be relevant to the current story.

After doing the research and setting up the interviews, the reporter and photog pack up the gear, drive to the location, and execute the schedule laid out in preproduction. Interviews would have been lined up for specific times. The press event itself will need some setup time for lights and microphones. And the b-roll at the event might be planned ahead of time, although often the photog will simply look around with the camera during breaks and shoot interesting visuals. For a governor's press conference, an exterior shot of the capitol building or governor's office might work for the story. Even though the reporter is most likely going to be the one editing the video, they'll still want options in post, especially since a news package can't be storyboarded or scripted out in preproduction. Like a documentary film, the story a news package tells usually comes together in post.

Participants

Like documentaries, there are ethical decisions to be made when shooting a news package. Paying actors would be completely unethical. We generally think that if people who support only one side of an issue are interviewed, the journalist isn't being ethical with their presentation of the issue. There are exceptions to that, however. If you only interview people who thought an accidental death was a tragedy, you wouldn't necessarily need to present people who thought the death was a good thing. The point here is that you should do your best to explore the issue and to interview people with differing viewpoints. The Society of Professional Journalists (SPJ) has a very good and detailed Code of Ethics. I would highly recommend reading through it if you want to produce news packages. One additional note on ethics: sometimes you shouldn't interview the person who is closest to the topic or event. Even if the family is willing to interview right after their house was destroyed by a fire, you're catching them at a very vulnerable time and showing them in a way they might regret later. You'll often see people interviewed after their house is destroyed by a tornado. As much as this captivates the viewer, for those people who have lost everything, you should treat their words with great care.

Because sit-down interviews take time to set up, they're not often used in news packages. Instead, many participants are interviewed right on the spot and not planned out as thoroughly as documentary interviews are. One extreme example of this is when a reporter will conduct "person on the street" interviews. Like it sounds, the reporter sets up the camera and a handheld microphone, then tries to stop people and interview them as they walk by on the sidewalk. This only works when you ask everyone similar questions (so you can edit them together better) and the reporter plays the part of the on-camera interviewer. The reporter will hold the microphone and ask their question, then hold it out to hear the answer. If the question requires back and forth between the reporter and the participant, the reporter will hold the mic and move it as needed. Person on the street interviews pretty much require a camera operator to be there, because the shots need to be framed on the fly as people come and go.

Person on the street interviews should be done for topics like elections or public reactions to something. The idea here is that a variety of thoughts need to be heard. However, it would be inappropriate in many situations. For instance, if there were a car accident, you wouldn't need to line up interviews just to hear each person say it was a tragedy. One eyewitness or two who can describe what happened would be enough. If you're planning on producing news packages, I cannot stress this enough: watch the news. The more you watch, the more you'll pick up on who the interviewees are, how they lend credibility to the topic, and how the reporter asks questions to elicit sound bites that are edited together in the package. You'll start to notice a formula. Google "Charlie Brooker's How to Report the News" and you'll find a satire video that absolutely nails the way news packages are put together (I'll also say "sorry" for the bad language in the video). Watching this satirical piece will actually educate you about the different types of interviews you might do in a news package and how you might present those people in your final cut.

Locations

As with interviews, there isn't a lot of time to set up permissions for different locations when producing a news package. And most often, the location is a key component of the story. If you know it might be difficult to get permission to shoot somewhere, you should definitely call ahead. If you can't get permission, then you set up in a public space and shoot with the location in the background. For example, when reporting on a potential merger happening between two large companies, you probably won't get access to the board room where the merger is being discussed. But you can set up on a public sidewalk with one of the company's buildings in the background of the shot. If you look at news packages, many of them are shot this way.

The general guideline is that if you set up your camera in a public space (typically sidewalks and parks) outdoors, you're probably okay to shoot there. If you're going inside a building, you need to ask for permission to set up inside, even if it is a public building. This is because even though you have a right to be there, the people inside that building have a certain expectation of privacy. The people who run the building also have to be able to conduct their business without interference. I had a student once who set their camera up outside of the student health center on campus. They were on a public sidewalk and were shooting towards the building. Legally, they had the right to be there. The campus police were called, though, because that student had not contacted the health center and received permission. The health center was conducting STD testing that day, and the presence of the camera had a chilling effect on the event. None of the students who might have used the health center at that time felt comfortable being in the background of the shot. There are exceptions to the rule that it is okay to shoot in a public space.

Another exception specifically for students is that you can't go into a classroom and set your camera up and start shooting without permission. Even though a public university is technically owned by the state, the camera would have a disruptive effect on the classroom. Another caveat to shooting in public is that people have a right to privacy. If you've set your camera up on a public sidewalk, but use technology like a zoom lens to look through someone's home windows, this is also illegal without permission. If it can be seen without technology, you can shoot it. If you need zoom lenses, infrared lenses, or anything else not available to your eyes, this is not only unethical, and the courts have generally ruled that it is also a violation of privacy.

Equipment

Equipment is usually cared for by station engineers, but it is often the reporter's or photog's job to check out a set of gear and make sure batteries get put on chargers when they return. Sometimes the SD card or other media belongs to the MMJ, and sometimes it gets returned to the camera after the footage is imported into the NLE and backed up. Often, the wireless mic set will be inside the camera bag, and the bag will have enough room

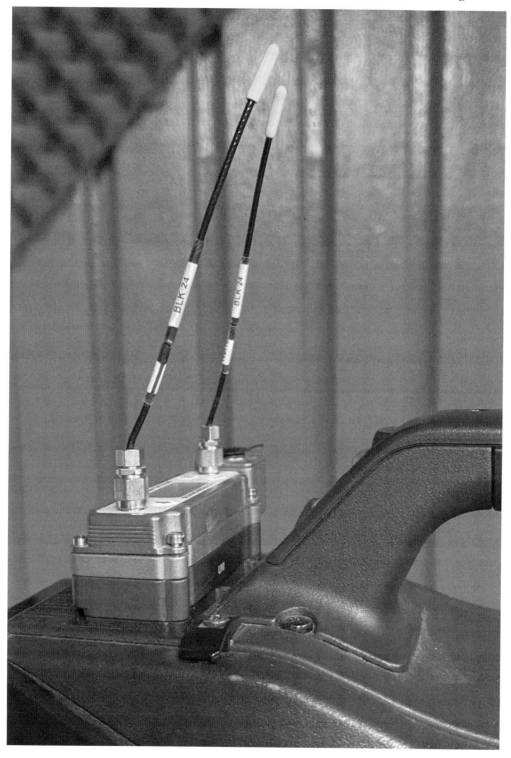

Figure 14.1 The ENG camera often has a microphone receiver built into it.

for extra batteries. There might also be a battery-powered light that mounts directly onto the camera's cold shoe. These lights aren't ideal, but they're better than nothing when shooting in low light.

The microphone set will likely have the receiver built into the camera and draw power from the camera battery, but the transmitter for the mic will often have two separate components. One will be an XLR plug attached to a transmitter (as seen in Chapter 6 in Figure 6.9). This plugs into a handheld mic, often with a foam "flag" that slides up underneath the mic's windscreen and has the station's logo on it. For any interview or standup where the reporter is seen, this is the microphone that will be used. For an interview where the participant is the only one in the shot, the reporter or photog will often use a wireless lavalier mic and place it on the person before shooting the interview. It's important to note that some systems will only allow one of these transmitters to connect to the receiver at any given time. Some receivers actually have two separate antenna systems and can handle more than one transmitter, but the microphones would still need to operate on separate frequencies to avoid interfering with each other.

The light kit will usually be inside a separate bag or hard case, and will usually consist of anywhere from three to four lights and stands. When I worked for the TV station, we had three-light kits that were open-faced hard light instruments. So, we carried gels that we could quickly clip onto the lights to diffuse them. Today, I imagine that news stations prefer softer LED panel lights for their interviews. There won't be flags or scrims on C-stands to shape the lights, but there may be barn doors to help block some of the spill.

Workflow

Reporters typically have two distinctive ways they get stories. First, they might work a beat where they are assigned to a specific region or a specific topic. A reporter might have the City Hall beat, for example, and cover City Council meetings and other city government decisions. Or they might be assigned to the North City beat and cover every breaking story in that area. Sometimes, whoever is on shift at the time goes out to cover any news that breaks during their shift. There are a lot of ways to assign beats, but the point is that there shouldn't be any seams. When breaking news happens, it should be determined well in advance who will be covering it. That way, no time is wasted trying to make phone calls and see who is available to cover it.

The second way stories are assigned is in pitch meetings or assignment meetings. These are usually the stories that are scheduled, or topics that aren't on a short timeline to get aired. For those news packages, the reporter might pitch the topic to the News Director, or the News Director might assign the topic to the reporter. If the topic is pitched, the News Director has the ability to say no, as they are in charge of news operations at the station and they usually decide what goes on air and what doesn't in terms of the newscast. Either way, the News Director or the reporter might have an idea for people to interview, approaches to the topic, or other guidance to begin putting the package together. From there, the reporter makes phone calls, sets up locations and interviews, and plans out questions. This can look a lot like the preproduction for a documentary film if the topic or event can be planned out ahead of time.

Production

The approach to shooting a news package is pretty straightforward. If you're the reporter or photog on the scene, shoot b-roll of the things you find interesting or relevant to the story whenever you have time before, in between, or after you shoot the interviews. Long shots are good for location information, but close ups will be necessary for the viewers to see any specific details. Interviews should be framed in loose close ups or medium shots, and often include the participant from the waist up (a "waist shot"). If the reporter is

Figure 14.2 A wireless XLR transmitter and mic with the station's flag slid up underneath the microphone's windscreen.

seen in the shot, then it should be a tighter 2-shot where we might see the waists of both people. We rarely see interviews in news packages that are further out than an MS, unless the participant's relationship to the location is important, in which case an LS will show more of the location with the participant in it. Even then, you don't want to conduct the entire interview like this. Just get some b-roll framed like that, or maybe only the first question or two. You want the viewer to really listen to the words being said and to focus on the people, so when that participant is on the screen, you want to minimize distractions.

Cameras

If an MMJ is setting the camera up and also shooting the standup, the LCD screen built into the side or top of the camera is extremely important. So is the autofocus. If you're working as an MMJ and doing the setup and reporting at the same time, set the camera in autofocus, then flip the screen around so you can see it while you stand in front of the camera. From there, go back and forth to the camera and pan, tilt, or zoom until you get the shot framed the way you want it. If autofocus isn't available on your camera, or if the background is extremely busy and will cause the autofocus to jump, then set up a

Figure 14.3 The LCD screen is turned to face the person in front of the camera. This allows the MMJ to frame the shot and ensure that it's in focus when they don't have a photog with them. This isn't ideal, and it often leads to poor framing and blurry shots, but it saves the station having to send two people out for a news story.

light stand or set something up at the distance you'll be standing from the camera, and set your focus to it. Then, do your best to stand at that distance and you'll stay in focus.

If you're doing a standup interview with someone, you can set your focus on them, then use the flipped LCD screen to frame the two of you together in the shot. This is much easier than trying to do it for a single standup. I can't tell you how distracting it is when I'm watching the local news and the reporters are doing a standup and they're out of focus. I might be more sensitive than the typical viewer, but I have to imagine that this comes across as amateurish. It also happens fairly often when reporters have to run their own cameras for their interviews and standups.

Like my advice for conducting documentary interviews, my preference for news packages is to stand behind and slightly to the side of the camera when shooting interviews where the reporter isn't in the shot. That way, the interviewee's eyeline is looking slightly off-camera and not wandering or looking directly into the camera. Do your best to maintain eye contact with the person while they're talking as well. If you're checking the camera shot or fiddling with it, they'll get distracted or start to look around as they talk. If you've ever had a conversation with someone who asks a question, then starts playing with their phone, you've done the same thing – you wonder what they're doing, why they even asked the question, and why they're not paying attention to your answer.

Lighting

For b-roll and run-and-gun interviews (like the person on the street interview style mentioned earlier), an on-camera light might be your only option. These used to be tiny but powerful hard lights that weren't at all flattering to the person being interviewed. Today, my preference is to mount a small LED panel light onto the camera's cold shoe, then aim it slightly downward so it illuminates the area the camera is pointed at. These LED panels should have diffusion gel on them to soften the light as much as possible. Even then, the light flattens out the subject since it comes from the same direction as the camera. But at least this way, you don't have a lot of setup time if you find someone at a scene who is willing to talk on camera. You just set the tripod up, throw the camera on it, and start recording. If there is a separate photog, then they might even just walk around with the camera on their shoulder and hold it very still while they shoot an interview.

If you're using a two-light kit, the lights should be used as a key and fill, unless the background is too dark to see. In that case, move the key light almost directly in line with the camera (it will give the same effect as an on-camera light will, but at least it will fill in the shadows on the person's face). The second light should then be placed slightly in front of the participant, but just out of the frame, and aimed at the background. This will light up the background, won't cast a strong shadow from the participant, and will hopefully fill in some of the shadows on the side of the face opposite the key light.

If you're using a three-light kit, you should use a standard three-point lighting setup. One light for the key, one for the fill, and one for the backlight/rimlight. If the background needs extra light, then remove the backlight and aim it at the background instead. This will cause the depth to flatten out, and the participant will look like they're plastered to the background, but it will be better than not having a light for the location. If you have a four-light kit, then you've got the key, fill, backlight, and background lights. Don't forget that overhead lights and windows work well for non-fiction. Since you're not going for a dramatic effect, your main goal is to fill in the shadows and show the relationship between the participant and the location.

Figure 14.4 An on-camera light panel. These should always be powered by their own battery so they don't drain the camera's battery too fast.

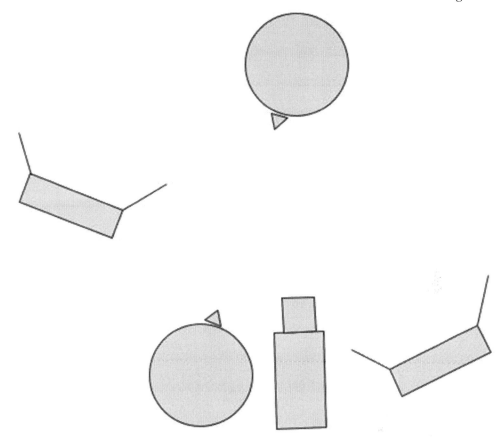

Figure 14.5 A two-light setup for an interview where the background needs extra light. Remember that the barn doors in the lighting plot indicate the direction the light is pointing.

Sound

I've talked about the equipment already, but I haven't mentioned headphones yet. If they're not part of the camera package you check out from the station, you'll need to purchase a good pair of headphones if you're a reporter or photog. News crews never have a sound person on location, so it's important that you know how to record and monitor good sound. Even when I'm interviewing a participant from behind the camera, I always wear my headphones and listen for audio trouble. This saves me a lot of headache in post. For one interview I shot at Balboa High School in San Francisco, buses kept driving past. When this happened, I simply waited for them to finish their answer, then asked the participant to repeat it and explained that the audio wasn't clean because of the buses. Or if they seem particularly nervous, wait for them to finish and then ask the question in a slightly different way, so they say roughly the same thing, but they think you're just asking for clarification. Follow-up questions like this often elicit sound bites that are clearer and more succinct anyway.

    You should also do a quick mic check on a participant before launching into the interview. If you're practiced at it, you can probably set levels manually while they're saying and spelling their name out in the beginning of the interview. During that time, it doesn't matter if they're looking off-camera or seem distracted. If you don't feel confident about your levels after they spell their name, just tell them you need a sound check and ask them your first question as a "rehearsal." If it takes you a minute to get the levels right, you can always ask the question again. If you have good levels quickly, you can just say, "actually, that was great! We can move on to the next question." This gives them confidence right out of the gate that they're doing well and will help them relax.

Your goal for levels should be −6 to −12 dB. This is slightly lower than my recommendations for narrative projects, but you won't be able to ride levels as closely if your participant gets loud all of a sudden. You can glance at the levels on the screen every once in a while (when you also check framing and focus), but don't do it too often or you'll lose their eye contact. And I would strongly caution against AGC (automatic gain control) for interviews. While the participant is thinking, the camera will boost the levels during the silence and your background noise levels will be all over the place. Usually in news packages, we don't actually record room tone. This is for two reasons: first, because of the fast turnaround times, laying down room tone and mixing levels isn't efficient; and second, the background noise during the interview actually lends it authenticity. As long as the viewer can clearly hear the words the interviewee is saying, anything in the background just gives the interview a more natural feel. After all, we don't expect polished, staged news. We expect actuality.

Post

Postproduction for news packages happens very quickly. And for MMJs, post will also include writing up a story for the station's website and sending it and the video package to the online editor for the web. When I worked in news, reporters had at least until the 6pm newscast to finish their editing. Today, the deadline is as soon as possible. Sometimes, MMJs are even shooting and editing on their phones at the location and posting the video to the web before they even get in the car and drive back to the station. This book isn't really about shooting news packages on your phone, but if you're going to be a journalist, it's something you might want to learn.

Workflow

Once the b-roll and interviews are captured, the MMJ begins editing. As with documentary films, it's worthwhile to take a few minutes and list out what you've got. You should absolutely take the time to rename the files, and at many stations, there is a centralized server to house all of the footage you shot. This allows the footage to be edited on any computer in the building, and if the server has enough room on it, it will also house archival footage that might be useful to your current story. Some larger networks generate entirely too much footage to archive on one server, so they might use a backup archival system of hard drives or cloud storage. In those cases, it's even more important to label the clips in a descriptive way, often with a topic, location, date, people involved, etc. and tag it with metadata so it can be found later by computer searches. Every station might have a slightly different workflow when it comes to labeling and archiving footage.

When it comes to post, though, I would start with the sound bites from interviews and figure out which ones are short enough and help tell the story in a way that makes your package flow. It's even better if you got b-roll of the things they're talking about in the sound bites. Once you've cataloged everything, figure out the order you want to show things in and sit down to start editing. Record any narration transitions you need to help it flow. You hopefully already did your standup intro and maybe a standup outro on location, but until you edit, you don't necessarily know which spots will need help transitioning from one topic or sound bite to another. After you get everything laid down on the timeline, add your graphics and then export. In a server environment, you'll likely be exporting directly to a playback server so the newscast can roll it into their 6pm or 10pm show. Most stations will also want you to export a copy for the web.

Editing

I almost always begin editing a news package by laying down my sound bites first. Once I have them in the right order to tell the story, I put in my intro and outro, then lay down transitions. Finally, I put the b-roll in on top to illustrate the points being made. After I have the visuals in place, I clean up the audio and fade the transitions in and out so the gaps between audio clips aren't noticeable. This isn't a hard, fast rule for workflow. Sometimes a story is fairly linear, and you can edit it more like a fictional film where you just lay the clips down from start to finish in order. Since this is non-fiction, though, you'll often be refining the story and finding the best way to tell it as you edit.

Because news packages are usually simple editing projects with few effects, coloring, or graphics (besides the lower-thirds), there are often different NLE software preferences. Sometimes, that's because only certain NLEs will interface with the station's server system. Sometimes, it's because Adobe Premiere, DaVinci Resolve, and AVID Media Composer are a bit cumbersome to launch a new project, import the footage, and edit. There are NLEs out there like the AVID Newscutter option, the Cut tab in DaVinci, and even things like iMovie and ShotCut that are built for speed.

Graphics

It doesn't hurt to know how to create graphics within your NLE for news packages, but most stations will have templates for their lower-thirds, or you will actually leave them out of the package altogether. For packages that are designed for air, your station might prefer to use the studio control room's switcher to create and lay in graphics live during the broadcast. You might still need to insert lower-thirds graphics for the web page, though. For full-screen graphics or information that is part of your story, you'll probably have some guidance from the station for how to create and format it. Many NLEs will let you lay down a photo background and put simple text over it, so knowing a bit about Adobe Photoshop can be helpful for creating full-screen graphics. If you're a photog and you're doing the editing, knowing more advanced programs like Adobe After Effects will be extremely helpful for creating motion graphics that enhance the visuals. Just be sure that however you create the text, you don't crowd the screen with too much information and your words are easy to read quickly. A good rule of thumb is to leave a graphic on the screen for twice as long as it takes you to read everything on it.

Airing

When your package is rolled into a newscast, it needs to be timed out to the exact second. The anchors and live production staff will need to know exactly how long it is so the anchor can come back in smoothly. The anchor will also likely want to know the outcue from the package. This is written into the live newscast script so the entire production crew knows the last words that are spoken in the package. It's a way to know you're coming back soon without even looking at the clock. Lastly, some anchors and stations want help to script out the transitions. You might be asked for a scripted intro and outro for the anchor to read to introduce the package and to come back out of it. Of course, different stations might choose to do things differently. A station usually spends the first few weeks of employment training their reporters and photogs on the process and formulas they prefer.

For the web distribution, you'll probably be asked to write a short story to go with the video. Most readers/viewers won't click on a news package video based solely on the thumbnail. The video will need a caption and probably a paragraph to several paragraphs of print to go with it. I'm certainly not an expert on print journalism, but when writing for the web, you should still use the inverted pyramid style. This means putting the most relevant information first with the lead, followed by more details in the body, and then the conclusion with the rest of the information.

Case Study: *Happy Half Hour*

Even though I worked in TV news, I never owned anything I produced, so instead I wanted to give a recent example of a news package. Last year, we started a new show at my university, called *Happy Half Hour*. My students were the producers for the show and produced all of the news packages. As the executive producer for the show, I helped guide students in the process and gave them feedback and suggestions on their packages. The show was styled after a late-night talk show, so I wouldn't consider it to be hard news, but it certainly reported news from the community in a way that required research, planning, shooting, and editing. To view the episodes, search on YouTube for the "UCM CTV" channel and *Happy Half Hour*. I'm going to talk about two packages we rolled into episode 5 (the Hot Rod Car Show around 8:30 and the Clay Clear Band spotlight around 15:00) for this case study. I'll also talk a little about the Cinderella package in episode 8 (at around 13:50). These three packages are very different and each required a different approach.

For the Hot Rod Car Show package, the City of Warrensburg, Missouri has an annual festival. The students knew the festival was coming up and researched the different events and happenings. They decided that the car show would be a good focus for a package. The potential for visuals and interviews was intriguing. The producer for the package did a little bit of research and some phone calls to figure out what streets the car show would take place on, and when it would run, but they didn't have any specific names to reach out and set up interviews or focus on specific cars. Instead, they recruited a photog to go out with them and run the camera while they walked around and interviewed people. The reporter, Roman Pfister, simply walked around the event and looked for interesting cars, like the VW Bus, with great stories behind them. After talking to the owners for a minute or two, he asked them if they would be willing to do an interview. Once they said yes, he miked them up while the photog set up the camera. No lights were needed because it was a bright sunny day, but care was taken so the sun didn't silhouette the participant. The car was in the background of the shot to give the interview a good backdrop. After the interview, the photog shouldered the camera and got some b-roll of the VW. Then the group walked on to the next street looking to repeat the process. In post, Roman laid down the interview sound bites first, then put in the standups he recorded on location, then put in the b-roll. Some b-roll of cars and streets helped him transition between cars he spotlighted. Then, lower-thirds graphics were put in. He probably needed to clean up the audio a little bit after that. He exported the clip and loaded it up into our cloud storage, and we downloaded it and played it back live into the show that week. This is essentially a person on the street interview setup, with the twist of having the cars as the backdrop.

Later in the episode, Mason Harding, our music reporter, did a package on the Clay Clear Band. Incidentally, this is the same band that my other students did the music video for in Chapter 12. Don't let their UCM connection fool you, though – Clay is a rising star in country music. We were just lucky enough that he's local and has connections to some of our students. Mason actually works at the guitar shop where Clay goes, and asked him if he would be willing to be interviewed. Once Clay and the band agreed, Mason did more research. He figured out when and where the next concert was, went and got b-roll at that concert, and asked the band for additional footage. The drone shots in the beginning were visuals provided by the band, as was some of the concert footage. In this situation, though, I believe Mason actually shot the b-roll before doing the interview. The timing just worked out that way, but the visuals are not specific enough that they had to be inserted at specific points of the interviews. The b-roll just has the band setting up for the concert and playing various venues. For the interviews, Mason decided to actually shoot the band in the guitar shop. If he had chosen to do the interviews at one of the venues where he was already shooting b-roll, it might have been more convenient. But the band would also have been more distracted. And the background noise would have been worse. The guitar shop provides a good visual background and allowed Mason to set up lights and mics, and conduct several really nice interviews. He got some great sound bites. In post, he took all of his interview footage and laid down the sound bites first. Where they didn't quite connect, Mason recorded his own voiceovers to bridge the gaps. He inserted those transitions into the audio track, then laid down all the b-roll. This is a great example that shows you can never have too much b-roll. There is a good variety of shots from a good variety of angles, so the viewer never gets bored and we don't have to see talking heads too much on the screen. Last, Mason put in the lower-thirds graphics and cleaned up the audio. One of Clay's songs also plays in the background until the end, when the audio transitions to the soundtrack of one of the concert clips for the outro. This is essentially a documentary-style feature news package.

The last news package example is from episode 8, when the student producers did a package on the Theater Department's upcoming play, *Cinderella*. For this package, the research was pretty straightforward. The students researched who the main people were, and details about the performance. At that point, they reached out to the Director of the play and found times they could come in and interview the actors and crew for the play. After completing the interviews, they shot b-roll of the backstage set pieces, the dress rehearsals, and other things that went into making the play. Then in post, the reporter, River Riley, recorded his voiceover intro and outro. The sound bites flowed well enough that he didn't need to record any narration for transitions. There is plenty of b-roll to illustrate the clock, which is talked about in one of the interviews, and to cover the transitions. Once the piece was put together, the graphics were added, including the full-screen poster for the play at the beginning and end. Then the package was uploaded to the server and played back live during the show.

Chapter 14: News Packages Main Points

- News packages are the only single-camera genre that are often made with limited pre-production. Due to the nature of breaking news, you often have to rely on experience to shoot a news package. Having said that, you should do as much planning as your timeline allows.
- During preproduction, you should connect with people and locations that are important to the story. As much as possible, you should schedule interviews and locations.
- When shooting, you should bring a standard package of gear: camera, light(s), mics. Being able to grab a set of gear quickly as you head to the scene of a story is important, as is your familiarity with the gear.
- Like documentary films, the story for a news package almost always comes together in post. Do your best to script out questions for people, and your standup intro and outros when you're on the scene, but it's okay if you have to record narration in post to transition from one idea to the next.
- Every news station will have a different way of assigning stories. And every story will require a different approach to report and shoot. Rely on past experiences and routines to guide you as much as possible.
- Each station might have a different process and formulas for producing and editing a news package. It's important to get trained at the station you're working for.
- Like documentary films, ethics are important when producing a news package. You'll want to consider how you will respond to various situations before they actually occur.

15 Corporate and Freelance Production

Some of this has been covered in other chapters. Commercials and music videos are often freelance projects. You might crew as a freelancer on a film set or a documentary. In this chapter, I'm going to try to cover many of the other types of single-camera videos you might be asked to produce, either by your employer, or by someone wanting to hire you. This includes instructional videos, promo videos, highlight videos, marketing videos, and even wedding videos. There are many opportunities out there to use your skills in video production to make money. My first job after college was as an audiovisual technician for the local med school and university hospital. I got to shoot videos of groundbreaking surgeries to be used as PR materials. I got to record guest lectures for archival use. And I got to edit together materials requested by doctors and professors to use as classroom materials. In that corporate environment, I used a variety of skills and produced many different kinds of videos. There are a lot of opportunities to do video production in the corporate world these days.

After that job, I moved out to San Francisco and did freelance work. I recorded live plays, recorded interviews for the university foundation, and produced commercials and promo videos. When I moved back to Missouri, I freelanced shooting some interviews for a remote research project, I produced many weddings, I shot a music video, and I got to do some commercials and promo videos. As a freelancer, I've been able to decide what projects I want to take on and which ones I don't. I hope some day to write an entire book on corporate and freelance production, but for this chapter, I'll focus on some basics.

DOI: 10.4324/9781003010357-20

Preproduction

Many of the things I said in Chapter 11 (Commercials) applies here. When you're doing work for your company (corporate video) or doing freelance work, the person who hired you probably already has an idea of what they want the video to look like. They probably have a good idea of what the goals of the video should be. Your job for these projects is to produce something that helps them accomplish those goals. For the preproduction process, there are slight differences between doing corporate video production and doing freelance work, so I'll go into detail on both. I generally believe that when you do video work, you're either working for someone else or you're working for yourself. So, I think almost everything I've talked about in the book applies to either one or the other.

Corporate Workflow

When I worked at the university hospital and shot and edited videos for them, it was definitely a corporate environment. What I mean by this is that I had a boss, and that person was able to come in and set my agenda for the day and for the week. When I was given a project, it was never something where I just had an idea and wanted to do it. There might have been room for me to pitch my boss ideas, but I hardly ever had the time. Instead, I kept a daily calendar and filled it with appointments to shoot videos and perform other tasks. When I didn't have a shoot lined up on my calendar for the day, I was working on editing previous projects, organizing the gear, performing maintenance tasks on the equipment, and other ongoing jobs.

When my boss had a video that needed to be done, they would come to us (I was actually one of three AV techs) and lay out their vision for the project. For example, the hospital was hosting a conference and needed us to set up AV projectors, microphones, and speakers for the sessions. They also wanted all of the sessions recorded on video so they would be available to doctors working in residence that couldn't make it to the conference. We went to work planning. We scouted the locations, figured out the equipment needs, and wrote out a schedule for the day. Between the three of us, we figured out who was going to do what, who would be in each session and run the cameras, and who would do the audio boards. After the conference, we also scheduled time to edit the videos and make copies to send out. We didn't need to write any scripts or draft any storyboards, but we did go back to our boss and pitch them our plan to make sure we weren't missing anything.

Scripting

In some cases, no scripts or storyboards will be necessary. If you're working in a corporate environment and your company has a pretty strong idea of how the video needs to look, a script for your actors or voice artists will probably be enough. If you're doing highlight videos or other documentary-style work, you won't be able to script out the things you're shooting. However, if you're doing something like an instructional video, a script and storyboard are probably essential, just so your employer and your crew all know exactly what each section of the video will look like. Instructional videos, highlight videos, product launch videos, and things of that nature should be planned out ahead of time. That way, you make sure all of the main points are covered in the video.

For a product launch video, the words about the product absolutely need to be scripted. You might even want to storyboard the shots and how you'll transition from one product feature to the next. For an instructional video, you might script out the words, or you might just outline the general flow and let your instructor or narrator have some ad-lib ability to make it seem more natural. You might not need to storyboard the shots at all. And like a documentary or news package, I will often wait to shoot the b-roll or do screen captures until after the narration or standup is recorded, since I might not actually know what shots I need until after the voicework is laid down and edited on the timeline. Regardless, before moving forward, you'll want to take your script and storyboard to your company and pitch them your idea before proceeding. This is usually a less formal pitch than a narrative film or commercial project because the people you're pitching to are the ones who asked you to make the video in the first place. So, my goal here is just to make sure everyone is on the same page and we're ready to proceed.

Pitching

In the corporate environment, having a detailed plan and a schedule to hit your deadline is usually more important than helping your boss visualize the final product. The "pitch" will be very informal, and sometimes non-existent. If your boss feels like you have a good handle on what their needs are, they may not even want to meet with you before you begin production. If this is the case, it still might be worth running your plans by someone else just to make sure you're not missing anything.

For example, they might just say something like, "we need a video for the website that shows people how to log in to the new app." Without any additional direction from them, your mind might come up with a number of ways to do this. You could shoot a quick 5-second video that just hits the steps quickly and easily, only to find out that your boss was hoping for a video that targeted people who aren't very tech-savvy that goes into more detail and explanation. Or, you might use humor as you walk your audience through the steps to log in and it might cross a line into condescending. My point here is that you can save yourself time and effort by asking if you're on the right track. If your boss doesn't have the time, find a colleague who is willing to give you some feedback when you're still in the idea stage. It doesn't have to be formal, and if you work with a production team, then they will certainly give you feedback along the way. Especially in a job where you're doing a lot of video projects all the time, your boss might feel comfortable giving you a lot of freedom, but it never hurts to double-check.

Scheduling

This is often the hardest part of doing corporate work. You'll likely be working on several projects at the same time, and figuring out when you're going to plan, shoot, and edit each one can be challenging. It's worth setting out a schedule for the project, as well as a weekly/monthly schedule for all your projects. Start with the due date(s) and work back from there in both cases. You don't want to put yourself in a situation where you need to be editing one project, but the only day you can do it is the same day you're scheduled to interview someone for a different project. Planning out how to navigate each one when you're still in the middle of other projects is a nightmare sometimes, but staying organized is essential to being successful in the corporate world. Unlike a film project, commercial project, music video, or even a news package, you can't usually dedicate all of your time to one project until it's complete. Using an online calendar or whiteboard calendar where you can put in dates, but moving them later as needed, is my method. Many newsrooms and production houses have elaborate calendar systems that allow for multiple producers to be working on multiple projects. This way, everyone on the team knows what others are working on and when their dates are lined up.

My other advice here is to work out detailed lists for your needs. You might work on a team where there are only two cameras, so knowing when those cameras are going out and coming back is important. In your planning phase, make a list of everything you'll need for the project and schedule out when you'll have that equipment and when you'll bring it back. The same thing goes for locations, props, voice actors, etc. Schedule them out ahead of time so you can juggle multiple projects at once. The last thing you want is to wing it in a corporate environment. The only way that works is if you are the only producer there and you're only working on one project at a time. Those positions exist, but they're rare.

Freelance Workflow

On the other hand, when you're a freelancer, you might be the only one working on a project. Your workflow might vary based on who your client is and what kind of project you're working on. For weddings, I would highly recommend an initial meeting with the couple to discuss their dreams and the costs. Then, I would do preproduction and pitch my ideas back to them to make sure everyone is on the same page before actually shooting the wedding. Many wedding freelancers have set packages and tend to rely on formulas for their projects. There isn't anything wrong with this, but I would still make sure the couple feels as though you're personalizing their special day. Even in post, I usually send a rough cut to see if any changes need to be made before sending them the final version.

For other freelance projects, it would be difficult to cover everything in one chapter. Sometimes, as a freelancer, I was hired to show up and shoot with very little planning. I always tried to get as much clarity and ask as many questions as I needed, but there were some jobs that didn't go smoothly because I wasn't there for preproduction meetings (the producers for the projects didn't want to pay me for those meetings). If you are the producer for freelance projects, it's worthwhile to factor in preproduction time for crew meetings and setup times. Production runs a lot smoother when everyone understands the shots that are needed and how they will fit into the overall story. In post, you're often doing the editing yourself. You might choose to hire out for graphics and effects, though, if the project demands more than your skillset can handle. There's no shame in getting help when you need it, but you do have to set aside room in your initial estimate to your client for those things. Any costs you incur should be covered by your estimate, as well as the profit you need to make from the job.

On that note, I cannot recommend strongly enough that you have contracts and scope of work documents with your clients when producing freelance video projects. For the class I teach in Corporate and Freelance Production, I require students to go through four steps. The first step is to meet with the client, assess their needs, and set the overall schedule for the project. The second step is to pitch the idea to the client and define the scope of work. "Scope of work" lays out what will be done, how the project will be delivered, who is responsible for providing locations, crew, talent, etc., and any specific shooting dates that affect the client. The goal here is to cover everything thoroughly enough that once you begin shooting (and spending money renting equipment and hiring crew), your client won't come back and say, "that's not what we talked about!"

The third step I have students do is to present a polished rough cut to the client and see if any changes need to be made. I say a "polished" rough cut because it should have graphics, transitions, effects, and coloring done already. I just don't call it a "final cut" because the client might want some things changed. In your contract and scope of work, you should limit the number of major changes you're willing to make in the third step. Re-shooting the entire project won't be feasible, for example, but re-shooting one shot or re-recording a narration might be. My advice in everything when it comes to freelancing is to be as transparent as possible and communicate well with your client.

The first wedding I ever shot was ... not great. I was in filmmaking mode, and even though I ran the camera the entire ceremony, I moved around to get different angles of the event. The end result was that parts of the ceremony are shaky and framed awkwardly. I learned a lot from the experience and did a much better job on future weddings, but I was so embarrassed to tell my clients (who were also my friends – I did this one at an extremely discounted rate) that I had messed up. Instead, I procrastinated on the editing, and I didn't return their phone calls and emails. When I finally told them what had happened, they were very understanding. They just wanted their video! From then on, I've always been up front and proactive in my freelance work. Sometimes things happen. You can always discount your initial rate or give a refund to make up for it. Be professional, though, and even if you mess up occasionally, your clients will respect you and you'll stay in business.

The last step in the process is to have your client sign off on the final cut. This is the easiest step, but if you and your client have both moved on from the project, it may be the most difficult to schedule. This is why I try to set the date for this step at the very beginning. If your client doesn't sign off, there could be legal implications later on, so this is a very important step. If your client decides later that they want a different graphic or shot in the video, they will have to hire you again to make the changes and they won't be able to claim that it was part of your initial agreement (and therefore the money they paid you should still cover it) since they signed off on the final product. It's also a great way to signal to all parties that the project is over and you're moving on to other things. Payments should be made, and the project should be moved to archival storage.

Treatment and Script

For freelance projects, you may or may not produce a treatment and/or script. For a wedding, you're probably better off showing your clients previous work and talking about what they liked and what they didn't like from those videos. For some of the freelance work I've done, I've had to script out interview questions and send them to the client before shooting the interviews to make sure I would get good sound bites. I've also videotaped court depositions as a freelancer, which required no script or treatment, and very little editing. For more elaborate projects, like a web video or commercial, you'll want

Comm 4565 Corporate and Freelance Production
Client and Producer Agreement Form for Projects

Project Title _____

Client Name _____

Client Department/Division/Company Name _____

Client Contact info (email/phone)   _____

Student Producer's Name   _____

Step 1: Initial Contact and Schedule
The Student Producer listed above will set up a time to meet with the client to plan, pitch, shoot, edit, and distribute the Project. Because this is a class, each of these 4 steps needs to be documented and signed off on by the Client.

Schedule (in step one, determine the project time line and fill in additional dates as needed)

Date	Time	Description of what will be done
		Step 1: Date to meet to discuss initial goals and needs (fill in to the left)
		List goal here:
		List target audience here:
		Step 2: Date to meet to pitch the idea back to the client (fill in to the left)
		Location scouting date (fill in to the left)
		Talent recruiting deadline (fill in to the left)
		Production Schedule : list date(s) to the left and/or below here
		Step 3: Date to discuss any suggested changes (fill in to the left)
		Complete the final project in this format/codec: _____
		Step 4: Date to finalized is tribution and Client Sign-off on the Project

After Step 1, the Student Producer will email a copy of this form to the professor (price@ucmo.edu) and the Client (see email above).

Student Producer Signature _____   Date _____

Client Signature _____   Date _____

Figure 15.1 Step one of the process. On this page of the client agreement form, it's important to figure out what the client's goals are, who their intended audience is, what the timeline is for completion, and any other important information.

Step 2: Pitch Meeting and Scope of Work

This will drive the project. As the Student Producer pitches the project details to the client, they w ill have identified specific needs for the project. The Scope of Work listed here constitutes an a greement between the Student Producer and the Client about what will be done.

Scope of Work (describe the project, expectations of the Student Producer, and expectations of the client in as much detail as possible)

Shooting Dates	
Client will Provide	Location? Talent?
Student Producer will secure	Crew, Equipment,
Talent will be recruited by	
Project deliverable will be	
Additional Notes	

After Step 2, the Student Producer will email a copy of this form to the professor and the Client.

Student Producer Signature _____ Date _____

Client Signature _____ Date _____

Step 3: Post Production Meeting and Summary of Suggested Changes

The Student Producer will shoot/record project elements, edit them together, and present a rough cut to the Client. At this point, the client is free to suggest changes. These changes will be made IF they do not require extensive planning or production and can be done in a reasonable amount of time. If no changes need to be made, the Client should sign here and then also sign the "Step 4: Assessment of the Project and Distribution" section below.

List of Suggested Changes:

After Step 3, the Student Producer will email a copy of this form to the professor and the Client.

Student Producer Signature _____ Date _____

Client Signature _____ Date _____

Figure 15.2 In steps two and three, the details need to be worked out and agreed upon. The scope of work will outline what will be done and anything the client will provide. "Deliverables" means the actual.mov file, the tape, the hard drive, etc. that you will give to the client on completion. This could also include raw footage, multiple versions, preproduction materials, or anything else you agree upon with the client. Typically, those extras cost more for the client.

a treatment to pitch to your client and a full script to help guide production. One of the freelance opportunities I've had recently was to record and edit interviews for a local church to play back during their Sunday service and to post on their website. I scripted specific questions and pitched my overall idea back to my client. The church's logo is in soft focus behind the people giving the interviews, and I asked each participant the same question, then edited their sound bites together vox pop style. It turned out well and my client was very happy. But if I hadn't discussed the questions ahead of time with them, the sound bites might not have fit with the message that Sunday.

Storyboarding

Like the treatment and script, you may or may not need to storyboard out your project as a freelancer. If the project is highly visual, or your client needs help visualizing the flow of everything, a storyboard is a great idea. I'll often use storyboards like the template in Figure 1.10 just to help organize my thoughts as I get my equipment lists and schedules together. Even if I'm the only one who will ever see them, I find them very helpful. And certainly, storyboards help your client to understand the visuals you're going to capture and how you'll edit everything together to accomplish their goals. For the music video project "No More Victims," we found ourselves going back to our storyboards constantly. We used them to pitch our storyline shots to our client, then used them to create our shooting schedule, and then used them to edit together the rough cut. We didn't stray from the storyboards much throughout the entire project.

Pitching

As a freelancer, I would never, ever, move into production without pitching my idea(s) back to my client. When you're in business for yourself, even the time you spend on something costs you money. At that point, it's just opportunity cost (if you could be making money by working on a different project during that time instead). But once you move into production, you will probably have actual costs. If you hire a crew, rent equipment, pay location rental fees, license music, or hire actors, either you will pay for those things up front, or your client will have to cover them. Regardless, real money will be spent. The last thing you want is to shoot and edit everything and then have your client tell you that you're way off from what they really wanted. Pitching your storyboards, scripts, and treatments to them is essential for preventing this kind of misunderstanding. If the client decides at this point that they want to part ways or that you're just not on the same page, it's better to find out before either of you spends actual money.

Scheduling

When you're freelancing, like corporate video, you might be juggling multiple projects at a time. Planning out your schedule for each project is important, but so is planning out your daily and monthly schedules. If you're doing a lot of wedding videography, you'll be meeting with clients several weeks before their wedding. You may end up shooting two or three weddings in the meantime, so staying organized with your notes for each one is important. If you're doing commercials, you may be able to work on one project at a time and schedule shoots that are efficient and packed into a day or two of production.

And you'll want to schedule time to rest, relax, and have a life outside of work. All of these things are important.

As a student, it's very easy to get into the trap of working obsessively on one project until it's finished, then moving on to the next project. If you're freelancing as your main source of income, this intense schedule can be a recipe for burnout. If you do find that your clients expect you to work long hours for quick turnarounds on projects, you'll definitely want to schedule some down time to relax in between projects. This is a bit how narrative films are made. On the other hand, if you do a lot of wedding videography, you'll be shooting on the weekends a lot. It's important that you take a day or two off during the week, as long as you can get your client meetings in and get your preproduction and editing done. Once this is your career, you have to think about developing a rhythm that's sustainable in the long term. Pulling all-nighters regularly is not. When I work on longer projects, I find it helpful to schedule specific times each day to work on it. When I don't have that structure in place, it's very hard to work because there isn't a cutoff in sight. That's when I feel overwhelmed and burned out. But when there's a stopping point in sight, it's easier to focus. This is called the "Pomodoro Technique" (not a film term, just a freelancing tip from a pro).

Production

As I freelancer, I often worked as crew for projects, and I wasn't always the producer. One of the keys to developing a career as a freelancer is to choose a specialty and stick with it. For example, when I worked with a national reality TV show, the Director was a freelancer who almost always directed shows for different reality networks. The sound person and Cinematographers were well known for their specialties and always had jobs lined up. Part of the reason for this is that freelancers are usually expected to provide their own equipment. The Cinematographers for the episode brought their own cameras, lights, and lenses. The sound person brought their mixer, boom, mics, wireless systems, headphones, and cables. Specializing also gives you the advantage of making a name in the specialty area. I know several drone operators who are now specialists in the area and are booked with enough drone work that they only do aerial cinematography. They're certainly capable of doing other things in the field, but they don't need to for work.

If you're going to freelance as a producer or a generalist, though, it's certainly not a bad thing. And in some areas of the country or some genres, this is even expected. Wedding video productions are usually done by a generalist who can plan, shoot, and edit. They might hire a second camera operator for the wedding day, but otherwise they're doing everything. Instructional videos, commercials, and music videos might be made this way as well. And even the Director, Cinematographers, and sound person I worked with on the reality show had the knowledge and skills to do everything on set.

Cameras

If you're going to be a generalist, or specialize as a Cinematographer or videographer, a good camera setup should be your first investment. I'm a big fan of the newer mirrorless photography cameras that are capable of shooting high-quality video (these have essentially replaced DSLR cameras, but all the things in the book about DSLRs also apply to them). There are even some hybrids on the market now that are designed to be a cinema camera first, but also a very good still photography camera. These are great options and are usually available for a much lower cost than a true cinema camera. I also subscribe to the growing belief that there aren't vast differences between sensors these days, but the lenses can make a huge difference. Getting high-quality lenses is important.

I've found that some lenses shoot "above their price point," meaning that the quality of the image is what you'd expect from a more expensive lens. As you purchase lenses as a freelancer, this is what you're looking for. You'll want a good overall range of focal lengths, or several good zoom lenses: 18mm will give you good wide shots; a 35mm and/or 50mm lens will give you a good normal look; and an 85mm or greater will be needed for close up shots. My personal kit has an 18mm–200mm zoom lens, a 50mm fixed focal length lens, and a 24–105mm high-quality zoom lens. I also have a 150mm–600mm lens I use for specialized shots, like when I shoot photos of the moon or outdoor portraits. I use the 50mm lens for interviews, indoor portrait photography, and for low-light shooting (the f-stop goes down to 1.2). I use the 24–105mm for general use (the f-stop only goes to 4, but it's a great all-around lens for shooting events). And I use the 18–200mm sparingly because the quality of the glass is not great (but that zoom range helps me cover live events where the shots vary a lot in an unpredictable way). The best way to choose lenses is to look at online reviews of them and to see pictures people post who shoot with those lenses. Remember that as a freelancer, keeping costs low helps increase profit, but your gear and skills will also lead to jobs. Balancing investing in gear and maximizing profit is the key to success.

In the corporate world, part of your job may be checking out new equipment and pitching the need for it to your employer. I was lucky at my hospital job that our boss set money aside each year for us to upgrade cameras, computers, and other gear. We still had a limited budget and had to prioritize our needs. We also had to make a case each year that the money was still necessary to keep the quality of our productions up. I've talked to some people in the corporate environment who have large budgets, several different cameras, light kits, audio gear, and even studios to shoot in. I've also talked to people in corporate roles where production is only a fraction of their job duties, and they have an old DSLR camera and nothing else. This is often the case when a company first hires someone to shoot videos for their social media. In these situations, you may have to make the case that the videos will provide a return on investment (ROI) for the company in terms of increased sales, better brand recognition, etc. in order to get them to purchase new gear or upgrade items on a regular basis. This can be a source of frustration in the corporate world compared to the freelance world where you can buy whatever you want (assuming your business profits can afford it).

Lighting

I'll offer similar advice about lighting, but add that lighting has gotten a lot better and a lot cheaper recently. When LED lights first came out, any lighting instrument was fairly expensive. As LEDs have gotten cheaper and companies have experimented with different designs, like the open-faced instruments seen in Figure 5.2 (in Chapter 5), a new world has opened up for freelancers. There are lights out there that can double as hard and soft lights. Some kits come with softboxes for their hard lights. Some open-faced instruments have Fresnel lenses that can be added to focus the light and make it harder. Finding some good, all-around lights for freelancing is a pretty good investment these days. I've also used floor lamps and open bulbs lately, and shaped them using a paper lantern (in film, we call this a "china ball") surround purchased at a furniture store. The point of lighting is that you get the quality of light you need, and that the shadows and highlights are placed well to tell your story. It doesn't necessarily matter what specific instrument you're using or how much it costs.

The same thing is true of gear to help shape the light. Shining a floor lamp through a white sheet or parchment paper will provide the same soft light as a more expensive light kit. Since LEDs don't get very hot, you can use a white foamboard from a local store to bounce light or to block the spill. There are videos online that show how to make a PVC pipe frame with a white T-shirt to use in place of a more expensive 4×4 metal frame with opal diffusion gel taped to it. These are great cost-saving ideas. However, and this is a big asterisk, as a freelancer you need to convey professionalism. If you roll in with duct tape and bubble gum holding trash together, it may work perfectly well. But it may not show your client that you're really a professional, either. As with your camera gear, balancing cost and quality is important. There are many DIY solutions out there that still look professional, though, and it is possible.

I'll add that the best first investment as a freelancer after a camera and audio gear is a low-cost light kit that works well for interviews or other high-key lighting. A three-light or four-light panel kit is probably a good start. An interview kit with two hard lights (that you can soften with Grip gear as needed) and a panel light for the fill or background light would be my preference. If you need additional lights, brighter lights, or just a different look, you can always rent them. Even in the corporate world, DIY solutions are great, but you might have a hard time explaining to your boss why you need to buy white bedsheets. A good diffusion frame or light kit might be an expense that's easy enough to justify.

Sound

After purchasing a camera, you should look at buying a good wireless mic system. A wireless lav is actually very versatile if you know how to conceal it inside clothing (like in Figure 10.4 in Chapter 10). After that, purchasing a shotgun mic with a boom and perhaps even a zeppelin would be my next step. I would get the microphones before looking at an external recorder or mixer because you can usually run them directly into your camera and still get decent audio. If you are shooting with a DSLR or mirrorless camera, you might want one of the DSLR audio mixers (like the one in Figure 6.12 in Chapter 6) to go with your mics. They're not that expensive and they will help you monitor and adjust sound levels as you shoot.

After microphones, a good audio mixer is a luxury, but it can be helpful. If you have the business income to support it, I would start with a 2-channel mixer that is light and portable. A mixer with more than two inputs will open up your ability to shoot projects with more than two mics, so you might look at those options as well. The sound person for the reality show I worked on had a 6-channel mixer. And even though there were only two people talking at any given time, this allowed him to leave the boom mic he had strapped to his bag open to record ambience on a separate channel. He could also record room tone quicker and easier through the boom mic than the wireless lavs clipped on the participants.

When recording sound on set, a good set of headphones is also a requirement. They should passively cancel the noise with thick, over-ear pads (I'm wearing mine in Figure 6.8

in Chapter 6). When I shoot weddings or other live events, I listen to the audio closely (usually while also running the camera, so it pays to practice doing both at the same time). I can't necessarily stop the ceremony if there is distracting noise in the background, but I might be able to minimize it. This is one advantage a separate mixer has over running the mics directly into the camera. You can adjust levels as you go, but you can also EQ as you go, or at least roll off the bass frequencies when they get distracting. Of course, if you can scout a location ahead of time, you can also think about how to minimize unwanted noise before you even start shooting.

The same goes for the corporate environment, although if you're lucky enough to have a studio to shoot in, many of the lights and audio gear may be hardwired in. I've worked in several studios where there was a lighting grid with a light board to adjust them. These studios are usually built with multiple audio plugs in the wall feeding into an audio board in the control room. They look a lot like a TV station's studio, and many even have separate control rooms where a crew can record a live multicamera session. Unlike a TV station's studio, though, corporate studios often don't have any cameras set up on pedestals. Cameras are too expensive to be limited to shooting inside a studio, even in a corporate setting. Most often, I've worked in corporate studios where the set design is fixed; some audio gear and lights are there, but we set up the tripods, cameras, and teleprompter only when we shot in there. The rest of the time, the camera gear was used out on location.

Directing

In the corporate and freelance worlds, you'll find a wide variety of projects, as well as a wide variety of directing needs. Slating takes, working with Cinematographers and others on your crew, communicating clearly and openly, and being able to clearly convey your vision are all important qualities when you're directing a project in corporate or freelance settings. The one thing I will add here, though, is that your ability to work well with others matters a lot. It might even matter more than your artistic abilities. It will be very hard to find new clients in the freelance world if you develop a reputation as a jerk. It will be equally hard to keep your job if you're a jerk around the office.

I was amazed at the level of comradery we developed as a crew in a very short period when I worked on the reality show. At one point, a fairly major setback occurred. Instead of pointing fingers and getting upset, everyone moved forward. We hashed out what needed to happen next without assigning any blame, and we put that new plan into action. No need to waste energy focusing on who was to blame. Use all the energy from then on to figure out and execute a solution. I learned a lot that day about working as a team. And I also realized that these freelancers were in it for the long haul. It was likely they would have to work together again at some point. It was also likely that they would need each other's help at some point, either lining up future jobs, or lining up crew for future projects. The freelance world is much smaller than you might imagine, and even though burning a bridge might make you feel better in the moment, it can have long-term effects on your career.

In the corporate environment, there may be a hierarchy for all productions. Someone may have the title of "Creative Director" and someone else may be "video producer" or something like that. In those situations, you should work to get really good at your job, but always be learning the other roles as well. At some point, the Creative Director may leave the company and give you the chance to move up into the role. In the hospital setting I worked at, we didn't have that kind of hierarchy. It worked well for us, as the three of us took turns directing or working on a specific project type. I liked shooting and editing more creative videos, so my coworkers often let me lead on those types of projects. Another co-worker really liked the planning and preproduction. Even when there isn't a hierarchy in the corporate environment, I'd recommend trying to expand your skillset and learn from each other. If one coworker leaves, you'll be left to fill in the gaps. So even if there is a dedicated sound person on your team, don't assume you'll never be needed to run sound. Instead, always be learning.

Post

For most of my freelance work, I've been the editor as well as the producer and camera operator. For weddings especially, I've always done everything. In the corporate world, we would sometimes work collaboratively on post. For some recent projects, I've hired former students to work on post, just because I find it difficult to prioritize editing over other duties I have with my teaching job. Ironically, when I produced the highlight videos for the Wakonse Conference on College Teaching the last couple of years, I've mainly focused on post as part of my freelancing job for the conference. The conference takes place up in Michigan, and the last two years I've been too busy to attend. Instead of going there, I've set up a cloud-based folder for conference participants to drop their photos and videos into an online account. This allows me to download the crowdsourced footage from the conference and edit it together into a highlight video for the participants of the conference to enjoy at the end.

You can see these videos on my YouTube channel. The older highlight videos for the conference on my channel are ones that I actually planned, shot, edited, and distributed. That was back when I was able to attend. You might also notice that I've been able to keep using the various drone shots I recorded back in 2017 and 2018, even for the videos in 2023 and 2024. They're fairly generic shots of the area, and they make good transitions from one part of the video to the next. Plus, I shot a lot of drone footage those last two years I was there in person, so there are enough shots I can use that haven't been used in videos for previous years. As a freelancer or even in the corporate world, you'll want to catalog your footage in case you ever want to reuse it in another project. For the Wakonse promo video in the case study (below), it was edited together entirely with video and drone shots that I had stored on my server from prior years.

Workflow

Like other types of production, the first step in post is to get organized. Renaming your footage into something that makes sense for the project you're working on is a good start. It's worth looking back through your preproduction as you begin post on corporate and freelance projects. Especially if you're juggling more than one project at a time, it's easy to forget about details and goals your clients had for the video. I always look back over the notes I took in preproduction meetings with my clients to make sure I'm editing the video into something the client will like. When I shot and edited the video for Balboa High School's "Action Academy," I was even able to sit down with my client and go through the edit to make sure they were happy with it. I won't always do this, but at times it makes sense.

After editing, I add music and graphics (if I didn't lay the music down first to help me develop a rhythm for the cuts. Then, I add transitions and do a screening for my client. With their feedback, I put the final touches on the project and export it out for them in the deliverable format we agreed on. Sometimes this is a digital file uploaded to the cloud and shared with them. Sometimes it's burning a DVD.

For corporate work, the postproduction process can look a bit different. You might be checking in with your boss more often and doing multiple edits before you're done with the project. When you freelance, your contract can specify how many changes you're willing to make for free before it will start to cost your client extra (because of the extra time you'll have to devote to it). In the corporate world, you keep working until your boss is happy, regardless of how much time it takes. In the corporate world, you might also be the one responsible for distributing the video. You may be the one managing the company's YouTube channel or website. You might be posting videos to social media on a daily basis. You're probably also the one responsible for archiving the video projects and any raw footage that might be useful in the future.

Editing

I usually begin editing the same way, regardless of whether it's a corporate video or free-lance video – actually, regardless of what type of video it is as well. I typically import and organize my assets in the bin first, then look through the footage. I plan out how I want the video to flow in my head or on paper. Then I lay down the music if the rhythm is an important part of the video, which is often the case. For instructional videos, the music may be an afterthought that's mostly there to cover up background noise. In some videos, I'll lay the visuals down first and find a music bed later to help transition and cover up unwanted sound. For all of the Wakonse videos, music is an important part of the flow, so I lay down the songs first.

In the corporate world, you'll probably be limited in the songs you can use. Most of the time, if it's a web video, instructional video, product launch video, or something other than a commercial, the company won't want to pay for the use of copyrighted music. Instead, they'll want you to use songs from a library the company has purchased, or they'll want you to find royalty-free music that is legal to use in such projects. Even with fairly generic-sounding music, you'll still have a beat that can help guide your editing rhythm and pleasant music to cover up unwanted noise. You should still envelope the music way down underneath any voices that you hear in the video, and raise the music levels for the intro, outro, and possibly transitions. Editing can be the most fun part of corporate and freelance productions. It's often where you get to use your creative muscles. If the product launch video required specific shots and highlights for specific features, shooting might not have given you much latitude to get creative. But in post, you can decide how those shots are presented.

Graphics

I'll be honest. (You'll see it in my videos on my YouTube channel anyway.) Graphics is where I really struggle with my freelance work. Instead of creating my own graphics for a project, I usually try to work with the client to use some of their existing graphics and designs. It helps them keep a consistent image across their videos, but it isn't always the best quality. They may have a logo with a white background, and your video really calls for the background to be transparent. In those cases, I often just try to figure out how to make the white background work instead of actually taking the time to re-create the graphic with a transparent background. My skills in programs like After Effects and Photoshop are also extremely limited, so I often make do with what I've got. I would recommend that if you have a client who needs it, either hiring someone who does good work with graphics, or taking some time to learn how to do a good job with them yourself.

In the corporate environment, you'll most likely have a library of graphics that your company prefers anyway. Our university, for example, has an entire web page full of approved graphics that we're allowed to use in our projects. We're not allowed to make our own anyway. If we want to use a specific image on our website, we have to go to the university's website and download the approved graphic. From there, we can make it fly into the screen, bounce, spin around, or other effects. I'm good at those things. That's just keyframing your movement. But my skills end when I have to create graphics from scratch. And templates are okay for many projects, but the generic nature of them will limit the professional look that custom-made graphics will give. It's worth it to me to hire someone to do graphics. For the film on Central State Hospital, my editor spent some time designing the custom-made graphics for the film and they look fantastic; much better than if I had just done them myself using templates available in an NLE.

Distribution and Archiving

For corporate projects, your company will likely have a server to upload to, a hard drive array to archive projects to, or some other system for distributing and archiving the projects. There may also be instructions on what kinds of raw footage to archive and what to delete once the project is complete. If you work for a smaller company, or you're the only person doing production at the location, then it may be up to you to create archival policies. Distribution is typically an.mp4 file type with an h.264 video codec for the web. But I would highly recommend archiving a.mov file with RAW, ProRes 422, or ProRes 444 video codecs. This way, if the project is needed for additional distribution later, you have a higher-quality version available compared to the one you used for initial web distribution. For example, if your company decides a few months later to pay for the commercial to air during local sporting events on cable TV, you'll want a higher-resolution version that you can transcode from (into whatever file type the TV or cable station needs) instead of using the compressed h.264 video. Same thing goes for raw footage. If you're going to take the time to archive it, do it in the same codecs you shot in. You can't create anything with a higher resolution than the files you archive, so it's worth it to archive in the resolution you shot in.

For freelance projects, it may or may not be worth it to archive raw footage. I have always archived the final cut as a high-resolution video file, but sometimes I've deleted the original footage. For the weddings I've done, I have no need for that footage after a few years. There's a slight chance that a client may change their mind and pay for the raw footage after seeing the final cut, so I keep the original footage for a year or two. After that, the chances aren't likely. And it's not like I can re-use footage from someone's wedding in another project down the road (at least, not without their permission), so there's limited use for it. Ultimately, you'll have to decide how much storage space to purchase for projects and archives. I currently have a 32TB RAID array (which duplicates all data in case one of the drives fails – this gives me 16TB of storage after the duplication). I have about 10TB of it filled with archives. Most of it is old projects, but I do have some projects where I've kept the raw footage. The Central State film raw footage is there currently. Since the film was completed last year, I think I'll hang onto the original footage for another year or two to see if I need it. If not, I'll look at how much space it's taking up on the RAID array and decide whether or not to keep it permanently. I have also kept all of the Wakonse footage and images I've shot over the years. More on this below, but I've found that I have needed to search these archives every year as I put together additional promo videos and highlight videos for the conference.

The distribution for freelance projects really comes down to whatever you and your client agree to. Most often, I find that this is probably a high-res.mov file as well as a web-friendly.mp4 file. This way, the client has the higher resolution version for their archives, and they also have the web version to distribute to their website, YouTube channel, social media outlets, etc. I should also point out here that you are under no obligation to archive a client's project for them unless you agree to do so. I keep old projects for my own portfolio, and occasionally I have a client reach out to me and ask for an old project when they've misplaced their file or their computer crashed. Many people don't adequately back up their files, so I'm happy to help them when I've still got a copy of the project. I'm also a bit of a hoarder of digital files because hard drives are getting bigger every year. When I start to fill up my 16TB RAID, I can always get a second one or upgrade to a larger array. But that does cost money.

If you and your client agree to use a physical medium for your distribution, you should add that cost into your charges for the project. For example, if they expect the file to be given to them on a USB thumb drive, you'll have to purchase one and give it to them when you complete the project. It may only cost you $25, but your client should be the one paying for that thumb drive in the end. Same goes for legacy media. If your client wants the project on a DVD, you'll probably need to find a company that can burn the disc(s) for you. I still have access to a DVD burner, but I'm not sure I still have any software that can author a DVD. Any and all of these costs need to be worked out with your client from the beginning.

Case Study: Wakonse Conference Promo Video

Since about 2014, I've done freelance videography for the Wakonse Conference on College Teaching. For a year or two before that, I attended the conference and shared the pictures I took with the producer of the video, which is how I got into the actual video production for the conference. For the first few years, I worked as a photographer only. I started shooting video clips as well as stills, but until 2017 the producers only used stills in the highlight video for the conference. In 2017, those producers weren't able to go to the conference, so the conference hired me as the sole producer for the highlight video. I hired a videographer and, together, we shot drone footage, stills, and videos during the weeklong conference and edited together the 2017 Wakonse In Review (you can see all the videos I've shot for Wakonse over the years if you search my YouTube channel for the Wakonse Videos Playlist or click here: https://www.youtube.com/playlist?list=PLsrT5A6t70nf-EZI1UKF0zWrBCzsqgBuM). In 2018, I did the same thing. I packed up two DSLR cameras, including a shoulder rig (the one you see in Figure 4.7 in Chapter 4), my drone (the one in Figure 4.21), my laptop, and some external hard drives. Both years, I shot a lot of landscape stills and captured a lot of drone footage of the camp, the lake, the canoes, and other ambience shots. I got even more shots of the participants each year, and those are primarily the ones that make up the highlight videos. I also

Figure 15.3 The drone, DSLR, and shoulder-mounted rig we used for the Wakonse Conference highlight video, "Wakonse In Review," in 2017.

Figure 15.4 Our editing room in 2017 at the Wakonse Conference. My videographer and I spent about 12 hours each day shooting, organizing, and ultimately editing together the highlight video for the conference.

conducted a series of interviews over the years for posterity. I interviewed and shot footage of three of the conference's founders telling the story of how the conference started. I didn't necessarily think all of this would make it into the highlight videos for those years, but I was there anyway, and the documentarian in me thought maybe I'd make a film about the Wakonse movement later in my career.

I'm glad I shot all the extra footage. In 2019, I didn't make it to the conference because my second son was born. The conference hired one of the previous producers to make the highlight video that year. In 2020, the conference was canceled due to the COVID-19 pandemic. In 2021 and 2022, the conference was online and didn't require a highlights video. In 2023 the conference wanted to hire me, but I wasn't able to make the drive up to Lake Michigan to attend in person. This is when we decided that I would produce the video remotely. I created a shared folder, and conference staff members collected photos and videos that they had shot. They also collected photos from participants and put them into the shared folder. I downloaded the photos, used old drone footage and video clips I had shot in previous years, and edited the video together. In 2024, I produced the video remotely. This time, I was able to create a QR code that allowed participants to upload their photos directly. I still used old drone footage and some old interviews to edit together the highlight video. You'll also hear copyrighted music in these videos. Although I'm generally against this, the Wakonse Conference really prefers popular music for these highlight videos. YouTube's algorithms flag it and prevent the videos from being seen in some countries. But since the videos aren't being sold commercially, it's not a violation of the copyright necessarily. YouTube also has an agreement where the copyright holders are paid whenever their songs are played on the platform, so many artists and record companies are okay with this kind of use. You absolutely need to look into the agreements in place before deciding to use copyrighted music in your videos as a freelancer, though.

I gave you all of that backstory to explain how I put together the conference promo video this year (2024). The conference board of directors reached out to me and asked if I could create a promo video they could use to recruit new participants from different universities and increase conference attendance. I agreed, and I actually had a practicum student interested in working for me on the project. Together, Thomas Delzeit and I went through all of the drone footage, video clips, and still images I had shot for the conference over the years. We settled on a set of raw imagery that I put on a hard drive for him to work from. I also purchased the rights to a song for the video. Because a promo video is commercial in nature – its purpose is to make money for the conference – I insisted to my client that we could not use copyrighted music for this kind of video. I bought commercial rights to the song from bensound.com. I did this for a few reasons. First, it was used legally this way. Second, the musician deserves to be paid for their work. Lastly, the song isn't a free-use song that other people will hear everywhere in other videos. While I don't have exclusive rights to the song, it's less likely that others will pay to use it when there are also free songs on the site (songs that I hear often in student projects).

Thomas put together a rough cut with drone footage and video highlights from previous conferences. He's also very talented with graphics and was able to make the Wakonse graphics and the conference contact info at the end look better than I could have. I gave him Director's notes on the rough cut, and he came back with the final cut of the project. The video is housed on my YouTube channel, and my client sends out the link to the video in their recruitment materials. The video will also be embedded from my channel onto the conference's new website when it is rolled out later this year. I wouldn't do this for all of my freelance clients. For most of them, I would simply give them a copy of the video and have them house it on their own YouTube channel or website. Since I've been with the conference for so long, I'm happy to serve as their video historian and house all of the video archives I can.

The promo video is here: https://www.youtube.com/watch?v=gWB4LNnwSW8, or you can find it on my channel by looking for "Wakonse Promo Video." There wasn't really any preproduction for this particular video because we were re-using stuff I had shot previously. During the production phase, we were choosing which shots we wanted to use to tell the story of what happens at the conference. My client's goal was to show people having fun, learning new things, and inspiring others. They also wanted to give a sense of the location because Lake Michigan is a large part of the draw for the conference. The mixture of drone shots, action shots, and still images of the beautiful sunsets helps convey what the conference is all about.

When Thomas edited the video, he first laid down the music. The beat and flow of the music helped him determine where to put the cuts and transitions. The music starts out slower, allowing the drone shot to build and for the graphics to come in. Because it's a promo video for the web, we wanted a shot that grabs attention, and then we wanted the graphic to come in almost immediately. Because attention spans are so short, it's important to accomplish these two things quickly. After the graphic, the music picks up a little. This allowed Thomas to edit in action shots and move more quickly through the edits. The pacing helped get a number of different shots in. The shots mostly have people smiling and having fun, as well as being blindfolded (challenging themselves), speaking passionately, and interacting with each other. The rough cut didn't have a call to action, so I had Thomas put graphics at the end with the conference website in the final version. Obviously, if this video was seen on the website, or if it was part of the recruitment materials, this wouldn't be necessary. But since this is housed on my YouTube channel, and because it could be found on the web out of context, I felt it was important to have the contact info embedded in the video.

You can see the other videos I've done for the conference on the YouTube playlist. There are several "Wakonse In Review" highlight videos. There are a few raw videos from the conference, like the Chautauqua performances and the sunset. And there is one called "Wakonse Inspirations," which is a short film I did using interviews I shot at the conference. That film was screened at a festival in Dallas, Texas.

The "Wakonse Origins" video on the playlist is a similar story to the promo video. About a week before the conference this year (2024), the board of directors reached out to me and asked if I would put together a video that could be played at the start of the conference. The goal was to explain how Wakonse began, and what it was about. The conference founders weren't able to make it to the conference this year to do the intro in person, so we wanted a video that could accomplish the task. Because it's a captive audience, the origins video is longer than the promo video and goes into more detail about Wakonse. You can see how the two videos might actually overlap on some of the goals – to get participants excited about the conference and explain what happens there – but because the audiences are very different, the videos are very different. Both of them used interviews and footage I shot previously (I didn't have time to drive or fly and interview people in a week to create the origins video). Eventually, I'll try to sit down with the other two original founders for the conference and add clips from them into the origins video. This will not only give a fuller picture of the origins of the conference, but it will also be a good homage to the founders, while connecting current participants to the origins and goals of the conference.

Chapter 15: Corporate and Freelance Production Main Points

- Corporate video and freelancing are similar modes of production, where your ideas and plans need to be approved along the way by your boss or your client. Unlike some other modes of production, you have to focus on someone else's goals as you produce the video.
- There are many kinds of corporate and freelance projects out there. Web videos, instructional videos, promo videos, commercials, music videos, highlight videos, archival interviews or footage, and some I'm probably not even thinking of right now. Each one might require a different approach to planning, shooting, and editing.
- Even though different projects might have different goals and require different approaches, when you produce corporate or freelance projects, you need to establish a process for checking in at each stage of the project. This helps make sure you're on track to accomplish the goals for the project.
- In either a corporate or a freelance setting, you might be working on many different projects at the same time. Staying organized and developing a daily, weekly, and monthly calendar is important.
- In a freelance setting, your time will be very flexible. Work towards a sustainable work-life balance where you're working enough hours in a day or week to finish projects, but not so many hours that you'll burn yourself out.
- In a corporate setting, you might have a catalog of music and graphics to use in your projects. In the freelance setting, you should look at hiring specialists in those things, especially if you're not strong in either. And any costs for a project need to be passed on to your client.
- In both the corporate world and the freelance world, you'll need to figure out how to distribute and archive your projects. It costs money to archive raw footage, but it might be worth it.

Index